Victorian Scrutinies

Victorian Scrutinies

Reviews of Poetry 1830–1870

ഗ ഗ ഗ

ISOBEL ARMSTRONG

THE ATHLONE PRESS *of the University of London*
1972

Published by
THE ATHLONE PRESS
UNIVERSITY OF LONDON
at 4 Gower Street London W C I
Distributed by Tiptree Book Services Ltd
Tiptree, Essex

PR
593
A73

0 485 11131 4

Printed in Great Britain by
WESTERN PRINTING SERVICES LTD
Bristol

For Mary and Richard Hoggart

Acknowledgements

My thanks go above all to Professor W. E. Houghton, who supplied me freely with information about authorship from the unpublished volumes of the *Wellesley Index to Victorian Periodicals*. Like all workers in this field, I am deeply indebted to him, not least for the way in which he responded to what must have been my many irksome requests with generous wit and kindness.

I thank A. S. Byatt and Barbara Hardy for reading and advising me about the manuscript of this book. My colleagues have been most generous with their help. I am grateful to John Chalker, Lilian Haddakin, Shirley Jones, Trevor Lloyd, T. McFarland, Elizabeth Quinn, Patrick Roberts, W. A. Smeaton and Keith Walker for the time and trouble they took to answer my requests for information. I thank Hans de Groot, John Hopkins and Joanne Shattuck for their willingness to talk over some of the problems of the book, Janet Martin for her hard work on the index, and Jacqueline Peverley and Anne Stanley for much practical help. I am especially grateful to Brenda Feig for her meticulous and painstaking assistance.

I.A.

Contents

Abbreviations

Broughton   L. N. Broughton, C. S. Northup, R. Pearsall, *Robert Browning: A Bibliography, 1930–1950* (Cornell Studies in English, no. 39, New York, 1953)

Gollin   R. M. Gollin, W. E. Houghton, Michael Timko, *Arthur Hugh Clough: A Descriptive Catalogue* (New York, 1967)

Hyder   C. K. Hyder, *Swinburne's Literary Career and Fame* (Durham N.C., 1933)

Mineka   F. E. Mineka, *The Dissidence of Dissent* (Chapel Hill, 1944)

Shannon   E. F. Shannon Jnr., *Tennyson and the Reviewers* (Cambridge Mass., 1952)

Shannon, *P.M.L.A.*   E. F. Shannon Jnr., 'The Critical Reception of Tennyson's *Maud*', *Publications of the Modern Language Association*, lxviii (1953), 397–417

W.I.   *The Wellesley Index to Victorian Periodicals*, vol. i. Where there is no indication of page number in references to the Wellesley Index the information is from the unpublished volumes of the Index supplied to me by Professor W. E. Houghton.

Further Reading in Periodical Reviews

The reviews listed in the bibliographies following each of the three sections of this book are intended as a brief guide to further reading in the critical issues and problems discussed in the introduction and raised in the reprinted articles. For convenience the reviews are listed under the names of the four poets discussed in the book, Tennyson, Browning, Clough and Arnold, but the items have been selected primarily to illuminate the general problem of the nature of Victorian assumptions about poetry; the growth of a poet's reputation and popularity, or the changing emphases in the critical assessment of an individual poet have been of secondary importance to me in selecting this bibliography. I have drawn attention to them where they throw light on mid-nineteenth-century poetics.

Introduction

This selection of periodical reviews of Tennyson, Browning, Arnold and Clough covers the years 1830 to 1870. I have chosen the essays to suggest what kinds of demands were made on the poet during this period and what problems these poets as 'modern' poets created for their critics. These are the prolific years of high Victorian poetry, beginning with *Poems, Chiefly Lyrical* (1830) and *Pauline* (1833), and ending in 1869 with *The Holy Grail*, the completion of *The Ring and the Book*, the first collected edition of Arnold's poems and Clough's *Poems and Prose Remains*. They take in Meredith's *Poems* (1851) and *Modern Love* (1862); the first part of Patmore's *The Angel in the House* appeared in 1854; Morris began to publish in 1858 and the best of Swinburne's early poetry was published during this time, *Atalanta in Calydon* in 1865 and *Poems and Ballads* in 1866. The range of reviews for a selection is therefore large and in order to avoid miscellaneousness and to give a coherent indication of attitudes to poetry at this time I have concentrated upon two occasions when critical debate was particularly lively and urgent. These are the discussions of Tennyson's early poems and of Arnold's 1853 volume and Preface. They reveal the most urgent concerns of mid-nineteenth-century criticism as well as producing some impressively fresh and penetrating discussions of individual works. The first two sections of the book contain reviews of Tennyson and Arnold and discussions related to them. The third section illustrates the changing emphases of criticism in the sixties. For the sake of unity and clarity the reviews are mainly of the poets who are important in the earlier debates. In this introduction I shall examine and compare the preoccupations which emerge in the two controversies of the 1830s and 1850s, show how they determine judgements and emphases, and discuss the importance of these judgements in the period as a whole, particularly their relationship to critical attitudes in the sixties. I shall refer to the reprinted reviews in detail and for this reason they are presented as far as possible complete. Only the lengthy quotations they invariably include have been omitted.* A more important consideration, however, governed my decision not to cut these essays: critical assumptions and evaluations emerge in the kind of tone a writer adopts; they are revealed in the way he discusses the theme, form and language of a poem, as much as in the explicit statements he makes.

THE TERMS OF CRITICAL DISCUSSION

'We cannot open a magazine or a review without finding something new said about our friend "*The* Poet," as distinguished from our other friend "*The* Prophet," and the like' David Masson wrote in 1853.[1] This remark suggests something of the strenuous and self-conscious exercise in criticism going on in the four decades between 1830 and 1870. The volume of poetry published might lead one to expect this to be a time of particularly active discussion; it was also a time when the number of periodical publications of all kinds increased with the expanding reading public and when there was a growing popular interest in literature.[2] Even reviews with, on the face of it, sectarian interests often carried fine essays on general and literary topics. The *Church of England Quarterly Review*, for instance, was described in the *Atlas* for 12 November 1842, as:

> ... the advocate of high church principles—of apostolical succession —baptismal regeneration—the power and authority of the church, and the efficacy of sacerdotal absolution; yet it is avowedly opposed to the Tractarians ... In politics the *Church of England Quarterly Review* is the hater of the Whigs and Whiggery ... (*Atlas*, 730)

Nothing, perhaps, could seem more restricted, yet the *Atlas* writer goes on to praise two lengthy discussions of the poetry of Tennyson and of Browning in the *Church of England Quarterly* for October 1842. The review of Tennyson was by Leigh Hunt and that of Browning by R. H. Horne. Both are fine pieces of criticism though Horne mercilessly dismembered his piece when he adapted it with a too ready economy for his *A New Spirit of the Age* (1844).[3]

* Minor cuts have been made in the reviews by John Sterling and Richard Simpson, originally the two longest in the book. Throughout the reviews, lengthy quotations are usually indicated by printing the first and last lines only and quotations of whole poems by the title alone.

Very often, of course, the political and religious positions of a particular periodical do influence contributors: it is as well to remember the utilitarian bias of the *Westminster Review* when one comes across the remarkable statement that the 'deepest significance' of *In Memoriam* is its 'sanctification of human love as a religion'. It is even more illuminating to know that the review is by George Eliot.[4] Similarly, one of the best discussions of Clough's excessively morbid concern with the conscience comes in the Catholic *Rambler*.[5] Clearly, the general concern with unhealthily subjective poetry is being reinforced by a theological position here. Yet except in the case of some utilitarian critics it is always difficult to say how far a religious or political bias shapes a critic's thought about the nature and function of poetry.[6] It is particularly striking, indeed, that the same kinds of worry about the state of contemporary poetry recur whatever the ideological bent of a periodical. Though I shall attempt to show where a particular ideological position may have determined a writer's views I am mainly concerned with a vigorous and urgent debate about the function of poetry.

The Victorian periodical critic had to get to grips with a new work for the first time, and the theories and generalisations about poetry which emerge from this process of assimilation, definition and interpretation have a peculiar immediacy lacking in the abstract treatises on poetry which we know better.[7] J. H. Newman's *Poetry, with Reference to Aristotle's Poetics* (1829), E. S. Dallas's *Poetics: an Essay on Poetry* (1852), G. H. Lewes's *The Principles of Success in Literature* (1865), and the theories of Carlyle or Ruskin are written with a hypothetical or ideal poet and poetry in mind. Periodical criticism supplements and even modifies such treatises because of its necessary concern with the actual and displays the immense variety of emphasis with which an idea can be interpreted. J. S. Mill's review of Tennyson's 1830 and 1832 volumes, which I shall discuss later, suggests that his reading of Tennyson and the controversy over Tennyson's early poems made him change his mind about the relationship of feeling and intellect in poetry. He has moved away from the extreme expressive theory of poetry established in his two highly abstract articles, 'What is Poetry?' and 'The Two Kinds of Poetry' in the *Monthly Repository* for 1833.[8] More important, periodical criticism is closer to cultural pressures than the abstract treatises and makes one powerfully aware of the literary situation in which it was written, aware of the anxieties, stresses and distresses from which Victorian criticism emerged. Romantic and post-Romantic writers had dissolved the old categories and vocabulary of criticism and it was necessary to find new ones: Victorian critics contemplated a new poetry which seemed strange and, difficult though it is to see how this could be now, almost revolutionary; they were also confronted with a social or cultural environment which seemed to be peculiarly hostile to the writing of poetry. Of *The Strayed Reveller*, for instance, Kingsley wrote that the age was hostile to poetry and produced only 'bunglers at verse-making', fit only to express 'a spice of mild Pantheism, of milder Medievalism, and as first, last, and chief of all their themes, the howlings of spiritual indigestion'.[9] G. H. Lewes, in a review of Browning's *Bells and Pomegranates,* had said the same thing with more eloquent and sensitive pessimism:

> ... there reigns an intellectual anarchy, ... There is prodigious intellectual activity, but it is not employed in opening up new tracks of thought. Great ideas are in the process of incarnation; great changes are taking place within the womb of society; but it is a period of gestation, and we are not yet on the eve of a new birth.[10]

I shall try to demonstrate the major preoccupations of the periodical critics through a close examination of the reviews reprinted here. But before this something has to be said about the frame of reference within which the Victorian critic worked. I shall keep such summary and generalisation to a minimum, however, for there is no substitute for the particular formulations of the reviewers themselves. The two remarks just quoted show how much depends on the *quality* of the mind at work on any theme; the same idea can be handled superficially or searchingly (as by Lewes) and becomes modified in the process.

✍   ✍   ✍

There is an imperial refusal in Victorian criticism to regard the poem as a self-contained, sealed-off entity on which moral and social questions external to it do not impinge. This, of course, is very often the source of an irritating philistinism but it is also one of its strengths. Exclusively 'literary' criticism did not exist and the Victorian critic would cross the boundaries established by the restrictions and delimitations of literary criticism today without even knowing that they were there. John Sterling could begin a discussion of Tennyson's 1842 volume in the *Quarterly Review* (see below, p. 125) with a survey of his society; Francis Garden could argue impressively against Arthur Hallam's contention that 'art should keep quite distinct from all that is not of itself', insisting that poetry must merge and mingle with the affairs of men because—and this might almost be called the classic Victorian position—'Call it a fine art as much as you will,—it is discourse; it is utterance; it is man speaking to man, man telling man his thoughts and feelings'. Such discourse necessarily impinges on morality, introduces things 'foreign to art', things that are 'not out of place in poetry, but that yet cannot easily be brought within a definition if it'.[11] There is a wonderful understanding of Hallam's aestheticism here—which makes the case against it the more compelling. Almost without exception critics stuck to this 'impure' view of art. If this meant the unintelligent anger with poems such as *Modern Love* or *Poems and Ballads*, it also meant that critics recognised the nastiness of Tennyson's advocacy of the Crimean war in *Maud* and could not easily explain it away with a dramatic or symbolic theory of the poem—'but what, in the name of logic, have these things to do with a thirty years' peace, or what proof is there that a thirty years' war would reform, or rather not render them infinitely worse?'—the *Christian Reformer* reviewer asked sharply, when faced with *Maud*'s statement that the adulteration of food and child-murder, the evils of peace, would be abolished by war.[12]

In the best discussions poetry is seen in a broad cultural context. This grand disregard of the purely aesthetic, which at its crudest looks like (and often is) an unsophisticated confusion between art and life, is also what gives the best criticism a rich amplitude and seriousness, a largeness of concern.

One of the consequences of this 'impure' view of art is an almost complete absence of a specialised or technical critical vocabulary in Victorian reviewing, a vocabulary capable of describing the formal or aesthetic qualities of a poem. To some extent, of course, one must attribute this to the kind of men who reviewed literature. If a poet can be reviewed by an eminent politician and a dean of Canterbury as Tennyson was (Gladstone in the *Quarterly Review*, and Henry Alford in the *Contemporary Review*),[13] it is probably too much to expect a technical critical language to evolve. Spacious all-round thinkers such as Bagehot, aspiring polymaths such as Lewes, men whose interests were never exclusively literary, these were the journalists who reviewed poetry. Typical is William Bodham Donne, who wrote for the *British and Foreign Review*, or Richard Simpson, Catholic theologian and Elizabethan scholar, who wrote some perceptive literary criticism for the *North British Review*, including outstanding discussions of Jane Austen and of Tennyson.[14] Yet the absence of a literary vocabulary must be explained by something more influential than the intellectual interests of the men who contributed to journals. Mid-nineteenth-century criticism was, to borrow the term used by Abrams in *The Mirror and the Lamp*, predominantly a 'pragmatic' criticism; that is, the emphasis was almost invariably on the human or social reference of the work of art, on its *effect on the reader*, and hence on the needs of the reader. Matthew Arnold's call for an 'adequate' literature in his lecture of 1857, 'On the Modern Element in Literature', with its firm direction of criticism towards the needs of the reader or the needs of the age, is a superlative embodiment of the assumptions of periodical reviewers during the decades I discuss here. All interests were subsumed under this pragmatic criticism. This is why the vocabulary, concepts and categories evolved during this period were not literary in the sense that we would recognise today. This is why one of the main preoccupations, perhaps even the obsession, of Victorian criticism was what the poem should be about.

Nearly all the commonest evaluative words in criticism at this time carry a psychological, human/social or moral reference. They have immediately so little to do with the artistic qualities of a poem, indeed, that it is easy not to notice them or not to see how important and how meaningful they were. Condemnatory words are 'affectation', 'mystical', 'vague'. The epithet 'subjective' can be used approvingly or disapprovingly (particularly when it is linked with 'Wertherism'). Words used approvingly are even further away from defining literary qualities —'human', 'sympathy', 'the sympathies' (often linked with 'human'), 'the affections', 'feelings', 'heart', 'natural', 'simple', 'vigour', 'healthful', 'manly', 'noble', 'distinct/distinctness'. The various collocations and combinations in which they were used tell us more than the words in isolation. Here are some typical ways of using them taken from reviews of *In Memoriam*, though discussions of almost any poem throughout the period would be bound to contain them.

It is a pathetic tale of real human sorrow, suggested rather than told. . . It is the record of a healthy and vigorous mind working its way, through suffering, up to settled equipoise and hopeful resignation. (*Examiner*, 8 June 1850, 356)

The concentrated nerve and pathos of Lycidas is far above comparison with the hundred and thirty mournful chants in whose too-easy rhyme Mr. Tennyson has diluted this elegy. Nor can we be unmindful of the manly eloquence in which Byron poured forth his lament for Sheridan. (*Inquirer*, 22 June 1850, 389)

The greatest heights are the fairest; the most universal minds the serenest, most healthful. (*Eclectic Review*, xxviii N.S. (Sept. 1850), 331)

. . . easy and natural manner in which profound truths are shed from delicate fancies. . . (*Examiner*, 8 June 1850, 356)

There is a homeliness and a simplicity about them which bear ample testimony to their truth. There is nothing ornate or elaborate in them. (*Atlas*, 15 June 1850, 379)

Sometimes, indeed, he betrays a Della Cruscan tendency to elaborate the pretty and affected, and not seldom conceals a too slender idea in obscurity of diction. (*Inquirer*, 22 June 1850, 389)

. . . and most of the volume is as remarkable for force and simplicity, as for other more characteristic and less masculine qualities. (*Guardian*, 26 June 1850, 477)

. . . in the midst of faults with which his readers are familiar—affected simplicity or affected mysticism, far-fetched originalities or eccentricities of style and diction. . . (*Britannia*, 29 June 1850, 410)

. . . representations of an emotion or a thought in a few lines, more like the suggestive simplicity of Uhland than anything in our literature. (*British Quarterly Review*, xii (August 1850), 292)

Mr. Tennyson is, far more than Wordsworth, mystical, and what an ignorant and money-getting generation, idolatrous of mere sensuous activity, calls 'dreamy'. . . But, in reality, the spirit of the poem is simply anti-Werterian. It is man rising out of sickness into health,—not conquered by Werterism, but conquering his selfish sorrow, and the moral and intellectual paralysis which it produces. . . (Charles Kingsley, *Fraser's Magazine*, xlii (Sept. 1850), 247, 249)

The reader must already have discovered that this poem is characterized by thorough 'subjectivity'. We pause to say a few words with reference to the outcry which has been raised from time to time, against this order of poetry. Self-conscious or 'subjective' art, is only bad when it is not self-conscious and subjective enough. (*North British Review*, xiii (August 1850), 551)

Flagrantly moral and even more flagrantly uninformative. Much less easy to grasp is the use of the word 'sympathy', or 'the sympathies', another almost imperceptible word in the Victorian critical vocabulary, yet one of the most powerfully evaluative words that could be used.

> . . . but the widest sympathy has been given to those who have shown a power to endure and surmount, as well as a sensibility to feel and express, their trials and sorrows. . . (*Inquirer*, 22 June 1850, 389)

> It is no new thing for the fancy of the poet to find in the outward world numerous echoes or representations that give back or image his inward feeling, but bereavement has never found before so many touching symbols, so many answering relationships in the common experience of life, as are here presented, peopling the neighbourhood of sadness with unlooked-for sympathies. (*British Quarterly Review*, xii (August 1850), 292)

> . . . the varied experiences of his fellow-men lie open to his gaze, and his sympathies flow out to all truth, be it to the prayer of the little child, to the earnest enquiry of the sceptic, or to the choiring of angels. (*Westminster Review*, liv (Oct. 1850), 93)

> Still he is democratic; democratic in his universal sympathies, democratic in his treatment of things lowly. . . (Gerald Massey, *Christian Socialist*, ii (August 1851), 156)

> His faults of taste and language are stereotyped, and he now writes his affectations in capitals. . . The hero is beyond our sympathies. (*Times*, 28 Nov. 1851, 8)

> These [scenes of familiar life] are exquisite in feeling, still more exquisitely wrought; of entire simplicity, eloquent of a spirit of sympathy with humanity. (*Eclectic Review*, xxviii N.S. (Sept. 1850), 335)

It is through the assertion of these broad relations with nature—colouring with our individual passions the largest features of the universe—that we exercise our most direct (if our most unconscious) action upon the sympathies of our fellow-beings, who are creatures of time and space like ourselves. The simplest and most familiar images are those which flatter most our home-bred fancies, and, consequently, those through which the artist can work on us most easily. (*Tait's Edinburgh Magazine*, xvii (August 1850), 501)[15]

The notion of sympathy has completely lost its richness and dense moral weight for us.[16] In the quotations above 'sympathy' is being used with much the same implications as it had in eighteenth-century discussions of the psychology of ethics, where it is far closer to its root meaning than in the twentieth century. Sympathy was the faculty of sharing and understanding the situation of another person by being able to change places with him in imagination. This sense of the word is directly maintained in Lushington's review in *Tait's Edinburgh Magazine* from which I have already quoted: 'It does not require any abnormal development of the organ of inhabitativeness to enter thoroughly into the feeling of the following picture' (504). Those philosophers who made feeling and not reason the basis of moral perception put great stress upon the faculty of sympathy, thus making moral understanding dependent upon an act of imagination. As early as Shaftesbury's *An Enquiry Concerning Virtue, or Merit* (1711) we find great emphasis being given to the capacity of the mind to image moral situations in which 'the Heart cannot possibly remain neutral; but constantly takes part one way or other', and on the basis of morality in the outgoing social feelings, the 'Pleasures of *Sympathy* or *Participation with others*'.[17] But Adam Smith's *The Theory of Moral Sentiments* (1759) gives one most insight into the weight that sympathy could bear and I shall use Smith as a touchstone for the meaning of the term. For Smith our moral sense is derived from being the attentive spectator of the actions of others and from the resulting development of judgements which we then apply to our own conduct. But we cannot test the moral validity of anything except 'by changing places in fancy' with the person we are judging: 'we enter as it were into his body, and become in some measure the same person with him, and thence form some idea of his sensations, and even feel something which, though weaker in degree, is not altogether unlike them.' The morality of a society will be created by a series of delicately reciprocal acts of imagination in which each person is able to call up an 'analogous emotion' in response to the feeling of another and is therefore able to check both his companion's conduct and his own.[18]

It is not surprising to see sympathy being appropriated by discussions of aesthetic matters since it is so directly based on imaginative insight, and especially when aesthetic matters themselves were felt, as they were in the nineteenth century, to be so firmly involved with social and moral needs. Certainly in the mid-nineteenth century the notion of sympathy played a major part in forming expectations about poetry even though this involves a concern with what is really a belief about human nature rather than a theory of poetry. It was assumed that the faculty of sympathy would be highly developed in a poet because he is capable of the supreme imaginative act of identification with feelings other than his own. Correspondingly, poetry would appeal to the sympathies and the affections of the reader, to those impulses which are aroused by the essentially 'human' ties and feelings which we can all share. J. W. Marston's very naïve discussion of sympathy in *Poetry as an Universal Nature* (1838) suggests how powerfully the eighteenth-century connotations of the word clung on to it in the nineteenth century. Marston equates sympathy with love, felt by both poet and reader (Smith had equated it, more mildly, with 'fellow-feeling'), an outgoing impulse which compels us to seek out that which unites us to others, feeling 'common to all'. Some perfunctory science is invoked as an illustration (a typically nineteenth-century innovation): 'In the external world, one drop of water *sympathises* with another, and the two *unite*'.[19] What unites human beings are the common ties and duties and poetry, by exercising our outgoing impulse, therefore consolidates these. Marston's simple-minded approach provides one with a beautifully clear, not to say crude, demonstration of the way sympathy was conceived at this time. It is also an illustration of the arbitrary limitations which could be set upon this promising and potentially subtle theory of art: we will only be able to share the experiences we *can* share; we will only sympathise with what we *can* or *expect* to sympathise with. More than hovering behind this discussion is the assumption that it is not morally possible or permissible to sympathise with some areas of experience (Smith had emphasised the impropriety of sympathising with anger). Our sympathies will necessarily be confined to the common ties and duties.

The use of the word sympathy in discussions of poetry at this time provides a very precise indication of the nature of the moral basis of Victorian criticism. It is a truism that this criticism is irredeemably moralistic but most theories of art turn out to be moral in the end and what is important is the *way* in which their moral criteria operate. The morality of Victorian criticism depended almost exclusively on the way in which the notion of sympathy could be interpreted and it is through subtly changing, diverse and even conflicting interpretations of the word that the moral demands made on poetry can be examined.

However much they were preoccupied with the moral function of poetry, critics almost invariably disclaimed didactic theory, and with a zeal puzzlingly like post-symbolist disclaimers. It is true that Browning was advised by the reviewer of the *Eclectic Review* to 'set before himself a great aim in poetry. That aim should be the advocacy of great principles, and inculcation of great sentiments'. 'There is a sensual taint about his writings', the reviewer summed up. And of course, particularly in reviews of Browning's poetry, there was dogmatism and moral prejudice. The *Metropolitan Journal* complained, for instance, that Browning introduced the word 'God' into *Paracelsus* sixty-four times. The *Spectator* objected to the prostitutes in *Pippa Passes*, one rejoicing over 'what such people in England call a "blow-out"'.[20] But crude didacticism was surprisingly rare. To choose almost at random from innumerable disclaimers, this discussion of Bailey's poems in the *Scottish Review* is typical: 'He says, "Poets henceforth are the world's teachers." But so they have ever been. It is no new office this. Poets have always taught, and never taught better than when least didactically.' Sterling's distinction between the moralist and the poet in his *Quarterly Review* article on Tennyson (see below, p. 143) is not unusual. Nor is his criticism of Wordsworth: 'But the poetry would have streamed out in a freer gush, and flushed the heart with ampler joy, had the moral been less *obtruded* as its constant aim.' When Spedding praises the predominance of the 'moral soul' in Tennyson's maturer poetry he adds a hasty parenthesis, 'not in the way of formal preaching'. Patmore attacked the use of vague words such as 'exalting', 'purifying', 'expanding', to describe the effect of poetry. 'A poem need not be avowedly didactic, in order to be expressly religious... Art has its peculiar and far more effective method of teaching.' When 'the meaning of a work of art is just, the work may be said, not so much to inculcate, as to be, the truth'. Later he said that the poet should know 'the nature of his singing robe too well to think of turning it into a surplice'.[21]

Patmore said that the highest art *suggests* rather than imposes itself upon the reader. It is common to find imagery of organic life, blood and warmth and imagery of colouring, painting and blending used to describe what is meant by suggestiveness, the poem which is moral without being didactic. When Henry Alford produced the full-scale Christian interpretation of *The Idylls of the King* which I have mentioned above (*Contemporary Review*, 1870), for instance, he was reprimanded by the *London Quarterly* reviewer, who pointed out that a moral scheme is in itself no guarantee of the unity of a series of poems and that the morality of a poem should be in any case 'blended into the lines of ... [a] work irregularly'. It should not be codifiable for 'morality is not merely anatomical, but actually cellular'.[22] 'A poem does not *live* upon men's lips and *mingle* with their life [my italics] because they approve of its principles', a *Christian Remembrancer* reviewer of Browning wrote.[23] An ecstatic and wordy discussion of Tennyson in the *Westminster Review* singles him out as among 'the world's highest moral teachers', yet qualifies this by asserting that his poetry achieves its effect by appealing to

> the spontaneous emotions of man, *blending* with the native movement of his soul, and not to be obeyed through the command of the intellect alone. In such there is unity and harmony of nature, and mental philosophers must retire from classifying their powers under intellectual, moral and animal, or more heads, for these words are names standing as nothing here. *One deep full warm circulation* is visible throughout, the conscience shedding streams of light and heat everywhere, by which the intuitions of the intellect are sure as they are deep, the imagination acting in concert with it...[24]

The morality of a poem is something felt along the heart and felt in the blood; this writer is trying to say something of the kind, though not very happily.

But statements about the morality of art actually tell us very little. It is more illuminating to see, as I have suggested, how writers interpreted the notion of the appeal of poetry to the sympathies and also to look at the categories being evolved to describe the uniqueness of what to the Victorian critic was 'modern' poetry.[25] I shall show briefly what the terms of this discussion were before going on to a detailed examination of the criticism of particular poems.

Probably at no other time has there been such intense concern with the *subjects* of poetry, with the simple matter of what poetry should be about. This is the recurrent and most important concern for the Victorian critic—what are the proper materials of poetry? And this, of course, bore directly for the critic of the time upon the function of poetry, what it did for the reader. Critics tended to define subjects in terms of direct oppositions between two kinds of poetry, one which dealt with contemporary themes and one which did not. Writing on *The Princess* in 1849, Aubrey De Vere distinguished 'two great schools of poetry', the Ideal and the National, 'the one characterised by its plastic power and its function of embodying the abstractedly great and the ideally beautiful; the other by its reality, its homebred sympathies, its affinities with national history, character, and manners'.[26] W. C. Roscoe made the same kind of distinction, more urbanely, in a discussion of *Maud*, when he talked of 'the Established Catholic Church of poesy' in contrast to the 'Dissenters'.[27] He meant a contrast between the poet who can 'vividly reproduce' the 'thought and sentiment of his own time' and the poet who can 'transport' the reader 'to some entirely new field of existence'. In 1869 H. B. Forman, discussing *The Ring and the Book*, distinguished between the Idyllic and Psychological schools of poetry.[28] The Idyllic School treats of 'contemporary subjects otherwise than dramatically'. The Psychological school is more indirect, dealing with states of mind and feeling in a more abstract way and depicting 'the idealisation of the intellectual and emotional phases of being which, in modern city life, are so intensified as to preponderate immensely in importance over the life of physical activity'. Psychological poetry may be caused by, but is not necessarily directly *about* the life of the city.

These divisions are not analogous in every detail and there are differences of emphasis but they do illustrate, in the first place, the attempt to invent new categories different from the traditional 'kinds' (and the critical approaches associated with them made obsolete by the romantic movement), which define poetry in terms of its content. Secondly, they illustrate the tendency to see a distinction between an autonomous, ideal, self-derived, imaginative creation and the poetry which is directly dependent on and evolving out of the circumstances of the age in which it is written. Of course, they are evaluative as well as descriptive categories and reveal not only the problems which the new poetry created for the critic but also the ways in which the critic wished to regard it. Clearly, if one is thinking in terms of the creative process there is no necessary contradiction between the two kinds of poetry, but the Victorian critic wished to look at the end-product, at the content of a poem, and the two kinds of subject looked so different that it seemed necessary to derive a different kind of creative process from them.[29] And certainly, whatever the logical manoeuvres involved, there is an insistent emphasis on the *problematical* nature of the subject of the poem: Tennyson's early poetry raised this problem for reviewers; Arnold raised it deliberately in his Preface of 1853. In the case of both poets the discussion of their works was in terms of the distinction between—to combine De Vere and Forman, the National and Psychological schools of poetry. The debate continued in the sixties and in all the decades it was complicated by the deference given to the notion of sympathy. These are the terms of the debates about poetry. They are surprisingly free both from the vocabulary and concepts of Coleridge and of German criticism, despite G. H. Lewes's popularisation of Hegel.[30] A few 'German' terms, such as objective and subjective, are used, but until the sixties, apart from one or two exceptions such as Donne and Masson, it is almost as if Coleridge had never been.

ISSUES RAISED BY TENNYSON'S EARLY POETRY

Tennyson's poetic career began, it is well known, with controversy, a controversy which has been very fully discussed. What is important about it for my purposes is that Tennyson's *Poems, Chiefly Lyrical* (1830) immediately raised nearly all the problems which were to pre-occupy critics during the next four decades. I shall look at the debate around *Poems, Chiefly Lyrical* and its aftermath in discussions of *Poems*, 1832, and *Poems*, 1842, referring also to discussions of Browning's poems during this period. The first three reviews reprinted in this book form a related and closely-knit discussion and introduce the recurrent themes of criticism in this period with a peculiar urgency and concern. William Johnson Fox's review in the *Westminster*, the first review of Tennyson's poems to appear in a major quarterly, is extraordinary in the way that it raises almost every theme of major importance. Arthur Hallam's review in the *Englishman's Magazine* is clearly written with Fox in mind, and John Wilson (Christopher North) takes on both writers in his review in *Blackwood's*, attempting to refute them both at the same time as attacking some elements in Tennyson's poetry.[31] I shall look first at these three reviews in some detail.

The outstanding importance of Fox's review is disguised by its ponderous style and by what looks like a particularly unhelpful utilitarian starting point—'The machinery of a poem is not less susceptible of improvement than the machinery of a cotton-mill'. But this review is full of excitement, for Fox is trying to show how Tennyson's poems justify a theory of modern poetry and suggest new possibilities for contemporary poets. He is also attempting to demonstrate that utilitarian theories actually liberate poets rather than restrict them. The appeal of this review is that Fox writes as if he had experienced almost a revelation about the nature of poetry.

The heavy-handed analogy between the progress of cotton-mills and the progress of poetry is intended to show that the materials of poetry are not exhausted and never will be, even though the traditional kinds and materials (the example Fox gives is straightforward descriptive poetry) are now thoroughly obsolete, for the modern poet has new and infinitely richer areas of experience to work with. Fox's insistence throughout this review that poetry cannot decay, that the 'elements of poetry are universal' and perpetual is not superogatatory but written against the pressure of prevailing gloom and scepticism about the future of poetry. The doubts expressed by Hazlitt concerning the work of the living poets at the end of his *Lectures on the English Poets* in 1818—'I have felt my subject gradually sinking from under me as I advanced. . . The interest has unavoidably decreased . . .', the iconoclasm of Peacock's *The Four Ages of Poetry*, which provoked Shelley's *Defence* in 1821, such attitudes were reinforced during the next decade. It was quite seriously maintained that 'the age' was inimical to poetry, either because there was simply nothing more for the poet to say, the materials of poetry having been 'used up', or because of a deep antipathy between a mechanistic way of living and thinking and the poetic imagination. It is difficult to take seriously Macaulay's assertion in his essay on Milton in 1825 that the experimental sciences are capable of continual progress, whereas 'language, the machine of the poet', is not and, indeed, 'is best fitted for his purpose in its rudest state'.[32] His belief that the language of abstraction and logic is antipathetic to poetic language is of more importance but it does not necessarily lead to the conclusion, 'We think that, as civilisation advances, poetry almost necessarily declines'. However, people took such opinions seriously,[33] and Fox begins by arguing that there is no reason why poetry 'should retrograde from the days of Milton'. It looks as though he had Macaulay in mind rather than the much more profound analysis of Carlyle's 'Signs of the Times', in the *Edinburgh*. For Carlyle the Age of Machinery had killed 'spontaneous growth' and had diminished poetry and religion to 'a product of the smaller intestines'.[34] Benthamite criticism was not actually as hostile to poetry as Carlyle implies but he would not have been made happier to see Coleridge described as a 'Benthamite in his poetry; a Utilitarian; a "greatest happiness" man' in the *Westminster*.[35] This would be another proof that 'Men are grown mechanical in head and heart, as well as in hand'.

In the context of such depression about the future of poetry Fox's review is extraordinarily adventurous and experimental. He claims that there are two new areas of experience for the poet to explore. In the first place, there are modern themes: 'Is not the French Revolution as good as the siege of Troy?' The old themes may be exhausted but contemporary Europe provides themes equal in stature and grandeur to those of the ancient epics. Nevertheless, the epic as a form, even the epic in modern dress, is anachronistic. Fox sees the hope for modern poetry much less in contemporary themes than in something more fundamental—recent developments in psychology. Now the 'real science of mind' provides 'unbounded and everlasting materials of poetry'. 'A new world is discovered for him [the poet] to conquer' because 'The most important department in which metaphysical science has been a pioneer for poetry is in the analysis of particular states of mind'. These are 'as good a subject for poetical description as even the shield of Achilles itself'.

The 'science of mind' Fox has in view is something quite specific: though he nowhere mentions James Mill's *Analysis of the Phenomena of the Human Mind*, published in 1829 and reviewed in the *Westminster* a few months later than his discussion of Tennyson, the terms of his discussion make it clear that he is attempting to base a theory of poetry on Mill's psychology, and therefore to show that utilitarianism allowed for poetry.[36] Just as Mill derived all mental phenomena from the physical organisation of man, so Fox makes the material of poetry dependent upon 'The exercise of the organs of sight and sense' common to us all. If Fox's insistence that the science of mind 'is the essence of poetic power, and he who possesses it never need furbish up ancient armour, or go to the East Kehama-hunting or bulbul-catching', seems a little odd when one thinks of Mill's grinding attempt to resolve all mental phenomena into the laws of sensation and association, it has to be remembered that to enthusiastic utilitarians it seemed that Mill had evolved a logical but subtle and precise way of analysing the *complexity* of the organisation of the human mind. To the *Westminster* reviewer of Mill it looked as though the whole organisation of society could be altered as a result, and to Fox it seemed that the discovery of the richness and complexity of states of consciousness revealed in 'the analysis of particular states of mind' could be the basis of a new movement in poetry. Certainly, there are moments when even Mill's uningratiating prose rises almost to lyricism as he contemplates the almost limitless combinations and variety of the trains of feeling created by the law of association—'capable of composing a train of states of consciousness, the diversities of which transcend the limits of computation', and 'Thought succeeds thought; idea follows idea, incessantly'.[37]

For Fox the discoveries of this psychology meant that the poet no longer described 'the outward expression of the thoughts, feelings and passions' but penetrated to the complexity of feeling within the consciousness, grasping the 'mutual relations and influences' of this inner world, feeling himself into the very 'physical organisation' of the being whose emotions he expresses. 'He does not merely assume their external shapes, and exhibit his own mind masquerading. He takes their senses, feelings, nerves and brain, along with their names and local habitations.' Fox's analysis of Tennyson's poetry, particularly *Supposed Confessions of a second-rate sensitive mind* and *The Merman* are attempts to demonstrate how the unique processes of feeling of any being can be imaginatively appropriated by the poet. What we see, interestingly enough, is that Mill's psychology has given a new meaningfulness to the ideas of his utilitarian forebear, Adam Smith. When Fox says that Tennyson 'seems to obtain entrance into a mind as he would make his way into a landscape... The author personates (he can personate anything he pleases...)', and that 'Our author has the secret of the transmigration of the soul. He can cast his own spirit into any living thing, real or imaginary. Scarcely Vishnu himself becomes incarnate more easily, frequently, or perfectly', he is invoking Smith's notion of sympathy, of dramatic projection, that capacity for 'changing places in fancy' with another which is the basis of our understanding both of other people and ourselves. In this review sympathy extends the imaginative world of the poet and throughout the next four decades a minority of critics associated sympathy with a dramatic extension of the self, but for the most part a less adventurous interpretation of sympathy prevailed.

As one would expect, Fox is anti-didactic and makes it clear that the poet's use of psychological discoveries does not mean 'Metaphysical systems and discussions in verse'. And to demonstrate a more inward morality he uses what will become a familiar analogy between the paintings of bones and 'the real substances in the human body'. However, he becomes timid towards the close of his essay. 'A genuine poet has deep responsibilities to his country and the world. . . They can influence the associations of unnumbered minds; they can command the sympathies of unnumbered hearts. . .' Fox warns against becoming a 'poetical harlequin', for a poet can act upon the 'national feelings'. He holds out the possibility of some great but ill-defined poetic enterprise (the notion of which was to dog Tennyson and Victorian criticism) and in doing so virtually takes back with one hand what he offers with the other.

Modern themes, ways of exploring the feelings through dramatic projection, the responsibilities of the poet, these are important topics in later reviewing. Of course, this is not the first time that they had been aired, but it is the first time that they are drawn together and related in the discussion of the work of a new poet. This is why it has been necessary to examine Fox's discussion at some length. Hallam's review of Tennyson is very much better known, but though Hallam shows himself to be aware of the significance of all the issues raised by Fox, the position he adopts is deliberately outside the usual ways of looking at poetry, and he is almost alone in his advocation of 'picturesque' poetry, the poetry of 'sensation', until writers in the sixties began to think along the same lines.

There are many points of agreement between the two reviewers but on one crucial issue Hallam challenges Fox. He disagrees with his optimism about contemporary material. 'The French Revolution may be a finer theme than the war of Troy; but it does not so evidently follow that Homer is to find his superior.' The influence of the poet will become more and more restricted because there has been a change in the relationship between the artist and the community which will enable him to have 'little immediate authority over public opinion'.

The reason for this is that the modern consciousness is split and fragmented: sensation, thought and feeling no longer work harmoniously together (Hallam here is extraordinarily prophetic of T. S. Eliot's dissociated sensibility) but have been cut off from one another and directed into many different kinds of social activity. We can never return to the earlier unity—'repentance is unlike innocence'. 'Hence the melancholy, which so evidently characterises modern poetry; hence the return of the mind upon itself, and the habit of seeking relief in idiosyncrasies rather than community of interest.'

Sometimes Hallam anticipates Arnold's position in the 1853 Preface but accepts rather than rejects the destructive 'dialogue of the mind with itself', as Arnold describes it there. (Compare the more conventional position of the *Tatler*, which had doubts about the hints of morbidity and 'sick writing' in Tennyson's poetry.)[38] Hallam's assured acceptance of the situation—it looks almost as if he welcomes it—is achieved because he is quite content to let the poetry of 'Sensation' develop in its own sphere of activity which, he feels, will almost certainly predominate over the impure poetry of 'reflection'. Morbidity, destructive analysis, cannot impinge on the poetry of sensation because it is created out of 'a world of images', by which he means *pictures* of the external world in the mind. Hallam admits that this poetry, which comes from the absorption of the whole being into the energy of sense', can degenerate into sensuality, but for the most part it will be a refining influence. The constant education of the senses produces a 'delicate sense of fitness . . . hardly inferior to the correspondent judgements of conscience'. Moreover, a continual responsiveness to the external world turns the mind away from the morbid complexities of the inner world and directs it to an 'energetic principle of love for the beautiful'. Hallam shows himself as much aware as Fox of the laws of association and the complexities of states of feeling but, by implication, he suggests that the poetry of sensation is likely to be healthier than the poetry which inhabits and analyses particular states of feeling. He is at one with Fox in seeing that Tennyson's great gift is to colour his depiction of the external world with a predominant emotion—'he holds all of them *fused*, to borrow a metaphor from science, in a medium of strong emotion', but because his emphasis is on the power of sensation rather than the complexities of the inner world his analysis of the poetry is on very different lines. Certainly, his analysis of individual poems is more convincing than the cumbersome accounts of Fox.

He concludes that the poetry of sensation must be inevitably esoteric, difficult, and often divorced from 'matters of daily experience'. The confidence, almost the arrogance, with which this is set forward infuriated John Wilson. His elaborately irritable review suggests the reasons why Hallam seemed to undermine fundamental assumptions about the importance of poetry. Wilson associates Fox and Hallam, seeing them as jointly propagating a thoroughly subversive view of poetry. Hallam is pretentious and Fox a 'crazy charlatan'. Interestingly enough, he does not quarrel with Hallam about the sensuousness of Tennyson's poetry and praises the same poems, but clearly feels that Hallam's views in general encourage the remoteness and affectation of Tennyson's poetry. He does not object to Fox's belief that the contemporary world furnishes material for the poet and, indeed, endorses this view, suggesting that the 'earthquake' of the French revolution should produce a race of new poets. His attack on Fox is on the same ground as his attack on Hallam—they condone the remoteness of the poet. Hallam in particular flouted Wilson's presupposition not so much because he had denied that the best poetry was reflective, that reasoning and 'logical relations' are improper material for poetry, but because he wished to free poetry from ordinary experiences, those fundamental and universally recognisable things, 'love, friendship, ambition, religion': 'whatever is mixed up with art, and appears under its semblance', may be gratifyingly simple and easy to respond to, requiring 'little effort', but they have essentially nothing to do with art proper. For Wilson 'matters of daily experience' have everything to do with poetry, and he attacks Fox as much as Hallam for excluding these. Angered by Fox's psychology of 'Cockney materialism' and enraged by his ungraceful phraseology, Wilson complains of the absence of 'common-sense' in the idea of 'the principle of thought injected by a strong volition into the cranium of the finny worthy' (a direct quotation from Fox). 'At present,' he says of Tennyson,

> . . . he has small power over the *common feelings and thoughts of men.* His feebleness is distressing at all times when he makes an appeal to their *ordinary sympathies.* And the reason is, that he fears to look such sympathies boldly in the face,—and will be—metaphysical. What *all the human race see or feel,* he seems to think cannot be poetical; he is not aware of the transcendant and eternal grandeur of *common-place and all-time truths,* which are the staple of all poetry

... [poets] shun not the sights of common earth—witness Wordsworth ... Scott, when eulogising our love of our native land, uses
the *simplest language* and gives vent to the *simplest feelings*.

I have italicised the words and phrases that reappear, with similar
arguments and in connection with other poets, throughout this period.
For Wilson and many other Victorian critics Tennyson's 'Cockney'
affectation is not merely a superficial verbal artifice such as is discussed
by the *Spectator* reviewer who criticised the 'piebald dialect' of the
poems.[39] It is symptomatic of a deep moral and emotional failure, a
failure of sympathy. The poet's job is not to explore strange and unknown areas of experience (such as the nervous system of a fish), but
to confirm and revitalise through an appeal to the emotions those
central and fundamental experiences with which we are already familiar.
This is where his moral responsibilities lie. This is the notion of
sympathy expressed by Marston and inherent in Adam Smith's belief
in propriety. In the 1802 Preface to *Lyrical Ballads* Wordsworth had
put great emphasis on the power of poetry to bind human society
together through passion and its power to induce this 'habitual and
direct sympathy connecting us with our fellow-beings'. One might
call Wilson's position common-sense or debased Wordsworthianism—
though it is arguable that Fox had read his Wordsworth to better
purpose. Wilson is a sensible critic and he does not slide into philistinism, but in the following discussion it will become evident how much
later criticism of Tennyson was governed and sometimes restricted by
the notion of sympathy. 'Every faculty in one man is the measure by
which he judges of the like faculty in another. I judge of your sight by
my sight ... of your reason by my reason ... of your love by my love.
I neither have, nor can have, any other way of judging about them',
Adam Smith wrote.[40] I judge of your poetic sensibility by my own,
some Victorian critics imply. A demand for the familiar became connected with a demand for the simplest language. Admiration of the
simple ballad-like poems and rejection of the more esoteric ones, as in
Wilson's review, went along with the emphasis on sympathy as also
did the idea of some exceedingly vaguely defined great national poem.
If Tennyson was as dependent on his critics as we have sometimes been
led to believe, it is a wonder that he did not write a poem on the French
Revolution.

∽ ∽ ∽

I turn now to the response to the 1832 and 1842 volumes and to Browning criticism in the 1830s and early 1840s. I shall show how the preoccupations I have discussed above shape discussion and form the context in which judgements were made. We see criticism attempting to find the ways—and the words—for exploring a poetry which dealt with states of feeling, demanding a poetry based on an appeal to the affections and the sympathies, and formulating the whole question of poetry and the age.

Attempts to see Tennyson in terms of the exploration of states of feeling expressed through a poetry of sensation were few and confined mainly to a very limited number of people who must have read the early articles of Fox and Hallam. Fox himself continued to write, both on Tennyson and Browning, in the same vein, though in his article in the *Monthly Repository* on *Poems*, 1832, he demanded more earnestness and a sense of responsibility from Tennyson. In his discussion of *Pauline*, however, he talked of Browning's ability to explore the 'universe' of the mind and 'the ties of association flowing hither and thither like the films of a spider's web'. The *Monthly Repository* also printed a review of *Paracelsus* along very much the same lines.[41] Apart from this there exists a very derivative discussion of Tennyson's *Poems*, 1842, which discusses *Mariana* in much the same way as Hallam and J. S. Mill and talks of 'These converse operations of making nature body forth mind, and mind invest nature with its own attributes'. Although the writer does not display such a firm grasp of Hallam and Fox as Mill in his earlier discussion of the Tennyson controversy (*London Review*, 1835), it is interesting that their theories do provide him with a vocabulary which enables him to get closer to the poetry than a good many contemporary critics. Distinguishing between the mood of *The Lotos-Eaters* and Thomson's *Castle of Indolence*, for instance, he says that 'The indolence which Thomson describes, is the indolence of the Sensualist: Tennyson's is the indolence of the Visionary'.[42] The same is true of Sara Coleridge's much later discussion of *The Princess* which also returns to Hallam for illumination of Tennyson's work. With the aid of Hallam and an analogy between the descriptions in *Locksley Hall* and the paintings of Turner, Sara Coleridge talks of the wild mood of 'lavish gorgeousness' achieved by the poetry of sensation.[43]

On the whole, though the strain of criticism created by Fox and Hallam was persistent enough to come under Arnold's attack, as we shall see in his Preface of 1853, it had little influence in the early thirties and forties and was seen as something to react sharply against. The *London University Magazine* echoes Wilson in advising Tennyson to avoid all fancy 'transmigrations, and metempsychoses'.[44] Even sympathetic writers modify and qualify what they adopt. Sara Coleridge uses Hallam, but argues persuasively that the poetry of sensation leads to a restricted conception of art: 'there must be some common ground on which cultivated minds in general and the mind of the painter and the poet can meet, and . . . this is the true ground of art' (*Quarterly*, 1848, lxxxii, 438). Mill, such an eloquent and sensitive explicator of the ideas both of Fox and Hallam, characteristically and intelligently seeks to synthesise and reconcile their notions with the mainstream of Victorian criticism. He gives a splendid account of *Mariana* in terms of the relation between feelings and landscape and is thoroughly aware of the potentialities of states of emotion embodied in 'sensuous imagery'. But he is at pains to show that there is no antipathy between this kind of poetry and reflective poetry. It is not and cannot be incompatible with 'the systematic culture of the intellect'.[45] Every poet must be philosophical to the extent that the imagination is bound up with the intellect and is, indeed, conditioned and nurtured by it. Here Mill adopts a much less ambiguous attitude to the poet of nature and the poet of culture which he had described in an earlier article in the *Monthly Repository*. Earlier he had seen the two as virtually antithetical: now they have a reciprocal relationship. Furthermore, Mill ends his review by taking up what I have called the classic Victorian position from which Hallam so carefully dissociated himself: 'Let our philosophical system be what it may, human feelings exist: human nature, with all its enjoyments and sufferings, its strugglings, its victories and defeats, still remain to us; and these are the materials of all poetry.'

Whether or not Tennyson was a 'human' poet—this, rather than any worry about the sensuousness of his poetry and its philosophical content, was the main preoccupation of critics through the 1830s and early 1840s. Hostile critics accused him of remoteness from the common sympathies, whereas friendly critics attempted to show—particularly in 1842—that he was improving, that his poems were *human*. In reviews of the 1832 volume William Jerdan, Bulwer-Lytton and J. W. Croker follow Wilson in associating Tennyson with Keats and the Cockney school (or the 'Baa-Lamb' school as Jerdan has it) and in

basing their infinitely more crude attacks on Tennyson's lack of
common-sense and common sympathy—not necessarily the same thing
but often conflated by these writers. Croker's notorious piece of
ponderous ridicule is aimed at demonstrating that Tennyson is rarefied
to the point of absurdity. The same intention is behind Jerdan's attack
in *The Literary Gazette* in which he accuses Tennyson of insanity. In
the *New Monthly Magazine* Lytton saw Tennyson as 'the incarnation
of Modern Poetry' and its dangerous tendencies, its 'eunuch strain', its
failure to reach 'the common springs of emotion', 'the Universal
Heart'; 'Common sense should be the staple of fine verse as of fine
prose'.[46] The same kind of complaint recurs in 1842. Leigh Hunt, for
instance, seizes ironically upon the fact that Tennyson had a self-
conscious need to show that *Godiva* was shaped in the busy hum of a
station, among 'grooms and porters'—'for why should not Mr Tennyson, in the universality of his poetry, be as content to be waiting on a
bridge, among "grooms and porters," as with any other assortment of
his fellow men?' The 'Bond-Street drawl' of such comments is distasteful. The *Westminster* advised Tennyson to keep in tune with 'the
sympathies of his daily life, the humanities of his own experience'. The
same suggestion was made by the *London University Magazine* (1842)
and by *Hogg's Weekly Instructor*. The latter reviewer praises Tennyson's capacity for sympathy wherever the poems involve a dramatic
projection of the self—'He loses himself in his subject, and thus, in
some intangible form of beauty, gains admission to the heart and
sympathy of his sympathetic auditor'—but denies him the power to
appeal to the universal feelings and emotions. The poetry is too
morbid and withdrawn—'he does not speak to us in the language of
sympathy, and of hope'.

John Sterling and James Spedding, both enthusiastic and influential
reviewers of the 1842 volume, rejoiced to find the very qualities of
humanity and sympathy which other critics found lacking in Tennyson's poetry. Sterling, for instance, praises the Idylls and sees them as
by far the most important part of Tennyson's work because they are
about familiar and therefore accessible experiences—far more accessible
than similar poems of Wordsworth. 'The human soul', wrote Spedding,
'in its infinite variety of moods and trials, is his favourite haunt; nor
can he dwell long upon any subject, however apparently remote from
scenes and objects of modern sympathy, without touching some strings
which brings it within the range of our common life' (*Edinburgh*

Review, 1843, 382). The *Atlas* reviewer made similar claims for Tennyson's poetry. It was 'nearer to our sympathies'.[47]

It is rare to find a careful and reasoned justification of the doctrine of sympathy such as the one by Francis Garden which I have already discussed (see above, p. 5), but the poems singled out for praise, and comments on the language of Tennyson's poetry, imply clearly enough what is the moral basis of the appeal to the sympathies. Hostile and friendly reviewers alike seized upon the rustic and domestic idylls— *The Gardener's Daughter, Dora, The May Queen, Lady Clare Vere de Vere*—and these poems were even praised for being potentially trite. Of *The May Queen* Spedding said, 'The theme is as trite as can be, and the treatment as simple; but it is not the less original'. A remark by a later *Edinburgh* reviewer, Coventry Patmore, suggests why this could be so: 'moral truth is usually important in proportion to its triteness . . . the poet is doing his noblest work in resuscitating moral truths from the inert condition of truisms and conferring upon them a perennial bloom and power.'[48] At its best, then, the doctrine of sympathy led to a notion of poetry as a profoundly enriching exercise in making us *know* emotionally and imaginatively the things we *already know*. The central and commonplace experiences and truisms of life are to be re-animated into central truths. The function of poetry was, as it were, to provide the moral imagination with its exercise, renewing its freshness through the emotions. One often finds musical images associated with sympathy; the reader's heart *vibrates* with sympathy, is literally played upon, in order that this renewal can be achieved. The great poet, wrote one reviewer, has 'a keen sympathy with every nerve that vibrates in humanity' (*Cambridge University Magazine*, 1842, 632).

This view of poetry can certainly restrict the poet's subject matter and his treatment of it. It was George Gilfillan who suggested its limitations most succinctly in the *Dumfries-shire and Galloway Herald and Advertiser* when he said that Tennyson was constantly falling from the sublime to the snug. Too often it was the snug, debased Words-worthianism of the rustic poems which was admired. No wonder critics were so baffled by Browning during this time. And yet, trivi-alised though it could be, and limited though it might seem today, this notion of the functions of poetry cannot be dismissed without some attempt to see what its importance was to people living in the mid-nineteenth century. In a society so full of anxieties and bewilderments as Victorian society, this view of poetry held out hope and comfort:

poetry could be the great cohesive force, making for wholeness; it could bind into one society, through an appeal to their sympathies, the groups of people who were becoming increasingly atomised and fragmented in the changing environment of industrial Britain. Poetry could be, as Arnold put it much later, a consolation and a stay. Very few orthodoxies can last without having the needs and longings of people behind them. This one lasted so long because it held out reassurance. In the end, perhaps, it was too reassuring, but this did not prevent people believing in it with urgency and feeling. There is more than a self-comforting myth behind this statement of the classic Victorian position.

> But it is one thing to trust in this separateness of our natures, and another to aim at producing evidences of it. The poet's true object should rather be to excite sympathy in spite of it, to strike upon those chords which prove the whole world kin; and to do this he must choose either topics which concern men alike—men as men—the hopes and fears we are born with, the sorrows, the affections that come to us with the air we breathe. . .[49]

I have said that demands for clarity and simplicity of style, for 'distinct' language, are associated with demands for what is common and familiar. In almost every review of Tennyson and Browning alike this is reiterated, whether it is the hostility of Jerdan's parody of the affected greengrocery language of *The Lady of Shalott*—'The yellow-leavèd piccalilly | The greensheathèd pepperchili'—or Mill's friendly discussion of the precision and distinctness of Tennyson's 'statuesque' poetry, an indirect attempt to show that the poetry of sensation does not lead to vagueness. 'The forms are not, as in painting, of unequal degrees of definiteness; the tints do not melt gradually into each other, but each individual object stands out in bold relief, with a clear decided outline.'[50] To take two typical examples of the insistent demand for plainness recurring in 1832 and 1842: the *Athenaeum* accused Tennyson of a perverse desire for '*singularity*' in reintroducing the anachronisms of 'the quaint conceits, the elaborate subtilties . . . the affectations' of the sixteenth-century lyric and the metaphysical school. A *Spectator* reviewer uses the distinction made by Reynolds between what is classical and general and what is singular and particular to show that Tennyson's poems do not attain 'general truth'. He attacks all the namby-pamby eccentricities—the use of obsolete words, strange innovations and irregular versification—which make Tennyson a 'singular' rather than a classical poet. The same kind of language, to take two representative descriptions from the *Weekly Dispatch* and the *Spectator*, describes Browning's linguistic outrages: 'eccentric conceits'; 'mystical' or 'dreamy' vagueness. Ten years later the complaint was still the same. *Fraser's Magazine* attacked the affectation of Browning's attempt to 'tell common things in an uncommon manner' and his 'scrannel pipe' numbers.[51]

Spedding's comment on Tennyson's 1842 volume—'there is more humanity with less imagery and drapery' (*Edinburgh Review*, 1843, 377)—suggests why these demands were so insistent. The permanent and basic human emotions and experiences must be revealed in precise, clear and simple outlines. 'Drapery' obscures the clarity of these outlines and any language used for its own sake ('affectation', eccentricity, aberration, vagueness or dreaminess) destroys the purity of the essential, primary human elements of these experiences. Properly, language should idealise, purging these things of the accidental and the contingent, and realise, presenting them with distinctness and clarity. A discussion of Browning's *Bells and Pomegranates* in the *Christian Remembrancer* for 1846 puts the point well. The basis of poetry is '*human*: founded that is upon no circumstances, no relations, no accidents of our own, but inward, elementary, and constitutive'. And for this writer it must necessarily follow that

> Its peculiar resource and excellence must, therefore, be traced to its unrivalled power of *distinct* representation. . . The philosopher, who wishes to classify, is content with some one great feature or property in each single object. Not so, the poet who has to touch the affections of mankind at large. The well-known property of affection is to circumscribe, and realise, and picture its objects.[52]

To '*picture* its objects': this is the essential function of the language of poetry. The vocabulary most commonly used by reviewers to describe the language of poetry accordingly is borrowed mainly from painting and drawing. It is a limited vocabulary, and where there is an attempt at close reading it is with a view to exposing the logical and grammatical errors which 'drape' or obscure the sense and therefore the experience of the poem. The Victorian critic is at his best when he has to rely on descriptive imagery to suggest the 'feel' of a poem's language, as in Charles Peter Chretien's account of the 'peculiar bloom' of

Tennyson's poetry (see below, pp. 213–14).[53] Sometimes, however, painting imagery can take a writer quite far, as with this description by Leigh Hunt of *Oenone*. The poem is

> as beautiful and graceful as if it had been painted by one of the Italian masters. . . Select beauty is in it; not the less true for being select; and a golden warmth pervades the grace, like Titian shining upon the Caracci, or the hue of the orange upon the beauty of its orb. (*Church of England Quarterly Review*, 1842, 369)

But in general painting and drawing imagery is used in a utilitarian way to suggest the qualities most valued in the 'delineations' or 'depictions' of poetic language. The *Hogg's Weekly Instructor* reviewer (1847, 282) is typical when he writes of *Mariana in the Moated Grange*, 'it is a picture perfect in outline, filling up, tone, keeping, and execution'. An undistracting, level harmoniousness, precision and, above all, clarity of outline, the throwing of the subject into relief, all these can be suggested by painting imagery. In the case of Browning, though some critics were fortunate enough to be able to see pictures in his poetry ('There is a picture in every verse': 'how rich they are in pictures'), the picture image was used as a norm from which Browning's language deviated.[54] Turner, the painter who seemed to violate all the canons of painterliness, was a very useful comparison for some critics. An *Examiner* critic wrote of the obscurity of parts of *Pippa Passes*: 'the whole air of the scene so shadowy and remote, that, with its great blots of gorgeous colour too, we are reminded of nothing so much as one of Turner's canvasses—pictures *of* Nothing, as some one called them . . .'[55]

∽ ∽ ∽

The question of poetry and the age raised the crucial problem of what poetry should be about. The relationship of the poet to his age was a side-issue in 1830 but by 1842 it had become very important and by the time Arnold wrote his 1853 Preface it was a major topic of debate. In the 1830s the attention claimed by Ebenezer Elliott and the Corn-Law poets perhaps encouraged the notion of a truly popular poetry which would deal with contemporary issues and reinforced the growing feeling that poetry should, in some often undefined way, reflect the age. Both Carlyle and John Wilson for instance, wrote on Corn-Law poetry, and in the *Monthly Repository* Fox argued that 'The life and soul of poetry are always the same; but to make them visible and tangible, they must become incarnate in various forms, which forms bear the peculiar features of age, class, or country.'[56] But a popular poetry and a poetry imbued with 'the spirit of this age' are not necessarily the same thing, though they were often confused in Victorian criticism and, particularly in assessments of Tennyson, discussions were muddled. Lytton, for instance, firmly connects the approval of the public with the poet who is 'rapt in the spirit of this age' and who will, therefore, 'command the next' (*New Monthly Magazine*, 1833, 74). Another writer in *Chambers' Journal* cites Tennyson's popularity as evidence that 'the age of poetry' is not past, not an argument that means anything.[57]

By far the most significant contribution to the debate on poetry and the age in 1842 is John Sterling's essay on Tennyson.[58] An astonishing document in many ways, it is the first really searching attempt to define what sort of poetry should emerge from the age and why the question should be so important. It is an outstanding example of the dignity and passion with which the subject could be argued. Sterling first surveys the energies at work in modern English life beginning with the death of Huskisson when the Manchester and Liverpool railway was opened —a human sacrifice to the violent and powerful forces released in contemporary Victorian society. He discusses the commercial, political and religious life of the nation, attempting to weigh the uses and misuses of the energies he finds there, and asks the poet to seize upon the inner spirit of the age, producing a 'creative survey of modern life' in its best and worst aspects. If the poet cannot make use of what is good and energising in the age, the spectacle of an 'overwrought materialism fevered by its own excess into spiritual dreams' is there for him to work upon. Where Sterling can find evidence of this (for instance in the 'darkened world' of *Locksley Hall*)—and even the most willing reader fails to find much analysis of the failures of the age in Tennyson's volume—he brings it forward; where he cannot, he turns to the idylls as a second best because they have to do with 'fresh feeling and the delightful affections'. Nowhere is there any hint in Sterling's essay of the facile view that the poet either automatically 'reflects' the age (like breathing in a pervasive smell) or that it is his *duty* to reflect the optimism of the age, a view expressed by the writers in *Hogg's Weekly* and *Chambers' Journal*. 'The poet has his mission to perform. . . If the impulse of the world is forward, he is the first to feel and know so. . .

He might have been the herald of a new era', the first critic wrote
(*Hogg's Weekly*, 1847, 284). The spirit of the age is one 'of energy, of
material progress', wrote the second; Tennyson, clinging to memories
of the past is 'the poet of scholars' and not 'the poet of the people'
(*Chambers' Journal*, 1845, 26).

Many of Tennyson's reviewers in 1842 considered the question of a
contemporary poetry and what this implied (the question is hardly
touched upon in Browning criticism of this period), but most of them
had reservations about it. A feeling still exists that the influence of
poetry must be restricted, that it has lost its traditional sphere of influence and must find another. One reviewer suggested in the *British
Quarterly Review* that a certain 'wilful carelessness', a 'wanton play
with language', was the result of an unconscious yielding on Tennyson's part to 'the influence of a prosaic and practical age', where poetry
is 'looked upon as a species of ingenious trifling, or, at best, an "unpro-
ductive industry"'. Except to suggest that there is little profit in imitative or derivative poetry, in 'manufacturing modern antiques, whose
best recommendation is a very indifferent imitation of rust', this writer
gives no indication of the sort of poetry to be expected in the contemporary situation, but points out that most of the functions of poetry
have been taken over by prose and that we shall see the age of the short
poem appearing.[59] Similarly, a discussion in the *Westminster Review*,
probably by Monckton Milnes, talked of the poet's difficulty in the
present situation of reconciling 'his practical and his poetical existence,
his dreams by night and his thoughts by day', though he qualifies this
by saying that every poet has felt his own age to be unsympathetic to
poetry. Several writers felt that the physical externals of the age were
too alien to be assimilated in poetry—railway trains cannot have
poetical associations, and the 'universal sympathies' to which poetry is
meant to appeal are outraged by 'fashionable parasoles and gentlemen
in grenadiers' caps'.[60] The *London University Magazine* (1842, 286)
believed that poetry could never die because the essential passions and
emotions which are always the material of poetry are always the same,
but the 'facts and circumstances of an age', whatever its 'wonderful
discoveries, grand improvements, and sublime inventions' are as yet
too reduced to the level of ordinary reality to satisfy the poetic
imagination:

A ship with its flowing sails, and easily gliding motion, is not in itself more full of beauty, or suggestive of grander thoughts, than a railway train ... hurrying from place to place hundreds of human beings, with almost as much facility as the enchanted tapestry of the Arabian romance; yet this latter would be looked upon ... as something essentially prosaic, while the former, by old usage, has been admitted as poetical.

Anticipating Arnold, some reviewers argued that classical material was still important and relevant as the subject of poetry. The *Christian Teacher* asserted, 'We belong not to those who think that the days of those dreams should be over. The mythology and fabulous history of Greece and Asia appear to us to be still capable of yielding forth' interest. George Gilfillan welcomed the classical poems in Tennyson's volume—'after all, the poetry of Greece is not dead ... Homer ... is still alive to the airy purposes of poetry'—and denigrated those critics who identified popularity with the portrayal of the mere physical externals of the age 'extracting poetic music from the bickering railway train'.[61] Apart from Sterling's essay, however, there is little sense of the pressure and urgency behind this topic which is to be found later. People discussed it in a leisurely way. It had not yet become the centre of controversy.

ARNOLD AND THE 1853 PREFACE

With Arnold's 1853 Preface, poetry and the age becomes one of the dominating issues, but it is also surprising how far other things raised in the Preface parallel the earlier debate around Tennyson's poems even though there are differences in emphasis. Arnold disliked many of the tendencies of Victorian criticism but he is not the isolated figure the Preface sometimes leads one to believe. Some aspects of the criticism of this time are more Arnoldian than he suggests.

The confidence and authority of the 1853 Preface has something in common with Hallam's piece on Tennyson and in both essays this is unusual in a first attempt at critical prose. The Preface was clearly written with the critics of Arnold's first two volumes in mind (*The Strayed Reveller and Other Poems*, 1849, and *Empedocles on Etna*, 1852), but like all Arnold's prose it had much wider implications than a personal apologia. Its importance was that it drew the sharpest attention to the major preoccupations of criticism at that time and forced critics to reassess or at least to clarify their positions. The Preface is very well known but the reader must be reminded of the points which were central in Victorian critical debates and central to the Preface. Arnold objected strongly to the view that the present, the contemporary world in all its energy and innovation, could provide the materials of poetry. He quotes from a review of Edwin Arnold's poems by R. S. Rintoul in the *Spectator*: 'The poet who would really fix the public attention must leave the exhausted past, and draw his subjects from matters of present import and therefore both of interest and novelty'.[62] For Arnold the past was by no means exhausted, and the search for novelty in the present meretricious, because the materials of poetry are permanent—those things 'which appeal to the great primary human affections: to those elementary feelings which subsist permanently in the human race'. Such an assumption should seem familiar to anyone who is acquainted with the Tennyson debate. It is the classic Victorian claim that poetry must appeal to the affections, to what is generally human, to the universal sympathies. Perhaps it is not immediately recognisable because Arnold invests it with such uncommon grandeur; the primary feelings can only be aroused by the portrayal of actions, and 'great' actions at that, which in Arnold's view automatically disqualifies matters of 'present import' from poetry and necessitates a return to ancient sources, particularly to those of Greece and the Greek drama. An extreme position.

Arnold's almost perversely classical emphasis on action is related to another element in contemporary poetry which he disliked—the poetry which concerned itself with 'the dialogue of the mind with itself', that is to poetry which was commonly called subjective. *Hamlet* epitomises this spirit. The dialogue of the mind with itself was morbidly unhealthy and introspective, depressing and *lowering*. He condemns David Masson's assertion in the *North British Review* that a true 'allegory of the state of one's own mind in a representative history, whether narrative or dramatic in form, is perhaps the highest thing that one can attempt in the way of fictitious art'.[63] In quoting Masson, Arnold omitted the phrase 'whether narrative or dramatic in form', a qualification which makes a difference to Masson's argument, and I shall later discuss the significance of this. Lastly, Arnold went on to advocate a concern for form, 'architectonicé' as he calls it, and chastity of style as against Keatsian abundance. The concern for form and chastity of style are connected. Arnold had in mind the poetry of 'single lines and passages', poetry which produced merely 'a shower of isolated thoughts and images', such as the ununified, inorganic collections of derivatively Keatsian and Shakespearian imagery being produced by the Spasmodic poets at this time, particularly by Alexander Smith, who had been praised both by Clough and Masson. Though one can understand his dislike of excess in imagery (a dislike similar to the early Tennyson reviewers' dislike of 'Cockneyisms'), it is much more difficult to make out what he means when he advocates a concern for form and unity. One's suspicion is that he means something simply as bare and austere as possible, whatever the form it takes.

ᴄᴀ   ᴄᴀ   ᴄᴀ

It is necessary to look no further than reviews of Arnold's earlier volumes to see that the positions he resents are very much in evidence. The themes they introduce are the ones made familiar by the discussion of Tennyson's early poems and they can be looked at in the same way, in terms of the appeal to our common sympathies, the question of poetry and the age, and the attempt to find ways of discussing the poetry which explores states of feeling. I shall look at reviews appearing before the Preface to show how far Arnold's diagnosis of the situation was justified and then at reviews both of Tennyson, Arnold and Clough, which suggest the extent to which Arnold was in fact in agreement with a substantial amount of Victorian criticism.

In stressing the all-importance of the subject, the human action which appeals to the 'great primary human affections', Arnold was indirectly replying to the critics who had found no central human interest in his earlier poems. The *Spectator* had complained that the poems in *The Strayed Reveller* had 'no subject': the *Literary Gazette* had noticed the 'miscellaneous contents' drawn from 'classic' rather than 'natural founts'. The *Times* critic found him 'too learned', too philosophical and therefore too remote. The dry philosophisings of Empedocles make the character and action of the play 'beyond the pale of rational sympathy and almost of probable conception'.[64] This echoes an earlier review in *Blackwood's Magazine* which had accused Arnold of retreating into a pose of coldly introspective aloofness from the affairs of ordinary life—'Sympathy, indeed, he cannot look for, so long as he appeals neither to the heart, the affections, nor the passions of mankind, but prefers appearing before them in the ridiculous guise of a misanthrope. He would fain persuade us that he is a sort of Timon, who, despairing of the tendency of the age, wishes to wrap himself up in the mantle of necessity, and to take no part whatever in the vulgar concerns of existence'.

The 'vulgar concerns of existence': it is interesting to compare this remark with Christopher North's very similar criticism of Tennyson in the same periodical seventeen years before for there is now an important difference in emphasis. North's appeal to the 'ordinary sympathies' was not related to the notion that the poet should make poetry out of the documentary facts, as it were, of contemporary realities; it was not related to the demand for realism, the portrayal of scenes and situations such as we find in the novel. The reviewer of Arnold goes on to criticise the equivocations of *To a Republican Friend* and asks him, ironically but seriously, to assimilate contemporary facts into his work: 'What would our friend be at? If he is a Tory, can't he find work enough in denouncing and exposing the lies of the League. . . ? If he is a Whig, can't he be great upon sewerage. . . ?'[65] It was Clough, Arnold's most acute and sensitive critic, who linked the appeal to the ordinary sympathies firmly to an appeal for realistic or naturalistic portrayals of contemporary life. Poems after classical models, he argues, are all very well,

> Yet there is no question, it is plain and patent enough, that people much prefer Vanity Fair and Bleak House. Why so? Is it simply because we have grown prudent and prosaic . . . Or is it, that to be widely popular, to gain the ear of multitudes, to shake the hearts of men, poetry should deal more than at present it usually does, with general wants, ordinary feelings, the obvious rather than the rare facts of human nature?

The modern novel, Clough argues, is preferred to the modern poem because it deals with all the familiar details of everyday reality—'these indispensable latest addenda', 'these positive matters of fact'. There follows a stern censure of Arnold's rarefied classical posturings and Clough, with almost perverse foresight, praises Alexander Smith, the Glasgow mechanic-poet, and any poems of Arnold's which resemble Smith's, for all the qualities which Arnold was to condemn in the 1853 Preface—intensity of introspective feeling, richness of imagery.[66]

Four years before he wrote his review of Arnold's *Empedocles* volume and in the same year as *The Strayed Reveller* appeared, Clough's first long poem, *The Bothie of Toper-Na-Fuosich*, had been highly praised by Kingsley in *Fraser's Magazine* and by W. M. Rossetti in the *Germ* for introducing the habits and preoccupations of daily life. Kingsley praised Clough's originality in introducing into poetry the bizarre 'Cockney-savage Walpurgis-dance' of the undergraduate reading party in Scotland. 'There runs all through the poem a general honesty, a reverence for facts and nature.' Similarly, Rossetti commended 'The aspect of Fact pervading *The Bothie*'.[67] Pre-Raphaelite literalism, known through painting rather than through the literary productions of the *Germ* and *Art and Poetry*, had certainly made an impact by 1853 and must have been one of the contributory causes of a general scepticism about Arnold's retreat to the classics. Such literalism is aptly described by David Masson as 'Aristotelian' in the review censured by Arnold in the 1853 Preface. It is not difficult to see how it could be made to subserve the interest in what is 'human', the familiar and accessible sympathies, for literalism can so easily be associated with everyday affairs and common experiences. A much later review of *Enoch Arden* in the *Westminster* makes the connection explicit, though it is certainly implicit in the critical writing of Clough and Kingsley as well as of Rossetti. The *Westminster* reviewer propounds the Victorian truism that the 'mysterious activity in our sympathies and antipathies' is the central preoccupation of the poet; but in order that these may be aroused, detail, 'circumstantial events', 'pre-Raphaelite particularity', must convince the reader that what he reads is 'real' and 'vivid'. 'Every man and every woman has an intense sympathetic interest in the feelings and fortunes [for this reviewer, the basic experiences, "the marriage-bell, the funeral trappings"] of every other man and every other woman. If this interest seems at times dormant, it is because the fortunes and feelings of others are for the most part either wholly unknown, or very imperfectly narrated and obscurely conceived.'[68] One might call this a pre-Raphaelite variation on the demand for distinctness and precision of realisation in poetry which is so noticeable in earlier Tennyson reviewing.

Once the sympathies become dependent upon contemporary realism, both things become directly connected with the question, what sort of poetry does the age need? Arnold was right to see this as one of the major topics of criticism but he does not do full justice to the intelligence with which it could be discussed, or to the extent to which it was regarded as a highly problematical question. Goldwin Smith, the *Times* critic (see above, p. 33), cast doubt on the Carlylean notion of the poet-prophet and thought this encouraged the poet to be too subservient to, too bound by the circumstances of his age. Artists always, involuntarily and inadvertently reflect their time—'Dante could not help taking a Papal view of religion and society', but 'a man who has ceased to be read for anything else may be read as a specimen of his age'. Generally, however, there is an air of anxiety and worry about such discussions. A review in the *North British*, possibly by Patmore, is typical in its tentativeness. There is, the writer notes, a scarcity of good poetry and the public is still waiting for the coming of a 'Vates sacer', though it is unclear what kind of poet he is to be. He suggests that such a poet will at least be one 'who has felt the difficulties, and perhaps solved the problems of the present time'. But he is entirely clear about the limits of Arnold's classicism. Greater 'sympathy with the wants of the present generation, will endear him to many who would now turn away contemptuously from the self-complacent reverie, and refined indolence, which too often disfigure his pages'.[69] Even the self-confident Kingsley, decided as he is about the irrelevance of Arnold's classical poems—'What does the age want with fragments of an Antigone?'—admits that contemporary poets are 'utterly at a loss what they shall sing'. He is not certain what will 'bear directly upon the cravings and ideas of the age . . . and transfigure it into melody'.[70] After the 1853 Preface, *Fraser's* was even more pessimistic in tone. It contemplates the possibility of the death of poetry. A democratic age has made the portrayal of heroic life impossible: the introspective, self-anatomising drift of modern poetry is self-defeating—poetry no longer concerns itself with the whole of life, with 'the deepest currents of man's thought'. Added to this, the 'realm of fancy' has contracted with the advance of the microscopist and geologist.[71]

I have already quoted from G. H. Lewes's diagnosis of the contemporary situation in the *British Quarterly*. Anticipating much of Arnold's *Function of Criticism* essay (1865), he argues that there is no longer a powerful body of ideas for the poet to build upon, that unless he is to construct an intellectual or philosophical groundwork for himself, and perhaps even if he does, poetry will lean to the eccentric and the grotesque. But critics could be more hopeful, and Tennyson seemed to bring out the optimists. Patmore in a more cheerful vein, and Aubrey de Vere, suggested that there must be some way in which the poet could seize upon the inner spirit of the age in whatever circumstances. Patmore condemns those poets who feel that it is necessary to make a conscious effort to capture 'the spirit of the age', and makes it fully clear that 'The material features of the present age are wholly unfitted to become the final subject-matter of the poet'. What he proposes is an allegorical poetry concerned with shadowing forth some essential quality or conflict in the modern consciousness and his elaborate and often rather absurd interpretation of *The Princess* attempts to show that Tennyson has achieved this.[72] Unlike Lewes he will not admit a relationship between the quality of a culture and that of its art. Art need not be as debased as the culture which produces it. Similarly, 'it is only in a qualified sense that we can admit our age to be unpoetical', De Vere writes. He argues that the imagination is always 'sure to work its way up into the light' and describes the two kinds of poetry, National and Ideal, which emerge according to the sympathetic or unsympathetic environment of the poet. 'If the age be a poetical one, the imagination will embody its sentiment, and illustrate its tendencies. If it be unpoetical, the imagination will not therefore be repressed. It will then create a world for itself.' The great National poet, of course, is Milton and such a poet really can reflect the spirit of the age which is distinct from 'the fashion of the moment or the sentiment of the hour'.[73] Crude accidentals such as the railway train have no place in De Vere's National poetry. De Vere and Patmore certainly escape from the doctrinaire position that the truly modern poet *must* portray the externals and physical environment of the age. Clough is in danger of too readily equating genuine modernity with superficial contemporary realism, though he does not ever present the rather simple-minded conception of modernity which we find in this review of *The Princess*:

> The babbling of running brooks is certainly a more poetical sound than the whirr of factory-wheels, and Roman valour and chivalric honour more inviting themes than the social grievances of the 19th century. It is easier, in short, to follow in the old ruts. . .[74]

However unclear they were about the nature of the poetry which was to have some relationship with the age, critics again and again imply that they mean some kind of sustained and ambitious effort. There is a yearning for a kind of Victorian Milton, or at least and very much a second best, a Victorian Wordsworth. Neither the poem nor the poet ever appeared.[75]

∽　∽　∽

By the 'dialogue of the mind with itself' and his reference to an 'allegory of the state of one's own mind' Arnold seems to have meant, in the first place, reflective, philosophical poetry and, in the second, and possibly more immediately in his mind, personal, lyrical poetry about the poet's own emotions and feelings. Most Victorian discussion is concerned with introspective, self-probing poetry, yet oddly enough, Arnold and his critics were very much in agreement about the dangerous tendencies of both these things. Arnold's early poetry was constantly criticised for its refined introspections and there is something flagrant about the graceful ease with which Arnold joins forces with his critics here. By quoting from Masson's *North British* article, which is not primarily concerned with either reflective or introspective poetry, Arnold seems to confuse matters further. Yet when one realises that, like Arnold, Masson is proposing a theory of poetry which he calls dramatic but which is not dramatic in Arnold's strictly classical sense, and that this theory of dramatic poetry derives from Keats and the letters of Keats, the reasons for Arnold's irritation with Masson become plainer. Masson's is a romantic theory. He saw the poet as projecting himself dramatically into different personae, experiences and states of feeling. With Masson we are back with Fox's notions of the poet's 'transmigration of the soul' and with Hallam's belief in the poetry of sensation: for once, Coleridge, Keats and James Mill join hands as the prompters of similar theory. Masson was reviewing E. S. Dallas's *Poetics* (this treatise is very important in the theory Masson built) and the poems of Alexander Smith, the spasmodic poet with whom Arnold associated all the hectically disorganised excess—sensuous, emotional, formal and stylistic—of Keats. Keats and the Spasmodics were clearly in Arnold's mind when the Preface was written ('What a brute you were to tell me to read Keats' letters', he had exclaimed to Clough) and Arnold's antipathy would have been reinforced by the fact that Masson's criticism had been obviously influenced by the letters of Keats.[76] For all their differences Arnold, in this matter at least, plays Christopher North to Masson's Fox and Hallam.

Yet a Puritan dislike of excess, however strongly Arnold may have felt it, was not the main reason for his dislike of Masson's theories. The great significance of Masson's review is that it proposes a quite different notion of the *subject* of poetry than the one assumed either by Arnold or by the orthodox Victorian belief in the limits of sympathy which I have shown to be so persistently at work in reviews of this time.

Masson's views also imply a very different conception of the moral function of poetry than the one governing criticism at this time.

Masson was clearly influenced by Coleridge but the immediate basis of his theory is, I think, Keats's letter about the 'chameleon poet' who can lose his own identity and imagine others at will—'But even now I am perhaps not speaking from myself, but from some character in whose soul I now live'—combined with the notion of sympathy expounded in the *Poetics* of Dallas (1852).[77] Richard Monckton Milnes had edited the *Life, Letters, and Literary Remains of John Keats* in 1848 and the chameleon poet letter clearly made an impact on some critics. In his *Edinburgh Review* article of 1849 De Vere discusses the whole notion of negative capability and calls this dramatic, projecting quality of the poet's imagination 'versatility' or 'sympathy'.[78] Masson uses Keats to argue that the imagination is free and liberated from the poet's personality and also from prescribed or traditional subjects, whether pre-Raphaelite literalism (he is at one with Arnold in being suspicious of this), or epic material. The poet's imagination is exercised mainly through the exploration of states of feeling alien to him and these are likely to be associated with character and thus to become essentially dramatic in spirit if not in presentation. Yet however much the poet works through interpreting moods and feelings, these are externalised by being translated into an objective equivalent, what he calls an 'artificial concrete', a kind of allegory, and are *not* the poet's own. De Vere had earlier said much the same—'all genuine poetry is in its spirit dramatic'. Versatility 'consists in mobility'.

What should be so subversive about these beliefs? Arnold, as I have said, does not even acknowledge the dramatic aspect of Masson's theory but simply implies that it exposes poetry to a riot of feeling. (Perhaps what Masson proposed was so far from the orthodox drama that Arnold mentions in the Preface that the definition seemed no more than a verbal sleight-of-hand. Arnold could always deal briskly with the pretentious.) Of course, the theory does expose poetry to feeling but it also does more. It grants the poet a freedom, a moral and imaginative licence, simply not envisaged by the Victorian critic. Dallas's writings suggest how this could happen. In his *Poetics* Dallas also proposed that the highest form of poetry was the dramatic and invoked the notion of sympathy (actually recommending Adam Smith to the reader) to support his claim. Dramatic poetry enables the poet to exercise the greatest imaginative and moral freedom, he says: 'we may, or may not, according to our pleasure, put ourselves into this or that situation, and adopt such or such sentiments'.[79] Drama is more truly creative than any other form, including the epic—'For, in the sympathy and appropriation of a dramatist, as already has been said, freedom is implied; and what is freedom, if not in some sort the power to originate?' Dramatic sympathy takes us 'through the gamut of human emotions', teaching by experience and not by precept. Unlike Masson, Dallas had in mind only formal drama though he allows that the modern lyric will always be dramatic in spirit.

It is clear that Dallas has every intention of producing a thoroughly religious and, indeed, Christian theory of poetry, based on eighteenth-century thinkers such as Berkeley and Smith, but in his emphasis on freedom he leaves out of the notion of sympathy—and nowhere implies—what every Victorian critic put in, that it confirms the common bonds man has with man, corroborates the familiar, basic facts of our moral and emotional experience and confirms us in the ordinary duties and obligations of existence. On the contrary, Dallas can be taken to imply that an infinite range of experience new and strange can be opened up for the poet (it is interesting to compare his discussion of sympathy with that of Marston, quoted above, p. 10). Masson certainly made this assumption and so, less happily, did De Vere. A whole range of new experience is open to the poet—'regions unknown and forms of life untried'. The poet requires 'large sympathies' and the 'imaginative insight of the affections', De Vere wrote, in order to extend both his own and the reader's mind to new feelings and experience. As a perpetually enlarging and expanding influence he compares sympathy with love. In these three writers the emphasis is always on the enlarging, extending power of poetry and the immense variety of new experience to be explored, whereas the bulk of Victorian critics, including Arnold at this time, stressed the circumscribing of experience. This was a restrictionist theory, whatever the urgency with which it could be argued.

If the poet could be released from his identity it followed that his informing moral grip on the work of art could not be achieved. De Vere, who sometimes seems anxious about the implications of the theory he expounds and not quite sure where it will lead him, will not allow this.

And it is truly when the heart is most fixed that the imagination can afford to be most flexible. It may wave like a pine tree in the breeze, if, like the pine, it sends its root deep into the rocky soil. On these conditions, the more versatile the genius is, the ampler will be its sweep, and the mightier its resilient power.[80]

Masson, more reluctantly, admits that the poet can never entirely escape from himself and in this sense the poem has to be an allegory of the poet's mind.

> In short, the imagination, though in one sense it acts loose and apart from the personality, flying freely round and round it, like a sea-bird round a rock, seems, in a deeper sense, restricted by the same law of the personality in its choice and apprehension of the concrete.

The pine and the sea-bird are convenient images for each critic and remind us how much critical discussion is metaphorical; the image of dramatic projection is itself a persuasive image. Image or not, however, Masson is extraordinarily rigorous in his attempt to distinguish what is 'dramatic' and what is 'personal' in a poem:

> The poet may imagine opinions, doctrines, heresies, cogitations, debates, expositions . . . from which his own soul stands royally dis-entangled. . . The moment any of the doctrines he is dealing with melts subjectively into his own personal state of being . . . that moment the poet ceases to be a poet pure. . .[81]

Masson's theory of pure poetry has interesting correspondences with Hallam's distinction between poets of sensation and reflection. Hallam limits the material of the poet far more than Masson but both emphasise that the poet's imaginations are to be realised by and embodied in, as Masson puts it, 'a peculiar richness of language'.

It is difficult to believe that Arnold was really convinced of the validity of the extreme position he put forward in the Preface yet juxtaposed with Masson's essay it becomes understandable. We know from *The Strayed Reveller*, the title-poem of his first volume, how much Arnold was attracted by and yet resisted the Keatsian abandon-ment of selfhood to diverse and intense experience: perhaps the Preface should be seen as an attempt to counter romantic licence and subjectivity by reviving, dignifying and ennobling the Victorian claim that poetry should appeal to the human and the familiar, an effort to rescue this notion from the homely and the snug. There is something forlorn about Arnold's attempt to invest the essential, simple, primary affections with more grandeur than they can stand. But the Preface commands respect, alluring though Masson is.

∽   ∽   ∽

Very few critics actually adopted the dramatic theories I have discussed and it was not until the sixties that one sees anything like a growing acceptance of these ideas. One of Browning's early reviewers was able to make better sense of him by seeing him as a dramatic and objective poet: 'The poet's genius is essentially dramatic, but not in the sense which the word vulgarly bears. Mr Browning's is mostly the drama of character, not of incident, or scenic effect.'[82] W. C. Roscoe in the *National Review* discusses Tennyson in this way, only to deny him the status of a dramatic poet even in an extended sense. The Hero of *Maud* is nothing but 'a mere morbid mouthpiece'.[83] Even though many of Arnold's critics were intensely irritated by the Preface (as no doubt they were intended to be) they were substantially in agreement with him about the importance of a large theme, about the subjectivity of modern poetry and about form and style.

There was, as reviews I have quoted of *The Princess* (see note 75) suggest, much demand for a sustained, ambitious poem which would escape from the fragmentary lyric and Arnold's grand proposal for a poem based on classical and objective action might be seen as a scheme for such a poem. Nobody disagreed with Arnold about the necessity of a noble theme and no one denied that the basic material of poetry was the primary human affections. The only problem was how they had best manifest themselves—in ancient or in modern dress. The division of opinion for or against is not what is important here, but the reasons and arguments which were put forward. There is no doubt that the Preface stimulated intelligent reconsideration.

Few attacks on the Preface were as violent and sweeping as that by J. D. Coleridge in the *Christian Remembrancer*. Coleridge called it 'fallacious' and illogical and argued that there was no reason why ancient subjects *in themselves* should be preferred if poetry is achieved, as Arnold himself implies, 'by means often the most homely and ordinary, by appeals to those emotions of the heart which are, indeed, all-powerful, but all-pervading, which all men share in common, and in which one age does not differ from another'. Undermining the basis of Arnold's argument as no other critic was to do he asks why poetry should be concerned with the grandiose and why necessarily with action. He ends with a somewhat inconsistent attack on Arnold for advocating 'the art that has no relevancy to actual life', the art which portrays no deep conflict with evil.[84]

In general, however, critics argued that modern themes *could* be universalised, that familiar things could be idealised, and that the permanent feelings to which poetry appeals might actually be destroyed and debased by the anachronistic introduction of distracting classical equipage. *Putnam's Monthly Magazine* reasoned that to depend upon classical 'accessories' rather than 'the necessary familiarity of circumstance' could only be destructive to the poet's aim. The *Dublin University Magazine* took a malicious pleasure in pointing out just how involuntarily modern and inappropriate became the 'household drudge' simile in *Sohrab and Rustum*, the supposedly 'classical' Virgilian simile of the rich woman contemplating her maid. It simply suggests 'a vision of a London cinder-wench, in chamois gloves, lighting the fire-wood with a lucifer match, while her mistress lies a-bed'.[85] A modern reader might add that it suggests a later Arnold, the theorist of culture, glimpsing the hidden, ugly world of Wragge and her sort as he came down at dawn to write his lectures. Typical of writers who felt that modern themes could be universalised and dignified, a belief rather different from Clough's everyday realism, is the *Eclectic* reviewer. The examples of poetry he finds in the 'bustling, perplexed life of the present' are woman and her 'silent heroism' and 'unconscious self-sacrifice'. If we write of Balaclava rather than Troy we will still write of heroic human action and 'that marvellous human heart which is beating beneath it'.[86] 'There is poetry in Australian emigrations' and heroism in modern life, Kingsley asserted in spite of the pessimistic beginning of his review in *Fraser's Magazine*.[87] The age of Napoleon and Wellington, the glorious possibilities of England and America, are surely capable of being absorbed into poetry. The Preface pushed people into reconsidering the nature of contemporaneity in modern poetry. Shairp in the *North British* suggested that the themes which Arnold proposed as grandly untinged by contemporary issues had at one time been of intense national relevance.[88] Patmore distinguished between the superficial, modish contemporaneity of the Spasmodics and the truly modern poetry which can assimilate and utilise the productions of its culture—'no sooner are the facts of science regarded in their widest reference to the universe and its source, than they may abandon the swaddling clothes of prose, and assume the singing robes of verse'.[89] The whole debate is conducted with an awareness of the complexity of the question. Lewes, not unfriendly to Arnold, but arguing against the dangers of imitation of past literature in contrast to creative assimilation of it, is not alone in his intelligence.[90]

When they considered the second great issue of the Preface, the harmfulness and 'modernity' of introspective poetry, the extent to which Arnold made people think is even more evident. The discussion of introspective poetry was strikingly more alert after the Preface than it was at the time of the publication of *In Memoriam* (1850) which hostile critics described as 'egotistical'. Significantly enough, approving critics of the poem described it in as nearly Arnoldian terms as such a poem could be described—as a noble universalisation of the domestic and the familiar, the primary emotions 'enlarged into relevance with universal humanity'.[91]

Probably introspection rather than philosophical reflection seems to have been uppermost in Arnold's mind when he described the dialogue of the mind with itself and it is certainly with this that most critics also are preoccupied. Put under pressure by the Preface, a few critics became more accommodating about subjective poetry than most of their contemporaries. Though J. A. Froude, for instance, was clearly attracted by a certain colourless loftiness in Arnold's poetry, he questioned whether it was not the treatment rather than the subject of *Empedocles* which was at fault. Who could say confidently that *Werther* was a mistake?

> But we must be careful how we narrow our theories in such matters. In *Werther* we have an instance of the same trial, with the same issue as Mr Arnold has described in *Empedocles*, and to say that *Werther* was a mistake, is to circumscribe the sphere of art by a definition which the public taste will refuse to recognise.[92]

Some reviewers argued that poetry was necessarily psychological and inward in the nineteenth century, and so even where they agreed with the principles of the Preface, they emended Arnold's universal human action to universal human *feeling*. 'The present age is a metaphysical and psychological one, and poetry, as the reflex of the age, must, to be popular, exhibit the inner life of man—mental action, feelings, passions, spiritualities', wrote the reviewer of the *Dublin University Magazine* (1854, 737). *Putnam's* (1855) and the *Eclectic* (1855) pointed out that it was sentiment, not action, feeling and not the construction of

Sohrab and Rustum, which accounted for its success. But only W. C. Roscoe, that independent and sophisticated critic, went so far as to question the *necessity* of representing what is universal and the permanent passions in poetry, claiming that complexity and variety were the stuff of poetry and insisting that the *poem* makes the subject, not the subject the poem—'to delineate a complex individual character as it existed in ancient Egypt, would be hard, to say the least of it'.[93]

Yet on the whole, both before and after the Preface, critics shied away from introspective, analytical lyricism almost with a reflex action of dislike. It was nagging, morbid, self-conscious and unhealthy. Typical of this reaction, and of the vocabulary in which it was expressed, is Shairp's highly perceptive discussion of Arnold's poetry in the *North British Review* (1854). The 'refreshingness' of *The Scholar-Gipsy* is destroyed by allusions to the restlessness of the present age and so does nothing to 'strengthen and restore' because its lamentations are 'unmanly'. There is a 'morbid languor' about some of the poems and Shairp demands 'some better, healthier spirit', appealing to 'men's energies, their hopes, their moral aspirations'. Shairp exhorts Arnold in curiously Keatsian terms to liberate himself from the frigidity of self-indulgent emotion, and instead to 'speak straight out of things which he has felt and tested on his own pulses'. He misses 'the one pervading poet's heart, that throb of feeling which is the true inspiration'.[94] Clearly, high passion is to be welcomed, but the low passion of the analytic, self-consciously exploratory lyric was unacceptable. The manliness and sweeping power of Browning's poetry was practically the only aspect of Browning ever to be praised at this time—it was emphasised, one feels, when the critic would respond to nothing else and when it mastered a reaction against an excess of abstruse philosophical reflection. *Douglas Jerrold's Shilling Magazine*, for instance, praised 'the passion with which every line of his productions is fraught' and found the fragmentariness and abruptness of Browning's poetry proof of 'genuine inspiration'. They 'display the terrible energy of his conceptions' and 'create in the reader's mind a heat and vehemence corresponding to the author's'. Comparing the poems of Elizabeth Barrett and Browning, the *English Review* talked of 'the sensation experienced in issuing from a cathedral to the open air: the one, consecrated all over, its atmosphere incense . . . the other, nature's own wide temple,—fresh, genial, invigorating, and free'. Quoting Procter, the *Examiner* reviewer remarked that 'the motion of verse corresponds with the power of the poet, as the swell and tumult of the sea answer to the winds that call them up', but he warned that Browning's passion and his intellect are continually strangling one another.[95]

This failure to find a way of exploring the dialogue of the mind with itself, a failure the more marked because so much nineteenth-century poetry is exploratory and analytical, the poetry of *processes* of feeling, can only be explained by the dogged persistence of the idea that the sympathies of the poet are outgoing, rather like love, moving out of the self; that the feelings of the reader and the poet are stirred involuntarily and unselfconsciously. Dallas begins his *Poetics*, for instance, by asserting the 'unconsciousness' of art. In his *Two Lectures on the Influence of Poetry on the Working Classes* (1852), F. W. Robertson said that a man is capable of responding to poetry who has felt 'those emotions which are uncalculating', which break through the 'crust' of 'selfishness'.[96] In his review of Arnold in the *Germ*, W. M. Rossetti noted that art was becoming more 'self-conscious' in the late forties, 'the only permanent trace of the now old usurping deluge of Byronism'.[97] Emotion, said the *North British* reviewer of *In Memoriam*, can corrupt into a 'loathsome independent life' if it is 'watched'. But in *In Memoriam* it is the 'manna which supports the life of man', presumably because it is un-watched.[98]

Although Arnold's Preface forced some critics to re-think their attitudes to subjective lyricism and to the implications of modern analytical poetry, Arnold, Clough and Tennyson were all attacked for their morbid, unhealthy introspections both before and after the Preface. Both Arnold and Clough were criticised in the *Guardian* for their indulgence in analysis. Though one had no right to see the poems as autobiographical, in Clough's poetry 'there runs a morbid self-consciousness, a critical and sensitive distrust of self'. The reviewer asserted that 'states of minds and feelings, however interesting, want to be associated with outward realities' as in *Locksley Hall*. Aytoun in his *Blackwood's* review of Arnold's poetry in 1849, whose remarks on Arnold's retreat from the age I have already quoted, complained of a general lack of 'heartiness' in *The Strayed Reveller* volume.[99] 'Both are very *sad*', the *English Review* complained with heavy irony of Arnold and Clough, though possibly its determination to see both poets as 'helpless, cheerless' doubters was the result of an evident high church antipathy to Dr Thomas Arnold.[100] It is interesting that reviewers of *Sohrab and Rustum* who disliked any kind of morbidity invariably criticised the final simile of the Oxus, complaining that it deprived the culminating situation of its pure, human, tragic outline and moved into unhealthy subjectivity. Both Kingsley and the *Blackwood's* reviewer of 1854 made this point. Hostile reviewers of *In Memoriam* managed to find almost as much 'watched' emotion in the poem as they did in *Maud*. 'They are too mournfully monotonous; there is too much of the egotism of grief in them. . .' Manley Hopkins headed his *Times* review the 'Poetry of Sorrow' and called parts of the poem almost blasphemous in the disproportion of feeling and language to the situation.[101] When *Maud* appeared the complaint against its morbidity was almost universal and it is almost as if every critic had read the 1853 Preface. The ravings of the hero 'do not contain a touch of pathos' and Tennyson reduces his madness to 'absolute nonsense', especially if we compare the treatment of madness in *King Lear*—the *Blackwood's* review is typical. The *Irish Quarterly* saw the poem as the decadence of Tennyson's genius:[102]

> What is the characteristic of *Maud*? Maudlin semi-insanity; words meaning nothing worth remembering; and a disjointed tale of love and blood, to be discovered after close and laborious application to the text, omitting the various gasps and gaps of passionate prose run mad which intervene. . .

Alexander Smith is actually preferable. Only Franklin Lushington's analysis of *In Memoriam* in terms of a slow evolution of feeling moving through many shifts and contradictions, and a solitary review of *Maud*, interestingly enough, by David Masson, in the *British Quarterly*, who saw the poem as essentially dramatic, show anything like an ability to grasp and analyse the poetry of the dialogue of the mind.

Masson's *British Quarterly* review is remarkable in its ability to respond to *Maud* as an experiment in form:

> He seems to have resolved in this instance to make the attempt, suggested by the partial example of some of his former poems, to write a work in which a continuous story, implying a certain moral lesson, should be evolved, not in the usual narrative manner, but in a series of songs, or lyrical effusions. This he has accomplished by the simple and yet happy device of concentrating the attention on the principal personage of the supposed history, and representing the facts of the history itself through the medium of twenty-six

lyrical soliloquies, each imagined as being uttered at a critical moment in the progress of the history. It would be well if those critics who have been accusing the poet of diseased 'subjectivity' and what not, were to attend to this peculiarity of the present poem. All songs or lyrical pieces are, in their very nature, 'subjective,' being expressions either of the poet's personal feelings or of feelings imagined by him as belonging to such and such circumstances; and the positive peculiarity of *Maud* is, that the poet has there contrived to weave together a poem which, though 'subjective' in its parts, is as 'objective' as any one could desire in its total impression. For our part we regard the poem, on this very account, as something of a novelty in English poetry, and as a new proof of Tennyson's exquisite skill as an artist.[103]

But this groping towards the dramatic autonomy of the poem—the very tentativeness suggests how new the idea was—is exceptional. It is as isolated as a review in the *Eclectic*, which talks of Browning's 'unformal' drama and begins by saying that a poem creates its own laws.[104] Indeed, notions of form and unity at this time are elementary —if they are discussed at all. Arnold's Aristotelian rigour went further than most critics thought of going but, as the discussions of *The Princess* described above suggest, his position was not unique. Unity and completeness meant for most critics a kind of surface homogeneity, tidy outlines and clear narrative with unsurprising transitions. At most they thought in terms of a 'leading idea' and 'unity of emotion'. The *Athenaeum* reviewer of *Pippa Passes*, for instance, does not remark on the peculiar structure of the poem but discovers a leading idea and proceeds to discuss it.[105] Objections to the Spasmodics were very much on Arnold's lines and generally critics had no more positive notions of form than of something which was *not* full of startling juxtapositions and confusing leaps from one kind of material to another. It is not until discussions of *Merope* that reviewers are prepared to say explicitly that a poem should take the form that its material suggests—that it should be 'organic'. W. C. Roscoe was the most positive of such critics, writing in the *National Review*. He makes a distinction between mechanical and organic form—'there is a form which is one with its spirit, and is its outer manifestation; there is another which is merely a sort of outside shell', and hints that Arnold has certainly not achieved this oneness in *Merope*. Though he has a 'nice sense of the beauty of form', his poem is well finished rather than truly organic. But at least Arnold understands that 'finish of execution and harmony of proportion are essential to the completeness of a poem'.[106] This is one of the rare hints of Coleridgean thinking in Victorian criticism. On the whole, however, it would be true to say that the Victorian critic had few ways of discussing a poem, particularly a long poem, in its entirety. No discussions of Tennyson's *Idylls of the King* or of Morris's *Earthly Paradise* attempt to see the poems as a formal whole. Sometimes one will find discussions of a poem in terms of the unifying quality of its imagery but this is very rare.

The strong need for consistency and homogeneity of outline felt by critics made most writers agree with Arnold's stipulation about language in the 1853 Preface. The most spirited assent came from Coventry Patmore in the *Edinburgh Review* which attacked the Spasmodic 'christmas-tree style':

> Sugar-plums, quick-silvered globes, oranges, gimcracks, and lighted candles are not more incongruous ornaments to the stunted fir tree which they decorate for the nonce at a Christmas party than the tinsel thoughts and images which illustrate the subjects chosen by these poets.[107]

Earlier the *Eclectic Review* had used the same kind of vocabulary while agreeing with Arnold's Preface and tracing the current excess of language to the Spasmodics.

> Look at the working up of the poetical scrap-books that we have had. The paste that has been made with the plums stuck in afterwards. The tinselling and tinkering, and artificial-flower making. The wealth of imagery hiding the poverty of thought.[108]

Ornate styles were frequently described in terms of decoration, something externally applied. Far preferable was the utterly 'simple style' discussed by *Fraser's Magazine* when it found Arnold's belief in restraint and austerity borne out in practice in *Sohrab and Rustum*. *Sohrab and Rustum* achieves 'a strain of masculine and truly heroical poetry' by the use of 'homely words and objects', transmuted by the loftiness of the epic into a 'noble homeliness'. High homeliness—this is what can be achieved by simple language. As usual, the Spasmodics are attacked and Arnold is praised for managing to write poetry 'without the slightest taint of "poetry"' in it.[109] Froude voiced a general feeling in the *Westminster*—'A perfect style does not strike at all'.[110] It is rare to find even the tentatively hesitant dissent of the *Blackwood's* reviewer, Aytoun, who found Greek tragedy 'deficient in richness and flexibility' and felt that Arnold demanded an artificial 'nakedness'.[111]

Almost without exception the reasons given for the importance of a simple style are the ones found in discussions of Tennyson's early poems: 'drapery', as Spedding put it, gets in the way of 'humanity'; the style which does not strike at all exposes the human heart. There were occasional attempts, like those of Masson, De Vere and Patmore, to find ways of exploring the rich associative properties of language but in general critics unconsciously adopted the criteria of Arnold's 'grand style' which were to be formulated in *On Translating Homer* (1861), simply extending its application to many varieties of poetry. Interestingly enough, when *On Translating Homer* was discussed by an *Edinburgh* reviewer, C. S. M. Phillipps, the grand style was found so universally applicable that 'it is attainable in many distinct styles'. 'It is not necessarily grand, because it is applicable to many purposes which are in themselves morally and esthetically mean and ignoble.' The plainness and clarity of the 'exquisite perfection of art' which Arnold calls the grand style is 'not necessarily grand, and is not, properly speaking, a style'.[112] For most critics a style should be a non-style and language should be transparent, like water. The innumerable attacks on Browning's language—grotesque, eccentric, perverse, obscure—to which I have referred were inevitable in this ascetic context.

CHANGE IN THE 1860S

I have chosen four reviews to suggest the critical preoccupations of the sixties, and I have restricted these to the poets I have previously discussed here. For the best way to demonstrate the kind of demands being made on poets in the sixties is by a comparison of the later with the earlier attitudes to the same poet. There is such a wide spread of critical position in this decade that it would be misleading to say that any one was typical. At the same time, it is indubitable that things were changing and one is forced to say that something was 'happening' to critical opinion in this decade, and what was happening is best suggested by comparison. There is no controversy in this decade from which one can locate critical attitudes, as in the Arnold or Tennyson debates, and perhaps this in itself is significant, suggesting that there was no central core of opinion as in the earlier decades, that opinion was becoming more varied, more difficult to define.

Of course, this is not to say that people did not hold strong opinions; the fury which greeted Meredith's *Modern Love* (1862) and Swinburne's *Poems and Ballads* (1866) and the publication of Rossetti's poems in 1870 gives the impression that nothing had changed much since the publication of *Maud,* for the response to these poems is a logical extension of the response to *Maud.* It displays the same unwillingness to see the poem as an autonomous dramatic entity, the same refusal to see the treatment of experience which is not the shared, basic experience of us all as anything but an aberration, the same refusal, in other words, to adhere to anything but the most limited notion of sympathy as a criterion of moral value. After the reception of *Maud,* how familiar these attacks on *Modern Love* will seem. The *Spectator* noted that the 'foolish-sublime' of Meredith's 'modern lust' resulted in the misuse of language, in verbal tricks instead of simplicity—'No clever man who prizes grandiloquent ornament above modest meaning is guilty of a mere verbal negligence, for this goes to the heart of the matter'.[113] The *Athenaeum* asked for 'a healthier purpose, a purer taste and a clearer style'.[114] The *Saturday Review* compared the treatment of Guinevere in Tennyson's *Idylls*—pure, simple and universalised— with the 'moral mistake' of the treatment of adultery in *Modern Love,* with its unhealthy particularity and morbid detail: 'It was no doubt his conviction, derived from French authorities, that there is a species of nineteenth-century infidelity, more recondite, more interesting, more intellectual forsooth, than those which have gone before...'[115] If adultery is to be described in poetry at all, then let it at least be the unrecondite adultery of Guinevere. R. W. Buchanan's attack on Swinburne in the *Athenaeum* is on very much the same lines, and resembles his later and more violent attack on Rossetti. As with Meredith, the pernicious French are blamed for the poet's depravity and the critic refuses to believe that this 'unclean' 'filth' can be sincere.[116] John Morley's discussion of Swinburne is very much more sensible: he is less prone to automatic moral outrage and makes a careful distinction between the attempt to revive 'the grand old Pagan conception of joy' and the 'bestial delights' with which Swinburne has confused his notion of joy. Morley really does go to the heart of the matter, pointing to the repetition and redundancy of Swinburne's language, to the way in which conceits do the duty for thoughts, and in doing so he describes what Arnold and every reviewer of *Maud* would have accepted as a description of the highest poetry—the note of 'enlarged *meditation*' missing from Swinburne's work.[117]

Yet the reaction to Meredith, Swinburne and Rossetti would be misleading if it were taken to represent critical opinion at this time. Far more illuminating is a comparison between the reaction to Tennyson's *Idylls of the King* (1859) and to *The Holy Grail* (1869)—ten years later. With the *Idylls*, general approval of Tennyson was probably at its highest so far as one can tell from the evidence of reviews alone. With *Enoch Arden* (1864) critics tend to say, interestingly enough, that the poem will make Tennyson even more popular than ever ('A child may understand it', was the dubious praise of *Chambers' Journal*),[118] while carefully dissociating the fact of popularity from the intrinsic value of the poem.[119] It is with *The Holy Grail* that adverse criticism begins to be noticeable and what is important is not so much the fact of adverse criticism itself as the reasons which are given both for disapproving *and* approving of the poem, for the grounds of criticism are quite different from those of ten years before.

Bagehot's approval of the *Idylls* and his reasons for it were echoed, though with less weight and authority, by almost every critic of this poem. Bagehot has been reading the 1853 Preface, and his discussion reads like an application of its principles to the poem.

Why is this poem so much preferable to *Maud*? he asks, and takes Arnold as his starting point. 'One of our poets has said, in answer to the critics, "a great action" is a great action anywhere; surely it is as good if it happened in former ages as if it had happened yesterday.' The reasons he gives for preferring the great action of the past are substantially Arnold's. In the first place, it is easier to select, refine and universalise. The novel is the form best suited to the portrayal of the copiousness of adventitious detail with which we are surrounded in modern life, but the action of the past can be reduced to its primary essentials—'If King Arthur existed, there were peasants in his time, and these peasants had wives, and these wives had children, and these children had measles'. Poetry was never meant to absorb the trivia of measles; its concern is with isolating the basic human actions such as love and war which we find in legend, free from the distractions of the modern world, where 'everything runs into everything else'. Poetry must provide a satisfyingly shaped and refined 'large-hand copy of life'. In the comparison of Tennyson with the earlier Romantic poets which ends the article Tennyson is placed above Keats for possessing 'meditative tact', the 'reflective gift of a mature man', and actually praised for being a kind of 'drawing-room Wordsworth', including a greater range of human experience than Wordsworth.[120]

Arnold and Bagehot together provide the rationale for some of the commonest mid-nineteenth-century critical positions: after reading them one can understand the unexpressed values which lie behind the many praises of the *Idylls* for their dignity, their 'human' qualities and their simplicity. Gladstone is typical.

> It is national: it is Christian. It is also human in the largest and deepest sense; and, therefore, though highly national, it is universal; for it rests upon those depths and breadths of our nature to which all its truly great developments in all nations are alike essentially and closely related. The distance is enough for atmosphere, not too much for detail; enough for romance, not too much for sympathy.

Like so many critics, Gladstone also praised Tennyson for the purity and simplicity of his style, the 'native' or 'Saxon' style, as it was often called—Tennyson's metaphors have the clarity of outline of shells, 'each individually with its outline as well drawn, its separateness as clear, its form as true to nature'.[121]

If we compare these reactions with hostile discussions of *The Holy Grail* it is like moving in a different critical element; Tennyson's poetry was attacked, to put it briefly, for not having caught the measles.[122] Critics want complexity and detail, psychological and otherwise, a richness of dramatic insight which they cannot find in the portrayals of the Arthurian poem. Tennyson's poetry is described as immature and naïve, limited and restricted in the area of experience with which it deals. The question of poetry and the age is much less important to these later critics; explicitly or implicitly they recognise the distinction between a determined or involuntary relationship between the poet and his environment—not necessarily good in itself—and a managed or manipulated one, also not necessarily good, and possibly deleterious, to poetry. The critical positives of North, of Sterling and of Arnold have been reversed. Ten years after Gladstone's eulogy the *Quarterly Review* described as defects those things of which Bagehot and Gladstone had approved:

there is one quality which some people have fancied they have seen in Mr Tennyson, which is unquestionably not to be found in him; and that is, the clear knowledge of *men*, of individual character. He is no dramatist . . . what Mr Tennyson knows of men is capable of being put into a very few lines. He knows that, of human beings, some fall in love, and . . . by report, that men sometimes fight . . .[123]

What is being looked for here is not the primary human experience, portrayed in simple outlines, but particular and complex psychological insight. This reviewer, J. R. Mozley, thought that the contemporary science and philosophy with which Tennyson's poems were garnished were the pale reflections of 'other minds'. It is significant that he had written on Coleridge two years before.[124] Similarly, Alfred Austin, in a sparklingly gay, iconoclastic essay, had seen Tennyson as a limited lyric poet of nature, not even great enough to commit faults, with the tame 'completeness of a limited mind'. He seizes acutely upon Tennyson's fascination with the garden and uses this as an image of the qualities of the poetry—pretty, consciously cultivated, withdrawn and enclosed, cut off from life. He attacks Tennyson for his interest in science and asserts that he has only been praised for expressing the age because he has managed to portray it as it wishes to be portrayed. He ends by refusing to believe that anybody will speak of the time as the age of Tennyson; the age of Railways, Destructive Criticism, Penny Newspapers, yes, but Tennyson is too remote from the central pre-occupations of his time to merit such a description.[125] Prophetic as Austin is of many later twentieth-century criticisms of Tennyson, he was wrong here.

Outstanding for the perceptiveness of their criticism are two discussions of Tennyson, the first in the *British Quarterly Review* and the second by Richard Simpson in the *North British Review*. The *British Quarterly* concentrates on the suitability of the Arthurian legends for a major modern poem and concludes that though these 'half-empty forms of fancy' may enable Tennyson to infuse them with his peculiarly modern, brooding scepticism, they are for this very reason remote and debilitating, allowing Tennyson to retreat into a 'close and over-heated' atmosphere or else breaking down altogether under the weight of modern significance imposed on them.[126] The main argument of Simpson's lengthy study of Tennyson's poetic career is the narrow range of his imagination—'dreaming is substituted for living, and thought is a trance'. Everything is pervaded by unreality and in his descriptions 'the scene is first in idea reduced to a picture; and then the picture, not the scene, is the immediate object of the poetical description'. Pathos, but not dramatic energy, is his strong point. Where previous critics had praised the domestic idylls Simpson finds them tame and self-indulgent, tentative and uncertain in intention. Finally, where Bagehot finds him mature, Simpson finds him unsophisticated and monotonously limited, intellectually and imaginatively—

> But the satisfaction of the mature reader with Mr Tennyson will hardly stand the test of too much repetition, and, still less, of comparison with profounder poets. His characters come out not as real men, but as boys and girls acting the parts of men and women in their Christmas games. The words he puts into their mouths are full of beauty and refinement; but they illustrate only a narrow segment of that humanity which it is the privilege of poetry, at its highest power, to exhibit in myriad-sided completeness. [127]

Things were loosening up. In a signed essay on 'French Aesthetics', in the *Contemporary Review*, Edward Dowden wrote:

> Art has an end of its own, enacts its laws freely with reference to this end, is a self-governing republic, and is not a dependency of utility, or science, or history, or politics, or morality, or religion. . . We are beginning to smile at the poetical justice without which, not long ago, it was considered improper to wind up a story . . . let it [the story] close leaving the sense of unity,—the sad or joyous story of a life on earth, one round of existence,—but not the sense of finality, as if the whole purpose of the life were told.

Disappointingly, Dowden either ignores or does not think relevant Baudelaire, Gautier, the Parnassians, and concentrates on Cousin's *Du Vrai, du Beau, et du Bien* (1818) and Taine's *Philosophie de l'Art*. But though he does not seem aware of some of the most interesting developments in French thought he is carefully self-conscious and carefully sophisticated about the relationship of art and morality. Earlier, belief in the moral efficacy of poetry is so much an *assumption* that there are not many sustained discussions of it: in the sixties overt discussions, such as the *London Quarterly*'s argument, arising out of a review of the *Idylls* (see above, p. 12), that the *morality* and the *unity* of a work of art are not the same thing, are more common. Dowden dismisses the portrayal of the 'huckstering virtues, of which the great result is called "success in life"' as irrelevant to art.[128] Oddly, his phrase anticipates Walter Pater's flagrantly aesthetic definition of 'success in life' in his review of William Morris's poems in the *Westminster Review* only two years later in 1868:

> To burn always with this hard gem-like flame, to maintain this ecstasy, is success in life. . . Of this wisdom, the poetic passion, the desire of beauty, the love of art for art's sake, has most; for art comes to you professing frankly to give nothing but the highest quality to your moments as they pass, and simply for those moments' sake.

Pater, of course, postulating as he does in this review 'the sense of escape' as one of the functions of art is a complete anomaly at this time, yet as an index of the variousness and the transitional quality of this decade it is worth remembering that Pater's aestheticism and the crude attacks on Swinburne existed side by side.[129]

Manifestly, a change was occurring but the arguments by which this change was defended were in the same terms as discussions in the previous decades; the same formulations were current, the same values assumed. In the reviews which form the third section of this book discussion is still in terms of the proper subject of poetry and of the moral importance of the sympathies. The difference is that the notion of the proper subject for poetry has been widened almost beyond recognition and correspondingly the interpretation of sympathy has been silently and imperceptibly redefined. It is the interpretation we find in Dallas, Masson, De Vere, not in Marston, Sterling and Arnold. Even in Swinburne's defence of *Poems and Ballads* in *Notes on Poems and Reviews* (1866), where one might fairly expect (and surely his critics deserved) a rigorous art for art's sake position to be taken up, there is instead an insistence on the *morality* of his poems—a wider, freer, more clear-eyed morality, perhaps, a chastity altogether higher than the 'prurient prudery and virulent virtue' of his contemporaries, but morality all the same. The defence resolves itself into a sustained discussion of the subject of poetry—the old worry of the Victorian critic—and Swinburne argues for enlarging the range of poetry by condemning that sacrosanct form, the idyll. His book is dramatic and not to be accepted as 'the deliberate outcome and result of the writer's conviction'. A 'many-faced, multifarious' poetry can only be achieved if Victorian verse can be liberated from the overwhelming triviality of its contents; as Arnold said, all depends on the subject.

We have idyls good and bad, ugly and pretty; idyls of the farm and the mill; idyls of the dining-room and the deanery; idyls of the gutter and the gibbet. (*Notes on Poems and Reviews*, p. 22)

The idyllic form is best for domestic and pastoral poetry. It is naturally on a lower level than that of tragic or lyric verse. Its gentle and maidenly lips are somewhat narrow for the stream and somewhat cold for the fire of song. It is very fit for the sole diet of girls; not very fit for the sole sustenance of men. (*Notes on Poems and Reviews*, p. 23)

About the willingness to accept and explore a wider range of experience, subtlety and complexity in poetry, the reviews I have re-printed in the last section of this book should speak for themselves. In the 1853 Preface Arnold had spoken distrustfully of Hamlet and of Faust as touch-stones of modernism: for John Morley, reviewing *The Ring and the Book* in the *Fortnightly Review*, and for John Addington Symonds, reviewing Clough's poetry also in the *Fortnightly Review*, Arnold's evaluation is reversed and Hamlet and Faust are invoked to suggest the breadth and subtlety of these poets' work.[130] The morality of a work of art rests in its rich imaginative response to its material and not in the nature of the material itself. There is an acknowledgement of the impersonality of the work of art, a greater willingness to accept poetry as dramatic exploration of feeling. 'To imagine that . . . he was expressing his *own* view would be to mistake the artist's nature alto-gether', Symonds wrote of Clough. This acceptance is too new to be glib. The case is argued afresh whenever it is introduced, thought through with impressive care and commitment. A new vocabulary is apparent. Subtlety, variety, multifariousness, are words of approbation now, and there is a strenuous attempt to find a descriptive vocabulary which will match the complexity of a poet's work. The unity required of a poem is almost Coleridgean in its acceptance of variousness and contradictions and quite unlike the *uniformity* required in the earlier decades. In his discussions of Arnold's poems, Swinburne uses imagery of colour and music (*not* painting) to get closer to the unifying feeling of Arnold's poetry.[131] 'An ironical tone runs through them', Symonds writes of the songs in *Dipsychus*, 'and is strangely blended with bitterness, gravity, and a kind of tender regret.'[132] Talking of the 'reckless-ness' of Browning's similes, Richard Simpson notes that 'he thinks by images, not by abstractions' and 'he treats each image as a word, not to be followed by a consequent image, as pictorial effect might demand, but by another image-word, which may carry on the sense, without reference to the congruity of the metaphor'.[133]

Bagehot's measles are everywhere. And yet what I have called the high Victorian criterion of sympathy was not abandoned but made to assimilate these changes. Simpson's recognition of Browning's sophistication did not prevent his seeing him as a popular writer, a journalist-poet who responded imaginatively to the feelings of 'collective corporations, organized aggregates of men'. But the notion of sympathy is subtilised here, for Simpson meant that Browning was able to *represent* the feelings of 'the people' by providing a 'popular running commentary' to *The Ring and the Book*, rather than *appealing* to common feeling. John Morley also redefines the notion of sympathy when defending the 'sordidity' of *The Ring and the Book*.

> The truth is that nothing can be more powerfully efficacious from the moral point of view than the exercise of an exalted creative art, stirring within the intelligence of the spectator active thought and curiosity about many types of character and many changeful issues of conduct and fortune, at once enlarging and elevating the range of his reflections on mankind, ever kindling his sympathies into the warm and continuous glow which purifies and strengthens nature, and fills men with that love of humanity which is the best inspirer of virtue.

Morley is connecting the enlarging of experience achieved in poetry with the *extension* and expansion of the sympathies. He is not thinking of the *consolidation* of the basic, primary feelings which was understood to be the essence of the appeal to sympathy in the earlier decades. Comparison with an earlier criticism of Browning shows how Morley's position could liberate discussion. In 1856 Margaret Oliphant compared Browning adversely with Tennyson because Browning betrayed the function of poetry, which was 'to make the whole world ring with joy over a cottage cradle, or weigh down the very wings of the winds with wailing over some uncommemorated grave'.[134] By the 1860s the interpretation of the limits of sympathy inherent in Masson and in Dallas are being developed, albeit unconsciously. And the poet's volatile ability to dramatise, to project himself into different feelings and situations, is always associated with this more liberal view of sympathy—not so much because it established the autonomy of the poem, perhaps, as because it granted a more flexible notion of the far-reaching *humanising* power of art. When Simpson talks of Browning striving to 'enter the animal brain, to open a new intercourse with fishes and insects, to feel in his own fibres the irrational consciousness', we are back with Fox's clumsy attempt to show how the complex human mind is capable of injecting the principle of volition into the 'finny worthy'. The vocabulary of sympathy survived so long, I think, and proved so capable of redefinition and of assimilating and containing fresh views of art because it asserted human values which a purely aesthetic view of art seemed to deny. Criticism could be aesthetic without rejecting a humanistic foundation, and humanistic without sacrificing aesthetic values. English criticism has never gone to extremes of aestheticism: one explanation is the staying power of this humane vocabulary.

NOTES

1 *North British Review*, xix (Aug. 1853), 297–344; 298. David Masson. *The Wellesley Index to Victorian Periodicals*, i, 677.

2 For discussion of the rise in periodical publications and the expanding reading public in the nineteenth century, see E. E. Kellett, 'The Press', in *Early Victorian England, 1830–1865*, ed. G. M. Young (1934), ii, 3–97; W. J. Graham, *English Literary Periodicals* (New York, 1930); A. Cruse, *The Victorians and their Books* (1935); R. D. Altick, *The English Common Reader* (Chicago, 1957), pp. 318–64; A. Ellegård, *Readership of the Periodical Press in Mid-Victorian Britain* (Göteborg, 1957) (for the decade 1860–70); Louis Dudek, *Literature and the Press* (Toronto, 1960).

3 *Church of England Quarterly Review*, xii (Oct. 1842), 361–76. For Leigh Hunt's authorship see E. F. Shannon, *Tennyson and the Reviewers* (Cambridge Mass., 1952), p. 200.

4 *Westminster Review*, viii N.S. (Oct. 1855), 597. For George Eliot's authorship see *Essays of George Eliot*, ed. T. Pinney (1963), p. 453.

5 *Rambler*, iv (July 1849), 201–5.

6 See below, pp. 16–17 for utilitarian thinking on poetry. Shannon's account of the political elements in the reception of Tennyson's early poems (he was associated with liberal thinking) is supplemented by W. D. Paden, 'Tennyson and the Reviewers (1829–35)', *Studies in English* (Kansas, 1940). Although one can discuss the part played by progressive and reactionary sentiment

with some confidence in this controversy, it is as well to remember, as Sheila Rosenberg has demonstrated, that the policy both of reviews and reviewers is rarely unchanging ('More Notes on Westminster Review Research', *Victorian Periodicals Newsletter*, ii (1968), 24).

7 The treatises described, for instance, by A. H. Warren jnr., *English Poetic Theory 1825–1865* (Princeton, 1950), and M. Abrams, *The Mirror and the Lamp* (Oxford, 1953).

8 For authorship of Mill's article on Tennyson, *London Review*, i (July 1835), 402–24, see Shannon, p. 193. Mill's articles on poetry appeared in the *Monthly Repository*, vii N.S. (Jan. and Oct. 1833), 60–70; 714–24. For Mill's authorship see F. E. Mineka, *The Dissidence of Dissent* (Chapel Hill, 1944), p. 417.

9 *Fraser's Magazine*, xxxix (May 1849), 570–86; 570; 571. For Kingsley's authorship see below, note 70.

10 *British Quarterly Review*, vi (Nov. 1847), 490–507; 492. For Lewes's authorship see G. S. Haight, *The George Eliot Letters*, vii (1955), 368.

11 *Christian Remembrancer*, iv N.S. (July 1842), 42–58; 49. For Francis Garden's authorship see Shannon, pp. 65, 199.

12 *Christian Reformer*, xi N.S. (Oct. 1855), 602–13; 610.

13 W. E. Gladstone, *Quarterly Review*, cvi (Oct. 1859), 454–85. H. Alford, *Contemporary Review*, xiii (Jan. 1870), 104–25. Alford's article is signed. For Gladstone's authorship see *W.I.*, p. 742.

14 Simpson's essays on Jane Austen and Tennyson appeared in the *North British Review*, xiii N.S. (April 1870), 129–52 and xiv N.S. (Jan. 1871), 378–425. For the extent of his interests see also *D.N.B.* and *W.I.*, p. 1086.

William Bodham Donne's range of interests is suggested by his contributions to the *British and Foreign Review*, where he wrote on ancient history and theology and contributed two outstanding articles on Coleridge and Shelley. His contributions to *Fraser's Magazine* range from essays on Elizabethan drama, to Tacitus and Swedenborg. See the list of his articles in C. B. Johnson, *William Bodham Donne and his Friends* (1905), 340–3.

15 The authors of the discussions of *In Memoriam* have been identified in the following cases. *North British Review*, xiii (Aug. 1850), 551. Coventry Patmore (*W.I.*, p. 673). *Fraser's Magazine*, xlii (Sept. 1850), 246; 249. Charles Kingsley (*W.I.*). *Christian Socialist*, ii (Aug. 1851), 156. Gerald Massey (signed). *The Times*, 28 Nov. 1851, 8. Manley Hopkins (Shannon, p. 174). *Tait's Edinburgh Magazine*, xvii (Aug. 1850), 499–505. Franklin Lushington (Shannon, p. 174).

16 Walter Jackson Bate has shown how the assumptions of eighteenth-century psychology influenced the concepts and vocabulary of Romantic criticism. The meaning of sympathy as imaginative projection is clearly crucial to Romantic aesthetic: in Victorian criticism, though perhaps in a humbler way, sympathy had the same very specific meaning. See W. J. Bate, 'The Sympathetic Imagination in Eighteenth-Century English Criticism', *English Literary History*, xii (1945), 144–64.

17 *Characteristics* (1711), ii, 29; 112.

18 *The Theory of Moral Sentiments*, ed. Dugald Stewart (1853), p. 4; 5.

19 p. 6.
20 *Eclectic Review*, xix N.S. (April 1846), 421; 422. *Metropolitan Journal*, ii (April 1836), 20. *Spectator*, 17 April 1841, 379.
21 *Scottish Review*, iii (Oct. 1855), 352. *Quarterly Review*, lxx (Sept. 1842), 385–416; 416. John Sterling (*W.I.*, p. 724). *Edinburgh Review*, lxxvii (April 1843), 373–91; 377. James Spedding (*W.I.*, p. 492). *North British Review*, ix (May 1848), 43–72; 49; 50. Coventry Patmore (*W.I.*, p. 671). *Edinburgh Review*, cii (Oct. 1855), 498–519; 504. Coventry Patmore (*W.I.*, p. 505).
22 *London Quarterly Review*, xxxiv (April 1870), 154–186; 155.
23 *Christian Remembrancer*, xi N.S. (April 1846), 316.
24 *Westminster Review*, li (July 1849), 265–90; 275.
25 It is often thought useful to examine assumptions about the morality of poetry in the mid-nineteenth century by looking at the notion of the poet as prophet. The remark of David Masson's quoted above (p. 2) suggests how widespread was the link between poet and prophet or poet and teacher, but I have found the word prophet used in so many different senses that it is useful only to record that such a link was made, rather than to explore the sense in which it was understood. Prophet could cover anything from the transcendentalism of Carlyle, who saw the poet as a man who penetrated to the inner spiritual reality of the universe, to the view that the poet should write about railways. James Spedding, for instance, calls the *vates sacer* one who returns to the interpretation of the ordinary realities of daily life (*Edinburgh Review*, lxxvii (April 1843), 382). For George Gilfillan, prophet means one who returns to the 'visionary' world as opposed to the mundane world signified, as for so many Victorian critics, by the railway train (*Dumfries and Galloway Herald and Advertiser*, 23 Oct. 1845, 4). For the reviewer of *Hogg's Instructor* (25 Dec. 1847, 281–4), prophet means reflecting the optimism of the age—and nothing else. A review of De Maistre in *Fraser's Magazine* (xxxix (April 1849), 383–96) makes a distinction between the artist and the prophet. We no longer live in an age capable of creating great art, the writer says, and the nineteenth century will encourage only prophets, and not great artists, because its really creative writers will always be alienated from it. 'The truest artist, in an age of art, must be he who incarnates best the age's artistic tendencies: the truest prophet must always be he who stands in directest antagonism to the tendencies of the age . . . in Titanic conflict with the cardinal vice of the community' (395). Yet another distinction is between prophet and critic, made in a comparison between Arnold and Ruskin in the *Westminster Review* (xxiv N.S. (Oct. 1863), 468–82). The reviewer tries to distinguish between a metaphysical and a pragmatic response to the whole English cultural situation in the nineteenth century. The approach of the pragmatic critic (Arnold) he regards as balanced, central and relevant. The metaphysical prophet (Ruskin), on the other hand, is eccentric and idiosyncratic. 'Critic' here, of course, does not mean the specialised literary critic—a concept alien to this period, as I have said. The writer understands a much more general operation of critical analysis—very much what Arnold meant in his essay on 'The Function of Criticism at the Present Time'.
  All that can be said about the notion of the prophet is that it connects the

writer closely with his age—or *the* age as the nineteenth century was often called. So the problem one is dealing with is the problem of the poet and the age as it was discussed in the nineteenth century.

For Spedding's authorship of the *Edinburgh* essay see note 21 above. For Gilfillan's authorship see Shannon, p. 202. The *Fraser's* essay is by William Maccall (*W.I.*). The *Westminster* essay is by Samuel Henry Reynolds (*W.I.*).

26 *Edinburgh Review*, xc (Oct. 1849), 388–433; 409. For Aubrey De Vere's authorship see *W.I.*, p. 499.

27 *National Review*, i (Oct. 1855), 377–410; 378. For W. C. Roscoe's authorship see E. F. Shannon jnr., 'The Critical reception of Tennyson's *Maud*', *P.M.L.A.*, lxviii (June 1953), 397–417; 416.

28 *London Quarterly Review*, xxxii (July 1869), 325–57; 330. For H. B. Forman's authorship see L. N. Broughton, C. S. Northup, R. Pearsall, *Robert Browning: A Bibliography, 1830–1950* (New York, 1953), p. 111.

29 Browning's distinction between the objective and subjective poet (a distinction very generally taken over from German criticism), which he made in his introduction to the (spurious) *Letters of Percy Bysshe Shelley* (1852), assumes that the content of the two kinds of poem will be so different that they are *created* in different ways. The objective poem derives from a mimetic process, the subjective poem from the autonomous 'golden world' of the imagination which is directly God-given.

30 See G. H. Lewes's review, mainly of Hegel's *Lectures on Aesthetics*, in the *British and Foreign Review*, xiii (1842), 1–49.

31 W. J. Fox, *Westminster Review*, xiv (Jan. 1831), 210–24. The review is sometimes attributed to Dr (later Sir) John Bowring. See Shannon, pp. 5; 184, nn. 17, 18. W. D. Paden (see note 6 above) has also discussed the disputed authorship of this article, though most writers agree that it was Fox. Arthur Hallam, *Englishman's Magazine*, i (Aug. 1831), 616–28 (Shannon, p. 185). John Wilson ('Christopher North'), *Blackwood's Edinburgh Magazine*, xxxi (May 1832), 721–41 (see *W.I.*, p. 40).

32 *Edinburgh Review*, xlii (Aug. 1825), 304–46; 307. For Macaulay's authorship see *W.I.*, p. 467.

33 B. W. Procter ('Barry Cornwall') repeats Macaulay's arguments in the essay which he later called 'A Defence of Poetry', *Edinburgh Review*, xlvii (Jan. 1828), 184–204 (*W.I.*, p. 470).

34 *Edinburgh Review*, xlix (June 1829), 439–59; 446. For Carlyle's authorship see *W.I.*, p. 471.

35 *Westminster Review*, xii (Jan. 1830), 3.

36 James Mill is reviewed in the *Westminster Review*, xiii (Oct. 1830), 265–92. The author is probably Thomas Southwood Smith (*W.I.*).

37 *Analysis of the Phenomena of the Human Mind* (1829), i, 51; 52. Some of Fox's ideas could also have been derived from translations of A. W. Schlegel's *A Course of Lectures on the Dramatic Art and Literature* (1815) or F. Schlegel's *Lectures on the History of Literature, Ancient and Modern* (1818), but if they were, they were thoroughly naturalised. Crabb Robinson made a similar distinction between internal poetry and external poetry in his discussions of Goethe in the *Monthly Repository* (vii, N.S. 1833), but this

was later than Fox. For Robinson's authorship see Mineka, p. 421. I am indebted to Michael Mason for this note.

38 *Tatler*, 24 Feb. 1831, 594.

39 *Spectator*, 21 Aug. 1830, 637.

40 1802 Preface to *Lyrical Ballads*, ed. R. L. Brett and A. R. Jones (revised edn., 1965), p. 259. *The Theory of Moral Sentiments*, ed. Dugald Stewart (1853), p. 18.

41 W. J. Fox on Tennyson, *Monthly Repository*, vii N.S. (Jan. 1833), 30–41. Fox on *Pauline*, *Monthly Repository*, vii N.S. (April 1833), 252–62. Fox on *Paracelsus*, *Monthly Repository*, ix N.S. (Nov. 1835), 716–27. For his authorship see Mineka, pp. 407; 408; 409.

42 *Cambridge University Magazine*, ii (Oct. 1842), 629–39; 633; 639.

43 *Quarterly Review*, xxviii (March 1848), 427–53; 438. Sara Coleridge (*W.I.*, p. 731).

44 *London University Magazine*, i (Dec. 1842), 286–314; 312. Possibly William Arthur Case (Shannon, p. 201).

45 See above, note 8 for Mill's authorship of the Tennyson essay in the *London Review*, i (July 1835), 402–24. The discussion of *Mariana* is on pp. 405–7. Other quotations, pp. 419; 423.

46 *Quarterly Review*, xlix (April 1833), 81–96. John Wilson Croker (*W.I.*, p. 713). *Literary Gazette*, 8 Dec. 1832, 772–4. William Jerdan (?) (Shannon, pp. 14–15; 170). *New Monthly Magazine*, xxxvii (Jan. 1833), 69–74; 71; 69; 73. Edward Bulwer-Lytton (Shannon, p. 170).

47 *Church of England Quarterly Review*, xii (Oct. 1842), 362. For Hunt's authorship see above, note 3. *Westminster Review*, xxxviii (Oct. 1842), 371–90; 372. R. Monckton Milnes (Shannon, p. 171). *Hogg's Weekly Instructor*, vi (25 Dec. 1847), 281–4; 283; 284. *Atlas*, 25 June 1842, 410.

48 *Edinburgh Review*, civ (Oct. 1856), 337–62; 339. For Patmore's authorship see *W.I.*, p. 505.

49 *Dumfries-shire and Galloway Herald and Advertiser*, 16 Oct. 1845. *Christian Remembrancer*, xxi N.S. (April 1851), 346–99; 347.

50 *London Review*, i (July 1835), 413–14.

51 *Athenaeum*, 1 Dec. 1832, 770. *Spectator*, 4 June 1842, 544. *Weekly Dispatch*, 16 Aug. 1835, 298; *Spectator*, 15 Aug. 1836, 781; *Fraser's Magazine*, xxxiii (June 1846), 715; 716.

52 *Christian Remembrancer*, xi (April 1846), 316–30; 317; 320.

53 *Christian Remembrancer*, xvii (April 1849), 381–401. For Charles Peter Chretien's authorship see Shannon, pp. 209; 211.

54 *Athenaeum*, 17 Jan. 1846, 58. *People's Journal*, ii (Aug. 1846), 104–6; 104.

55 *Examiner*, 2 Oct. 1841, 629.

56 W. J. Fox, 'The Poor and their Poetry', *Monthly Repository*, vi N.S. (March 1832), 189–201; 190 (Mineka, p. 407). Carlyle's Corn-Law essay appeared in the *Edinburgh Review*, lv (July 1832), 338–61 (*W.I.*, p. 475). John Wilson's essay appeared in *Blackwood's Edinburgh Magazine*, xxxv (May 1834), 815–35 (*W.I.*, p. 46).

57 For Lytton's authorship see note 46 above. The writer in *Chambers' Journal*, 12 July 1845, 25, is unknown.

58 *Quarterly Review,* lxx (Sept. 1842), 385–416. For John Sterling's authorship see *W.I.,* p. 724.
59 *British Quarterly Review,* ii (Aug. 1845), 46–71; 47; 66.
60 *Westminster Review,* xxxviii (Oct. 1842), 371–90; 372. R. Monckton Milnes (Shannon, p. 171). *Foreign and Colonial Review,* iii (Jan. 1844), 202–15; 204. Parts of this essay appear in R. H. Horne's essay on Tennyson in *A New Spirit of the Age* (2 vols., 1844).
61 *Christian Teacher,* iv N.S. (Oct. 1842), 414–23; 417. *Dumfries-shire and Galloway Herald and Advertiser,* 23 Oct. 1845, 1; 4.
62 R. S. Rintoul, *Spectator,* 2 April 1853, 325. For Rintoul's authorship see *The Poems of Matthew Arnold* (ed. K. Allott, 1965), p. 593, note to ll. 77–80. All quotations from the Preface of 1853 are from this edition, Appendix A, pp. 590–607.
63 *North British Review,* xix (Aug. 1853), 338.
64 *Spectator,* 10 March 1849, 231. *Literary Gazette,* 17 March 1849, 188. *Times,* 4 Nov. 1853, 5. The *Times* article is by Goldwin Smith. See S. M. B. Coulling, 'Matthew Arnold's 1853 Preface', *Victorian Studies,* vii (March 1964), 233–263; 239, n. 17.
65 *Blackwood's Edinburgh Magazine,* lxvi (Sept. 1849), 340–6; 345; 346. W. E. Aytoun (*W.I.,* p. 87).
66 *North American Review,* lxxvii (July 1853), 1–30. Reprinted in *Poems and Prose Remains of Arthur Hugh Clough* (1869), i, 357–83.
67 *Fraser's Magazine,* xxxix (Jan. 1849), 103–10; 105. On 2 Dec. 1848, Charles Kingsley wrote to Clough asking permission to review *The Bothie* in *Fraser's.* See *Correspondence of Arthur Hugh Clough* (ed. F. Mulhauser, 1957), i, 229. *Germ,* i (Jan. 1850), 34–46; 36. W. M. Rossetti.
68 *Westminster Review,* xxvi N.S. (Oct. 1864), 396–414; 398.
69 *North British Review,* xix (May 1853), 209–18; 210; 214. Coulling, p. 236, n. 8, gives Patmore as the author but *W.I.,* p. 676, gives either Coventry Patmore or George David Boyle.
70 *Fraser's Magazine,* xxxix (May 1849), 570–86; 578; 570. For Charles Kingsley's authorship see Coulling, p. 239, n. 18.
71 *Fraser's Magazine,* xlix (Feb. 1854), 140–9; 140. Charles Kingsley (*W.I.*).
72 *North British Review,* ix (May 1848), 43–72; 62; 61; 44. For Coventry Patmore's authorship see *W.I.,* p. 671.
73 *Edinburgh Review,* xc (Oct. 1849), 388–433; 407; 408; 418. For De Vere's authorship see note 26 above.
74 *Christian Reformer,* iv (Feb. 1848), 111–13; 111.
75 A critic of Browning in the *English Review* (iv (Dec. 1845), 273–7; 275) was prepared to treat *Paracelsus* as a step in the right direction and wondered at the largeness of aim and control displayed in it. But in general Browning, like Tennyson, was exhorted to forsake the poetry of *disjecta membra*—'they are mere fragments, varying in length from half a dozen lines upwards—apparently thoughts jotted down for after use—or rejected from their places in longer pieces' (*Athenaeum,* 22 April 1843, 385). As one would expect, *The Princess* drew forth innumerable attacks on its grotesque heterogeneity. Critics simply could not accept the juxtaposition of different modes and

idioms. The *Examiner* felt Tennyson had fallen from the 'largeness of his view' to mere burlesque (8 Jan. 1848, 20–1; 21) and the *Atlas* asserted that in 'structure, it outrages all consistency . . . the ages of chivalry and steam are made to dance together' (15 Jan. 1848, 42–3; 42). 'The grand error of the story is the incoherency of its characteristics. Its different parts refuse to amalgamate', J. W. Marston wrote (*Athenaeum*, 1 Jan. 1848, 6–8; 7). The *Rambler* critic denied the poem stature: 'A medley can never take a high flight. It cannot possess any unity of design or conception, and must necessarily, therefore, be deficient in true dignity and collective grace' (i, 11 March 1848, 210–13; 210). The *Eclectic* reviewer said that the poem 'rather resembles grotto-work, where the spar glitters beside the common pebble stone, and the agate and jasper are embedded in sand,—than the stately building, perfect in design, which our great poets have delighted to construct' (xxiii N.S. (April 1848), 415–23; 422). The same Arnoldian notion of design was put forward before Arnold had written by Charles Peter Chretien in the *Christian Remembrancer* review reprinted here. What is surprising is that critics took this burlesque so seriously and did not see it for what it was in spite of its underlying seriousness—a joke.

For John Forster's authorship of the *Examiner* essay and J. W. Marston's authorship of the *Athenaeum* article see Shannon, p. 171.

76 *Letters of Matthew Arnold to Arthur Hugh Clough* (ed. H. F. Lowry, Oxford, 1932), p. 96.
77 *Life, Letters, and Literary Remains of John Keats* (1848), i, 221–3.
78 *Edinburgh Review*, xc (Oct. 1849), 426–9 (negative capability); 405; 403. For De Vere's authorship see note 26 above.
79 E. S. Dallas, *Poetics* (1852), pp. 256; 257–8; 291.
80 *Edinburgh Review*, xc (Oct. 1849), 404. For De Vere's authorship see note 26 above.
81 *North British Review* (1853), 315; 314.
82 *Eclectic Review*, xxvi N.S. (Aug. 1849), 203–14; 211. C. Edmunds is cited as author by Broughton, p. 92.
83 *National Review*, i (Oct. 1855), 395. For W. C. Roscoe's authorship see Shannon, *P.M.L.A.*, 416.
84 *Christian Remembrancer*, xxvii N.S. (April 1854), 310–33; 318; 320; 332. For J. D. Coleridge's authorship see Coulling, p. 250, n. 31.
85 *Putnam's Monthly Magazine*, vi (Sept. 1855), 235–8; 236. *Dublin University Magazine*, xliii (June 1854), 736–52; 738. Probably by J. F. Walker (*W.I.*).
86 *Eclectic Review*, ix N.S. (March 1855), 276–84; 276; 277; 278.
87 *Fraser's Magazine*, xlix (Feb. 1854), 140–9; 141. Charles Kingsley (*W.I.*).
88 *North British Review*, xxi (Aug. 1854), 493–504; 498. For J. C. Shairp's authorship see *W.I.*, p. 678.
89 *Edinburgh Review*, civ (Oct. 1856), 337–62; 338. For Patmore's authorship see *W.I.*, p. 505.
90 *Leader*, 1853, 1147; 1170. For G. H. Lewes's authorship see Coulling, p. 251, n. 30.
91 *Eclectic Review*, xxviii N.S. (Sept. 1850), 330–41; 331. 'A passion, deep-felt throughout it, has informed his ever subtle thoughts and delicate

imagery with a massive grandeur and a substantial interest', John Forster wrote in the *Examiner* (8 June 1850, 356). 'It has led the poet to meditations deep and sad and hopeful, on life and death and immortality', the *British Quarterly* reviewer wrote, discussing the universality of the poem (xii (Aug. 1850), 291–2; 291). Outstanding both for its understanding of the nature of *In Memoriam* and for its continual and sensitive demonstration of its relevance to the universal sympathies is Franklin Lushington's discussion of the poem in *Tait's Edinburgh Magazine* (xvii (Aug. 1850), 499–505; 501). 'The subject runs through the whole diapason of human sympathy', he writes, and 'The illustration of the deepest feelings through the commonest uses of daily life' ensures that the shepherd 'in the plains of Chaldæa, the ferryman over the waters of the Euphrates, the most untaught agricultural intellect that ever stepped behind an English plough' would all understand Tennyson's imagery. Of course, this is an optimistic claim, but it suggests the hopes that the notion of sympathy could encourage.

For John Forster's authorship of the *Examiner* article see Shannon, p. 173. For Franklin Lushington's *Tait's* article see Shannon, p. 174; p. 217, n. 14.

92 *Westminster Review*, v N.S. (Jan. 1854), 146–59; 154. For Froude's authorship see Coulling, p. 250, n. 31.

93 *Prospective Review*, x (Feb. 1854), 99–118; 113. For W. C. Roscoe's authorship see Coulling, p. 250, n. 30.

94 *North British Review* (1854), 500; 504, 502. For Shairp's authorship see note 88 above.

95 *Douglas Jerrold's Shilling Magazine*, ii (Dec. 1845), 565–6. *English Review*, iv (Dec. 1845), 259–77; 273. *Examiner*, 15 Nov. 1845, 723–4; 723.

96 p. 11.

97 *Germ*, ii (Feb. 1850), 84–96; 84.

98 *North British Review*, xiii (Aug. 1850), 532–55; 551.

99 *Guardian*, 28 March 1849, 209. See above, note 65 for Aytoun's *Blackwood's* authorship.

100 *English Review*, xiii (March 1850), 207–13; 213.

101 *Atlas*, 15 June 1850, 379. *Times*, 28 Nov. 1851, 8. For Manley Hopkins's authorship see Shannon, p. 174.

102 *Blackwood's Edinburgh Magazine*, lxxviii (Sept. 1855), 311–21; 319. W. E. Aytoun (*W.I.*, p. 100). *Irish Quarterly Review*, v (Sept. 1855), 453–72; 454.

103 *British Quarterly Review*, xxiii (Oct. 1855), 467–98; 482. David Masson (*W.I.*).

104 *Eclectic Review*, xxvi N.S. (Aug. 1849), 203–14.

105 *Athenaeum*, 11 Dec. 1841, 952.

106 *National Review*, vi (April 1858), 259–79; 260; 264. W. C. Roscoe (*W.I.*).

107 *Edinburgh Review*, civ (Oct. 1856), 337–62; 341. For Coventry Patmore's authorship see *W.I.*, p. 505.

108 *Eclectic Review*, ix N.S. (March 1855), 276–84; 280.

109 *Fraser's Magazine*, xlix (Feb. 1854), 140–9; 143; 144.

110 *Westminster Review*, v N.S. (Jan. 1854), 146–59; 156. For Froude's authorship see note 92 above.

111 *Blackwood's Edinburgh Magazine,* lxxv (March 1854), 303–14; 306–7. For W. E. Aytoun's authorship see *W.I.,* p. 97.

112 *Edinburgh Review,* cxxix (April 1869), 486–583; 502; 501. For C. S. M. Philipps's authorship see *W.I.,* p. 518.

113 *Spectator,* 24 May 1862, 580–1; 581.

114 *Athenaeum,* 31 May 1862, 719–20; 720.

115 *Saturday Review,* 24 Oct. 1863, 562–3; 563.

116 *Athenaeum,* 4 Aug. 1866, 137. For R. W. Buchanan's authorship see C. K. Hyder, *Swinburne's Literary Career and Fame* (Durham N.C., 1933), p. 275, n. 23. Buchanan's attack on Rossetti is 'The Fleshly School of Poetry', *Contemporary Review,* xviii (Oct. 1871), 334–50.

117 *Saturday Review,* 4 Aug. 1866, 145–7; 147. For John Morley's authorship see Hyder, p. 275, n. 18.

118 *Chambers' Journal,* 24 Sept. 1864, 620–3; 620. The *British Controversialist* printed a debate article called 'Is Tennyson's "Enoch Arden" morally objectionable?' xiii 3rd series (Jan.-April 1865), 28–34; 100–6; 181–90; 261–70. It had previously printed a debate topic, 'Is the Poetry of Tennyson as Healthy in its Tendencies as that of Longfellow?' iii, iv 3rd series (April-August 1860), 241–54; 317–24; 391–405; 27–39; 101–16. Possibly more research on Victorian periodicals of a popular nature or addressed to a lower- or working-class audience will suggest that the bed-rock popularity we assume to have been Tennyson's was never as secure as it seemed, or rather, it will make us far more tentative in speaking of 'popularity'. See Michael Wolff, '*The British Controversialist*', *Victorian Periodicals Newsletter,* ii (June 1968), 27–45.

119 In his *Collections and Recollections* (1890), vol. i, G. W. E. Russell described a growing disillusionment with Tennyson's poetry among the sophisticated literary public after *Enoch Arden.* This disillusion certainly found some expression in reviews—if the foremost intellectual and literary journals of the time are a sure indication of tastes and values of the educated reading public. To be quite sure of Russell's statement, and to be sure of his other contention, that Tennyson was still appreciated by his popular audience, one would have to explore opinion expressed in reviews in a sociological way in a very wide range of periodicals, and this has not been my aim.

120 *National Review,* ix (Oct. 1859), 368–94; 375; 375; 378; 390. For Walter Bagehot's authorship see Norman St John Stevas, *T.L.S.,* 26 April 1963.

121 *Quarterly Review,* cvi (Oct. 1859), 454–85; 468; 473. For Gladstone's authorship see note 13 above.

122 John Nichol, in the *Westminster Review,* xvi N.S. (Oct. 1859), 503–26; 523, is one of the rare voices of disapproval of the *Idylls.* He attacked the cult of medievalism and the retreat from modernity. But most writers persuaded themselves that the poem was relevant to the modern world. *W.I.* gives Nichol as author.

123 *Quarterly Review,* cxxviii (Jan. 1870), 1–17; 3. For J. R. Mozley's authorship see *W.I.,* p. 752.

124 'Coleridge as a Poet', *Quarterly Review,* cxxv (July 1868), 78–106. See *W.I.,* p. 750 for Mozley's authorship.

125 *Temple Bar*, xxvi (May 1869), 179–94; 181; 193. Signed.

126 *British Quarterly Review*, li (Jan. 1870), 200–14; 204; 209.

127 *North British Review* (1871), 385; 390; 425. For Simpson's authorship see note 14 above.

128 *Contemporary Review*, i (Feb. 1866), 279–310; 285; 285; 287.

129 *Westminster Review*, xxxiv N.S. (Oct. 1868), 300–12; 311; 312. Reprinted in *Studies in the History of the Renaissance* (1873).

130 *Fortnightly Review*, v N.S. (March 1869), 331–43. John Morley's review is signed. *Fortnightly Review*, iv N.S. (Dec. 1868), 589–617; 597. John Addington Symonds's review is signed.

131 *Fortnightly Review*, ii N.S. (Oct. 1867), 414–45. Reprinted in Swinburne's *Essays and Studies* (1875).

132 *Fortnightly Review*, iv N.S. (Dec. 1868), 597.

133 *North British Review*, li (Oct. 1869), 97–126; 104. For Richard Simpson's authorship see *W.I.*, p. 693.

134 *Blackwood's Edinburgh Magazine*, lxxix (Feb. 1856), 125–38; 125. For Margaret Oliphant's authorship see *W.I.*, p. 101.

Tennyson controversy to 1842

I

Tennyson ↶ *Poems, Chiefly Lyrical* ↶ 1830

William Johnson Fox, *Westminster Review,* xiv
(January 1831), 210–24

It would be a pity that poetry should be an exception to the great law of progression that obtains in human affairs; and it is not. The machinery of a poem is not less susceptible of improvement than the machinery of a cotton-mill; nor is there any better reason why the one should retrograde from the days of Milton, than the other from those of Arkwright. Of course we do not mean that the cases are precisely parallel, but the difference is not so much in favour of the perfectibility of the cotton-mill as is often imagined. Man cannot be less progressive than his own works and contrivances; in fact it is by his improvement that they are improved; and the mechanical arts are continually becoming superior to what they were, just because the men who are occupied in or about those arts have grown wiser than their predecessors, and have the advantage of a clearer knowledge of principles, an experience more extended or more accurately recorded, and perhaps a stronger stimulus to invention. Their progressiveness is merely a consequence from, a sort of reflection of, the progressiveness of his nature; but poetry is far nearer and dearer; it is essential to that nature itself; it is part and parcel of his constitution; and can only retrograde in the retrogradation of humanity.

There is nothing mysterious, or anomalous, in the power of producing poetry, or in that of its enjoyment; neither the one nor the other is a supernatural gift bestowed capriciously nobody knows how, when, or why. It may be a compound, but it is not incapable of analysis; and although our detection of the component parts may not enable us to effect their combination at pleasure, it may yet guide us to many useful

William Johnson Fox, 1786–1864, unitarian preacher, radical and editor of the *Monthly Repository* from 1833–6. For the problem of Fox's authorship see Introduction, note 31.

conclusions and well-grounded anticipations. The elements of poetry are universal. The exercise of the organs of sight and sense stimulates man to some degree of descriptive poetry; wherever there is passion, there is dramatic poetry; wherever enthusiasm, there is lyric poetry; wherever reflection, there is metaphysical poetry. It is as widely diffused as the electric fluid.[1] It may be seen flashing out by fits and starts all the world over. The most ignorant talk poetry when they are in a state of excitement, the firmly-organized think and feel poetry with every breeze of sensation that sweeps over their well-tuned nerves. There is an unfathomable store of it in human nature; the species must fail before that can be exhausted; the only question is, whether there be any reason why these permanent elements should not be wrought into their combined form, in the future, with a facility and power which bear some direct ratio to the progress of society.

So far as poetry is dependent upon physical organization; and doubt-less it is to some extent so dependent; there is no reason why it should deteriorate.[2] Eyes and ears are organs which nature finishes off with very different gradations of excellence. Nervous systems vary from the finest degree of susceptibility down to the toughness of a coil of hempen cable. *Poeta nascitur* in a frame the most favourable to acute perception and intense enjoyment of the objects of sense; and it would be difficult to show that poets are not, and will not continue to be, produced as excellent as they have been, and as frequently. Why, then, should not those species of poetry which may be termed its music and its painting, which spring from, and appeal to, our sense of the beautiful in form or colour and of harmonious modulation, abound as much as

---

[1] In talking of electric fluid Fox is drawing upon well established scientific theory. From about 1750 various scientists, notably Benjamin Franklin, postulated an electric fluid which was believed to pervade the entire universe and was always present in all material bodies. This notion (which persisted until the end of the nineteenth century) provides Fox with a very convenient image for the common nineteenth-century belief that 'poetry' is a kind of amorphous, free-floating series of moods and emotions, experiences which need not necessarily be attached to verse forms at all. This aspect of Victorian poetic theory is dealt with in the conclusion (ch. 11) of A. H. Warren's *English Poetic Theory, 1825–1865* (Princeton, 1950).

[2] James Mill's associationist theory is dependent upon the physical basis of perception. In tying poetry to physical processes Fox is not so much behaving like a doctrinaire utilitarian as demonstrating that physical processes, and there-fore poetry, are permanent things. Arthur Hallam also stresses the physical basis of poetry.

heretofore? He is no lover of nature who has any notion that the half of her loveliness has ever yet been told. Descriptive poetry is the most exhaustible; but our coal mines will fail us much sooner. No man ever yet saw all the beauty of a landscape. He may have watched it from the rising to the setting sun, and through the twilight, and the moonlight, and the starlight, and all round the seasons, but he is deceived if he thinks then that it has nothing more for him. Indeed it is not he who ever will think so, but the man who drove down one day and back the next because he found the place so dull. The world has tired of descriptive poetry because it has been deluged with what was neither poetical nor descriptive. The world was quite right to be no longer tolerant of the repetition of conventional, traditionary, unfelt, and unmeaning phrases. But Cowper did not find the ground preoccupied. Bucolics, and Georgics, and Eclogues, and Pastorals, all made reverential room for his honest verses; and the shelf on which they took their stand is far from crowded. Nature will never cease to be poetical, nor society either. Spears and shields; gods, goddesses, and muses; and all the old scenery and machinery may indeed wear out. That is of little consequence. The age of chivalry was but one, and poetry has many ages. The classical and romantic schools are both but sects of a religion which is universal. Even the fields which have been most frequently reaped will still bear harvests; and rich ones too. Bards began with battles some thousands of years ago, and yet nobody ever wrote the Fight of Flodden field till it was indited by Scott, nor did any one anticipate Campbell's glorious ballad of the battle of Hohenlinden. Genius is never anticipated. No wit ever complained that all the good things had been said; nor will any poet, to the world's end, find that all worthy themes have been sung. Is not the French Revolution as good as the siege of Troy? And the landing of the Pilgrim Fathers on the shores of America, as that of the Trojan fugitives on the coast of Italy? The world has never been more disposed to make the want of a hero 'an uncommon want' than in these supposed unpoetical days on which we are fallen. And were they not provided, poetry might do without them. The old epics will probably never be surpassed, any more than the old coats of mail; and for the same reason; nobody wants the article; its object is accomplished by other means; they are become mere curiosities. A long story, with a plot to be ravelled and unravelled, and characters to be developed, and descriptions to be introduced, and a great moral lesson at the end of it, is now always done, and best done, in prose. A large portion always was prose in fact, and necessarily so; but literary superstition kept up the old forms after every body felt them intolerably wearisome and soporific, though few dared be so heretical as to say so, until the utilitarian spirit showed itself even in poetical criticism, and then the dull farce ended. This we take to be a great reformation. We have left off singing what ought only to be said, but the singing is neither the less nor the worse on that account. Nor will it be. The great principle of human improvement is at work in poetry as well as everywhere else. What is it that is reforming our criminal jurisprudence?[3] What is shedding its lights over legislation? What purifies religions? What makes all arts and sciences more available for human comfort and enjoyment? Even that which will secure a succession of creations out of the unbounded and everlasting materials of poetry, our ever-growing acquaintance with the philosophy of mind and of man, and the increasing facility with which that philosophy is applied. This is the essence of poetic power, and he who possesses it never need furbish up ancient armour, or go to the East Kehama-hunting, or bulbul-catching. Poetry, like charity, begins at home. Poetry, like morality, is founded on the precept, know thyself. Poetry, like happiness, is in the human heart. Its inspiration is of that which is in man, and it will never fail because there are changes in costume and grouping. What is the vitality of the *Iliad?* Character; nothing else. All the rest is only read either out of antiquarianism or of affectation. Why is Shakespeare the greatest of poets? Because he was one of the greatest of philosophers. We reason on the conduct of his characters with as little hesitation as if they were real living human beings. Extent of observation, accuracy of thought, and depth of reflection, were the qualities which won the prize of sovereignty for his imagination, and the effect of these qualities was practically to anticipate, so far as was needful for his purposes, the mental philosophy of a future age. Metaphysics must be the stem of poetry for the plant to thrive; but if the stem flourishes we are not likely to be at a loss for leaves, flowers, and fruit. Now whatever theories may have come into fashion, and gone out of fashion, the real science of mind advances with the progress of society like all other sciences. The poetry of the last forty years already shows symptoms of life in exact proportion as

[3] Here Fox is thinking of Jeremy Bentham (founder of the *Westminster* with James Mill in 1824) whose *Introduction to the Principles of Morals and Legislation* was published in 1789.

it is imbued with this science. There is least of it in the exotic legends
of Southey, and the feudal romances of Scott. More of it, though in
different ways, in Byron and Campbell. In Shelley there would have
been more still, had he not devoted himself to unsound and mystical
theories. Most of all in Coleridge and Wordsworth. They are all going
or gone; but here is a little book as thoroughly and unitedly metaphysical and poetical in its spirit as any of them; and sorely shall we be
disappointed in its author if it be not the precursor of a series of
productions which shall beautifully illustrate our speculations, and
convincingly prove their soundness.

Do not let our readers be alarmed. These poems are any thing but
heavy; anything but stiff and pedantic, except in one particular, which
shall be noticed before we conclude; anything but cold and logical.
They are graceful, very graceful; they are animated, touching, and
impassioned. And they are so, precisely because they are philosophical;
because they are not made up of metrical cant and conventional
phraseology; because there is sincerity where the author writes from
experience, and accuracy whether he writes from experience or observation; and he only writes from experience or observation, because he
has felt and thought, and learned to analyze thought and feeling;
because his own mind is rich in poetical associations, and he has wisely
been content with its riches; and because, in his composition, he has
not sought to construct an elaborate and artificial harmony, but only to
pour forth his thoughts in those expressive and simple melodies whose
meaning, truth, and power, are the soonest recognized and the longest
felt.

The most important department in which metaphysical science has
been a pioneer for poetry is in the analysis of particular states of mind;
a work which is now performed with ease, power, and utility as much
increased, as in the grosser dissections of the anatomical lecturer.
Hence the poet, more fortunate than the physician, has provision made
for an inexhaustible supply of subjects. A new world is discovered for
him to conquer. The poets of antiquity rarely did more than incidentally touch this class of topics; the external world had not yet lost its
freshness; situations, and the outward expression of the thoughts,
feelings and passions generated by those situations, were a province so
much nearer at hand, and presented so much to be done and enjoyed,
that they rested there content, like the two tribes and a half of Israel,
who sought not to cross the narrow boundary that separated them

from a better and richer country. Nor let them be blamed; it was for the philosophers to be the first discoverers and settlers, and for poetry afterwards to reap the advantage of their labours. This has only been done recently, or rather is only beginning to be done at all. Metaphysical systems and discussions in verse, there have been indeed, from Lucretius down to Akenside. But they have generally had just argument enough to spoil the poetry, and just poetry enough to spoil the argument. They resembled paintings of the bones, arteries, veins, and muscles; very bad as a substitute to the anatomist for the real substances in the human body, and still worse for the artist as the materials for a pleasant picture. Science, mental or physical, cannot be taught poetically; but the power derived from science may be used poetically; and metaphysics may do as much for the poet as anatomy has done for the painter, in truth, more, for the painter's knowledge of the human frame does not furnish him with distinct subjects for the exercise of his art; we have just remarked the unfitness. The benefit which the painter derives is that of being able to delineate the external appearances of the living body with greater truth and effect. And while the poet has an analogous advantage from mental science in the greater truth and effect of his delineations of external action, character, passion, and all that belongs to situation and grouping; he also finds in the phenomena exhibited in moral dissection (though not in the operation itself, in the application of the logical scalpel) some of the finest originals for his pictures; and they exist in infinite variety.

Mr Tennyson has some excellent specimens of this class. He seems to obtain entrance into a mind as he would make his way into a landscape; he climbs the pineal gland as if it were a hill in the centre of the scene; looks around on all objects with their varieties of form, their movements, their shades of colour, and their mutual relations and influences; and forthwith produces as graphic a delineation in the one case as Wilson or Gainsborough could have done in the other, to the great enrichment of our gallery of intellectual scenery. In the 'Supposed Confessions of a second-rate sensitive mind not in unity with itself', there is an extraordinary combination of deep reflection, metaphysical analysis, picturesque description, dramatic transition, and strong emotion. The author personates (he can personate anything he pleases from an angel to a grasshopper) a timid sceptic, but who must evidently always remain such, and yet be miserable in his scepticism; whose early associations, and whose sympathies, make religion a necessity to his heart; yet who has not lost his pride in the prowess of his youthful infidelity; who is tossed hither and thither on the conflicting currents of feeling and doubt, without that vigorous intellectual decision which alone could 'ride in the whirlwind and direct the storm', until at last he disappears with an exclamation which remains on the ear like

> the bubbling cry
> Of some strong swimmer in his agony.

Now without intruding any irreverent comparison or critical profanity we do honestly think this state of mind as good a subject for poetical description as even the shield of Achilles itself. Such topics are more in accordance with the spirit and intellect of the age than those about which poetry has been accustomed to be conversant; their adoption will effectually redeem it from the reproach of being frivolous and enervating; and of their affinity with the best pictorial qualities of poetry we have conclusive evidence in this very composition. The delineations of the trustful infant, the praying mother, the dying lamb, are as good as anything of the kind can be; while those of the supposed author's emotions as he gazes on 'Christians with happy countenances', or stands by the Christian grave, or realizes again, with a mixture of self-admiration and self-reproach, 'the unsunned freshness of his strength', when he 'went forth in quest of truth', are of a higher order, and are more powerfully, though not less gracefully finished.

Our author has the secret of the transmigration of the soul. He can cast his own spirit into any living thing, real or imaginary. Scarcely Vishnu himself becomes incarnate more easily, frequently, or perfectly. And there is singular refinement, as well as solid truth, in his impersonations, whether they be of inferior creatures or of such elemental beings as Syrens, as mermen and mermaidens. He does not merely assume their external shapes, and exhibit his own mind masquerading. He takes their senses, feelings, nerves, and brain, along with their names and local habitations; still it is himself in them, modified but not absorbed by their peculiar constitution and mode of being. In *The Merman* one seems to feel the principle of thought injected by a strong volition into the cranium of the finny worthy, and coming under all the influences, as thinking principles do, of the physical organization to which it is for the time allied: for a moment the identification is complete; and then a consciousness of contrast springs up between the reports of external objects brought to the mind by the senses and those which it has been accustomed to receive; and this consciousness gives to the description a most poetical colouring:

> There would be neither moon nor star;
> But the wave would make music above us afar—
> Low thunder and light in the magic night—
> Neither moon nor star.
> We would call aloud in the dreary dells, &c.

The Mermaid is beautifully discriminated, and most delicately drawn. She is the younger sister of Undine; or Undine herself before she had a soul. And the Syrens, who could resist these Sea Fairies, as the author prefers calling them? We must introduce a fragment of their song, though it is barbarous to break such a piece of coral for a specimen:

> Day and night to the billow the fountain calls
>   . . .
> Whither away, whither away, whither away with the sail and the oar?

The poet has here done, in the character of the Sea-Fairies, that which he has several times done in his own person, and always admirably; he has created a scene out of the character, and made the feeling within generate an appropriate assemblage of external objects. Every mood of the mind has its own outward world, or rather makes its own outward world. But it is not always, perhaps with sensitive and imaginative minds it is seldom, that the external objects, and their qualities will be seen through the medium of congeniality. It is thus in *L'Allegro* and *Il Penseroso*; but Milton was a happy man; the visions of both those poems were seen with the eyes of happiness, the only difference being that the one depicts a state of light-hearted, and the other of sober-minded enjoyment. There is not less truth, perhaps a more refined observation, in the opposite course which our author has taken in the two poems *Nothing Will Die*, and *All Things Will Die*. The outward objects, at the commencement of each, are precisely the same; the states of mind, are in contrast; and each seizes with avidity on some appearance which is uncongenial with itself. He who thinks that nothing will die, yet looks with wondering, and almost wearied eye on the ever-flowing stream, &c.; and he, who feels that all things must die, gazes mournfully on those same objects in the 'gayest, happiest attitude', which his own fancy has unconsciously compelled them to assume. There is this difference, however, that the felicitous conviction, in the first poem, enables the mind to recover itself with a sort of elastic bound; while in the second the external beauty and enjoyment, being at permanent variance with the tone of feeling, the mind after a melancholy recognition of their loveliness sinks into unmixed gloom, and surrounds itself with objects of deeper and darker shade. We shall be better understood by quoting the commencement of each.

NOTHING WILL DIE

ALL THINGS WILL DIE

Both poems conclude nearly in the same terms, with the exception of a discriminative epithet or two; but expressing in the one case an exulting joyousness, 'So let the wind range'; and in the other a reckless and desperate gaiety, just as religion and infidelity sometimes approximate, in terms, to the inculcation of the same moral; and while the preacher of immortality cries 'rejoice evermore', the expectant of annihilation shouts, 'Let us eat and drink, for tomorrow we die'.

Mariana is, we are disposed to think, although there are several poems which rise up reproachfully in our recollection as we say so, altogether, the most perfect composition in the volume. The whole of this poem, of eighty-four lines, is generated by the legitimate process of poetical creation, as that process is conducted in a philosophical mind, from a half sentence in Shakespeare. There is no mere amplification; it is all production; and production from that single germ. That must be a rich intellect, in which thoughts thus take root and grow. Mariana, the forsaken betrothed of Angelo, is described in *Measure for Measure*, as living in seclusion at 'the moated grange'. Mr Tennyson knows the place well; the ruinous, old, lonely house, the neglected garden, the forlorn stagnation of the locality.

> About a stonecast from the wall
> . . .
> The level waste, the rounding grey.

And here it was, that the deserted one lingered day after day in that 'hope deferred which maketh the heart sick'. The dreariness of the abode and the surrounding scenery was nothing to her;

> She only said, 'My life is dreary,
>   He cometh not,' she said;
> She said, 'I am aweary, aweary,
>   I would that I were dead!'

The poem takes us through the circuit of four-and-twenty hours of this dreary life. Through all the changes of the night and day she has but one feeling, the variation of which is only by different degrees of acuteness and intensity in the misery it produces; and again and again we feel, before its repetition, the coming of the melancholy burthen,

> And ever when the moon was low
>   . . .
> I would that I were dead.

The day, by its keener expectancy, was more harassing and agitating than the night; and by its sights and sounds, in that lonely place, and under the strange interpretations of a morbid fancy and a breaking heart, did yet more 'confound her sense'. Her deserted parents, the greyheaded domestics that had nursed her infancy in her father's house, seemed to be there; she recognized them, and what would they with her?

> Old faces glimmered through the doors,
> Old footsteps trod the upper floors,
> Old voices called her from without.

Again the hour passed at which Angelo used to arrive; again the evening is come when he used to be there, where he never would be again; the bright sunshiny evening, blazing and fading; and

> ——most she loathed the hour
>   . . .
> Oh God, that I were dead!'

A considerable number of the poems are amatory; they are the expression not of heartless sensuality, nor of a sickly refinement, nor of fantastic devotion, but of manly love; and they illustrate the philosophy of the passion while they exhibit the various phases of its existence, and embody its power. An arrangement of them might be made which should depict the whole history of passion from its birth to its apotheosis, or its death. We have even

THE BURIAL OF LOVE

Had we space we should discuss this topic. It is of incalculable importance to society. Upon what love is, depends what woman is, and upon what woman is, depends what the world is, both in the present and the future. There is not a greater moral necessity in England than that of a reformation in female education. The boy is a son; the youth is a lover; and the man who thinks lightly of the elevation of character and the extension of happiness which woman's influence is capable of producing, and ought to be directed to the production of, in society, is neither the wisest of philosophers nor the best of patriots. How long will it be before we shall have read to better purpose the eloquent lessons, and the yet more eloquent history, of that gifted and glorious being, Mary Wollstonecraft?[4]

Mr Tennyson sketches females as well as ever did Sir Thomas Lawrence. His portraits are delicate, his likenesses (we will answer for them) perfect, and they have life, character, and individuality. They are nicely assorted also to all the different gradations of emotion and passion which are expressed in common with the descriptions of them. There is an appropriate object for every shade of feeling, from the light touch of a passing admiration, to the triumphant madness of soul and sense, or the deep and everlasting anguish of survivorship.

Lilian is the heroine of the first stage:

> Airy, fairy Lilian,
> . . .
> Cruel little Lilian.

Madeline indicates that another degree has been taken in the free-masonry of love, 'smiling frowning evermore'. And so we are conducted, through various gradations, to Isabel, 'the stately flower of female fortitude, and perfect wifehood', to the intense and splendid passion of *Hero*, and to the deep pathos of the ballad and dirge of *Oriana*.

We had noted many other passages for extract or remark, but our limits are prescribed and almost arrived at. We should also have illustrated the felicitous effect often produced by the iteration of a word or sentence so posited that it conveys a different meaning or shade of meaning, excites a varied kind of emotion, and is involuntarily uttered in a different tone. There are many beautiful instances of this kind. In the ballad of Oriana, and in the songs, repetition, with a slight variation

---

[4] Mary Wollstonecraft, *Vindication of the Rights of Woman* (1792).

of epithet, is also practised with great power. Rousseau's *air des trois notes* is only a curiosity;[5] Mr Tennyson has made some very touching, and some very animating melodies, of little more than that number of words. He is a master of musical combinations. His songs set themselves, and generate their own tunes, as all songs do which are good for anything; but they are not many. Perhaps our author is only surpassed, among recent poets, by Coleridge, in the harmony of his versification.

It would also have been pleasant to have transcribed and analyzed such pictures as those of the Dying Swan, the Sleeping Beauty, Adeline, &c.; and to have shown how the author can breathe his own spirit into unconscious things, making them instinct with life and feeling. One stanza of an autumnal song may intimate to some readers the facility and grace with which he identifies himself with nature.

> A spirit haunts the year's last hours
>   . . .
> Heavily hangs the tigerlily.

We must protest against the irregularities of measure, and the use of antiquated words and obsolete pronunciation, in which our author indulges so freely. He exposes himself thereby to the charge, and we think not unfairly, of indolence and affectation. There are few variations of effect which a skilful artist cannot produce, if he will but take the pains, without deviating from that regularity of measure which is one of the original elements of poetical enjoyment; made so by the tendency of the human frame to periodical movements; and the continued sacrifice of which is but ill compensated to the disappointed ear by any occasional, and not otherwise attainable correspondence between the movement of a verse and the sense which it is intended to convey. Nor certainly is any thing gained by a song's being studded with words which to most readers may require a glossary.

Mr Tennyson has the propensity which Shelley had, to use a word or two which young ladies of the present day are not accustomed to read or sing in the parlour; in singing, we believe, the toleration is greater than in reading or conversation; sentences, avoiding the words, but meaning much worse, are not generally proscribed.

That these poems will have a very rapid and extensive popularity we do not anticipate. Their very originality will prevent their being

---

[5] The philosopher, Jean Jacques Rousseau, was well known as a composer of opera and (through *Lettre sur la Musique Française*, 1753) theorist of music.

generally appreciated for a time. But that time will come, we hope, to a not far distant end. They demonstrate the possession of powers, to the future direction of which we look with some anxiety. A genuine poet has deep responsibilities to his country and the world, to the present and future generations, to earth and heaven. He, of all men, should have distinct and worthy objects before him, and consecrate himself to their promotion. It is thus that he best consults the glory of his art, and his own lasting fame. Mr Tennyson has a dangerous quality in that facility of impersonation on which we have remarked, and by which he enters so thoroughly into the most strange and wayward idio-syncrasies of other men. It must not degrade him into a poetical harlequin. He has higher work to do than that of disporting himself amongst 'mystics' and 'flowing philosophers'. He knows that 'the poet's mind is holy ground'; he knows that the poet's portion is to be

> Dower'd with the hate of hate, the scorn of scorn,
>   The love of love;

he has shown, in the lines from which we quote, his own just concep-tion of the grandeur of a poet's destiny; and we look to him for its fulfilment. It is not for such men to sink into mere verse-makers for the amusement of themselves or others. They can influence the associations of unnumbered minds; they can command the sympathies of un-numbered hearts; they can disseminate principles; they can give those principles power over men's imaginations; they can excite in a good cause the sustained enthusiasm that is sure to conquer; they can blast the laurels of the tyrants, and hallow the memories of the martyrs of patriotism; they can act with a force, the extent of which it is difficult to estimate, upon national feelings and character, and consequently upon national happiness. If our estimate of Mr Tennyson be correct, he too is a poet; and many years hence may be read his juvenile descrip-tion of that character with the proud consciousness that it has become the description and history of his own work:

> So many minds did gird their orbs with beams
>   · · ·
> Her beautiful bold brow.

2

Tennyson ∽ *Poems, Chiefly Lyrical* ∽ 1830

Arthur Henry Hallam, 'On Some of the Characteristics of
Modern Poetry', *Englishman's Magazine*, i
(August 1831), 616–28

So Mr Montgomery's *Oxford*, by the help of some pretty illustrations,
has contrived to prolong its miserable existence to a second edition!
But this is slow work, compared to that triumphant progress of the
Omnipresence, which, we concede to the author's friends, was 'truly
astonishing'.[1] We understand, moreover, that a new light has broken
upon this 'desolator desolate'; and since the 'columns' have begun to
follow the example of 'men and gods', by whom our poetaster has long
been condemned, 'it is the fate of genius', he begins to discover, 'to be
unpopular'. Now, strongly as we protest against Mr Montgomery's
application of this maxim to his own case, we are much disposed to
agree with him as to its abstract correctness. Indeed, the truth which it
involves seems to afford the only solution of so curious a phenomenon
as the success, partial and transient though it be, of himself, and others
of his calibre. When Mr Wordsworth, in his celebrated Preface to the
Lyrical Ballads, asserted that immediate or rapid popularity was not
the test of poetry, great was the consternation and clamour among

Arthur Henry Hallam, 1811–33, close friend of Tennyson at Trinity College,
Cambridge (his death occasioned *In Memoriam*) and co-member of the Cambridge 'Apostles' society. Hallam's prose is collected in *The Writings of Arthur
Hallam* (ed. T. H. Vail Motter, 1943). This brilliant essay is claimed by Marshall
McLuhan as an anticipation of symbolist thought, but Hallam is far less concerned with the 'interior' landscape of the mind than with the energising properties
of a response to the external world. See *Critical Essays on the Poetry of Tennyson*
(ed. John Killham, 1960), pp. 67–85.

[1] Robert Montgomery (1807–55): *The Omnipresence of the Deity* (1828), went
into twenty-eight editions by 1855. *Oxford* appeared in 1831. Hallam introduces
Montgomery in order to argue that despite the evidence of his poetry neither
popularity nor didacticism will be characteristic of modern poetry.

those farmers of public favour, the established critics. Never had so audacious an attack been made upon their undoubted privileges and hereditary charter of oppression. 'What! *The Edinburgh Review* not infallible!' shrieked the amiable petulance of Mr Jeffrey. '*The Gentleman's Magazine* incapable of decision!' faltered the feeble garrulity of Silvanus Urban.[2] And straightway the whole sciolist herd, men of rank, men of letters, men of wealth, men of business, all the 'mob of gentlemen who think with ease', and a terrible number of old ladies and boarding-school misses began to scream in chorus, and prolonged the notes of execration with which they overwhelmed the new doctrine, until their wits and their voices fairly gave in from exhaustion.

Much, no doubt, they did, for much persons will do when they fight for their dear selves: but there was one thing they could not do, and unfortunately it was the only one of any importance. They could not put down Mr Wordsworth by clamour, or prevent his doctrine, once uttered, and enforced by his example, from awakening the minds of men, and giving a fresh impulse to art. It was the truth, and it prevailed; not only against the exasperation of that hydra, the Reading Public, whose vanity was hurt, and the blustering of its keepers, whose delusion was exposed, but even against the false glosses and narrow apprehensions of the Wordsworthians themselves. It is the madness of all who loosen some great principle, long buried under a snow-heap of custom and superstition, to imagine that they can restrain its operation, or circumscribe it by their purposes. But the right of private judgement was stronger than the will of Luther; and even the genius of Wordsworth cannot expand itself to the full periphery of poetic art.

It is not true, as his exclusive admirers would have it, that the highest species of poetry is the reflective: it is a gross fallacy, that, because certain opinions are acute or profound, the expression of them by the imagination must be eminently beautiful. Whenever the mind of the artist suffers itself to be occupied, during its periods of creation, by any other predominant motive than the desire of beauty, the result is false in art. Now there is undoubtedly no reason, why he may not find beauty in those moods of emotion, which arise from the combinations

---

[2] Silvanus Urban was the pseudonym for the editor of the *Gentleman's Magazine*. Francis Jeffrey made three notable contributions to the Wordsworth controversy in the *Edinburgh Review*: xii (April 1808), 131–51 (a digression in an essay on Crabbe): xxiv (Nov. 1814), 1–30: xxv (Oct. 1815), 355–63.

of reflective thought, and it is possible that he may delineate these with fidelity, and not be led astray by any suggestions of an unpoetical mood. But, though possible, it is hardly probable: for a man, whose reveries take a reasoning turn, and who is accustomed to measure his ideas by their logical relations rather than the congruity of the sentiments to which they refer, will be apt to mistake the pleasure he has in knowing a thing to be true, for the pleasure he would have in knowing it to be beautiful, and so will pile his thoughts in a rhetorical battery, that they may convince, instead of letting them glow in the natural course of contemplation, that they may enrapture. It would not be difficult to show, by reference to the most admired poems of Wordsworth, that he is frequently chargeable with this error, and that much has been said by him which is good as philosophy, powerful as rhetoric, but false as poetry. Perhaps this very distortion of the truth did more in the peculiar juncture of our literary affairs to enlarge and liberalize the genius of our age, than could have been effected by a less sectarian temper. However this may be, a new school of reformers soon began to attract attention, who, professing the same independence of immediate favour, took their stand on a different region of Parnassus from that occupied by the Lakers,* and one, in our opinion, much less liable to perturbing currents of air from ungenial climates.[3]

We shall not hesitate to express our conviction, that the Cockney school (as it was termed in derision, from a cursory view of its accidental circumstances) contained more genuine inspiration, and adhered more speedily to that portion of truth which it embraced, than any *form* of art that has existed in this country since the day of Milton. Their *caposetta* was Mr Leigh Hunt, who did little more than point the way, and was diverted from his aim by a thousand personal predilections and political habits of thought. But he was followed by two men

---

* This cant term was justly ridiculed by Mr Wordsworth's supporters; but it was not so easy to substitute an inoffensive denomination. We are not at all events the first who have used it without a contemptuous intention, for we remember to have heard a disciple quote Aristophanes in its behalf. ʽΟὗτος ὂυ τῶν ἠθάδων τωνδ' ὦν ὁρᾶθ' ὑμεῖς ἀεὶ, ἀλλὰ ΛΙΜΝΑΙΟΣ. 'This is no common, no barn-door fowl: No, but a *Lakist*!'[3]

[3] 'That's not the usual kind (of bird) that you see everywhere about, but a marsh bird.' Aristophanes, *Birds*, i, 271–2. The Flamingo, first of the birds summoned to a conference by the Hoopoe, is introduced as the marsh bird. Hallam is making a pun on marsh fowl and 'lakist', meaning the Lake Poets, and in particular of course, Wordsworth.

of a very superior make; men who were born poets, lived poets, and went poets to their untimely graves. Shelley and Keats were, indeed, of opposite genius; that of the one was vast, impetuous, and sublime: the other seemed to be 'fed with honey-dew', and to have 'drunk the milk of Paradise'. Even the softness of Shelley comes out in bold, rapid, comprehensive strokes; he has no patience for minute beauties, unless they can be massed into a general effect of grandeur. On the other hand, the tenderness of Keats cannot sustain a lofty flight; he does not generalize or allegorize Nature; his imagination works with few symbols, and reposes willingly on what is given freely. Yet in this formal opposition of character there is, it seems to us, a ground-work of similarity sufficient for the purposes of classification, and constituting a remarkable point in the progress of literature. They are both poets of sensation rather than reflection. Susceptible of the slightest impulse from external nature, their fine organs trembled into emotion at colours, and sounds, and movements, unperceived or unregarded by duller temperaments. Rich and clear were their perceptions of visible forms; full and deep their feelings of music. So vivid was the delight attending the simple exertions of eye and ear, that it became mingled more and more with their trains of active thought, and tended to absorb their whole being into the energy of sense. Other poets *seek* for images to illustrate their conceptions; these men had no need to seek; they lived in a world of images; for the most important and extensive portion of their life consisted in those emotions, which are immediately conversant with sensation. Like the hero of Goethe's novel, they would hardly have been affected by what are called the pathetic parts of a book; but the *merely beautiful* passages, 'those from which the spirit of the author looks clearly and mildly forth', would have melted them to tears.[4] Hence they are not descriptive; they are picturesque. They are not smooth and *negatively* harmonious; they are full of deep and varied melodies. This powerful tendency of imagination to a life of immediate sympathy with the external universe, is not nearly so liable to false views of art as the opposite disposition of purely intellectual contemplation. For where beauty is constantly passing before 'that inward eye, which is the bliss of solitude'; where the soul seeks it as a perpetual and necessary refreshment to the sources of activity and intuition; where all the other sacred ideas of our nature, the idea of good, the idea of perfection, the idea of truth, are habitually contem-

[4] *Wilhelm Meisters Lehrjahre*, book v, ch. 6.

plated through the medium of this predominant mood, so that they assume its colour, and are subject to its peculiar laws—there is little danger that the ruling passion of the whole mind will cease to direct its creative operations, or the energetic principle of love for the beautiful sink, even for a brief period, to the level of a mere notion in the understanding. We do not deny that it is, on other accounts, dangerous for frail humanity to linger with fond attachment in the vicinity of sense. Minds of this description are especially liable to moral temptations, and upon them, more than any, it is incumbent to remember that their mission as men, which they share with all their fellow-beings, is of infinitely higher interest than their mission as artists, which they possess by rare and exclusive privilege. But it is obvious that, critically speaking, such temptations are of slight moment. Not the gross and evident passions of our nature, but the elevated and less separable desires are the dangerous enemies which misguide the poetic spirit in its attempts at self-cultivation. That delicate sense of fitness, which grows with the growth of artist feelings, and strengthens with their strength, until it acquires a celerity and weight of decision hardly inferior to the correspondent judgements of conscience, is weakened by every indulgence of heterogeneous aspirations, however pure they may be, however lofty, however suitable to human nature. We are therefore decidedly of opinion that the heights and depths of art are most within the reach of those who have received from Nature the 'fearful and wonderful' constitution we have described, whose poetry is a sort of magic, producing a number of impressions too multiplied, too minute, and too diversified to allow of our tracing them to their causes, because just such was the effect, even so boundless, and so bewildering, produced on their imaginations by the real appearance of Nature.

These things being so, our friends of the new school had evidently much reason to recur to the maxim laid down by Mr Wordsworth, and to appeal from the immediate judgements of lettered or unlettered contemporaries to the decision of a more equitable posterity. How should they be popular, whose senses told them a richer and ampler tale than most men could understand, and who constantly expressed, because they constantly felt, sentiments of exquisite pleasure or pain, which most men were not permitted to experience? The public very naturally derided them as visionaries, and gibbeted *in terrorem* those inaccuracies of diction, occasioned sometimes by the speed of their conceptions, sometimes by the inadequacy of language to their peculiar conditions of thought. But, it may be asked, does not this line of argument prove too much? Does it not prove that there is a barrier between these poets and all other persons, so strong and immovable, that, as has been said of the Supreme Essence, we must be themselves before we can understand them in the least? Not only are they not liable to sudden and vulgar estimation, but the lapse of ages, it seems, will not consolidate their fame, nor the suffrages of the wise few produce any impression, however remote or slowly matured, on the judgements of the incapacitated many. We answer, this is not the import of our argument. Undoubtedly the true poet addresses himself, in all his conceptions, to the common nature of us all. Art is a lofty tree, and may shoot up far beyond our grasp, but its roots are in daily life and experience. Every bosom contains the elements of those complex emotions which the artist feels, and every head can, to a certain extent, go over in itself the process of their combination, so as to understand his expressions and sympathize with his state. But this requires exertion; more or less, indeed, according to the difference of occasion, but always some degree of exertion. For since the emotions of the poet, during composition, follow a regular law of association, it follows that to accompany their progress up to the harmonious prospect of the whole, and to perceive the proper dependence of every step on that which preceded, it is absolutely necessary *to start from the same point*, i.e., clearly to apprehend that leading sentiment in the poet's mind, by their conformity to which the host of suggestions are arranged. Now this requisite exertion is not willingly made by the large majority of readers. It is so easy to judge capriciously, and according to indolent impulse! For very many, therefore, it has become *morally* impossible to attain the author's point of vision, on account of their habits, or their prejudices, or their circumstances; but it is never *physically* impossible, because nature has placed in every man the simple elements, of which art is the sublimation. Since then this demand on the reader for activity, when he wants to peruse his author in a luxurious passiveness, is the very thing that moves his bile, it is obvious that those writers will be always most popular, who require the least degree of exertion. Hence, whatever is mixed up with art, and appears under its semblance, is always more favourably regarded than art free and unalloyed. Hence, half the fashionable poems in the world are mere rhetoric, and half the remainder are perhaps not liked by the generality for their substantial merits. Hence, likewise, of the really pure compositions those are most universally agreeable, which take for their primary subject the *usual* passions of the heart, and deal with them in a simple state, without applying the transforming powers of high imagination. Love, friendship, ambition, religion, &c., are matters of daily experience, even amongst imaginative tempers. The forces of association, therefore, are ready to work in these directions, and little effort of will is necessary to follow the artist. For the same reason such subjects often excite a partial power of composition, which is no sign of a truly poetic organization. We are very far from wishing to depreciate this class of poems, whose influence is so extensive, and communicates so refined a pleasure. We contend only that the facility with which its impressions are communicated, is no proof of its elevation as a form of art, but rather the contrary.

What then, some may be ready to exclaim, is the pleasure derived by most men from Shakespeare, or Dante, or Homer, entirely false and factitious? If these are really masters of their art, must not the energy required of the ordinary intelligences, that come in contact with their mighty genius, be the greatest possible? How comes it then that they are popular? Shall we not say, after all, that the difference is in the power of the author, not in the tenor of his meditations? Those eminent spirits find no difficulty in conveying to common apprehension their lofty sense, and profound observation of Nature. They keep no artistocratic state, apart from the sentiments of society at large; they speak to the hearts of all, and by the magnetic force of their conceptions elevate inferior intellects into a higher and purer atmosphere. The truth contained in this objection is undoubtedly important; geniuses of the most universal order, and assigned by destiny to the most propitious eras of a nation's literary development, have a clearer and larger access to the minds of their compatriots, than can ever be open to those who are circumscribed by less fortunate circumstances. In the youthful periods of any literature there is an expansive and communicative tendency in mind, which produces unreservedness of communion, and reciprocity of vigour between different orders of intelligence. Without abandoning the ground which has always been defended by the partisans of Mr Wordsworth, who declare with perfect truth that the number of real admirers of what is really admirable in Shakespeare and Milton are much fewer than the number of apparent admirers might lead one to imagine, we may safely assert that the intense thoughts set in circulation by those 'orbs of song', and their noble satellites, 'in great Eliza's golden time', did not fail to awaken a proportionable intensity in the natures of numberless auditors. Some might feel feebly, some strongly; the effect would vary according to the character of the recipient; but upon none was the stirring influence entirely unimpressive. The knowledge and power thus imbibed, became a part of national existence; it was ours as Englishmen; and amid the flux of generations and customs we retain unimpaired this privilege of intercourse with greatness.

But the age in which we live comes late in our national progress. That first raciness, and juvenile vigour of literature, when nature 'wantoned as in her prime, and played at will her virgin fancies', is gone, never to return. Since that day we have undergone a period of degradation. 'Every handicraftsman has worn the mark of Poesy.' It would be tedious to repeat the tale, so often related, of French contagion, and the heresies of the Popian school. With the close of the last century came an era of reaction, an era of painful struggle, to bring our overcivilised condition of thought into union with the fresh productive spirit that brightened the morning of our literature. But repentance is unlike innocence: the laborious endeavour to restore has more complicated methods of action, than the freedom of untainted nature. Those different powers of poetic disposition, the energies of Sensitive,* of Reflective, of Passionate Emotion, which in former times were intermingled, and derived from mutual support an extensive empire over the feelings of men, were now restrained within separate spheres of agency. The whole system no longer worked harmoniously, and by intrinsic harmony acquired external freedom; but there arose a violent and unusual action in the several component functions, each for itself, all striving to reproduce the regular power which the whole had once enjoyed. Hence the melancholy, which so evidently characterises the spirit of modern poetry; hence that return of the mind upon itself, and the habit of seeking relief in idiosyncracies rather than community of interest. In the old times the poetic impulse went along with the general impulse of the nation; in these, it is a reaction against

---

* We are aware that this is not the right word, being appropriated by common use to a different signification. Those who think the caution given by Caesar should not stand in the way of urgent occasion, may substitute 'sensuous,' a word in use amongst our elder divines, and revived by a few bold writers in our own time.

it, a check acting for conservation against a propulsion towards change. We have indeed seen it urged in some of our fashionable publications, that the diffusion of poetry must necessarily be in the direct ratio of the diffusion of machinery, because a highly civilized people must have new objects of interest, and thus a new field will be opened to description. But this notable argument forgets that against this *objective* amelioration may be set the decrease of *subjective* power, arising from a prevalence of social activity, and a continual absorption of the higher feelings into the palpable interests of ordinary life. The French Revolution may be a finer theme than the war of Troy; but it does not so evidently follow that Homer is to find his superior. Our inference, therefore, from this change in the relative position of artists to the rest of the community is, that modern poetry, in proportion to its depth and truth, is likely to have little immediate authority over public opinion. Admirers it will have; sects consequently it will form; and these strong under-currents will in time sensibly affect the principal stream. Those writers, whose genius, though great, is not strictly and essentially poetic, become mediators between the votaries of art and the careless cravers for excitement.* Art herself, less manifestly glorious than in her periods of undisputed supremacy, retains her essential prerogatives, and forgets not to raise up chosen spirits, who may minister to her state, and vindicate her title.

One of this faithful Islam, a poet in the truest and highest sense, we are anxious to present to our readers. He has yet written little, and published less; but in these 'preludes of a loftier strain', we recognise the inspiring god. Mr Tennyson belongs decidedly to the class we have already described as Poets of Sensation. He sees all the forms of nature with the *eruditus oculus*, and his ear has a fairy fineness. There is a strange earnestness in his worship of beauty, which throws a charm over his impassioned song, more easily felt than described, and not to be escaped by those who have once felt it. We think he has more definiteness, and soundness of general conception, than the late Mr Keats, and is much more free from blemishes of diction, and hasty capriccios of fancy. He has also this advantage over that poet, and his friend Shelley, that he comes before the public, unconnected with any

---

* May we not compare them to the bright, but unsubstantial clouds which, in still evenings, girdle the sides of lofty mountains, and seem to form a natural connection between the lowly valleys, spread out beneath, and those isolated peaks above, that hold the 'last parley with the setting sun?'

political party, or peculiar system of opinions. Nevertheless, true to the theory we have stated, we believe his participation in their characteristic excellencies is sufficient to secure him a share in their unpopularity. The volume of *Poems, chiefly Lyrical*, does not contain above 154 pages; but it shows us much more of the character of its parent mind, than many books we have known of much larger compass, and more boastful pretensions. The features of original genius are clearly and strongly marked. The author imitates nobody; we recognise the spirit of his age, but not the individual form of this or that writer. His thoughts bear no more resemblance to Byron or Scott, Shelley or Coleridge, than to Homer or Calderon, Ferdusi or Calidas. We have remarked five distinctive excellencies of his own manner. First, his luxuriance of imagination, and at the same time his control over it. Secondly, his power of embodying himself in ideal characters, or rather moods of character, with such extreme accuracy of adjustment, that the circumstances of the narration seem to have a natural correspondence with the predominant feeling, and, as it were, to be evolved from it by assimilative force. Thirdly, his vivid, picturesque delineation of objects, and the peculiar skill with which he holds all of them *fused*, to borrow a metaphor from science, in a medium of strong emotion.[5] Fourthly, the variety of his lyrical measures, and exquisite modulation of harmonious words and cadences to the swell and fall of the feelings expressed. Fifthly, the elevated habits of thought, *implied* in these compositions, and imparting a mellow soberness of tone, more impressive, to our minds, than if the author had drawn up a set of opinions in verse, and sought to instruct the understanding, rather than to communicate the love of beauty to the heart. We shall proceed to give our readers some specimens in illustration of these remarks, and, if possible, we will give them entire; for no poet can fairly be judged of by fragments, least of all a poet, like Mr Tennyson, whose mind conceives nothing isolated, nothing abrupt, but every part with reference to some other part, and in subservience to the idea of the whole.

Recollections of the Arabian Nights! What a delightful, endearing title! How we pity those to whom it calls up no reminiscence of early enjoyment, no sentiment of kindliness as towards one who sings a song

---

[5] A metaphor from chemistry. Tennyson's emotion is the flux, which dissolves or melts the picturesque elements as a mineral is dissolved in a solution before it is analysed.

they have loved, or mentions with affection a departed friend! But let nobody expect a multifarious enumeration of Viziers, Barmecides, Fireworshippers, and Cadis; trees that sing, horses that fly, and Goules that eat rice pudding! Our author knows what he is about: he has, with great judgement, selected our old acquaintance, 'the good Haroun Alraschid', as the most prominent object of our childish interest, and with him has called up one of those luxurious garden scenes, the account of which, in plain prose, used to make our mouths water for sherbet, since luckily we were too young to think much about Zobeide! We think this poem will be the favourite among Mr Tennyson's admirers; perhaps upon the whole it is our own; at least we find ourselves recurring to it oftener than to any other, and every time we read it, we feel the freshness of its beauty increase, and are inclined to exclaim with Madame de Sevigné, 'à force d'être ancien, il m'est nouveau'. But let us draw the curtain.

> When the breeze of a joyful dawn blew free
> . . .
> I saw him—in his golden prime,
> The good Haroun Alraschid!

Criticism will sound but poorly after this; yet we cannot give silent votes. The first stanza, we beg leave to observe, places us at once in the position of feeling, which the poem requires. The scene is before us, around us; we cannot mistake its localities, or blind ourselves to its colours. That happy ductility of childhood returns for the moment; 'true Mussulmans are we, and sworn', and yet there is a latent knowledge, which heightens the pleasure, that to our change from really childish thought we owe the capacities by which we enjoy the recollection. As the poem proceeds, all is in perfect keeping. There is a solemn distinctness in every image, a majesty of slow motion in every cadence, that aids the illusion of thought, and steadies its contemplation of the complete picture. Originality of observation seems to cost nothing to our author's liberal genius; he lavishes images of exquisite accuracy and elaborate splendour, as a common writer throws about metaphorical truisms, and exhausted tropes. Amidst all the varied luxuriance of the sensations described, we are never permitted to lose sight of the idea which gives unity to this variety, and by the recurrence of which, as a sort of mysterious influence, at the close of every stanza, the mind is wrought up, with consummate art, to the final disclosure. This poem is a perfect gallery of pictures; and the concise boldness, with which in a few words an object is clearly painted, is sometimes (see the 6th stanza) majestic as Milton, sometimes (see the 12th) sublime as Æschylus. We have not, however, so far forgot our vocation as critics, that we would leave without notice the slight faults which adhere to this precious work. In the 8th stanza, we doubt the propriety of using the bold compound 'black-green', at least in such close vicinity to 'gold-green': nor is it perfectly clear by the term, although indicated by the context, that 'diamond plots' relates to shape rather than colour. We are perhaps very stupid, but 'vivid stars un-rayed' does not convey to us a very precise notion. '*Rosaries* of scented thorn', in the 10th stanza, is, we believe, an entirely un-authorized use of the word. Would our author translate *biferique rosaria Pæsti*—'And *rosaries* of Pæstum, twice in bloom'? To the beautiful 13th stanza, we are sorry to find any objection: but even the bewitching loveliness of that 'Persian girl' shall not prevent our performing the rigid duty we have undertaken, and we must hint to Mr Tennyson, that 'redolent' is no synonym for 'fragrant'. Bees may be redolent *of* honey: spring may be 'redolent *of* youth and love', but the absolute use of the word has, we fear, neither in Latin nor English, any better authority than the monastic epitaph on Fair Rosamond. *Hic iacet in tomba Rosa Mundi, non Rosa Munda, non redolet, sed olet, quæ redolere solet.*[6]

We are disposed to agree with Mr Coleridge, when he says 'no adequate compensation can be made for the mischief a writer does by confounding the distinct senses of words'. At the same time our feelings in this instance rebel strongly in behalf of 'redolent'; for the melody of the passage, as it stands, is beyond the possibility of improvement, and unless he should chance to light upon a word very nearly resembling this in consonants and vowels, we can hardly quarrel with Mr Tennyson

[6] In bringing forward this clumsy piece of medieval dog Latin as authority for Tennyson's use of the word 'redolent', Hallam implies that he has no authority. This is an elegiac couplet supposedly inscribed on the tomb of Rosamund Clifford, mistress of Henry II, at Godstow nunnery, hence the pun in the first line. The second line, 'Non redolet sed olet, quae redolere solet', plays feebly upon the synonyms *olere* and *redolere*, both meaning to smell, while *redolere* is found in Virgil and Ovid meaning to smell of or like flowers or honey etc. As a sweet smell apparently emanated from the tomb the second line's inept compli-ment runs, 'She does not smell, but emits a (sweet) scent, she who is accustomed to smell (of roses).'

if, in spite of our judgement, he retains the offender in his service.

Our next specimen is of a totally different character, but not less complete, we think, in its kind. Have we among our readers any who delight in the heroic poems of Old England, the inimitable ballads? Any to whom Sir Patrick Spens, and Clym of the Clough, and Glorious Robin, are consecrated names? Any who sigh with disgust at the miserable abortions of simpleness mistaken for simplicity, or florid weakness substituted for plain energy, which they may often have seen dignified with the title of Modern Ballads? Let such draw near, and read the Ballad of Oriana. We know no more happy seizure of the antique spirit in the whole compass of our literature; yet there is no foolish self desertion, no attempt at obliterating the present, but every where a full discrimination of how much ought to be yielded, and how much retained. The author is well aware that the art of one generation cannot *become* that of another by any will or skill: but the artist may transfer the spirit of the past, making it a temporary form for his own spirit, and so effect, by idealizing power, a new and legitimate combination. If we were asked to name among the real antiques that which bears greatest resemblance to this gem, we should refer to the ballad of *Fair Helen of Kirconnel Lea* in the *Minstrelsy of the Scottish Border*.[7] It is a resemblance of mood, not of execution. They are both highly wrought lyrical expressions of pathos; and it is very remarkable with what intuitive art, every expression and cadence in *Fair Helen* is accorded to the main feeling. The characters that distinguish the language of our *lyrical*, from that of our *epic* ballads, have never yet been examined with the accuracy they deserve. But, beyond question, the class of poems, which, in point of harmonious combination, Oriana most resembles, is the Italian. Just thus the meditative tenderness of Dante and Petrarch is embodied in the clear, searching tones of Tuscan song. These mighty masters produce two-thirds of their effect by *sound*. Not that they sacrifice sense to sound, but that sound conveys their meaning, where words would not. There are innumerable shades of fine emotion in the human heart, especially when the senses are keen and vigilant, which are too subtle and too rapid to admit of corresponding phrases. The understanding takes no definite note of them; how then can they leave signatures in language? Yet they exist; in plenitude of being and beauty they exist; and in music they find a medium

[7] 'Fair Helen', *Minstrelsy of the Scottish Border* (ed. Sir Walter Scott, 1802), i, 72.

through which they pass from heart to heart. The tone becomes the sign of the feeling; and they reciprocally suggest each other. Analogous to this suggestive power, may be reckoned, perhaps, in a sister art, the effects of Venetian colouring. Titian *explains* by tints, as Petrarch by tones. Words would not have done the business of the one, nor any groupings, or *narration by form*, that of the other. But, shame upon us! we are going back to our metaphysics, when that 'sweet, meek face' is waiting to be admitted.

> My heart is wasted with my woe,
> Oriana.
>
> . . .
>
> I hear the roaring of the sea,
> Oriana.

We have heard it objected to this poem, that the name occurs once too often in every stanza. We have taken the plea into our judicial consideration, and the result is, that we overrule it, and pronounce that the proportion of the melodious cadences to the pathetic parts of the narration, could not be diminished without materially affecting the rich lyrical impression of the ballad. For what is the author's intention? To gratify our curiosity with a strange adventure? To shake our nerves with a painful story? Very far from it. Tears indeed may 'blind our sight', as we read; but they are 'blissful tears'; the strong musical delight prevails over every painful feeling, and mingles them all in its deep swell, until they attain a composure of exalted sorrow, a mood in which the latest repose of agitation becomes visible, and the influence of beauty spreads like light, over the surface of the mind. The last line, with its dreamy wildness, reveals the design of the whole. It is transferred, if we mistake not, from an old ballad (a freedom of immemorial usage with ballad mongers, as our readers doubtless know), but the merit lies in the abrupt application of it to the leading sentiment, so as to flash upon us in a few little words a world of meaning, and to consecrate the passion that was beyond cure or hope, by resigning it to the accordance of inanimate Nature, who, like man, has her tempests, and occasions of horror, but august in their largeness of operation, awful by their dependence on a fixed and perpetual necessity.

We must give one more extract, and we are almost tempted to choose by lot among many that crowd on our recollection, and solicit our preference with such witchery, as it is not easy to withstand. The poems towards the middle of the volume seem to have been written at an earlier period than the rest. They display more unrestrained fancy, and are less evidently proportioned to their ruling ideas, than those which we think of later date. Yet in the *Ode to Memory*—the only one which we have the poet's authority for referring to early life—there is a majesty of expression, united to a truth of thought, which almost confounds our preconceived distinctions. The *Confessions of a second-rate, Sensitive Mind*, are full of deep insight into human nature, and into those particular trials, which are sure to beset men who think and feel for themselves at this epoch of social development. The title is perhaps ill chosen: not only has it an appearance of quaintness, which has no sufficient reason, but it seems to us incorrect. The mood portrayed in this poem, unless the admirable skill of delineation has deceived us, is rather the clouded season of a strong mind, than the habitual condition of one feeble and 'second-rate'. Ordinary tempers build up fortresses of opinion on one side or another; they will see only what they choose to see; the distant glimpse of such an agony as is here brought out to view, is sufficient to keep them for ever in illusions, voluntarily raised at first, but soon trusted in with full reliance as inseparable parts of self. Perhaps, however, Mr Tennyson's mode of 'rating' is different from ours. He may esteem none worthy of the first order, who has not attained a complete universality of thought, and such trustful reliance on a principle of repose, which lies beyond the war of conflicting opinions, that the grand ideas, 'qui planent sans cesse au dessus de l'humanité', cease to affect him with bewildering impulses of hope and fear. We have not space to enter farther into this topic; but we should not despair of convincing Mr Tennyson, that such a position of intellect would not be the most elevated, nor even the most conducive to perfection of art. The *How and the Why* appears to present the reverse of the same picture. It is the same mind still; the sensitive sceptic, whom we have looked upon in his hour of distress, now scoffing at his own state with an earnest mirth that borders on sorrow. It is exquisitely beautiful to see in this, as in the former portrait, how the feeling of art is kept ascendant in our minds over distressful realities, by constant reference to images of tranquil beauty, whether touched pathetically, as the Ox and the Lamb in the first piece, or with fine humour, as the 'great bird' and 'little bird' in the second. The *Sea Fairies* is another strange title; but those who turn to it with the very natural curiosity of discovering who these new births of mythology may be, will be unpardonable if they do not linger over it with higher feelings. A stretch of lyrical power is here exhibited, which we did not think the English language had possessed. The proud swell of verse, as the harp tones 'run up the ridged sea', and the soft and melancholy lapse, as the sounds die along the widening space of waters, are instances of that right imitation which is becoming to art, but which in the hands of the unskilful, or the affecters of easy popularity, is often converted into a degrading mimicry, detrimental to the best interests of the imagination.

A considerable portion of this book is taken up with a very singular, and very beautiful class of poems, on which the author has evidently bestowed much thought and elaboration. We allude to the female characters, every trait of which presumes an uncommon degree of observation and reflection. Mr Tennyson's way of proceeding seems to be this. He collects the most striking phenomena of individual minds, until he arrives at some leading fact, which allows him to lay down an axiom, or law, and then, working on the law thus attained, he clearly discerns the tendency of what new particulars his invention suggests, and is enabled to impress an individual freshness and unity on ideal combinations. These expressions of character are brief and coherent: nothing extraneous to the dominant fact is admitted, nothing illustrative of it, and, as it were, growing out of it, is rejected. They are like summaries of mighty dramas. We do not say this method admits of such large luxuriance of power, as that of our real dramatists; but we contend that it is a new species of poetry, a graft of the lyric on the dramatic, and Mr Tennyson deserves the laurel of an inventor, an enlarger of our modes of knowledge and power. We must hasten to make our election; so, passing by the 'airy, fairy Lilian', who 'clasps her hands' in vain to retain us; the 'stately flower' of matronly fortitude, 'revered Isabel'; Madeline, with her voluptuous alternation of smile and frown; Mariana, last, but oh not least—we swear by the memory of Shakespeare, to whom a monument of observant love has here been raised by simply expanding all the latent meanings and beauties contained in one stray thought of his genius—we shall fix on a lovely, albeit somewhat mysterious lady, who has fairly taken our 'heart from out our breast'.

ADELINE

Is not this beautiful? When this Poet dies, will not the Graces and the Loves mourn over him, fortunataque favilla nascentur violae?[8] How original is the imagery, and how delicate! How wonderful the new world thus created for us, the region between real and unreal! The gardens of Armida were but poorly musical compared with the roses and lilies that bloom around thee, thou faint smiler, Adeline, on whom the glory of imagination reposes, endowing all thou lookest on with sudden and mysterious life. We could expatiate on the deep meaning of this poem, but it is time to twitch our critical mantles; and, as our trade is not that of mere enthusiasm, we shall take our leave with an objection (perhaps a cavil) to the language of cowslips, which we think too ambiguously spoken of for a subject on which nobody, except Mr Tennyson, can have any information. The 'ringing bluebell' too, if it be not a pun, suggests one, and might probably be altered to advantage.

One word more, before we have done, and it shall be a word of praise. The language of this book, with one or two rare exceptions, is thorough and sterling English. A little more respect, perhaps, was due to the *jus et norma loquendi*, but we are inclined to consider as venial a fault arising from generous enthusiasm for the principles of sound analogy, and for that Saxon element, which constitutes the intrinsic freedom and nervousness of our native tongue. We see no signs in what Mr Tennyson has written of the Quixotic spirit which has led some persons to desire the reduction of English to a single form, by excluding nearly the whole of Latin and Roman derivatives. Ours is necessarily a compound language; as such alone it can flourish and increase; nor will the author of the poems we have extracted be likely to barter for a barren appearance of symmetrical structure that fertility of expression, and variety of harmony, which 'the speech, that Shakespeare spoke' derived from the sources of southern phraseology.

In presenting this young poet to the public, as one not studious of instant popularity, nor likely to obtain it, we may be thought to play the part of a fashionable lady, who deludes her refractory mate into doing what she chooses, by pretending to wish the exact contrary, or of a cunning pedagogue, who practises a similar manoeuvre on some self-willed Flibbertigibbet of the schoolroom. But the supposition would do us wrong. We have spoken in good faith, commending this volume to feeling hearts and imaginative tempers, not to the stupid

[8] 'And from your blest ashes shall violets grow.' A translation of Hamlet's speech over Ophelia's grave.

readers, or the voracious readers, or the malignant readers, or the readers after dinner![9] We confess, indeed, we never knew an instance in which the theoretical abjurers of popularity have shown themselves very reluctant to admit its actual advances; so much virtue is not, perhaps, in human nature; and if the world should take a fancy to buy up these poems, in order to be revenged on the *Englishman's Magazine*, who knows whether even we might not disappoint its malice by a cheerful adaptation of our theory to 'existing circumstances'?[10]

[9] Hallam's assertion of the autonomy of art possibly owes something to German thinking (perhaps to Schiller's *Letters on the Aesthetic Education of Man*, 1795) but the rigorousness of his position is all his own. The finest Victorian answer to his essay—and possibly the only answer—was by Francis Garden, writing over ten years later (*Christian Remembrancer*, iv N.S. (July 1842), 42–58). Hallam's theory is 'mistaken', he says, not so much because it denies the subservience of art to politics or morals but because of the narrowness of its basis. In the first place, Garden condemns the notion of the poet's privileged isolation by asserting the simple wholeness of the human personality, which both dreams *and* acts, moves in the world of beauty *and* public interests—'energetic, human, and sympathising' (47). The dichotomy between the real world and the world of imagination is false. Secondly, a much more important argument, poetry has a very different status from the other arts because speech, 'human discourse', is its material. Therefore poetry *must* exploit not only the image-making capacities of language, its power to bring sensuous life before us as 'pictures' (and he reminds us that language is fairly limited in this direction in comparison with some arts), but *all* aspects of speech, the utterance of thoughts and feelings. Whereas 'sculpture and painting have no opinions to profess, no persuasions to urge, few direct *duties* of any sort, poetry is in a predicament altogether different. Call it a fine art as much as you will, it is discourse; it is utterance; it is man speaking to man, man telling man his thoughts and feelings. Now, speech can never be long without having a direct moral character, without having aims in themselves foreign to art, without having a good deal to do that is not out of place in poetry, but yet that cannot easily be brought within a definition of it' (49).

[10] The *Englishman's Magazine*, owned and edited by Edward Moxon, the publisher later of Tennyson's *Poems*, 1832, had a brief existence from April to October 1831. It had radical associations which made John Wilson (see below, p. 107) readier to connect Tennyson with Leigh Hunt and his circle of 'Cockney' poets.

3

Tennyson ❧ Poems, Chiefly Lyrical ❧ 1830

John Wilson, 'Christopher North', *Blackwood's Edinburgh Magazine*, xxxi (May 1832), 721–41

Almost all men, women, and children, are poets, except those who write verses. We shall not define poetry, because the Cockneys have done so; and were they to go to church, we should be strongly tempted to break the Sabbath. But this much we say of it, that every thing is poetry which is not mere sensation. We are poets at all times when our minds are makers. Now, it is well known, that we create nine-tenths at least of what appears to exist externally; and that such is somewhere about the proportion between reality and imagination. Millions of supposed matters-of-fact are the wildest fictions—of which we may mention merely two, the rising and the setting of the sun. This being established, it follows that we live, breathe, and have our being in Poetry—it is the Life of our Life—the heart of the mystery, which, were it plucked out, and to beat no more, the universe, now all written over with symbolical characters of light, would be at once a blank obscurely scribbled over with dead letters; or rather, the volume would be shut up—and appear a huge clumsy folio with brass clasps, bound in calf-skin, and draperied with cobwebs. But instead of that, the leaves of the living Book of Nature are all fluttering in the sunshine; even he who runs may read; though they alone who sit, stand, or lie, pondering on its pages, behold in full the beauty and the sublimity, which their own immortal spirits create, reflected back on them who are its authors, and felt, in that trance, to be the spiritual sound and colouring which vivifies and animates the face and the form of Nature.

John Wilson, 1785–1854, professor of moral philosophy in the university of Edinburgh, 1820–51, tory, and main contributor to 'Noctes Ambrosianae' in *Blackwood's*. Despite the hostility of the magazine to the early romantic poets, Wilson admired Wordsworth, Coleridge and Shelley. He had lived in the Lake District by choice before he began his literary career and contributed to Coleridge's *Friend*.

All men, women, and children, then, are manifestly poets, except those who write verses. But why that exception? Because they alone make no use of their minds. Versifiers—and we speak but of them—are the sole living creatures that are not also creators. The inferior animals—as we are pleased to call them, and as indeed in some respects they are—modify matter much in their imaginations. Rode ye never a horse by night through a forest? That most poetical of quadrupeds sees a spirit in every stump, else why by such sudden start should he throw his master over his ears? The blackbird on the tip-top of that pine-tent is a poet, else never could his yellow bill so salute with rapturous orisons the reascending Sun, as he flings over the woods a lustre again gorgeous from the sea. And what induces those stock-doves, think ye, to fill the heart of the grove with soft, deep, low, lonely, far-away mournful, yet happy—*thunder*; what, but Love and Joy, and Delight and Desire, in one word, Poetry—Poetry that confines the universe to that wedded pair, within the sanctuary of the pillared shade impervious to meridian sunbeams, and brightens and softens into splendour and into snow divine the plumage beautifying the creatures in their bliss, as breast to breast they croodendoo on their shallow nest!

Thus all men, women, and children, birds, beasts, and fishes, are poets, except versifiers. Oysters are poets. Nobody will deny that, who ever in the neighbourhood of Prestonpans beheld them passionately gaping, on their native bed, for the flow of tide coming again to awaken all their energies from the wide Atlantic. Nor less so are snails. See them in the dewy stillness of eve, as they salute the crescent Dian, with horns humbler indeed, but no less pointed than her own. The beetle, against the traveller borne in heedless hum, if we knew all his feelings in that soliloquy, might safely be pronounced a Wordsworth.

Thus are we all poets—high and low—except versifiers. They, poor creatures, are a peculiar people, impotent of good works. Ears have they, but they hear not—eyes have they, but they will not see—nay, naturalists assert that they have brains and spinal marrow, also organs of speech; yet with all that organization, they seem to have but little feeling, and no thought; and but by a feeble and monotonous fizz, are you made aware, in the twilight, of the useless existence of the obscure ephemerals.[1]

[1] This is a half-serious, half-satirical treatment of Coleridgean ideas, and illustrates the uneasy combination of real sensitivity and facetiousness in Wilson's reviewing manner. His belief in the shaping, projecting imagination is not

But we fear that we are getting satirical, than which nothing can well be more unbecoming the character of a Christian: So let us be serious. Many times a month do we hint to all such insects, that Maga looks upon them as midges. But still will they be seeking to insinuate themselves through her long deep veil, which nunlike she wears at gloaming; and can they complain of cruelty, if she brush them away with her lily hand, or compress them with her snow-white fingers into unlingering death? There is no such privileged place in this periodical world now as the fugitive Poets' Corner. All its regions are open to the inspired; but the versifier has no spot now wherein to expand his small mealy wings; and you see him sitting disconsolate as one of those animal-culæ, who, in their indolent brownness, are neither flies, bees, nor wasps, like a spot upon dandelion or bunweed, till he surprises you by proving that he has wings, or something of that sort, by a feeble farewell flight in among nettles some yards off, where he takes refuge in eternal oblivion.

It is not easy to find out what sets people a-versifying; especially nowadays, when the slightest symptoms of there being something amiss with them in that way, immediately subject them not only to the grossest indignities, but to the almost certain loss of bread. We could perhaps in some measure understand it, were they rich, or even tolerably well-off; in the enjoyment, let us suppose, of small annuities, or of hereditary kail-yards, with a well in the corner, overshadowed with a bourtree bush; but they are almost always, if in at the knees, out at the elbows; and their stockings seem to have been compiled originally by some mysterious process of darning upon nothing as a substratum. Now nothing more honourable than virtuous poverty; but then we expect to see him with a shuttle or a spade in his hand, weaving 'seventeen hunder linen', or digging drains, till the once dry desert is all one irrigated meadow, green as the summer woods that fling their shadows o'er its haycocks. He is an insufferable sight, alternately biting his nails and his pen, and blotching whitey-brown with hieroglyphics that would have puzzled Champollion. Versifying operatives are almost always half-witted creatures, addicted to drinking; and sell their songs for alms. Persons with the failing, in what are sometimes called

substantially weaker than that of Fox and Hallam but his idealism found their stress on the physical basis of perception repugnant. He was also readier (see the last paragraph of his review) to associate Wordsworth happily with eighteenth-century descriptive poetry than they were.

the middle-classes, or even in more genteel or fashionable life, such as the children of clerks of various kinds, say to canal or coal companies, are slow to enter upon any specific profession, trusting to their genius, which their parents regard with tears, sometimes of joy, and sometimes of rage, according as their prophetic souls see the brows of their off-spring adorned with laurels, or their breeches with tatters. Sensible parents crush this propensity in the bud, and ruthlessly bind the Apollos apprentices to Places; but the weaker ones enclose contributions to Christopher North, as if they had never heard of his crutch, and thus is the world defrauded of many a tailor. What becomes of all the versifiers when they get old—if, indeed, they ever do get old—we never yet heard any plausible conjecture; though we have ourselves seen some in middle age, walking about, each by himself, looking as if he were sole survivor of the Seven Young Men, with his unmeaning face, and his umbrella under his arm, though the dust may have been lying three inches thick, and laughing to scorn the thin-spurting showers of the water-carts, that seemed sent there rather to raise than to lay the ghost of a dry summer. 'Tis said that from this class is drawn the supply of theatrical critics.

Now and then, by some felicity of fortune, a versifier enjoys a temporary revenge on stepdame Nature, and for a while is seen fluttering like a butterfly among birds; or rather heard cheeping like a mouse among a choir of nightingales. People take it into their heads to insist upon it that he is a poet. They solicit subscriptions, get him into print, and make interest with newspaper editors to allow him to review himself twice a week through the season. These newspapers he files; and binds the folio. He abuses Blackwood, and is crowned King of all the Albums.

We had no intention of being so, but suspect that we have been somewhat, severe; so let us relieve all lads of feeling and fancy, by assuring them that hitherto we have been sneering but at sumphs and God-help-you-silly-ones, and that our hearts overflow with kindness towards all the children of genius. Not a few promising boys have lately attempted poetry both in the east and west of Scotland, and we have listened not undelighted to the music. Stoddart and Aytoun—he of the Death-Wake, and he of Poland—are graciously regarded by Old Christopher; and their volumes—presentation-copies—have been placed among the essays of those gifted youths, of whom in riper years much may be confidently predicted of fair and good. Many of the small poems of John Wright, an industrious weaver, somewhere in Ayrshire, are beautiful, and have received the praise of Sir Walter himself, who, though kind to all aspirants, praises none to whom nature has not imparted some portion of the creative power of genius.[2]

One of John's strains we have committed to memory—or rather, without trying to do so, got by heart; and as it seems to us very mild and touching, here it is.

THE WRECKED MARINER

England ought to be producing some young poets now, that there may be no dull interregnum when the old shall have passed away; and pass away many of them soon must—their bodies, which are shadows, but their spirits, which are lights—they will burn for ever—till time be no more. It is thought by many that almost all the poetical genius which has worked such wonders in our day, was brought into power— it having been given but in capacity to the Wordsworths, and Scotts, and Byrons—by the French Revolution. Through the storm and tempest, the thunder and the lightning, which accompanied that great moral and intellectual earthquake, the strong-winged spirits soared; and found in their bosom, or in the 'deep serene' above all that turmoil, in the imperturbable heavens, the inspiration and the matter of im-mortal song. If it were so, then shall not the next age want its mighty poets. For we see 'the deep-fermenting tempest brewed in the grim evening sky'. On the beautiful green grass of England may there glisten in the sun but the pearly dewdrops; may they be brushed away but by the footsteps of Labour issuing from his rustic lodge. But Europe, long ere bright heads are grey, will see blood poured out like water; and there will be the noise of many old establishments quaking to their foundations, or rent asunder, or overthrown. Much that is sacred will be preserved; and, after a troubled time, much will be re-paired and restored, as it has ever been after misrule and ruin. Then— and haply not till then—will again be heard the majestic voice of song from the renovated nations. Yet, if the hum which now we heard be

---

[2] Wilson takes three very different poets to show the catholic generosity of his taste—an intense, highly gothic poem by T. T. Stoddart, *The Death-Wake, or Lunacy. A Necromaunt in three Chimeras* (1831); a poem on public themes by W. E. Aytoun, *Poland* (1832); John Wright's *The Wrecked Mariner*. Wright's chief poem is *The Retrospect*, an autobiographical nature poem in Spenserian stanzas and hectic but derivative eighteenth-century poetic diction.

indeed that of the March of Intellect, that voice may ascend from the earth in peace.[3] Intellect delights in peace, which it produces; but many is the mean power that apes the mighty, and often for a while the cheat is successful—the counterfeit is crowned with conquest—and hollow hymns hail victories that issue in defeats, out of which rise again to life all that was most lovely and venerable, to run a new career of triumph.

But we are getting into the clouds, and our wish is to keep jogging along the turnpike road. So let all this pass for an introduction to our Article—and let us abruptly join company with the gentleman whose name stands at the head of it, Mr Alfred Tennyson, of whom the world, we presume, yet knows but little or nothing, whom his friends call a Phoenix, but who, we hope, will not be dissatisfied with us, should we designate him merely a Swan.

One of the saddest misfortunes that can befall a young poet, is to be the Pet of a Coterie; and the very saddest of all, if in Cockneydom. Such has been the unlucky lot of Alfred Tennyson. He has been elevated to the throne of Little Britain, and sonnets were showered over his coronation from the most remote regions of his empire, even from Hampstead Hill. Eulogies more elaborate than the architecture of the costliest gingerbread, have been built up into panegyrical piles, in commemoration of the Birth-day; and 'twould be a pity indeed with one's crutch to smash the gilt battlements, white too with sugar as with frost, and begemmed with comfits. The besetting sin of all periodical criticism, and nowadays there is no other, is boundless extravagance of praise; but none splash it on like the trowelmen who have been be-daubing Mr Tennyson. There is something wrong, however, with the compost. It won't stick; unseemly cracks deform the surface; it falls off piece by piece ere it has dried in the sun, or it hardens into blotches; and the worshippers have but discoloured and disfigured their Idol. The

[3] March of Intellect, the satirical term for the current (often utilitarian) zeal for 'improvement' and education of the uneducated with which Brougham's Society for the Diffusion of Useful Knowledge (1827) was associated. Cf. the 'March of Mind' and the 'Steam Intellect Society' satirised in Peacock's *Crotchet Castle* (1831). While accepting the French Revolution as a subject for poetry, Wilson warns the utilitarians against a superficial optimism about it. Three things made him wrongly interpret Tennyson as a coterie poet of the Cockney school with advanced political opinions. The *Englishman's Magazine* had radical connections; he had been reviewed in the utilitarian *Westminster*, and he had been reviewed by Leigh Hunt in the *Tatler* (see below, p. 148).

worst of it is, that they make the Bespattered not only feel, but look ridiculous; he seems as absurd as an Image in a teagarden; and, bedizened with faded and fantastic garlands, the public cough on being told he is a Poet, for he has much more the appearance of a Post.

The *Englishman's Magazine* ought not to have died; for it threatened to be a very pleasant periodical. An Essay 'on the Genius of Alfred Tennyson', sent it to the grave. The superhuman—nay, supernatural—pomposity of that one paper, incapacitated the whole work for living one day longer in this unceremonious world. The solemnity with which the critic approached the object of his adoration, and the sanctity with which he laid his offerings on the shrine, were too much for our irreligious age. The Essay 'on the genius of Alfred Tennyson', awoke a general guffaw, and it expired in convulsions. Yet the Essay was exceedingly well-written—as well as if it had been 'on the Genius of Sir Isaac Newton'. Therein lay the mistake. Sir Isaac discovered the law of gravitation; Alfred had but written some pretty verses, and mankind were not prepared to set him among the stars. But that he has genius is proved by his being at this moment alive; for had he not, he must have breathed his last under that critique. The spirit of life must indeed be strong within him; for he has outlived a narcotic dose administered to him by a crazy charlatan in the *Westminster*, and after that he may sleep in safety with a pan of charcoal.

But the Old Man must see justice done to this ingenious lad, and save him from his worst enemies, his friends. Never are we so happy—nay, 'tis now almost our only happiness—as when scattering flowers in the sunshine that falls from the yet unclouded sky on the green path prepared by gracious Nature for the feet of enthusiastic youth. Yet we scatter them not in too lavish profusion; and we take care that the young poet shall see, along with the shadow of the spirit that cheers him on, that, too, of the accompanying crutch. Were we not afraid that our style might be thought to wax too figurative, we should say that Alfred is a promising plant; and that the day may come when, beneath sun and shower, his genius may grow up and expand into a stately tree, embowering a solemn shade within its wide circumference, while the daylight lies gorgeously on its crest, seen from afar in glory —itself a grove.

But that day will never come, if he hearken not to our advice, and, as far as his own nature will permit, regulate by it the movements of his genius. This may perhaps appear, at first sight or hearing, not a little unreasonable on our part; but not so, if Alfred will but lay our words to heart, and meditate on their spirit. We desire to see him prosper; and we predict fame as the fruit of obedience. If he disobey, he assuredly goes to oblivion.

At present he has small power over the common feelings and thoughts of men. His feebleness is distressing at all times when he makes an appeal to their ordinary sympathies. And the reason is, that he fears to look such sympathies boldly in the face,—and will be—metaphysical. What all the human race see and feel, he seems to think cannot be poetical; he is not aware of the transcendant and eternal grandeur of commonplace and all-time truths, which are the staple of all poetry. All human beings see the same light in heaven and in woman's eyes; and the great poets put it into language which rather records than reveals, spiritualizing while it embodies. They shun not the sights of common earth—witness Wordsworth. But beneath the magic of their eyes the celandine grows a star or a sun. What beauty is breathed over the daisy by lovingly blessing it because it is so common! 'Sweet flower! whose home is everywhere!' In like manner, Scott, when eulogizing our love of our native land, uses the simplest language, and gives vent to the simplest feelings—

> Lives there the man with soul so dead,
> Who never to himself hath said,
> This is my own, my native land?

What less—what more, could any man say? Yet translate these three lines—not omitting others that accompany them equally touching—into any language, living or dead—and they will instantly be felt by all hearts, savage or civilized, to be the most exquisite poetry. Of such power, conscious, as it kindles, of its dominion over men, because of their common humanity, would that there were finer and more frequent examples in the compositions—otherwise often exquisite—of this young poet. Yet two or three times he tries it on—thus,

NATIONAL SONG

A national song that could be characteristically sung but by—Tims. Tims, too, would be grand in the following war-song—and an *encore* would assuredly be called for in a voice of thunder sufficient to sour small-beer.

> Who fears to die? Who fears to die?
> . . .
> England for aye!

Think of Tims going off the stage, with right arm uplifted, shouting so—

> There standeth our ancient enemy;
> . . .
> CHOR.—Shout for England, &c.

Miserable indeed.

These are almost the only lines in the volume in which Mr Tennyson condescends to be patriotic; and they do not by resemblance remind us of Tyrtæus.[4] It would not be safe to recite them by the sea-shore, on an invasion of the French. Yet our friend is a lover of liberty, as he leaves us to gather from the following strain, which must have been composed before he had acquired much skill in the 'sedentary art of penmanship', or experienced the painful awkwardness which every man-child must pass through on his first entrance into breeches. Samuel Johnson, long before he was a doctor, and but in his fourth year, indited some stanzas to a duck, after which 'We are Free' will, we fear, be read at a disadvantage. Here is the whole concern:

> The winds, as at their hour of birth,
> . . .
> Atween the blossoms, 'We are free.'

That is drivel.

But there is more dismal drivel even than that—and as seeing is said to be believing—here it is.

LOST HOPE

But there is more dismal drivel even than that—and as seeing is believing—here *it* is,

LOVE, PRIDE, AND FORGETFULNESS

The only excuse for such folly—and it is so bad a one as to be indeed an aggravation of the guilt—is, that it is a poor imitation of a wretched model mouldered away to dust in a former age.

---

[4] Tyrtaeus was a Spartan poet and general, living in the 7th century B.C., who led his troops to the second Messenian war and encouraged them with war songs.

The worst of all the above is, that they betray a painful and impotent straining after originality—an aversion from the straightforward and strong simplicity of nature and truth. Such cold conceits—devoid of ingenuity—would seem to us of evil omen—but for our faith in genius, which can shake itself free even from the curse of Cockneyism, under the timeous administration of the exorcising crutch. But for that faith, we should have no hope of the author of the following sonnet:

> Shall the hag Evil die with child of Good . . .

In cases of rare inspiration, the two gifts may go together; but most commonly it is one thing to be idiotic and another oracular. Not thus spoke the oaks of Dodona; we should expect a more sensible response from one of Sir Henry Steuart's thirty-times-transplanted sycamores, that are no sooner in the ground than they are out again, and have not a single small spot on all the estate of Allanton they can call their own.

Yet Mr Tennyson is manifestly prouder of his lays, than of his laws was Alfred the Great; and he is ready with his shafts of satire, tipped with fire, and barbed with fury, to shoot all that sneer at his songs.

THE POET'S MIND

Most of that is silly—some of it prettyish—scarcely one line of it all true poetry; but as it has been admired, we quote it entire, that, should we be in error, the Poet may triumph over the critic, and Christopher North stand rebuked before the superior genius of Alfred Tennyson.

Our young friend is a philosopher—sometimes a crying, sometimes a laughing one—and sometimes 'says a smile to a tear on the cheek of my dear'; but what it says can only be given in its own words. We offer to match the following composition for a cool hundred, against any thing alive of the same inches—and give a stone.

THE 'HOW' AND THE 'WHY'

Mr Tennyson opines, that in these verses he displays his genius before an admiring, a delighted, and an instructed world, in the garb of an orthodox philosophy venturing for a while sportively to give utterance to its sense of the nothingness of all human knowledge, which is but another word for our ignorance of the mysteries of creation. But it is from beginning to end a clumsy and unwieldy failure, and shows no fancy in the region of metaphysics; though it is plain from many a page that he has deluded himself, and suffered others to delude him, into the belief that there lies his especial province. To some of his queries Thomas Aquinas himself, or any other celestial doctor, might be puzzled to give a satisfactory answer; but the first little boy or girl he may meet will set his mind at rest on the last two, though no man who has ever walked the streets of Edinburgh in a high wind, will be able to bring his mind to believe in the propriety—whatever he may think of the necessity—of a house with a chimney-pot, for which there is no substitute like an Old Woman.

Mr Tennyson's admirers say he excels wonderously in personating mermen and mermaids, fairies, *et id genus omne*, inhabiting sea-caves and forest glades, 'in still or stormy weather', the 'gay creatures of the element', be that element air, earth, fire, or water, so that the denizens thereof be but of 'imagination all compact'. We beg of you to hear, for a few sentences, the quack in the *Westminster*.

> Our author has the secret of the transmigration of the soul. He can cast his own spirit into any living thing, real or imaginary. Scarcely Vishnu himself becomes incarnate more easily, frequently, or perfectly. And there is singular refinement, as well as solid truth, in his impersonations, whether they be of inferior creatures, or of such elemental beings as sirens, as mermen, and mermaidens. He does not merely assume their external shapes, and exhibit his own mind masquerading. He takes their senses, feelings, nerves, and brain, along with their names and local habitations; still it is himself in them, modified but not absorbed by their peculiar constitution and mode of being. In the 'Merman', one seems to feel the principle of thought injected by a strong volition into the cranium of the finny worthy, and coming under all the influences, as thinking principles do, of the physical organization to which it is for the time allied: for a moment the identification is complete; and then a consciousness of contrast springs up between the reports of external objects brought to the mind by the senses, and those which it has been accustomed to receive, and this consciousness gives to the description a most poetical colouring.

We could quote another couple of critics—but as the force of nature could no farther go, and as to make one fool she joined the other two, we keep to the *Westminster*. It is a perfect specimen of the super-hyperbolical ultra-extravagance of outrageous Cockney eulogistic foolishness, with which not even a quantity of common sense less than nothing has been suffered, for an indivisible moment of time, to mingle;

the purest mere matter of moonshine ever mouthed by an idiot-lunatic, slavering in the palsied dotage of the extremest superannuation ever inflicted on a being, long ago, perhaps, in some slight respects and low degrees human, but now sensibly and audibly reduced below the level of the Pongos. 'Coming under all the influences, as thinking principles do, of the physical organization to which it is for the time allied!' There is a bit of Cockney materialism for you! 'The principle of thought injected by a strong volition into the cranium of the finny worthy!' Written like the Son of a Syringe. O the speculative sumph! 'Tis thus that dishonest Cockneys would fain pass off in their own vile slang, and for their own viler meaning, murdered and dismembered, the divine Homeric philosophy of the Isle of Circe. Was not Jupiter still Jove—aye, every inch the thunderous king of heaven, whose throne was Olympus—while to languishing Leda the godhead seemed a Swan? In the eyes of a grazier, who saw but Smithfield, he would have been but a bull in the Rape of Europa. Why, were the Cockney critic's principle of thought injected by a strong volition into the skull of a donkey—has he vanity to imagine, for a moment, that he would be a more consummate ass than he now brays? Or if into that of the Great Glasgow Gander, that his quackery would be more matchless still? O no, no, no! He would merely be 'assuming their external shapes'; but his asinine and anserine natural endowments would all remain unchanged—a greater goose than he now is, depend upon it, he could not be, were he for a tedious lifetime to keep waddling his way through this weary world on web-feet, and with uplifted wings and outstretched neck, hissing the long-red-round-cloaked beggar off the common; a superior ass he might in no ways prove, though, un-tethered in the lane where gipsy gang had encraal'd, he were left free to roam round the canvass walls, eminent among all the 'animals that chew the thistle'.

Here is most of the poem which 'proves that our author has the secret of the transmigration of the soul'.

> Who would be
> A merman bold
> . . .
> Laughingly, laughingly.

'Tis, after all, but a sorry affair—and were fifty of the 'Οι πολλοι[5] to

[5] *Hoi polloi*—the majority, the many-headed, the common herd.

compose prize verses on 'the Merman', Oxford and Cambridge must be changed for the worse since our days, if two dozen copies did not prove about as bad as this—one dozen rather worse—one dozen far better, while the remaining brace, to the exclusion of Mr Tennyson's attempt, had the prize divided between them, the authors having been found entitled to an equality of immortal fame. The pervading character of the verses is distinguished silliness; and Alfred cuts a foolish figure, 'modified but not absorbed by the peculiar constitution and mode of being' of a merman. He kisses like a cod-fish, and, we humbly presume, he is all the while stark-naked under the sea; though, for the sake of decency, we recommend next dip a pair of flannel drawers. Poetry and criticism must be at a low ebb indeed on the shores of the Thames. Should he persist in writing thus to the end of the Dean and Chapter, Alfred Tennyson may have a niche in the *Westminster Review*, but never in Westminster Abbey.

The Mermaid, we are told by the Tailor's Trump, 'is beautifully discriminated and most delicately drawn. She is the younger sister of Undine; or Undine herself before she had a soul.' Here is a specimen of the sea-nymph without a soul, who is younger sister to herself, that is Undine. Her mother ought to keep a sharp look out upon her; for she is of an amorous temperament, and a strong Anti-Malthusian.

> And all the mermen under the sea
> Would feel their immortality
>   . . .
> In the branching jaspers under the sea.

So much for Mermen and Mermaidens, and for the style in which the Westminster Pet of the Fancy 'takes their senses, feelings, nerves, and brain, along with their local habitations and their names'. 'And the Sirens, who could resist these Sea-Fairies, as the author prefers calling them?' And pray what may be their alluring enticements?

> Drop the oar
>   . . .
> Whither away, whither away, whither away with the sail and the oar?

Shakespeare—Spenser—Milton—Wordsworth—Coleridge—The Etrick Shepherd—Allan Cunninghame,[6] and some others, have loved,

---

[6] Allan Cunningham, 1784–1842, stonemason-poet from Dumfries, whose

and been beloved by mermaidens, sirens, sea and land fairies, and revealed to the eyes of us who live in the thick atmosphere of this 'dim
spot which men call earth', all the beautiful wonders of subterranean
and submarine climes—and of the climes of Nowhere, lovelier than
them all. It pains us to think, that with such names we cannot yet rank
that of Alfred Tennyson. We shall soon see that he possesses feeling,
fancy, imagination, genius. But in the preternatural lies not the sphere
in which he excels. Much disappointed were we to find him weak where
we expected him strong; yet we are willing to believe that his failure has
been from 'affectations'. In place of trusting to the natural flow of his
own fancies, he has followed some vague abstract idea, thin and
delusive, which has escaped in mere words—words—words. Yet the
Young Tailor in the *Westminster* thinks he could take the measure of
the merman, and even make a riding-habit for the sirens to wear on
gala days, when disposed for 'some horseback'. 'Tis indeed a jewel of
a Snip. His protégé has indited two feeble and fantastic strains entitled
Nothing will Die, *All things will Die*. And them, Parsnip Junior,
without the fear of the shears before his eyes, compares with
L'Allegro and *Il Penseroso* of Milton, saying, that in Alfred's 'there
is not less truth, and perhaps more refined observation!' That
comes of sitting from childhood cross-legged on a board beneath a
skylight.

The Young Tailor can with difficulty keep his seat with delight,
when talking of Mr Tennyson's descriptions of the sea. ' 'Tis barbarous', quoth he, 'to break such a piece of coral for a specimen'; and
would fain cabbage the whole lump, with the view of placing it among
other rarities, such as bits of Derbyshire spar and a brace of mandarins,
on the chimney-piece of the show-parlour in which he notches the
dimensions of his visitors. So fired is his imagination, that he beholds
in a shred of green fustian a swatch of the multitudinous sea; and on
tearing a skreed, thinks he hears him roaring. But Mr Tennyson should
speak of the sea so as to rouse the souls of sailors, rather than the soles
of tailors—the enthusiasm of the deck, rather than of the board. Unfortunately, he seems never to have seen a ship, or, if he did, to have
forgotten it. The vessel in which the landlubbers were drifting, when
the Sea-Fairies salute them with a song, must have been an old tub of
a thing, unfit even for a transport. Such a jib! In the cut of her mainsail

Remains of Nithsdale and Galloway Song (1810), ballads and imitations of Scots
songs, attracted both Scott and Wilson.

you smoke the old table-cloth. To be solemn—Alfred Tennyson is as
poor on the sea as Barry Cornwall—and, of course, calls him a serpent.[7]
They both write like people who, on venturing upon the world of
waters in a bathing machine, would ensure their lives by a cork-jacket.
Barry swims on the surface of the Great Deep like a feather; Alfred
dives less after the fashion of a duck than a bell; but the one sees few
lights, the other few shadows, that are not seen just as well by an
oyster-dredger. But the soul of the true sea-poet doth undergo a sea-
change, soon as he sees Blue Peter; and is off in the gig,

> While bending back, away they pull,
> With measured strokes most beautiful—

There goes the Commodore!
'Our author having the secret of the transmigration of the soul',
passes, like Indur, into the bodies of various animals, and

> Three will I mention dearer than the rest,

the Swan, the Grashopper, and the Owl. The Swan is dying; and as
we remember hearing Hartley Coleridge praise the lines, they must be
fine; though their full meaning be to us like the moon 'hid in her vacant
interlunar cave'. But Hartley, who is like the River Wye, a wanderer
through the woods, is aye haunted with visions of the beautiful; and
let Alfred console himself by that reflection, for the absent sympathy of
Christopher. As for the Grashopper, Alfred, in that green grig, is for
a while merry as a cricket, and chirps and chirrups, though with less
meaning, with more monotony, than that hearth-loving insect, who is
never so happy, you know, as when in the neighbourhood of a baker's
oven. He says to himself as Tithon, though he disclaims that patrony-
mic,

> Thou art a mailed warrior, in youth and strength complete.

a line liable to two faults; first, absurdity, and, second, theft; for the
mind is unprepared for the exaggeration of a grashopper into a
Templar; and Wordsworth, looking at a beetle through the wonder-
working glass of a wizard, beheld

> A mailed angel on a battle-day.

[7] B. W. Procter, 'Barry Cornwall', 1787–1874, well known as a literary figure,
poet, and writer for periodicals, produced no more poetry after *English Songs
and other smaller poems*, 1832.

But Tennyson out-Wordsworths Wordsworth, and pursues the knight, surnamed Longshanks, into the fields of chivalry.

> Arm'd cap-a-pie,
> . . .
> The Bayard of the Meadow!!

Conceived and executed in the spirit of the celebrated imitation—'Dilly—dilly Duckling! Come and be killed!' But Alfred is greatest as an Owl.

SONG—THE OWL

SECOND SONG. TO THE SAME

All that he wants is to be shot, stuffed, and stuck into a glass-case, to be made immortal in a museum.

But, mercy on us! Alfred becomes a—Kraken! Leviathan, 'wallowing unwieldy, enormous in his gait', he despises, as we would a minnow; his huge ambition will not suffer him to be 'very like a whale'; he must be a—Kraken. And such a Kraken, too, as would have astounded Pontoppidan.

THE KRAKEN

The gentle reader who understands that sonnet, will perhaps have the goodness to interpret for us the following oracular sentence, which from childhood has been to us a great mystery. 'An old horse came in to be shaved; curse you, where's the suds? The estate was entailed to male heirs; and poor Mrs Molly lost all her apple-dumplings.'

Thin as is this volume we are now reviewing, and sparse the letterpress on its tiny pages, 'twould yet be easy to extract from it much more unmeaningness; but having shown by gentle chastisement that we love Alfred Tennyson, let us now show by judicious eulogy that we admire him; and, by well-chosen specimens of his fine faculties, that he is worthy of our admiration.

Odes to Memory are mostly mummeries; but not so is the *Ode to Memory* breathed by this young poet. In it, Memory and Imagination, like two angels, lead him by the hands back to the bowers of paradise. All the finest feelings and the finest faculties of his soul, are awakened under that heavenly guidance, as the 'green light' of early life again blesses his eyes; and he sees that the bowers of paradise are built on this common earth, that they are the very bushes near his father's house, where his boyhood revelled in the brightening dawn. We have many quotations yet to make—and therefore cannot give the whole ode, but the half of it; and none will deny, all will feel, that, with perhaps the exception of some harmless mannerisms—affectations we shall not call them—the lines are eminently beautiful.

> Come forth, I charge thee, arise,
> . . .
> Thou dewy dawn of memory.

There is fine music there; the versification would be felt delightful to all poetical ears, even if they missed the many meanings of the well-chosen and happily-obedient words; for there is the sound as of a various-voiced river rejoicing in a sudden summer shower, that swells without staining its translucent waters. But the sound is echo to the sense; and the sense is sweet as that of life's dearest emotions enjoyed in 'a dream that is not all a dream'.

Mr Tennyson, when he chooses, can say much in few words. A fine example of that is shown in five few-syllabled four-lined stanzas on a Deserted House. Every word tells; and the short whole is most pathetic in its completeness—let us say perfection—like some old Scottish air sung by maiden at her wheel—or shepherd in the wilderness.

THE DESERTED HOUSE

Mr Tennyson is sometimes too mystical; for sometimes we fear there is no meaning in his mysticism; or so little, that were it to be stated perspicuously and plainly, 'twould be but a point. But at other times he gives us sweet, still, obscure poems, like the gentle gloaming saddening all that is sad, and making nature's self pensive in her depth of peace. Such is the character of

A DIRGE

Many such beautiful images float before us in his poetry, as 'youthful poets fancy when they love'. He has a delicate perception of the purity of the female character. Any one of his flesh and blood maidens, walking amongst flowers of our own earth, is worth a billowy wilderness of his Sea-Fairies. Their names and their natures are delightful—sound and sight are spiritualized—and yet, as Wordsworth divinely saith, are they

Creatures not too bright or good
For human nature's daily food,
For transient sorrows, simple wiles,
Praise, blame, love, kisses, tears and smiles!

We are in love—as an old man ought to be—as a father is with his ideal daughters—with them all—with Claribel, and Lilian, and Isabel, and Mariana, and Adeline, and Hero, and Almeida, and the Sleeping Beauty, and Oriana. What different beings from King Charles's beauties! Even in bodily charms far more loveable; in spiritual, pure

As heavenly Una with her milk-white lamb—

objects, for a moment's thought, of passion; but of affection, for ever and a day. In face, form, figure, circumstance and character, delicately distinguished from one another are all the sweet sisterhood. 'Seven lilies in one garland wrought'—'alike, but oh, how different!' Budding, blossoming, full-blown; but if on leaf or flower any touch of decay, 'tis not the touch of time but of sorrow, and there is balmy beauty in the very blight—lovely to the last the lily of the garden, of the field, or of the valley. The rose is the queen of flowers—but should she ever die, the lily would wear the crown—and her name is

ISABEL

There is profound pathos in *Mariana*. The young poet had been dreaming of Shakespeare, and of Measure for Measure, and of the gentle lady all forlorn, the deserted of the false Angelo, of whom the Swan of Avon sings but some few low notes in her distress and desolation, as she wears away her lonely life in solitary tears at 'the moated grange'. On this hint Alfred Tennyson speaks; 'he has a vision of his own'; nor might Wordsworth's self in his youth have disdained to indite such melancholy strain. Scenery—state—emotion—character—are all in fine keeping; long, long, long indeed is the dreary day, but it will end at last; so finds the heart-broken prisoner who, from sunrise to sunset, has been leaning on the sun-dial in the centre of his narrow solitude!

MARIANA

It is not at all necessary that we should understand fine poetry to feel and enjoy it, any more than fine music. That is to say, some sorts of fine poetry—the shadowy and the spiritual; where something glides before us ghostlike, 'now in glimmer and now in gloom', and then

away into some still place of trees or tombs. Yet the poet who composes it, must weigh the force of every feeling word—in a balance true
to a hair, for ever vibrating, and obedient to the touch of down or dew-
drop. Think not that such process interrupts inspiration; it sustains and
feeds it; for it becomes a habit of the heart and the soul in all their
musings and meditations; and thus is the language of poetry, though
human, heavenly speech. In reading it, we see new revelations on each
rehearsal—all of them true, though haply different—and what we at
first thought a hymn, we may at last feel to be an elegy—a breathing
not about the quick, but the dead. So was it with us in reading over and
over again *Claribel*. We supposed the lady slept beneath the 'solemn
oak-tree, thick-leaved, ambrosial'; and that the 'ancient melody' was
dimly heard by her in her world of dreams. But we know now that only
her dust is there; and that the character of her spirit, as it dwelt on
earth, is shadowed forth by the congenial scenery of her burial-place.
But *Adeline* is alive—faintly-smiling—shadowy—dreaming—spiritual Adeline—such are the epithets bestowed by the poet on that Lady
of Light who visits his visions—though doomed to die—or rather
to melt away back to her native heaven.

ADELINE

The life of Claribel was shadowed forth by images of death—the
death of Adeline seemed predicted by images of life—and in the lovely
lines on the Sleeping Beauty, life and death meet in the stillness of that
sleep—so profound that it is felt as if it were immortal. And is there not
this shading and blending of all feeling and all thought that regards the
things we most tenderly and deeply love on this changeful earth?

THE SLEEPING BEAUTY

Some of our old ballads, breathed in the gloom of forests or glens by
shepherds or woodsmen, are in their earnest simplicity inimitable by
genius born so many centuries since they died, and overshadowed by
another life. Yet genius has often delighted to sink away into such
moods as those in which it imagines those lowly men to have been lost
when they sang their songs, 'the music of the heart', with nothing that
moved around them but the antlers of the deer, undisturbed by the bard
lying among the breckens or the broom, beneath the checkered light
that came through the umbrage of the huge oak-tree, on which spring
was hourly shedding a greener glory, or autumn a more golden decay.

Shepherds and woodsmen, too, there have been in these later days, and other rural dwellers, who have sometimes caught the spirit of the antique strain—Robert, James, and Allan—whose happiest 'auld ballants' are as if obsolete forest-flowers were brought back to life on our banks and braes. Perhaps the most beautiful of all Alfred Tennyson's compositions, is the *Ballad of Oriana*.

THE BALLAD OF ORIANA

But the highest of all this young poet's achievements, is the visionary and romantic strain, entitled, *Recollections of the Arabian Nights*. It is delightful even to us, who read not the Arabian Nights, nor ever heard of them, till late in life—we think we must have been in our tenth year; the same heart-soul-mind-awakening year that brought us John Bunyan and Robinson Crusoe, and in which—we must not say with whom—we first fell in love. How it happened that we had lived so long in this world without seeing or hearing tell of these famous worthies, is a mystery; for we were busy from childhood with books and bushes, banks and braes, with libraries full of white, brown, and green leaves, perused in schoolroom, whose window in the slates showed the beautiful blue braided skies, or in fields and forests (so we thought the birch coppice, with its old pines, the abode of linties and cushats—for no long, broad, dusty, high-road was there—and but footpaths or sheep-walks winded through the pastoral silence that surrounded that singing or cooing grove), where beauty filled the sunshiny day with delight, and grandeur the one-star-red gloaming with fear. But so it was; we knew not that there was an Arabian Night in the whole world. Our souls, in stir or stillness, saw none but the sweet Scottish stars. We knew, indeed, that they rose, and set, too, upon other climes; and had we been asked the question, should have said that they certainly did so; but we felt that they and their heavens belonged to Scotland. And so feels the fond, foolish old man still, when standing by himself at midnight, with withered hands across his breast, and eyes lifted heavenwards, that show the brightest stars somewhat dim now, yet beautiful as ever; out walks the moon from behind a cloud, and he thinks of long Loch Lomond glittering afar off with lines of radiance that lift up in their loveliness, flush after flush—and each silvan pomp is statelier than the last—now one, now another, of her heron-haunted isles!

But in our egoism and egotism we have forgot Alfred Tennyson. To his heart, too, we doubt not that heaven seems almost always an English heaven; he, however, must have been familiar long before his tenth year with the Arabian Nights' Entertainments; for had he discovered them at that advanced period of life, he had not now so passionately and so imaginatively sung their wonders.

RECOLLECTIONS OF THE ARABIAN NIGHTS

Our critique is near its conclusion; and in correcting it for press, we see that its whole merit, which is great, consists in the extracts, which are 'beautiful exceedingly'. Perhaps, in the first part of our article, we may have exaggerated Mr Tennyson's not unfrequent silliness, for we are apt to be carried away by the whim of the moment, and in our humorous moods, many things wear a queer look to our aged eyes, which fill young pupils with tears; but we feel assured that in the second part we have not exaggerated his strength—that we have done no more than justice to his fine faculties—and that the millions who delight in Maga will, with one voice, confirm our judgement—that Alfred Tennyson is a poet.

But, though it might be a mistake of ours, were we to say that he has much to learn, it can be no mistake to say that he has not a little to unlearn, and more to bring into practice, before his genius can achieve its destined triumphs. A puerile partiality for particular forms of expression, nay, modes of spelling and of pronunciation, may be easily overlooked in one whom *we* must look on as yet a mere boy; but if he carry it with him, and indulge it in manhood, why it will make him seem silly as his sheep; and should he continue to bleat so when his head and beard are as grey as ours, he will be truly a laughable old ram, and the ewes will care no more for him than if he were a wether.

Farther—he must consider that all the fancies that fleet across the imagination, like shadows on the grass or the tree-tops, are not entitled to be made small separate poems of—about the length of one's little finger; that many, nay, most of them, should be suffered to pass away with a silent 'God bless ye', like butterflies, single or in shoals, each family with its own hereditary character mottled on its wings; and that though thousands of those grave brown, and gay golden images will be blown back in showers, as if upon balmy breezes changing suddenly and softly to the *airt* whence inspiration at the moment breathes, yet not one in a thousand is worth being caught and pinned down on paper into poetry, 'gently as if you loved him'—only the few that are bright with the 'beauty still more beauteous'—and a few such belong to all the orders—from the little silly moth that extinguishes herself in your taper, up to the mighty Emperor of Morocco at meridian wavering his burnished downage in the unconsuming sun who glorifies the wondrous stranger.

Now, Mr Tennyson does not seem to know this; or if he do, he is self-willed and perverse in his sometimes almost infantile vanity; (and how vain are most beautiful children!) and thinks that any Thought or Feeling or Fancy that has had the honour and the happiness to pass through *his* mind, must by that very act be worthy of everlasting commemoration. Heaven pity the poor world, were we to put into stanzas, and publish upon it, all our thoughts, thick as mots in the sun, or a summer evening atmosphere of midges!

Finally, Nature is mighty, and poets should deal with her on a grand scale. She lavishes her glorious gifts before their path in such profusion, that Genius—reverent as he is of the mysterious mother, and meeting her at sunrise on the mountains with grateful orisons—with grateful orisons bidding her farewell among the long shadows that stretch across the glens when sunset sinks into the sea—is yet privileged to tread with a seeming scorn in the midst of imagery that to common eyes would be as a revelation of wonders from another world. Familiar to him are they as the grass below his feet. In lowlier moods he looks at them—and in his love they grow beautiful. So did Burns beautify the daisy—'wee modest crimson-tipped flower!' But in loftier moods, the 'violet by the mossy stone', is not 'half-hidden to the eye'—it is left unthought of to its own sweet existence. The poet then ranges wide and high, like Thomson, in his Hymn to the Seasons, which he had so gloriously sung, seeing in all the changes of the rolling year 'but the varied god', like Wordsworth, in his Excursion, communing too with the spirit 'whose dwelling is the light of setting suns'.

Those great men are indeed among the 'Lights of the world and demigods of fame'; but all poets, ere they gain a bright name, must thus celebrate the worship of nature. So is it, too, with painters. They do well, even the greatest of them, to trace up the brooks to their source in stone-basin or mossy well, in the glen-head, where greensward glades among the heather seem the birthplace of the Silent People—the Fairies. But in their immortal works they must show us how 'red comes the river down'; castles of rock or of cloud—long withdrawing vales, where midway between the flowery foreground, and in the distance of blue mountain ranges, some great city lifts up its dim-seen spires through the misty smoke beneath which imagination hears the hum of life—'peaceful as some immeasurable plain', the breast of old ocean sleeping in the sunshine—or as if an earthquake shook the pillars of his caverned depths, tumbling the foam of his breakers, mast-high, if mast be there, till the canvass ceases to be silent, and the gazer hears him howling over his prey—See—see!—the foundering wreck of a three-decker going down head-foremost to eternity.

With such admonition, we bid Alfred Tennyson farewell.

4

Tennyson ~ *Poems* ~ 1842

John Sterling, *Quarterly Review*, lxx
(September 1842), 385–416

What poetry might be in our time and land, if a man of the highest powers and most complete cultivation exercised the art among us, will be hard to say until after the fact of such a man's existence. Waiting for this desirable event, we may at least see that poetry, to be for us what it has sometimes been among mankind, must wear a new form, and probably comprise elements hardly found in our recent writings, and impossible in former ones.

Of verses, indeed, of every sort but the excellent there is no want: almost all, however, so helpless in skill, so faint in meaning, that one might almost fancy the authors wrote metre from mere incapacity of expressing themselves at all in prose—as boys at school sometimes make nonsense-verses before they can construct a rational sentence. Yet it is plain that even our magazine stanzas, album sonnets, and rhymes in corners of newspapers aim at the forms of emotion, and use some of the words in which men of genius have symbolized profound thoughts. The whole, indeed, is generally a lump of blunder and imbecility, but in the midst there is often some turn of cadence, some attempt at an epithet of more significance and beauty than perhaps a much finer mind would have hit on a hundred years ago. The crowds of stammering children are yet the offspring of an age that would fain teach them—if it knew how—a richer, clearer language than they can learn to speak.

It is hard in this state of things not to conceive that the time, among us at least, is an essentially unpoetic one—one which, whatever may be

John Sterling, 1806–44, preceded Tennyson at Trinity College, Cambridge, where he was a member of the 'Apostles' society. He was influenced by Coleridge and Carlyle who wrote a *Life* in 1851. Sterling's liking for Tennyson's pseudo-Wordsworthian idyllic poetry is perhaps explained by his own idyll, *The Sexton's Daughter*, in his *Poems* (1839).

the worth of its feelings, finds no utterance for them in melodious words.

Yet our age is not asleep. Great movements, various activities, are heard and seen on all sides. In the lowest department, that of mere mechanics, consider what fifteen years have done. It was only in the autumn of 1830, following close on the French three memorable days of July, that the Duke of Wellington opened the Manchester and Liverpool Railroad. The population of the busiest region on this earth were assembled round him, whom all acknowledged as the greatest man in England, at the inauguration of a new physical power, then felt to double the strength and swiftness of human beings. While, among myriads of gravely joyous faces, the new machines travelled at a speed matching that of eagles, the life of a great statesman shot off on a darker and more distant journey, and the thrill of fear and pain at his destruction gave the last human tragic touch to an event which would at any rate have retained for ever an historic importance. The death of Mr Huskisson startled the fixed bosom of the veteran soldier, and those who were near perceived a quiver of the lip, a movement of the eye, such as had hardly been caused by the most unlooked-for and dreadful chances of his mighty wars.[1] To a calm observer, the emotion of the whole multitude, great and small, might strangely have recalled far-distant ages and the feelings with which ancient peoples held every great event as incomplete, wanting the blood of a victim—too often human—solemnly shed. In the most prosperous and peaceful of national triumphs the dark powers again claimed a share, and would not be forgotten.

Since then, about twelve years have passed, and behold what they have brought forth. Some seventy millions of money have been expended—more, at the lowest estimate, than four times as much as the Papacy was able to raise in a century and a half for the construction of its greatest monument, the costliest the world has ever seen. These seventy millions of pounds have been subscribed by private persons at

---

[1] The bloodless July revolution of 1830 in France overthrew the Bourbons and instated Louis Philippe, still ruling when Sterling wrote this review, as constitutional monarch. The Liverpool and Manchester Railway was opened in September 1830. Huskisson's death is a dramatic illustration of Sterling's view of the energies of his society: Huskisson's liberalism and free-trading economics represented the fresh ideas invading English political life, and Sterling sees his death as the forces of progress being themselves destroyed by another agent of progress—the railway train.

their own choice in one small country, and have created nearly fifteen hundred miles of railroads—structures that surpass all pyramids and Cyclopean walls, and machines that would puzzle Archimedes, by which myriads of men are perpetually travelling like the heroes of fairy tales. It is probable that the roads of the Roman empire, the work of many centuries, did not cost so much of human labour, and they certainly did not exhibit so much greatness of thought, as those that we have built in less than twenty years. In the state of society that has produced such results there may be, we know there is, enough torpor, even rottenness. But it cannot be, on the whole, an insignificant stage of human existence, one barren for imaginative eyes.

Or look at one of our general elections. The absurdities are plain, no doubt—has not the ocean froth and bubbles? But take the thing altogether, and observe the mixture and spread of interests and faculties brought into action—above all, the open boldness with which a nation throws itself into the streets and markets, casting off, in the faith that it can reproduce, its company of rulers, and letting the fools clamour, the poor groan, the rich humble themselves, and all men bring all to judgement, without a moment's fear but that quiet will spring out of the tumult, and a government be born from a mob. From the castle of the highest peer to the clay-stained tipplers in the alehouse, from the bench of bishops to the ranters in the moor-side smithy, all are stirred and fluttered, feverish with the same anxieties, debating in their different dialects the same questions, and all alike dependent on the omnipotence of an event which no man can absolutely control. Most of what they say is folly—most of their objects of hope and fear chimeras: but how full of throbbing business is the whole land, how braced are all the wishes and devices of all! Among so much of make-believe and sound, it is a great thing that the whole country must at least be willingly deceived if it is to be gained over—must seem to itself rationally persuaded; and that the most futile pretender can only cheat by aping, and so strengthening in others, the qualities in which he is most deficient. At the blast of the newsmen's tin trumpets all shadows must walk out of their darkness into sunshine, and there be tried; when if many of the umbratile fraudulently pass muster, there is at least a public recognition of the laws of light.

Not merely is there a debate and seeming adjudication in every country-town on all matters over the whole globe which any tailor or brazier may choose to argue, but at last the tailor's and the brazier's voice does really influence the course of human affairs. The vote of the cobbler in an alley turns the poll for a candidate; the vote of the member gains the triumph of his party; and the success of his party decides on every question of peace or war over the globe, makes commercial treaties with Abyssinia, creates a white commonwealth among the savages of the Pacific Ocean, sends armaments to Pekin, and raises or lowers the price of silk grown among the Druses of Lebanon, and of opium sold on the frontiers of Tartary. Within a year after the election in an English village, its result is felt in the more or less cost of food and clothes in Kaffir huts, and in the value of the copper saucepan trafficked at Timbuctoo for palm-oil and black babies. This is not a vapid, insubstantial political existence for the mass of men, not one devoid of topics and emotions, however little they may hitherto have been used in any books but those of statistics and trade.

Or glance at the matter in another of its phases. In the midmost rush of London business, and all the clatter of its vehicles, turn aside through an open door, and what do we see? A large and lofty room, every yard of its floor and galleries crammed with human, chiefly female life—a prodigious sea of bonnets, and under each of these a separate sentient sea of notions, and feelings, and passions, all in some measure stirred by the same tides and gales—every one of them, however narrow at the surface, in depth unfathomable.

Altogether irrespectively of our present purpose, and on the most general grounds, it may be safely said that in one of these great Exeter Hall meetings there is more to strike us than almost anywhere else we know.[2] The room is said to hold four thousand persons, and from its form they are all clearly visible at once—all of the middle or upper classes, well dressed, though often many of them in Quaker uniform, and at these times probably three-fourths of them women. Such assemblages are in truth, for a large part of the members, by far the most exciting outward events of life. The faces themselves are alone quite enough to prove no small share of moral culture in the mass. The delicately-curved mouths and nostrils, the open yet quiet and observant eyes, and a look of serious yet pleasurable elevation, mark very clearly a chosen class of our country. The men are of course less pure and single in their stamp of feeling—business has marked on them its contractedness with its strength. Yet these also have an appearance of

[2] Exeter Hall, Strand, built 1831, a huge nonconformist chapel, so big that it was frequently hired for concerts.

thought, although with some coxcombical importance and complacent theological primness. Take, however, the whole assemblage, all it is and all its represents, we know not where anything like it could be discovered. No Roman Catholic, no despotic, no poor, no barbarous, no thoroughly demoralised, we fear we must add no very instructed and well-organised community could ever exhibit such a gathering— voluntary be it remembered, chiefly female, all with money to spare, united for such remote and often fantastic objects: above all, under such leaders. For in the kind of persons guiding these bodies, and in their discourse, consists more than half the wonder. In the House of Commons, in the Courts of Law, we may hear nonsense enough. But in these places it is not the most vehement, the most chimerical—in other words, the most outrageous and silly, who bear the chiefest sway, but much the contrary. Now in such Strand-Meetings, for the purest and noblest purposes, it is plain enough that a loud tongue, combined with a certain unctuous silkiness of profession, and the most dismal obscuration of brain, may venture with success upon the maddest assertions, the most desperate appeals. . . Very strange it is to witness the single thrill of some two thousand bonnets, to hear the deep long sigh from as many warm and gentle breasts, all inspired by the raving folly of some declaimer, or by the gravely numerical statements of moral facts as to distant countries proceeding from ill-informed and well-paid agents, and which those who know their falsity are sure enough not to seek the odium of refuting. The sure tact of goodness leads the greater part of the hearers right in home-concerns, but has no measure of probability for new experiments in remote lands. The faith which lives in the Infinite and Eternal, and is perpetually baffled in its search among present things, adds joyfully its charms, the transcendant element of all romance, to the faintest glimpse between distant clouds, and feels it a duty and delight to believe in the realised visions of credulous fancy.

Yet who can think without a certain approval of the immense annual revenue, larger than that of some continental kingdoms, raised by these marvellous addresses to our best feelings? Who can compare, without some admiration mixed in his contempt, the coarse and brainless weakness of the talk on these occasions with the honest virtue, the moral elegance of heart in those whom it influences? Or who that lives in England can be unaware that very many among the auditors of these brazen mouth-pieces show in the whole course of their private lives, and in hard stern trials of all kinds, a simple self-forgetting nobleness and truth, beautifully contrasted with the ostentatious emptiness of the charitable melodrame?

On the whole, the country in which these varieties of good and evil are found mixed on such a scale can hardly be considered in a state of lifeless inertness. Its want cannot be of themes and interest, but rather of those able to seize what lies before them, and turn it to right imaginative use. For every one indeed knows that all our activities, mechanical, political, missionary, celestial, or diabolical, are the immediate outgrowths of the human beings engaged in such matters, and might be found with much more inside and beneath them in the hearts and lives of the individuals. This is all the poet requires; a busy, vigorous, various existence is the matter *sine qua non* of his work. All else comes from within, and from himself alone. Now, strangely as our time is racked and torn, haunted by ghosts, and errant in search of lost realities, poor in genuine culture, incoherent among its own chief elements, untrained to social facility and epicurean quiet, yet unable to unite its means in pursuit of any lofty blessing, half-sick, half-dreaming, and whole confused—he would be not only misanthropic, but ignorant, who should maintain it to be a poor, dull, and altogether helpless age, and not rather one full of great though conflicting energies, seething with high feelings, and struggling towards the light with piercing though still hooded eyes. The fierce, too often mad force, that wars itself away among the labouring poor,[3] the manifold skill and talent and unwearied patience of the middle classes, and the still unshaken solidity of domestic life among them—these are facts open to all, though by none perhaps sufficiently estimated. And over and among all society the wealth of our richer people is gathered and diffused as it has never been before anywhere else, shaping itself into a thousand arts of luxury, a million modes of social pleasure, which the moralist may have much to object against, but which the poet, had we a truly great one now rising among us, would well know how to employ for his own purposes.

Then, too, if we reflect that the empire and nation seated here as in its centre, and at home so moving and multifarious, spreads its

[3] The 'mad force' is Chartism. The curious tone of despairing self-reassurance and anxious hope in this review must be seen in the context of the political and economic troubles of the forties—'but in 1841 the recession moved into depression again and there was no gloomier year in the whole nineteenth century than 1842' (Asa Briggs, *The Age of Improvement* (1959), p. 295).

dominions all round the globe, daily sending forth its children to mix in the life of every race of man, seek adventures in every climate, and fit themselves to every form of polity, or it to them—whereafter they return in body, or at least reflect their mental influences among us—it cannot be in point of diversity and meaning that Britain disappoints any one capable of handling what it supplies.

See how Chaucer exhibits to us all that lay around him, the roughness and ignorance, the honour, faith, fancy, joyousness of a strong mind and a strong age, both tranquil within bounds which, as large enough for their uses, neither had tried to pass. How strikingly for us are those grating contrasts of social condition harmonised by the home-bred feeling that men as they then were had the liberty and space they then needed: the king and priest the all-sufficient guides of men's higher life, and all powers and even wishes finding ample room, each within the range marked out by custom! Every figure is struck off by as clear and cutting a stroke as that of a practised mower with his scythe—and of all these peculiarities of character, so blended in that world are strength and unconsciousness, not one ever rises into individuality of principle. . .

In Shakespeare again, who never meant anything of the kind, that period, with its far deeper wants and more abundant forces, all lies softly, firmly drawn by every random jotting of his pen. For that, with all his unmatched reflectiveness, much was thus lightly done, seems no less certain at the hundredth perusal than obvious at the first. The stately courtesies and consecrated forms of the past, all still untroubled, but a new spirit rising within those antique walls, and as yet professing peaceful reverence, though it must one day shake them down. . . And he who has best shown us all this as it truly was, yet sent forth at every breath a fiery element, of which he was himself scarce conscious, that should some day kindle and burn much still dear and venerable to him.

A gulf of generations lies between us and him, and the world is all changed around his tomb. But whom have we had to feel and express like this man the secret of our modern England, and to roll all out before him the immense reality of things as his own small embroidered carpet, on which he merely cared to sit down at his ease and smoke his pipe?

There have been but two writers among us whom every Englishman with a tincture of letters has read or heard of, aiming to shape poetically an image of human life. These are of course Sir Walter Scott and Lord

Byron. But see how different their aim has been from such a one as we hint at. The elder poet, with his wholesome sense and clear felicity, has indeed given us much of human fact, and this, as it could not be otherwise, in the colours of the time that he himself belonged to. But he has swayed the sympathies of the world in a great measure through their curiosity after the past, which he, more than all men in the annals of mankind, has taught us all to regard as alive and still throbbing in spirit, though its bones be turned to dust.

Byron has sought, through distance of place and foreign costume, the interest which Scott obtained from the strangeness of past ages; and it is but a small though a profound and irrepressible part of our farspread modern mind that he has so well embodied in his scornful Harolds and despairing Giaours.

We have indeed one of his works, the only one, which is a splendid attempt at a creative survey of modern life, and contains all the essential elements of such performance. And in spite of the puerile egotisms and dawdling prate into which the poem so often wanders, the first five cantos of *Don Juan*, forming in point of bulk about a half, have more of fiery beauty and native sweetness in them than anything we know of in our modern literature. There is also a wide range and keenness of observation; and were some trivialities struck out, as they so easily might be, no capital defect would remain but the weakness of speculative culture visible in all Lord Byron's philosophical excursions. In the latter half of the poem, and unhappily when he is on English ground, the lax shapelessness of structure, the endless slipshod, yawny loungings, and vapid carelessness of execution, become very disagreeable in spite of passages rich with imperishable beauty, wit, and vigour, such as no other modern Englishman or man could have approached. On the whole, with all its faults, moral and poetic, the earlier portion of this singular book will probably remain, like the first half of *Faust*, the most genuine and striking monument of a whole recent national literature. But the weakness as to all deeper thought, and the incomplete groundplan, place it somewhat lower than could be wished. And at best it is but one book, in an age that produces annual thousands.

Little therefore as is all that has been done towards the poetic representation of our time—even in the looser and readier form of prose romance—it is hard to suppose that it is incapable of such treatment. The still unadulterated purity of home among large circles of the nation presents an endless abundance of the feelings and characters, the want of which nothing else in existence can supply even to a poet. And these soft and steady lights strike an observer all the more from the restless activity and freedom of social ambition, the shifting changes of station, and the wealth gathered on one hand and spent on the other with an intenseness and amplitude of will to which there is at least nothing now comparable among mankind. The power of self-subjection combined with almost boundless liberty, indeed necessitated by it, and the habit of self-denial with wealth beyond all calculation—these are indubitable facts in modern England. But while recognised as facts, how far do they still remain from that development as thoughts which philosophy desires, or that vividness as images which is the aim of poetry! It is easy to say that the severity of conscience in the best minds checks all play of fancy, and the fierceness of the outward struggle for power and riches absorbs the energies that would otherwise exert themselves in shapeful melody. But had we minds full of the idea and the strength requisite for such work, they would find in this huge, harassed, and luxurious national existence the nourishment, not the poison, of creative art. The death-struggle of commercial and political rivalry, the brooding doubt and remorse, the gas-jet flame of faith irradiating its own coal-mine darkness—in a word, our overwrought materialism fevered by its own excess into spiritual dreams—all this might serve the purposes of a bold imagination, no less than the creed of the antipoetic Puritans became poetry in the mind of Milton, and all bigotries, superstitions, and gore-dyed horrors were flames that kindled steady light in Shakespeare's humane and meditative song.

Of all our recent writers the one who might seem at first sight to have most nearly succeeded in this quest after the poetic *Sangreal* is Crabbe. No one has ranged so widely through all classes, employed so many diverse elements of circumstance and character. But nowhere, or very, very rarely, do we find in him that eager sweetness, a fiery spirituous essence. . .

Crabbe is always an instructive and forceful, almost always even an interesting writer. His works have an imperishable value as records of his time; and it even may be said that few parts of them but would have found an appropriate place in some of the reports of our various commissions for inquiring into the state of the country. Observation, prudence, acuteness, uprightness, self-balancing vigour of mind are everywhere seen, and are exerted on the whole wide field of common life. All that is wanting is the enthusiastic sympathy, the jubilant love, whose utterance is melody, and without which all art is little better than a laborious ploughing of the sand, and then sowing the sand itself for seed along the fruitless furrow.

In poetry we seek, and find, a refuge from the hardness and narrowness of the actual world. But using the very substance of this Actual for poetry, its positiveness, shrewdness, detailedness, incongruity, and adding no new peculiar power from within, we do no otherwise than if we should take shelter from rain under the end of a roof-spout.

To Mr Wordsworth of course these remarks on Crabbe would be by no means applicable. Yet even he has exhibited only one limited, however lofty region of life, and has made it far less his aim to represent what lies around him by means of self-transference into all its feelings, than to choose therefrom what suits his spirit of ethical meditation, and so compel mankind, out alike of their toilsome daily paths and pleasant nightly dreams, into his own severe and stately school of thought. The present movements of human life, nay its varied and spontaneous joys, to him are little, save so far as they afford a text for a mind in which fixed will, and stern speculation, and a heart austere and measured even in its pity, are far more obvious powers than fancy, emotion, or keen and versatile sympathy. He discourses indeed with divine wisdom of life and nature, and all their sweet and various impulses; but the impression of his own great calm judicial soul is always far too mighty for any all-powerful feeling of the objects he presents to us. . .

In thus pointing to the problem which poetry now holds out, and maintaining that it has been but partially solved by our most illustrious writers, there is no design of setting up an unattainable standard, and then blaming any one in particular for inevitably falling short of it. Out of an age so diversified and as yet so unshapely, he who draws forth any graceful and expressive forms is well entitled to high praise. Turning into fixed beauty any part of the shifting and mingled matter of our time, he does what in itself is very difficult, and affords very valuable help to all his future fellow-labourers. If he has not given us back our age as a whole transmuted into crystalline clearness and lustre, a work accomplished only by a few of the greatest minds under the happiest circumstances for their art, yet we scarce know to whom we should be equally grateful as to him who has enriched us with any shapes of lasting loveliness 'won from the vague and formless infinite'.

Mr Tennyson has done more of this kind than almost any one that has appeared among us during the last twenty years. And in such a task of alchemy a really successful experiment, even on a small scale, is of great worth compared with the thousands of fruitless efforts or pretences on the largest plan, which are daily clamouring for all men's admiration of their nothingness.

The first of these two volumes consists of republished poems, and may be regarded, we presume, as all that Mr Tennyson wishes to preserve of his former editions. He has sifted in most cases his earlier harvests, and kept the better grain. There are some additions of verses and stanzas here and there, many minute changes, and also beneficial shortenings and condensations. The second volume, however, is on the whole far advanced in merit beyond the first. There is more clearness, solidity, and certainty of mind visible in it throughout: especially some of the blank-verse poems—a style almost unattempted in the earlier series—have a quiet completeness and depth, a sweetness arising from the happy balance of thought, feeling, and expression, that ranks them among the riches of our recent literature.

The collection includes poems of four markedly different kinds: 1. The Idyllic, in which there is sometimes an epic calmness in representing some event or situation of private life, sometimes a flow of lyrical feeling, but still expanding itself in a narrative or description of the persons, events, and objects that fill the poet's imagination. 2. The purely Lyrical—odes, songs, and the more rapid ballads, where the emotion is not only uppermost, but all in all, and the occasions and interests involved appear but casually and in hints. 3. Fancy pieces; those, namely, of which the theme is borrowed or imitated from those conceptions of past ages that have now become extremely strange or quite incredible for us. In these the principal charm of the work can spring only from the vividness and grace of the imagery, the main idea making no direct impression on our feelings. 4. There is a class of Allegories, Moralities, didactic poems. We might add another, of Facetiae; but in these the writer, though not unmeaning or without talent, seems far inferior to himself, and they happily fill but a small part of his pages.

The first and third of these classes—the Idylls and Fancies—are, in our view, of the greatest merit, and differ in little but the stranger and more legendary themes of the latter series, while they resemble each other in a somewhat spacious and detailed style of description, with, however, an evident general predominance of personal feeling, sometimes masked by the substitution of an imaginary narrator for the real poet.

We shall speak first of the second class, which we have called Odes. *Claribel, Lilian, Isabel, Madeline, Adeline, Eleanore,* and *Margaret,* all are raptures in honour of ladies. *Isabel* is similar in style and plan to the rest, but differs by being addressed to a matron, not a maiden; and though, like the others euphuistic enough, and coldly ingenious, is pleasant as a relief from the unrealities of rhetorical sentiment. There is a beautiful idea in it—with much verbal melody and many dainty phrases, far beyond the reach of any but a man of genius, however inaptly genius may be spent in dressing make-believe emotions with far-fetched rhythmic ornament. *Claribel* is a sort of lament over a dead woman. The other young ladies seem to have the advantage of being still alive, but their poetic environment is not for that the less ghostly and preternatural. In all of these pieces the will to write poetry seems to us to have supplied (insufficiently) the place of poetic feeling; though one sees that only a poet could have written them. The heroines are moonshine maidens, in the number of whom Mr Tennyson is really as unconscionable as Solomon or Mahomet. It may be suspected that neither the Arab prophet nor Jewish king would much have approved such questionable charms as *black-beaded* eyes, and *crimson-threaded* lips. We of a more metaphysical generation grow heartily weary of the delicacies, and subtleties, and super-fineries of so many mysterious passions, and phantom objects, as carefully discriminated as varieties of insects by Ehrenberg, or fossils by Owen.[4] The whole style smells of musk, and is not without glimpses of rouge and pearl-powder. We have found nothing here at once more distinct and graceful than the following lines, and these are marred by the two final epithets:

> His bowstring slacken'd, languid Love,
> Leaning his cheek upon his hand,
> Droops both his wings, regarding thee;

---

[4] C. G. Ehrenberg, German naturalist and microscopist, published his observations on micro-organisms (bacteria) in 1833. Sterling calls microbes 'insects', presumably because Ehrenberg thought (wrongly) that they had elaborate structures—muscles, digestive systems etc.—and were therefore analagous to insects. [Sir] Richard Owen was a famous palæontologist. Some of his work on fossils had been published by 1842 but this was quite early in his career. Sterling, showing himself a true follower of Carlyle, argues that Tennyson's worse poems have been composed on a scientific method.

And so would languish evermore,
Serene, imperial Eleanore.

Of the poem 'To ——', much need not be said. 'Clearheaded friend' is the most ludicrously flat beginning of a serious poem that we have ever seen proceed from a real poet; and the construction of the final strophe is so obscure that we have in vain attempted to disentangle it into any meaning. Yet few readers can be required to spend as much time on such a matter as we are both bound and glad so to employ. In the same verses 'kingly intellect' is at least in that connection a phrase of vague rhetoric. The two little poems to the 'Owl' are at best ingenious imitations of the manner of some of Shakespeare's and his contemporaries' songs; well done enough, but not worth doing.

The *Recollections of the Arabian Nights* is of a better kind. The writer does not in this seem painfully striving after topics, images, variations, and originalities, but writing from lively conception of a theme which offered in abundance the material suited to his fancy and ear. The poem is at once brilliant and pleasing: but we may remark that its merit is of a kind which presents itself somewhat too easily to a reader of the tales it recalls; that there is little progress in imagery, and none in thought, beyond the first stanza, in all the following thirteen; and that some meaning adapted to our modern European brains might perhaps have been insinuated under those gorgeous eastern emblems without injury to their genuine Asiatic import. The gold and red arabesque repeats itself, square after square of the pattern, with undeniable splendour, but somewhat wearying monotony.

The *Ode to Memory* aims at a far higher sort of excellence. Had it preceded, instead of following, Mr Wordsworth's *Platonic Ode*, it would have been a memorable poem. The elder poet's solemn rapture on the *Recollections of Childhood* is comparable, in its way, to the Portland funeral vase, were that lighted, as it ought to be, from within: on a purple ground, dark as midnight, still and graceful snow-white figures, admitting of endless interpretations, all more or less fitting, but none, perhaps, conclusive. Mr Tennyson has caught some of the same feeling, and much of the rhythm, but has not even earned what was still within his power, the praise of a greater variety and richness of painting, nor has precipitated with Shelleyan passion the stream that slept so calmly in Mr Wordsworth's mountain-lake.

There could hardly be a more decisive proof of Mr Tennyson's inaptitude for *Orphic* song than the last six lines of this poem:

> My friend, with thee to live alone,
> Methinks were better than to own
> A crown, a sceptre, and a throne.
> O strengthen me, enlighten me!
> I faint in this obscurity,
> Thou dewy dawn of memory.

To tell Memory, the mystic prophetess to whom in these transcendant initiations we owe all notices connecting our small individuality with the Infinite Eternal, that converse with her were better than crowns and sceptres! Memory might perhaps reply—'My friend, if you have not, after encircling the universe, traversing the abyss of ages, and uttering more than a hundred lines, forgotten that there are such toys on that poor earth as crowns and sceptres, it were better for you to be alone, not with, but without me.' Think how sublime a doctrine, that to have the beatific vision is really better than the power and pomp of the world. Philosophy, that sounds all depths, has seldom approached a deeper *bathos*.

Of the little poem called *Circumstance* we shall quote the whole, pleased to find something that we can produce in support of our admiration for a large class of Mr Tennyson's poems, on which we have not yet touched:

> Two children in two neighbouring villages
> . . .
> So runs the round of life from hour to hour.

Much is not attempted here, but the more performed. How simple is the language; how quietly flowing the rhythm; how clear the images; and with what pleasant enigmatic openness do the few lines set before us all the little tale of the two villagers, playing, parted, meeting, loving, wedding, dying, and leaving behind them two orphan children! It is a small tone of natural feeling, caught and preserved with genuine art, and coming home to every bosom that sweet words can penetrate at all.

Fatima is of a far higher pitch, but seems oddly misnamed. It is full of true and vehement, yet musical passion; and it suggests the strong flow of Lesbian poetry, and particularly the well-known fragment of Sappho addressed to a woman. Whence, then, the name? Lesbos has hardly gained by becoming a part of Turkey, or Sappho by turning into Fatima. But the poem is beautiful: we scarcely know where in English we could find anything so excellent, as expressing the deep-hearted fulness of a woman's conscious love. Many will read it as if it belonged only to some Fatima or Sappho to feel with this entireness of abandonment. But there are hundreds of women in the West end of London—and in the East end too—who would find it only a strain that nature had already taught them.

Lady Clara Vere de Vere aims at less, and though of no very rare cast, is successful in all that it attempts. Mr Tennyson seems to have intended to be very severe in this remonstrance to a flirt. But the damsel who deserved it would certainly rather have been flattered than provoked by such a tribute to her powers.

The Blackbird, *The Death of the Old Year*, and *Edward Gray*, are all sufficiently good for publication, but not for detailed criticism. *Sir Launcelot and Queen Guinevere* is of similar tone, but not extraordinary merit. The last but one appears to be the best stanza:

> Now on some twisted ivy-net,
> 　· · ·
> With jingling bridle-reins.

In one less careful of his melody—and we have few very recent writers so successfully careful of it—we should hardly make any remark on the harsh *r*'s in these latter lines, so unsuitable to the vague and gliding fluency of the image.

Under the head of Fancies we class all those poems relating to distant and marvellous circumstances and persons such as we can only conceive, and that very imperfectly, by a conscious removal of our thoughts into regions of which we have no experience, and which seem to us half impossible. In some instances the poet only attempts to reproduce outward relations of society and a kind of feeling which have departed from our common life—as in *The Sisters*, *The Beggar Maid*, *St Simeon*, and *St Agnes*. In others, and the greater number of these pieces, he rushes away with us into the ruins and sepulchres of old supernatural beliefs—dear to him, however, not as still partly credible, or as ever having been sacred and awful to mankind, but for the graceful strangeness of the figures that they suggest and are linked with. This mythological poetry is not of equal interest and difficulty with that which produces as brilliant and deep effects from the ordinary realities of our own lives. But it is far from worthless. Some German ballads of this kind by Goethe and Schiller—nay, by Bürger and by Heine—have great power over every one, from the art with which the imagination is won to accept as true what we still feel to be so strange. This is done mainly by a potent use of the mysterious relation between man and nature, and between all men towards each other, which always must show itself on fitting occasions as the visionary, the ominous, the spectral, the 'eery', and awful consciousness of a super-natural somewhat within our own homely flesh. It appears to us that Mr Tennyson has neither felt so deeply as some other poets—Coleridge, for instance, in *Christabel*—the moral ground on which this oracular introsentient part of man is firmly built, nor has employed its phantas-magoric power with such startling witchery. But there is almost always a vivid elegance and inward sweetness in his elfin song, whether Gothic or Grecian, and he sometimes even uses the legends of Pagan antiquity with a high perfection of dreamy music.

The Dying Swan, *The Merman*, and *The Mermaid*, are figments which he has not connected with any feeling that could render us willing to believe, nor with any meaning that would give them value as symbols. There is a kind of unhappy materialism in some of these attempts at spiritualising nature, and in the midst of some beautiful images we are stopped short by fancies equally farsought and un-pleasant. . .

There are, however, hardly any of these legendary poems that might not well be cited as examples of solid and luminous painting. We must admit that Mr Tennyson has scarcely succeeded, perhaps has not tried, to unite any powerful impression on the feelings with his coloured blaze. It is painted—though well painted—fire. But in animated pomp of imagery, all in movement, like a work of Paolo Veronese, few things that we know could rival these compositions. His figures are distinct as those of brazen statuary on tombs, brilliant as stained glass, musical as the organ-tones of chapels. And as some of these romantic songs remind us of Paul Cagliari, others—those especially that have been dreamt upon the lap of the Greek Muse—are akin to the creations of a still greater painter than the Veronese, Correggio. So mild and mourn-ful in interest are these, so perfect in harmony of images and rhythm, we almost grieve at last to waken from our trance and find we have been deluded by a Pagan vision, and by the echoes of oracles now dumb. Scarcely fabled magic could be more successful. The effect is the result evidently of great labour, but also of admirable art. As minstrel conjurations, perhaps, in English, *Kubla Khan* alone exceeds them. The verse is full of liquid intoxication, and the language of golden oneness. While we read, we too are wandering, led by nymphs, among the thousand isles of old mythology, and the present fades away from us into a pale vapour. To bewitch us with our own daily realities, and not with their unreal opposites, is a still higher task; but it could not be more thoroughly performed.

The *Morte d'Arthur*, the first poem in the second volume, seems to us less costly jewel-work, with fewer of the broad flashes of passionate imagery, than some others, and not compensating for this inferiority by any stronger human interest. The miraculous legend of 'Excalibar' does not come very near to us, and as reproduced by any modern writer must be a mere ingenious exercise of fancy. The poem, however, is full of distinct and striking description, perfectly expressed; and a tone of mild, dignified sweetness attracts, though it hardly avails to enchant us. The poet might perhaps have made the loss of the magic sword, the death of Arthur, and dissolution of the Round Table, a symbol for the departure from earth of the whole old Gothic world, with its half-pagan, all-poetic faith, and rude yet mystic blazonries. But it would be tyrannical exaction to require more philosophy in union with so fiery and productive a fancy. No one but Coleridge among us has ever combined a thoroughly speculative intellect with so restless an abundance of beautiful imagery as we find in Mr Tennyson; and the younger minstrel has as much of the reflection proper to an age like ours as any living poet except Mr Wordsworth, and as any but a very few deceased ones.

The gift of comprehensive thoughtfulness does not, however, show itself to advantage in *St Simeon Stylites*, a kind of monological personation of a filthy and mad ascetic. We find exhibited, with the seriousness of bitter poetic irony, his loathsome, yet ridiculous attempts at saintship, all founded on an idea of the Divinity fit only for an African worshipping a scarecrow fetish made of dog's bones, goose-feathers, and dunghill-rags. This is no topic for Poetry: she has better tasks than to wrap her mantle round a sordid, greedy lunatic.

How different, how superior is *Ulysses*! There is in this work a delightful epic tone, and a clear unimpassioned wisdom quietly carving its sage words and graceful figures on pale but lasting marble. Yet we know not why, except from schoolboy recollections, a modern English poet should write of Ulysses rather than of the great voyagers of the modern world, Columbus, Gama, or even Drake. Their feelings and aims lie far nearer to our comprehension—reach us by a far shorter line. Even of *Godiva*, different as is the theme, a similar observation holds. It also is admirably well done; but the singularity and bar-barousness of the fact spur, no doubt, the fancy, even told in plain prose, yet are far from rendering the topic favourable for poetry. The *Day-Dream*, the old and pretty tale of the *Sleeping Beauty*, is open to no such objection. Here the poetry was made to the writer's hand, and one cannot but wish that his grace, liveliness, and splendour had been employed on a matter of his own invention;* or, if borrowed, of some more earnest meaning. Yet, as graceful and lively description, as truth playing behind the mask of fairy-tale, the whole poem is most agreeable. It opens thus:

> The varying year with blade and sheaf
> . . .
> Through all the world she follow'd him.

The poems which we would class under the head MORALITIES, in which Reflection lifts the rod to silence Feeling, are scattered up and down the volumes under various titles. They almost all appear to us decided and remarkable failures, and only one or two of the shorter and slighter at all worthy of Mr Tennyson.

The Palace of Art, indeed, has the tints and force of poetry, and shows the author's characteristic power of distinct and deeply-dyed painting. But there is considerable affectation in some of the groupings both of words and things, and what is worse, the meaning, the *morality*, is trivial, and even mistaken. The writer's doctrine seems to be, that the soul, while by its own energy surrounding itself with all the most beautiful and expressive images that the history of mankind has pro-duced, and sympathizing wholly with the world's best thoughts, is perpetrating some prodigious moral offence for which it is bound to repent in sackcloth and ashes. A more rational and not less religious view would seem to be, that we should repent of the errors we commit from the *in*activity of our higher powers and feelings. We hardly know a notion worthier of Simeon [Stylites], or of some crack-brained sot repenting in the stocks, than this doctrine that the use of our noblest faculties on their right objects is an outrage against our best duties.

* It is difficult to suppose that the poem was written before the exhibition of Mr Maclise's picture of 'The Sleeping Beauty' (1841)—a work displaying, like most of that rising artist's, great wealth and boldness of fancy and execution, but, like too many both of the paintings and the poems of our day, too ambitiously crowded, and forced and glaring in its περιεργια.

Happily, Mr Tennyson's practice is wiser than the theory propounded in this piece; and his theory itself, if we may judge from the doctrinal parts of his second and more mature volume, is also much improved. The long and dull production called the *Two Voices*, a dispute on immortality, adding nothing to our previous knowledge, and of which the substance might have been better given in three pages (or one) than thirty, has yet no such folly in it as the many-coloured mistake of *The Palace of Art*.

In all Mr Tennyson's didactic writing one sees too clearly that, unless when the Image enchains his heart, the Thought has far too little hold upon him to produce any lively movement of soul. His speculations have the commonplaceness, vagueness, and emptiness of dreams, though the dreams of genius; and hopefully do we trust that the poet will not again throw off his magic mantle for either the monkish gown or stoic robe.

We have now reached that class of poems which stand first in our list, and which we have entitled IDYLLS. We have reserved till now all special mention of them, as holding them the most valuable part of Mr Tennyson's writings, a real addition to our literature. They have all more or less of the properly Idyllic character, though in three or four of them marked with the rapid and suggestive style of the ballad. In all we find some warm feeling, most often love, a clear and faithful eye for visible nature, skilful art and completeness of construction, and a mould of verse which for smoothness and play of melody has seldom been equalled in the language. The heartfelt tenderness, the glow, the gracefulness, the strong sense, the lively painting, in many of these compositions, drawn from the heart of our actual English life, set them far above the glittering marvels and musical phantasms of Mr Tennyson's mythological romances, at first sight the most striking portion of his works.

Among the happier specimens of this class two are pre-eminent— *The Gardener's Daughter*, and *Dora*. These are both of them Idylls in the strictest sense of the term, and might rank with the eclogues of Theocritus and Virgil, and with some poems of Goethe—as anecdotes drawn from rustic life and rounded into song. Especially, as compared with the antique models, we see in them all the gain that Christianity and civilization have brought to the relation of the sexes, and to the characters of women.

The Gardener's Daughter is a husband's recollection of his successful love, the object of which has been withdrawn from him by death. The unrhymed verse has a quiet fulness of sound, and all the delineation a clear yet rich completeness of truth, that render the little work, though far from the loftiest, yet one of the most delightful we know. As English landscape-painting, what can exceed this?

> Not wholly in the busy world, nor quite
> Beyond it, blooms the garden that I love
> . . .
> The lime a summer home of murmurous wings.

Or take the companion picture, where this view is alive with human passion:

> There sat we down upon a garden mound
> . . .
> The central wish, until we settled there.

Dora, though not so luxuriously beautiful, has less, indeed nothing, that could be spared without serious loss, and being only half the length of the former one, we shall extract it entire:

> With farmer Allan at the farm abode
> . . .
> But Dora lived unmarried till her death.

Audley Court, and *Walking to the Mail*, are in a lighter style, and with less of interest. *The Talking Oak* is more important, but does not satisfy us so well. This also, like most of Mr Tennyson's better poems, is love-inspired and love-breathing. But an ancient oak, that is won by a poet to utter Dodonaean oracles, would hardly, we conceive, be so prolix and minute in its responses. In *Locksley Hall* the fancy is again at home. It is, perhaps, on the whole, the one of all these poems in which far-extended thought is best involved in genuine and ardent imagination. A quick and generous heart pours out through the lips of a young man who has been deceived by the woman he loved, and who, inflamed with disappointment, reviews at passionate speed—far unlike the prosaic slowness of professional reviewers—the images that the darkened world now presents to him, and the diverse paths of action that he is tempted to try. We know not what the author means by his hero's talk of comrades and bugle-horns; for all the rest is the direct outbirth and reflection of our own age. The speaker tells his former happiness in the following lines:

> Then her cheek was pale and thinner than should be for one so young,
> And her eyes on all my motions with a mute observance hung
> . . .
> Is it well to wish thee happy?—having known me—to decline
> On a range of lower feelings, and a narrower heart than mine!

The images that haunt him, of the faithless maiden's married life with a despised husband, are full of bitter strength; but we prefer a small specimen of his more indistinct and wider notions:

> Can I but relive in sadness? I will turn that earlier page.
> Hide me from my deep emotion, O thou wondrous Mother-Age!
> . . .
> Far along the world-wide whisper of the south-wind rushing warm,
> With the standards of the peoples plunging thro' the thunder-storm.

Lady Clare is not memorable; but *The Lord of Burleigh* well deserves citation, as an example of the skill with which a poet can find a true and complete imaginative interest in an anecdote of our actual refined life:

> In her ear he whispers gaily
> . . .
> That her spirit might have rest.

Every thoughtful reader of the poems which we have thus glanced through will be led to compare them with those on similar themes, of present human existence in the country, by the most profoundly reflective of our living poets, Mr Wordsworth. *Michael, The Brothers*, the story of Margaret in the beginning of *The Excursion, Ruth*, these also are English Idylls, drawn from the well-springs of Nature, and finished with the painful care of a great artist. How naked and bare they all are in their solemn stillness! Nor is it only in these poems, but even in works of lighter and gladder movement, that we are compelled to listen to the bard as to a grave teacher of moral truth, whom the spirit of spontaneous enjoyment, and even the sympathy with whatever is pathetic or grand in man, cannot hurry beyond the school of his compassionate but austere stoicism. Ignorance only, or lunacy, could deny him a deeper internal power of true poetry. But even this, and not merely the manly passions and the soft affections, even the shaping and inspired imagination itself, is always subject to the considerate dominion of the moral idea. *Emotion*, the most general and obvious, the necessary impulse of all poetry in every age, is restrained in all his writings by the awful presence of self-centred will. The feelings are described rather than shared; the tragic passions summoned up only to be rebuked by a more solemn conjuration than their own; the free enjoyment of life and nature approved only within the bounds of unrelaxing caution; and love—the name bubbled by every wave of Hippocrene, and thundered in all the floods and storms of the main ocean of our being—is here a grave ritual sound spoken over the still waters drawn from the well of Truth for a penitential baptism.

Of course it would be far from our design to charge this great writer with want of feeling. A poet without feeling! Fire without warmth, and a heart without pulsation! But it is clear that his feelings are always strictly watched by his meditative conscience, too strictly, not for wisdom, but for rapture. Not a prophet in the wilderness lifting up his testimony against an evil generation, for the heart of the seer must be red and fierce as molten iron—not a hermit in his cave retired from human joys, for the anchorite floats above his rocky floor, forgetful of laws and retributions, in an ecstasy of self-denying love, that supplies the place of decalogue and duties—but like the prophet and the monk, this poet turns aside from the busy ways of life to speculate, in sage and sometimes awful rhetoric, on the wondrousness of existence, and the care with which we must tend the purity of its fountain in the heart. There is no face so lovely, no act so gushing over with keen life, that it can kindle at once the minstrel into song, hurrying him beyond all thought of wrong and right, and having warrant enough in the zealous heat which it inspires. Only in communion with the stars, the mountains, and the sea, the flowers of spring and autumn leaves, and all the simple mysteries of natural things, does his heart pour, without pause, a stream of melodious gladness, and fear no danger in its own happy ecstasies. Even in these solemn elevations of soul he does not forget to impose a scheme of toils on human life. Among streams and rocks he begins with discourse of virtue; and when he has risen on the ladder of his vision to the stars, we still hear him singing from the solar way, that it is by temperance, soberness, and chastity of soul he has so climbed, and that the praise of this heroic discipline is his last message to mankind. A noble temper of heart! A truly great man! He has strangely wedded his philosophic lore to the sweetness of poetry. But the poetry would have streamed out in a freer gush, and flushed the heart with ampler joy, had the moral been less *obtruded* as its constant aim.

In the younger of these two idyllic writers, on the whole the most genial poet of English rural life that we know—for Burns was of another language and country, no less than school—there is a very different stamp of soul. In his works there has been art enough required and used to give such clear and graceful roundness; but all skill of labour, all intellectual purpose, kept behind the sweet and fervid impulse of the heart. Thus, all that we call affection, imagination, intellect, melts out as one long happy sigh into union with the visibly beautiful, and with every glowing breath of human life. In all his better poems there is this same character—this fusion of his own fresh feeling with the delightful affections, baffled or blessed, of others—and with the fairest images of the real world as it lies before us all today. To this same tendency all legend and mystery are subordinate—to this the understanding, theorizing and dogmatizing, yet ever ministers, a loyal giant to a fairy mistress. In his better and later works the fantastic and ingenious brain, abounding in gold-dust and diamond-powder, and the playmate of sphinxes and hieroglyphic beasts, pours out its wealth, and yokes its monsters only for the service of that homely northern nature, without whose smile all wealth is for us but dead stones, and all mysteries but weary task-like puzzles.

Further Reading in Periodical Reviews

TENNYSON

Reviews of *Poems, Chiefly Lyrical*, 1830 and *Poems*, 1832, pay much attention to Tennyson's language. His poetry is compared variously to Elizabethan and metaphysical poetry, to Keats and to Shelley. Some of these comparisons were made in a benign spirit (see *Atlas* below) but attitudes harden after Arthur Hallam's provocative *Englishman's Magazine* essay in August, 1831.

Atlas, v, 27 June 1830, 411, *Poems, Chiefly Lyrical*, 1830. Robert Bell? (Shannon, p. 169.)

Spectator, 21 August 1830, 637–9, *Poems, Chiefly Lyrical*, 1830.

Tatler, 24 February 1831, 593–4: 26 February 1831, 601–2, *Poems, Chiefly Lyrical*, 1830. Leigh Hunt. (Shannon, p. 169.)

New Monthly Magazine, 33 (March 1831), 111–12, *Poems, Chiefly Lyrical*, 1830.

Athenaeum, 1 December 1832, 770–2, *Poems*, 1832.

Literary Gazette, 8 December 1832, 772–4, *Poems*, 1832. William Jerdan? (Shannon, p. 170.)

Monthly Repository, 7 N.S. (Jan. 1833), 30–41, *Poems*, 1832. W. J. Fox. (Shannon, p. 170.)

New Monthly Magazine, 37 (Jan. 1833), 69–74, *Poems*, 1832. Edward Bulwer-Lytton? (Shannon, p. 170.)

Quarterly Review, 49 (April 1833), 81–96, *Poems*, 1832. John Wilson Croker. (*W.I.*, p. 713.)

London Review, 1 (July 1835), 402–24. J. S. Mill. (Shannon, p. 170.)

The following reviews of Tennyson's *Poems*, 1842, have been selected to show in the first place the almost universal approval of Tennyson's attempts to appeal to the essential, basic human sympathies and secondly, the ways in which the question of poetry and the age was discussed. Most writers approve of the domestic idylls and *Locksley Hall*. Henry Sutton's close reading of *The Lady of Shallot* in *Howitt's Journal* (see below) is a curiosity. It is the only Victorian 'close reading' that I know of and seems to have been based on methods of explicating a text in a sermon. *The Lady of Shallot* is the

poet-prophet whose creative power would have survived and strengthened
had she remained in isolation, but she gave in to the lure of popularity—
Lancelot.

Sun, 28 May 1842, 4, *Poems*, 1842.
Spectator, 4 June 1842, 544, *Poems*, 1842.
Atlas, 17, 25 June 1842, 410–11, *Poems*, 1842.
Morning Post, 9 August 1842, 6, *Poems*, 1842.
Cambridge University Magazine, 2 (Oct. 1842), 629–39, *Poems*, 1842.
Christian Teacher, 4 N.S. (Oct. 1842), 414–23, *Poems*, 1842.
Church of England Quarterly Review, 12 (Oct. 1842), 361–76, *Poems*, 1842.
  Leigh Hunt. (Shannon, p. 170.)
Westminster Review, 38 (Oct. 1842), 371–90, *Poems*, 1842. R. Monckton
  Milnes. (Shannon, p. 171.)
London University Magazine, 1 (Dec. 1842), 286–314, *Poems*, 1842. Possibly
  William Arthur Case. (Shannon, p. 171.)
Edinburgh Review, 77 (April 1843), 373–91, *Poems*, 1842. James Spedding.
  (*W.I.*, p. 492.)
Chambers' Journal, 4 N.S. (July 1845), 25–9, *Poems*, 1842.
British Quarterly Review, 2 (Aug. 1845), 46–71, *Poems*, 1842.
Dumfries and Galloway Herald and Advertiser, 16 Oct. 1845, 1, 4: 23 Oct.
  1845, 1, 4, *Poems*, 1842. George Gilfillan. (Shannon, p. 171.)
Hogg's Weekly Instructor, 6 (1847), 281–4, *Poems*, 1842.
Howitt's Journal, 3, 15 Jan. 1848, 39–42. Henry Sutton (signed).

BROWNING

The following selection of reviews of Browning complement reviews of
Tennyson and display much the same values. Very few critics wrote approvingly or perceptively about Browning during this period. W. J. Fox, G. H.
Lewes and the writer of a discussion in the *Eclectic Review* for 1849 (see
below) are exceptions. *The Examiner* was a loyal but disapproving friend.
Browning's poetry was rarely seen in the context of the question of poetry
and the age. A rare exception is the *Metropolitan Journal* (see below).
Writers concentrated on what seemed to them the perverse obscurity and
eccentricity of his work. Nevertheless, he was acknowledged from the
beginning as a poet of stature, worthy of comparison with Tennyson.
Although the Victorian critic's limited ways of dealing with poetic language
hindered his response to Browning, frustration and respect are mingled. Only
the critics who approved of passion and energy, or the exceptional *Eclectic*
critic who saw Browning primarily as the portrayer dramatically of 'abstract
mental life' (a view not developed fully until the sixties) had a chance of
coming to terms with Browning at this time. I have included one or two

reviews of *Strafford* (1837) as the views on the nature of drama expressed compare interestingly with Arnold's much later 1853 Preface.

Monthly Repository, 7 N.S. (April 1833), 252–62, *Pauline*, 1833. W. J. Fox. (Mineka, p. 408.)

Athenaeum, 6 April 1833, 216, *Pauline*, 1833.

Fraser's Magazine, 8 (Dec. 1833), 658–70, *Pauline*, 1833. William Maginn? (*W.I.*)

Spectator, 15 August 1835, 780–1, *Paracelsus*, 1835.

Leigh Hunt's London Journal, 21 Nov. 1835, 405–8, *Paracelsus*, 1835. Leigh Hunt. (Broughton, p. 84.)

Monthly Repository, 9 N.S. (Nov. 1835), 716–27, *Paracelsus*, 1835. W. J. Fox. (Mineka, p. 409.)

Fraser's Magazine, 13 (March 1836), 362–74, *Paracelsus*, 1835. J. A. Heraud, perhaps with William Maginn. (*W.I.*)

New Monthly Magazine, 46 (March 1836), 289–308, *Paracelsus*, 1835. J. Forster (*W.I.*). Not a very perceptive review but it makes a comparison between Paracelsus and Rousseau which possibly throws some light on Browning's aims and on his political position during this period.

Metropolitan Journal, 1, 16 April 1836, 19–20, *Paracelsus*, 1835.

The Times, 2 May 1837, *Strafford*, 1837.

Athenaeum, 6 May 1837, 330, *Strafford*, 1837.

Weekly Dispatch, 7 May 1837, 224.

Edinburgh Review, 65 (July 1837), 132–51, *Strafford*, 1837. Herman Merivale. (*W.I.*, p. 483.)

Athenaeum, 30 May 1840, 431–2, *Sordello*, 1830.

Examiner, 2 Oct. 1841, 628–9, *Pippa Passes*, 1841.

Athenaeum, 11 Dec. 1841, 952, *Pippa Passes*, 1841.

Examiner, 26 Nov. 1842, 756–7, *Dramatic Lyrics*, 1842.

Athenaeum, 22 April 1843, 385, *Dramatic Lyrics*, 1842.

Examiner, 15 Nov. 1845, 723–4, *Dramatic Romances*, 1845.

English Review, 4 (Dec. 1845), 273–7, *Dramatic Romances*, 1845.

Christian Remembrancer, 11 N.S. (April 1846), 316–30, *Dramatic Romances*, 1845.

Eclectic Review, 19 N.S. (April 1846), 413; 421–6, *Dramatic Romances*, 1845.

Examiner, 25 April 1846, 259–60, *Luria, A Soul's Tragedy*. 1845.

British Quarterly Review, 6 (Nov. 1847), 490–509, *Dramatic Romances*, 1845. G. H. Lewes. *The George Eliot Letters*, ed. G. S. Haight, 1955, vol. vii, p. 368.

North American Review, 66 (April 1848), 357–400, Browning's work up to 1848. J. R. Lowell. (Broughton, p. 92.) This American study contrasts with most English reviews in its willingness to accept Browning's work.

Eclectic Review, 26 N.S. (Aug. 1849), 203–14, *Poems*, 1849. C. Edmunds (Broughton, p. 92.)

The debate around Arnold's 1853 Preface
and two related reviews of Tennyson

5

Arnold ✍ *The Strayed Reveller and Other Poems* ✍ 1849
Empedocles on Etna, and Other Poems ✍ 1852
Alexander Smith ✍ *Poems* ✍ 1853
William Sydney Walker ✍ *The Poetical Remains* ✍ 1852
William Allingham ✍ *Poems* ✍ 1850

Arthur Hugh Clough, *North American Review*, lxxvii (July 1853), 1–30

Poems by Alexander Smith, a volume recently published in London, and by this time reprinted in Boston, deserve attention. They have obtained in England a good deal more notice than is usually accorded there to first volumes of verse; nor is this by any means to be ascribed to the mere fact that the writer is, as we are told, a mechanic; though undoubtedly that does add to their external interest, and perhaps also enhances their intrinsic merit. It is to this, perhaps, that they owe a force of purpose and character which makes them a grateful contrast to the ordinary languid collectanea published by young men of literary habits; and which, on the whole, may be accepted as more than compensation for many imperfections of style and taste.

   Arthur Hugh Clough, 1819–61, friend of Arnold at Rugby and Oxford. He went to America in 1852 and wrote this review there. Arnold could have read it as his Preface is dated 1 October 1853. The review continues Clough's private debate with Arnold, so evident in *Letters of Matthew Arnold to Arthur Hugh Clough* (ed. H. F. Lowry, Oxford, 1932), on the nature of poetry and is a contribution to the public debate on modern poetry.

The models, whom this young poet has followed, have been, it would appear, predominantly, if not exclusively, the writers of his own immediate time, *plus* Shakespeare. The antecedents of the Life-Drama, the one long poem which occupies almost the whole of his volume, are to be found in *The Princess*, in parts of Mrs Browning, in the love of Keats, and the *habit* of Shakespeare. There is no Pope, or Dryden,* or even Milton; no Wordsworth, Scott, or even Byron to speak of. We have before us, we may say, the latest disciple of the school of Keats, who was indeed no well of English undefiled, though doubtless the fountain-head of a true poetic stream. Alexander Smith is young enough to free himself from his present manner, which does not seem his simple and natural own. He has given us, so to say, his Endymion; it is certainly as imperfect, and as mere a promise of something wholly different as was that of the master he has followed.[1]

We are not sorry, in the mean time, that this Endymion is not upon Mount Latmos. The natural man does pant within us after *flumina silvasque*; yet really, and truth to tell, is it not, upon the whole, an easy matter to sit under a green tree by a purling brook, and indite pleasing stanzas on the beauties of Nature and fresh air? Or is it, we incline to ask, so very great an exploit to wander out into the pleasant field of Greek or Latin mythology, and reproduce, with more or less of modern adaptation,

> the shadows
> Faded and pale, yet immortal, of Faunus, the Nymphs, and the Graces?

Studies of the literature of any distant age, or country; all the imitations and *quasi*-translations which help to bring together into a single focus, the scattered rays of human intelligence; poems after classical models, poems from Oriental sources, and the like, have undoubtedly a great literary value. Yet there is no question, it is plain and patent enough, that people much prefer *Vanity Fair* and *Bleak House*. Why so? Is it simply because we have grown prudent and prosaic, and should not welcome, as our fathers did, the Marmions and the Rokebys, the Childe

---

* The word *spoom*, which Dryden uses as the verb of the substantive *spume*, occurs also in Beaumont and Fletcher. Has Keats employed it? It seems hardly to deserve re-impatriation.

[1] Compare Clough's fairly charitable view of Keats with Arnold's strictures in the Preface.

Harolds, and the Corsairs? Or is it, that to be widely popular, to gain the ear of multitudes, to shake the hearts of men, poetry should deal more than at present it usually does, with general wants, ordinary feelings, the obvious rather than the rare facts of human nature? Could it not attempt to convert into beauty and thankfulness, or at least into some form and shape, some feeling, at any rate, of content—the actual, palpable things with which our every-day life is concerned; introduce into business and weary task-work a character and a soul of purpose and reality; intimate to us relations which, in our unchosen, peremptorily-appointed posts, in our grievously narrow and limited spheres of action, we still, in and through all, retain to some central, celestial fact? Could it not console us with a sense of significance, if not of dignity, in that often dirty, or at least dingy, work which it is the lot of so many of us to have to do, and which some one or other, after all, must do? Might it not divinely condescend to all infirmities; be in all points tempted as we are; exclude nothing, least of all guilt and distress, from its wide fraternization; not content itself merely with talking of what may be better elsewhere, but seek also to deal with what *is* here? We could each one of us, alas, be so much that somehow we find we are not; we have all of us fallen away from so much that we still long to call ours. Cannot the Divine Song in some way indicate to us our unity, though from a great way off, with those happier things; inform us, and prove to us, that though we are what we are, we may yet, in some way, even in our abasement, even by and through our daily work, be related to the purer existence.

The modern novel is preferred to the modern poem, because we do here feel an attempt to include these indispensable latest addenda—these phenomena which, if we forget on Sunday, we must remember on Monday—these positive matters of fact, which people, who are not verse-writers, are obliged to have to do with.

> Et fortasse cupressum
> Scis simulare; quid hoc, si fractis enatat expes
> Navibus, aere dato qui pingitur?[2]

The novelist does try to build us a real house to be lived in; and this common builder, with no notion of the orders, is more to our purpose

---

[2] 'Perhaps you know how to paint a cypress? But what of that, if your commission is to paint a sailor who has escaped from a shipwreck?' Horace, *Epistula ad Pisones, de Arte Poetica*, 19–21.

than the student of ancient art who proposes to lodge us under an Ionic portico. We are, unhappily, not gods, nor even marble statues. While the poets, like the architects, are—a good thing enough in its way—studying ancient art, comparing, thinking, theorizing, the common novelist tells a plain tale, often trivial enough, about this, that, and the other, and obtains one reading at any rate; is thrown away indeed tomorrow, but is devoured today.

We do not at all mean to prepare the reader for finding the great poetic desideratum in this present Life-Drama. But it has at least the advantage, such as it is, of not showing much of the *litterateur* or connoisseur, or indeed the student; nor is it, as we have said, mere pastoral sweet piping from the country. These poems were not written among books and busts, nor yet

> By shallow rivers, to whose falls
> Melodious birds sing madrigals.

They have something substantive and lifelike, immediate and first-hand, about them. There is a charm, for example, in finding, as we do, continual images drawn from the busy seats of industry; it seems to satisfy a want that we have long been conscious of, when we see the black streams that welter out of factories, the dreary lengths of urban and suburban dustiness,

> the squares and streets,
> And the faces that one meets,

irradiated with a gleam of divine purity. There are moods when one is prone to believe that, in these last days, no longer by 'clear spring or shady grove', no more upon any Pindus or Parnassus, or by the side of any Castaly, are the true and lawful haunts of the poetic powers: but, we could believe it, if anywhere, in the blank and desolate streets, and upon the solitary bridges of the midnight city, where Guilt is, and wild Temptation, and the dire Compulsion of what has once been done—there, with these tragic sisters around him, and with Pity also, and pure Compassion, and pale Hope, that looks like Despair, and Faith in the garb of Doubt, there walks the discrowned Apollo, with unstrung lyre; nay, and could he sound it, those mournful Muses would scarcely be able as of old, to respond and 'sing in turn with their beautiful voices'.

To such moods, and in such states of feeling, this Life-Drama will be an acceptable poem. Under the guise of a different story, a story unskilful enough in its construction, we have seemed continually to recognize the ingenuous, yet passionate, youthful spirit, struggling after something like right and purity amidst the unnumbered difficulties, contradictions, and corruptions of the heated and crowded, busy, vicious, and inhuman town. Eager for action, incapable of action without some support, yet knowing not on what arm to dare to lean; not untainted; hard-pressed; in some sort, at times, overcome, still we seem to see the young combatant, half combatant, half martyr, resolute to fight it out, and not to quit this for some easier field of battle, one way or other to make something of it.

The story, such as we have it, is inartificial enough. Walter, a boy of poetic temperament and endowment, has, it appears, in the society of a poet friend now deceased, grown up with the ambition of achieving something great in the highest form of human speech. Unable to find or make a way, he is diverted from his lofty purposes by a romantic love-adventure, obscurely told, with a 'Lady' who finds him asleep, Endymion-like, under a tree. The fervour and force of youth wastes itself here in vain; a quick disappointment—for the lady is betrothed to another, sends him back enfeebled, exhausted, and embittered, to essay once again his task. Disappointed affections, and baffled ambition, contending henceforward in unequal strife with the temptations of scepticism, indifference, apathetic submission, base indulgence, and the like; the sickened, and defeated, yet only too strong, too powerful man, turning desperately off, and recklessly at last plunging in mid-unbelief into joys to which only belief and moral purpose can give reality; out of horror-stricken guilt, the new birth of clearer and surer, though humbler, conviction, trust, resolution; these happy changes met, perhaps a little prematurely and almost more than half-way, by success in the aims of a purified ambition, and crowned too, at last, by the blessings of a regenerate affection, such is the argument of the latter half of the poem; and there is something of a current and tide, so to say, of poetic intention in it, which carries on the reader (after the first few scenes) perforce, in spite of criticism and himself, through faulty imagery, turgid periods, occasional bad versification and even grammar, to the close. Certainly, there is something of a real flesh-and-blood heart and soul in the case, or this could not be so.

Of the first four or five scenes, perhaps the less said the better. There are frequent fine lines, occasional beautiful passages; but the tenor of the narrative is impeded and obstructed to the last degree, not only by accumulations of imagery, but by episode, and episode within episode, of the most embarrassing form. It is really discouraging to turn page upon page, while Walter is quoting the poems of his lost friend, and wooing the unknown lady of the wood with a story of another lady and an Indian page. We could almost recommend the reader to begin with the close of scene IV, where the hero's first love-disappointment is decided, and the lady quits her young poet.

> I must go,
> Nay, nay, I go alone!
>   . . .
> As in a little wind, thou 'lt know 'tis I.

The ensuing scene, between Walter and a Peasant, is also obscurely and indecisively given; and before Part VI, it would have been well, we think, to place some mark of the lapse of time. The second division of the poem here commences. We are reintroduced to the hero in a room in London, reading a poetical manuscript. Edward, a friend, enters and interrupts. We quote from a speech of Walter's.

> Thou mock'st at much:
>   . . .
> Is hurrying up the great world's side with light.

Two scenes of conversation are given between Walter and this friend, Edward, cold, clear-sighted, a little cynical, but patient, calm, resigned, and moral. He, as it happens, is going on the morrow to Bedfordshire, to visit

> Old Mr Wilmott, nothing in himself,
> But rich as ocean.
>   . . .
> Yet wealthier in one child than all of these.

Thither Walter accompanies him. We subjoin part of a dialogue between him and the 'one child', in whom, more than in all his land, old Mr Wilmott was blest. Walter had been describing his own story under the name of another person.

> *Violet.* Did you know well that youth of whom you spake?
>   . . .
> Dearer is Earth to God for her sweet sake.

The issue and catastrophe of a new love-adventure here, in this unhappy and distempered period of baffled and disappointed ambition, and power struggling vainly for a vent, may be conjectured from the commencement of a scene, which perhaps might be more distinctly marked as the opening of the third part.

> [*A bridge in a City. Midnight. Walter alone.*]
> Adam lost Paradise—eternal tale,
> Repeated in the lives of all his sons.
>   . . .
> They swarm and feed upon me.

Three years appear to have gone by, when Walter, like a stag sore-hunted, returns to the home of his childhood.

> 'Twas here I spent my youth, as far removed
>   . . .
> Starts the completed moon.

Here, in this determination, he writes his poem, attains in this spirit the object which had formerly been his ambition. And here, in the last scene, we find him happy, or peaceful at least, with Violet.

> *Violet.* I always pictured you in such a place
>   . . .
> A long day stretches to the very end.

So be it, O young Poet; Poet, perhaps it is early to affirm; but so be it, at any rate, O young man. While you go forth in that 'armour of pure intent', the hearts of some readers, be assured, will go with you.

Empedocles on Etna and other Poems, with its earlier companion volume, *The Strayed Reveller and other Poems*, are, it would seem, the productions (as is, or was, the English phrase) of a scholar and a gentleman; a man who has received a refined education, seen refined 'society', and been more, we dare say, in the world, which is called the world, than in all likelihood has a Glasgow mechanic. More refined, therefore, and more highly educated sensibilities, too delicate, are they, for common service? a calmer judgement also, a more poised and steady intellect, the *siccum lumen* of the soul; a finer and rarer aim perhaps, and certainly a keener sense of difficulty, in life; these are the characteristics of him whom we are to call 'A'. Empedocles, the sublime Sicilian philosopher, the fragments of whose moral and philosophic poems testify to his genius and character, Empedocles, in the Poem before us, weary of misdirected effort, weary of imperfect thought, impatient of a life which appears to him a miserable failure, and incapable, as he conceives, of doing any thing that shall be true to that proper interior self,

> Being one with which we are one with the whole world,

wandering forth, with no determined purpose, into the mountain solitudes, followed for a while by Pausanias, the eager and laborious physician, and at a distance by Callicles, the boy-musician, flings himself at last, upon a sudden impulse and apparent inspiration of the intellect, into the boiling crater of Etna; rejoins there the elements. 'Slave of sense', he was saying, pondering near the verge,

> Slave of sense
> I have in no wise been: but slave of thought?
> And who can say, he has been always free,
> Lived ever in the light of his own soul?
> I cannot:
> . . .
> ere the mists
> Of despondency and gloom
> Rush over it again,
> Receive me! save me!
> [*He plunges into the crater.*]

The music of the boy Callicles, to which he chants his happy mythic stories, somewhat frigidly perhaps, relieves, as it sounds in the distance, the gloomy catastrophe.

Tristram and Iseult (these names form the title of the next and only other considerable poem) are, in the old romantic cycle of North-France and Germany, the hero and the heroine of a mournful tale. Tristram of Lyonness, the famed companion of King Arthur, received in youth a commission to bring from across the sea the Princess Iseult of Ireland, the destined bride of the King of Cornwall. The mother of the beautiful princess gave her, as a parting gift, a cup of a magic wine, which she and her royal husband should drink together on their marriage-day in their palace at Tyntagil; so they should love each other perfectly and forever. But on the voyage it befell—

> The calm sea shines, loose hang the vessel's sails,
> Before us are the sweet green fields of Wales,

And overhead the cloudless sky of May.
'Ah, would I were'—

(saith Iseult)

'Ah, would I were in those green fields at play,
. . .
Reach me my golden cup which stands by thee,
And pledge me in it first for courtesy.'

On the dreamy seas it so befell, that Iseult and Tristram drank together of the golden cup. Tristram, therefore, and Iseult should love each other perfectly and for ever. Yet nothing the less for this must Iseult be wedded to the King of Cornwall; and Tristram, vainly lingering, fly and go forth upon his way.

But it so chanced that, after long and weary years of passion vainly contended with, years of travel and hard fighting, Tristram, lying wounded in Brittany, was tended by another, a youthful, innocent Iseult, in whose face he seemed to see the look of that Iseult of the past, that was, and yet could not be, his. Weary, and in his sad despondency, Tristram wedded Iseult of Brittany, whose heart, in his stately deep distress, he had moved to a sweet and tender affection. The modern poem opens with the wedded knight come home again, after other long years, and other wars, in which he had fought at King Arthur's side with the Roman emperor, and subdued the heathen Saxons on the Rhine, lying once more sick and sad at heart, upon what ere long he feels shall be his death-bed. Ere he die, he would see, once yet again, her with whom in his youth he drank of that fatal cup.

> *Tristram.* Is she not come? the messenger was sure
> . . .
> *The Page.* The lanterns of the fishing-boats at sea.

And so through the whole Part I of our poem, lies the sick and weary knight upon his bed, reviewing sadly, while sadly near him stands his timid and loving younger Iseult, reviewing, half sleeping, half awake, those old times, that hapless voyage, and all that thence ensued; and still in all his thought recurring to the proud Cornish Queen, who, it seems, will let him die unsolaced. He speaks again, now broad awake.

> Is my page here? Come turn me to the fire.
> Upon the window panes the moon shines bright;

> The wind is down; but she'll not come to-night.
> Ah no,—she is asleep in Tyntagil—
> . . .
> To bed—good night.

And so (our poet passing without notice from Tristram's semi-dramatic musings and talkings, to his own not more coherent narrative)—

> She left the gleam-lit fireplace,
> She came to the bed-side
> . . .
> Are not more innocent than thine.

Sleeping with her little ones, and, it may be, dreaming too, though less happily than they, lies Iseult of Brittany. And now—

> What voices are those on the clear night air? . . .

Yes, the Queen Iseult of Cornwall, Iseult that was of Ireland, Iseult of the ship upon the dreamy seas long since, has crossed these stormy seas tonight, is here, holds his hand. And so proceeds, through some six or seven pages of Part II, the fine colloquy of the two sad, world-worn, late-reunited lovers. When we open upon Part III,

> A year had flown, and in the chapel old
> Lay Tristram and Queen Iseult dead and cold.

Beautiful, simple, old medieval story! We have followed it, led on as much by its own intrinsic charm as by the form and colouring—beautiful too, but indistinct—which our modern poet has given it. He is obscure at times, and hesitates and falters in it; the knights and dames, we fear, of old North-France and Western Germany would have been grievously put to it to make him out. Only upon a fourth re-reading, and by the grace of a happy moment, did we satisfy our critical conscience that, when the two lovers have sunk together in death, the knight on his pillows, and Queen Iseult kneeling at his side, the poet, after passing to the Cornish court where she was yesternight, returns to address himself to a hunter with his dogs, worked in the tapestry of the chamber here, whom he conceives to be pausing in the pictured chase, and staring, with eyes of wonder, on the real scene of the pale knight on the pillows and the kneeling lady fair. But

> Cheer, cheer thy dogs into the brake
> . . .
> A thousand years ago.

Fortunately, indeed, with the commencement of Part III, the most matter-of-fact quarterly conscience may feel itself pretty well set at ease by the unusually explicit statements that

> A year had fled; and in the chapel old
> . . .
> Creeps over it from the tilled fields behind.

Yet anon, again and thicker now perhaps than ever, the mist of more than poetic dubiousness closes over and around us. And as he sings to us about the widowed lady Iseult, sitting upon the sea-banks of Brittany, watching her bright-eyed children, talking with them and telling them old Breton stories, while still, in all her talk and her story, her own dreamy memories of the past, and perplexed thought of the present, mournfully mingle, it is really all but impossible to ascertain her, or rather his, real meanings. We listen, indeed, not quite unpleased, to a sort of faint musical mumble, conveying at times a kind of subdued half-sense, or intimating, perhaps, a threequarters-implied question; Is any thing real?—is love any thing?—what is any thing?—is there substance enough even in sorrow to mark the lapse of time?—is not passion a diseased unrest?—did not the fairy Vivian, when the wise Merlin forgot his craft to fall in love with her, wave her wimple over her sleeping adorer?

> Nine times she waved the fluttering wimple round
> . . .
> For she was passing weary of his love.

Why or wherefore, or with what purport, who will venture exactly to say?—but such, however, was the tale which, while Tristram and his first Iseult lay in their graves, the second Iseult, on the sea-banks of Brittany, told her little ones.

And yet, dim and faint as is the sound of it, we still prefer this dreamy patience, the soft submissive endurance of the Breton lady, and the human passions and sorrows of the Knight and the Queen, to the high, and shall we say, pseudo-Greek inflation of the philosopher musing above the crater, and the boy Callicles, singing myths upon the mountain.

Does the reader require morals and meanings to these stories? What shall they be, then?—the deceitfulness of knowledge, and the illusive-ness of the affections, the hardness and roughness and contrariousness of the world, the difficulty of living at all, the impossibility of doing any thing, *voilà tout?* A charitable and patient reader, we believe (such as is the present reviewer) will find in the minor poems that accompany these pieces, intimations—what more can reader or reviewer ask?—of some better and further thing than these; some approximations to a kind of confidence, some incipiences of a degree of hope, some roots, retaining some vitality, of conviction and moral purpose.

> And though we wear out life, alas,
>   . . .
> Nor lightness wisdom any more.

In the future, it seems, there is something for us; and for the present also, which is more germane to our matter, we have discovered some precepts about 'hope, light, and *persistence*', which we intend to make the most of. Meantime, it is one promising point in our author of the initial, that his second is certainly on the whole an improvement upon his first volume. There is less obvious study of effect; upon the whole, a plainer and simpler and less factitious manner and method of treat-ment. This, he may be sure, is the only safe course. Not by turning and twisting his eyes, in the hope of seeing things as Homer, Sophocles, Virgil, or Milton saw them; but by seeing them, by accepting them as he sees them, and faithfully depicting accordingly, will he attain the object he desires.

In the earlier volume, one of the most generally admired pieces was *The Forsaken Merman.*

> Come, dear children, let us away
>   Down, and away below,

says the Merman, standing upon the sea-shore, whither he and his children came up to call back the human Margaret, their mother, who had left them to go, for one day—for Easter-day—to say her prayers with her kinsfolk in the little grey church on the shore:

> 'T will be Easter-time in the world—ah me,
> And I lose my poor soul, Merman, here with thee.

And when she staid, and staid on, and it seemed a long while, and the little ones began to moan, at last, up went the Merman with the little ones to the shore, and so on into the town, and to the little grey church, and there looked in through the small leaded panes of the window. There she sits in the aisle; but she does not look up, her eyes are fixed upon the holy page; it is in vain we try to catch her attention.

> Come away, children, call no more,
> Come away, come down, call no more.

Down, down to the depths of the sea. She will live up there and be happy, among the things she had known before. Yet sometimes a thought will come across her; there will be times when she will

> Steal to the window and look at the sand
> . . .
> And the gleam of her golden hair.

Come away, children, come down. We will be happy in our bright home under the sea—happy, though the cruel one leaves us lonely for ever. Yet we too, sometimes at midnight, when winds blow softly, and the moonlights falls clear,

> Up the still glistening beaches,
> . . .
> The Kings of the Sea.

It is a beautiful poem, certainly; and deserves to have been given at full length. *The Strayed Reveller* itself is more ambitious, perhaps a little strained. It is a pleasing and significant imagination, however, to present to us Circe and Ulysses in colloquy with a stray youth from the train of Bacchus, who drinks eagerly the cup of the enchantress, not as did the sailors of the Ithacan king, for gross pleasure, but for the sake of the glorious and superhuman vision and knowledge it imparts.

> But I, Ulysses,
> . . .
> Sometimes a Faun with torches.

But now, we are fain to ask, where are we, and whither are we unconsciously come? Were we not going forth to battle in the armour of a righteous purpose, with our first friend, with Alexander Smith? How is it we find ourselves here, reflecting, pondering, hesitating, musing, complaining, with 'A'. As the wanderer at night, standing under a stormy sky, listening to the wild harmonies of winds, and watching the wild movements of the clouds, the tree-tops, or possibly the waves, may, with a few steps, very likely, pass into a lighted sitting-room, and a family circle, with pictures and books, and literary leisure, and ornaments, and elegant small employments, a scene how dissimilar to that other, and yet how entirely natural also; so it often happens too with books. You have been reading Burns, and you take up Cowper. You feel at home, how strangely! in both of them. Can both be the true thing? and if so, in what new form can we express the relation, the harmony, between them? Such a discrepancy there certainly does exist between the two books that have been before us here. We close the one and open the other, and feel ourselves moving to and fro between two totally different, repugnant, and hostile theories of life. Are we to try and reconcile them, or judge between them?

May we escape from all the difficulty by a mere quotation, and pronounce with the shepherd of Virgil,

> Non nostrum inter vos tantas componere lites
> Et vitulâ tu dignus, et hic.[3]

Or will the reader be content to bow down with us in this place, and acknowledge the presence of that highest object of worship among the modern Germans, an *antinomy*. (That is, O unlearned reader, ignorant, not impossibly, of Kant and the modern German religion, in brief, a contradiction in terms, the ordinary *phenomenal* form of a *noumenal* Verity; as, for example, *the world must have had a beginning*, and, *the world cannot have had a beginning*, in the transcendental fusion or confusion of which consists the Intelligible or unintelligible truth.) Will you be content, O reader, to plod in German manner over miles of a straight road, that seems to lead somewhere, with the prospect of arriving at last at some point where it will divide at equal angles, and lead equally in two opposite directions, where you may therefore safely pause, and thankfully set up your rest, and adore in sacred doubt the Supreme Bifurcation?[4] Or do you hold, with Voltaire, who said (*apropos* of the question then debated among the French wits, whether there were or were not a God) that 'after all, one must take a side'?

With all respect for the Antinomies and Germans, and 'most dis-

---

[3] 'It is not for us to settle the issue of such strife between you; both of you deserve a calf (as prize).' Virgil, *Eclogues* 3. 108–9. In other words—it is not for us to decide in favour of either of you in such a great competition.

[4] Veyriras thinks that Clough read Kant's *Critique of Pure Reason* in the mid-1840s. See Paul Veyriras, *Arthur Hugh Clough* (Paris, 1964), p. 204.

tinguished consideration' for Voltaire and Parisian persiflage, still, it may not be quite necessary for us, on the present occasion, either to stand still in transcendental doubt, or toss up, as it were, for our side. Individuals differ in character, capacity, and positions; and, according to their circumstances, will combine, in every possible variety of degree, the two elements of thoughtful discriminating selection and rejection, and frank and bold acceptance of what lies around them. Between the extremes of ascetic and timid self-culture, and of un-questioning, unhesitating confidence, we may consent to see and tolerate every kind and gradation of intermixture. Nevertheless, upon the whole, for the present age, the lessons of reflectiveness and the maxims of caution do not appear to be more needful or more approp-riate than exhortations to steady courage and calls to action. There is something certainly of an over-educated weakness of purpose in Western Europe—not in Germany only, or France, but also in more busy England. There is a disposition to press too far the finer and subtler intellectual and moral susceptibilities; to insist upon following out, as they say, to their logical consequences, the notices of some single organ of the spiritual nature; a proceeding which perhaps is hardly more sensible in the grown man than it would be in the infant to refuse to correct the sensations of sight by those of the touch. Upon the whole, we are disposed to follow out, if we must follow out at all, the analogy of the bodily senses; we are inclined to accept rather than investigate; and to put our confidence less in arithmetic and antinomies, than in

A few strong instincts and a few plain rules.

Let us remark also in the minor Poems, which accompany *Em-pedocles*, a disposition, perhaps, to assign too high a place to what is called Nature. It may indeed be true, as the astronomers say, though after all it is no very great piece of knowledge, that the heavenly bodies describe ellipses; and go on, from and to all the ages, performing that self-repeating, unattaining curve. But does it, therefore, of neces-sity follow that human souls do something analogous in the spiritual spaces? Number is a wonderful thing, and the laws of nature sublime; nevertheless, have we not a sort of intuition of the existence, even in our own poor human selves, of something akin to a Power superior to, and transcending, all manifestations of Nature, all intelligible forms of Number and Law. We quote one set of verses, in which our author does appear to have escaped for once from the dismal cycle of his rehabilitated Hindu-Greek theosophy—[5]

MORALITY

It is wonderful what stores of really valuable thought may lie neglected in a book, simply because they are not put in that form which serves our present occasions. But if we have been inclined to yield to a preference for the picture of simple, strong, and certain, rather than of subtle, shifting, and dubious feelings, and in point of tone and matter to go along with the young mechanic, in point of diction and manner, we must certainly assign the palm to 'A', in spite of a straining after the rounded Greek form, such as, to some extent, vitiates even the style of Milton. Alexander Smith lies open to much graver critical carping. He writes, it would almost seem, under the impression that the one business of the poet is to coin metaphors and similes. He tells them out as a clerk might sovereigns at the Bank of England. So many comparisons, so much poetry; it is the sterling currency of the realm. Yet he is most pleased, perhaps, when he can double or treble a similitude; speaking of A, he will call it a B, which is, as it were, the C of a D. By some maturer effort we may expect to be thus conducted even to Z. But simile within simile, after the manner of Chinese boxes, are more curious than beautiful; nor is it the true aim of the poet, as of the Italian boy in the street, to poise upon his head, for public exhibition, a board crowded as thick as they can stand with images, big and little, black and white, of anybody and everybody, in any possible order of disorder, as they happen to pack. *Tanquam scopulem, insolens verbum,*[6] says the precept of ancient taste, which our author seems to accept freely, with the modern comment of—

> In youth from rock to rock I went
> With pleasure high and turbulent,—
> Most pleased, when most uneasy.

The movement of his poem is indeed rapid enough; there is a sufficient impetus to carry us over a good deal of rough and 'rocky' ground; there is a real continuity of poetic purpose; but it is so perpetually presumed upon; the attention, which the reader desires to devote to the pursuit of the main drift of what calls itself a single poem, *simplex*

---

[5] Arnold pressed the *Bhagavad Gita* on Clough in 1848. See Lowry, p. 69.
[6] I have been unable to find the source of this quotation.

et unum, is so incessantly called off to look at this and look at that; when, for example, we would fain follow the thought and feeling of Violet and of Walter, we are with such peremptory and frequent eagerness summoned to observe how like the sky is to x and the stars are to y, that on the whole, though there *is* a real continuity of purpose, we cannot be surprised that the critic of the *London Examiner* failed to detect it.[7] Keats and Shelley, and Coleridge, perhaps, before them, with their extravagant love for Elizabethan phraseology, have led to this mischief. Has not Tennyson followed a little too much in their train? Coleridge, we suppose, would have maintained it to be an excellence in the 'myriad-minded' dramatist, that he so often diverts us from the natural course of thought, feeling, and narrative, to see how curiously two trifles resemble each other, or that, in a passage of deep pathos, he still finds time to apprise us of a paronomasia. But faults which disfigure Shakespeare are not beauties in a modern volume.

> I rot upon the waters when my prow
> Should *grate* the golden isles

may be a very Elizabethan, but is certainly rather a vicious expression. Force and condensation are good, but it is possible to combine them with purity of phrase. One of the most successful delineations in the whole poem is contained in the following passage, which introduces scene VII.

> [*A balcony overlooking the sea.*]
> The lark is singing in the blinding sky,—
> Hedges are white with May.
> . . .
>
> A few half-withered flowers;—I love and pity it.

It may be the fault of our point of view; but certainly we do not find even here that happy, unimpeded sequence which is the charm of really good writers. Is there not something incongruous in the effect of the immediate juxtaposition of these two images? We have lost, it may be, that impetuosity, that *élan*, which lifts the young reader over hedge and ditch at flying leaps, across country, or we should not perhaps entertain any offence, or even surprise, at being transferred *per saltum* from the one field to the other. But we could almost ask, was the passage, so beautiful, though perhaps a little prolonged, about the

[7] *Examiner*, 9 April 1853, 227–9.

June day in November, written consecutively, and in one flow, with the previous, and also beautiful one about ocean and his bride. We dare say it was; but it does not read, somehow, in the same straight line with it,

Tantum series juncturaque pollet.[8]

We venture, too, to record a perhaps hypercritical objection to 'the *blinding* sky' in this particular collocation. Perhaps in the first line of a scene, while the reader has not yet warmed to his duty, simplicity should be especially observed; a single image, without any repeated reflection, so to speak, in a second mirror, should suffice. The following, which open scene XI, are better.

> Summer hath murmured with her leafy lips
> Around my home, and I have heard her not;
> I've missed the process of three several years
> From shaking wind flowers to the tarnished gold
> That rustles sere on Autumn's aged limbs.

Except the two last lines. Our author will not keep his eye steady upon the thing before him; he goes off, and distracts us, and breaks the impression he had begun to succeed in giving, by bidding us look now at something else. Some simpler epithets than *shaking*, and some plainer language than *tarnished gold* or *aged limbs*, would have done the work better. We are quite prepared to believe that these faults and these *disagreeables* have personally been necessities to the writer, are awkwardnesses of growth, of which the full stature may show no trace. He should be assured, however, that though the rude vigour of the style of his Life-Drama may attract upon the first reading, yet in any case, it is not the sort of writing which people recur to with pleasure and fall back upon with satisfaction. It may be a groundless fancy, yet we do fancy, that there is a whole hemisphere, so to say, of the English language which he has left unvisited. His diction feels to us, as if between Milton and Burns he had not read, and between Shakespeare and Keats had seldom admired. Certainly there is but little inspiration in the compositions of the last century; yet English was really best and most naturally written, when there was, perhaps, least to write about. To obtain a real command of the language, some familiarity with the

---

8 'Of such importance are due sequence and connexion.' Horace, *de Arte Poetica*. 242. A free translation would be— The order and inner coherence and (careful) connection are what make (your writing) take hold.

prose writers, at any rate, of that period, is almost essential; and to write out, as a mere daily task, passages, for example, of Goldsmith, would do a verse-composer of the nineteenth century as much good, we believe, as the study of Beaumont and Fletcher.

If our readers wish to view real timidity, real shrinking from actual things, real fear of living, let them open the little volume of Sidney Walker's *Poetical Remains*. The school-fellow and college friend of Praed, marked from his earliest youth by his poetic temper and faculty, he passed fifty-one years, mostly in isolation and poverty, shivering upon the brink, trembling and hesitating upon the threshold of life. Fearful to affirm any thing, lest it haply might be false; to do any thing, because so probably it might be sin; to speak, lest he should lie; almost, we might say, to feel, lest it should be a deception, so he sat, crouching and cowering, in the dismal London back-street lodging, over the embers of a wasting and dying fire, the true image of his own vitality. 'I am vext', is his weak complaining cry,

> . . . With many thoughts, the kindly spirit of hope
> Is sick within me;
> . . .
> Round the beloved knees.

Except some translations, of which one from the Persae of Æschylus, describing the morning of Salamis, and three of the three finest fragments of Ennius, may be recommended, there is hardly any thing that is not of this sad personal kind:

> Ah, woe is me, that I am forced to wrong
> . . .
> Of hope and natural joy, and build for peace a bower.

The flowers of hope and natural joy and simple feeling, the reader will find growing abundantly in the pages of William Allingham, a young Irish poet, whose vein of poetic thought and pure felicitous diction has won him the praise of good judges in England. We have already, we believe, overstepped the limits which can be allowed to the levities of verse; otherwise we would gladly quote from his charming tale of *The Music Master*. The volume, however, is already not unknown in America. It would have been better, certainly, for more perfect elaboration of several of the minor pieces, and perhaps for the entire omission of a considerable number.

The *Serenade* begins well,

> Oh! hearing sleep, and sleeping hear,
> The while we dare to call thee dear . . .

but it is not sustained. We will quote the following description.

> By the shore a plot of ground
> . . .
> And stars move calmly overhead.

6

Arnold ↜ *Poems* ↜ 1853

Charles Kingsley, *Fraser's Magazine*, xlix
(February 1854), 140–9

It is impossible to listen to those who argue that lofty poetry has
henceforth become impossible for man, without a painful misgiving
that their seemingly incredible theory may, after all, have some solid
foundation. They say, Men are not now as colossal for good or for
evil, as of old; and, even if they were, individual energy, individual
character, has no longer the same chance of distinction: it is not an
aristocratic age, an age of heroes; but a democratic one, in which men
think and act in masses. And a democratic age having once arisen, and
arisen apparently, too, for the whole world, all future ages must be
democratic also. At least there can be no return to heroism; only a
possible decline into some artificial and Byzantine despotism, in which
thought becomes pedantry, and poetry stereotyped concettism.[1]

'Moreover', they say, 'man thinks too much, now-a-days, for poetry.
He has become too self-anatomizing to clothe his heart's experience, as
of old, in symbols borrowed from all heaven and earth. He must, on the
contrary, strip it out of what scanty vesture it may have possessed, at
its first appearance, in his imagination, and hold it up to the microscope
upon a pin's point, to see exactly what it is, and, indeed, whether, after
all, it is anything.'

'Moreover'—and this, in the minds of some wise men, forms the
heaviest count of all—'poetry has ceased to be the natural expression of
the deepest currents of man's thought. We no longer think in verse
concerning God and nature, like the old Hebrew and Brahmin poets;

Charles Kingsley, 1819–75. Kingsley's very active social concern, his connection with F. D. Maurice and the Christian Socialists, made him almost inevitably
hostile to Arnold's ideas.

[1] Kingsley is speaking in the language of Carlyle's *On Heroes, Hero-worship,
and the Heroic in History* (1841).

not even of wars and genealogies, like the old Greek ones; and per-haps', say they, 'we are right; such subjects have lost their songfulness for us; they have ceased to convey to our ears any note of the spheral harmonies. The individualizing tendencies of our modern Protestant-ism have abolished theologic poetry, as the emasculating tendencies of our Mammonism have abolished martial song. And, again, that very realm of fancy, which has been, in all ages, the ground where poets made and found what they would, has been now narrowed to the merest strip. When Spenser wrote his *Fairy Queen*, or Ariosto his *Orlando*, no reader felt shocked by their wild conceptions. After all they might be true. Who knew but that Prester John's kingdom was still mighty in the heart of Asia, or could disprove that the unknown tracts of Africa held 'Anthropophagi and men whose heads do grow beneath their shoulders', not to mention the boundless field for fancy, which lay in the new and untried marvels of America? Besides, people believed in witches, then, and ghosts, and fairies, and could not com-plain of a poet, for using them; nay, they might thank him for raising them to a higher power, as Spenser did, and giving them a more moral and rational meaning than that which they had in the minds of the mob.

'But, now, no man can overstep plain scientific matter-of-fact, with-out lying and talking nonsense; if those unpleasant terms are, as of old, to be applied to the act of him who says what he does not believe him-self, and what he does not wish others to believe either. The mere praise of physical prowess, moreover, is now impossible, unless we be content to sing of Robert Coombes or the 'Notting Stag'. No Hercules can henceforth earn immortality by slaying the Nemaean lion, or Regnar-shaggy-breeks choke dragons single-handed. Man has out-stripped the wild beasts by cunning. Captain Mayne Reid's charming boy-hunters are heroes more terrible to bear and buffalo than Theseus' self; and when a man of the old thews and sinews, like Mr Gordon Cumming, tries his prowess on the desert beast, the result is painful, butcher-like; so much too feeble are the monsters for the man.[2]

'No', they say, 'a living poetry is impossible, henceforth; and all that

[2] Robert Coombes was champion rower of the Thames from 1846–52. He won large sums of money and perhaps this is why Kingsley thinks of him as crude and unheroic. Mayne Reid's fourth novel, *The Boy Hunters*, was published in 1852, R. G. Gordon Cumming's *Five Years of a Hunter's Life in South Africa* was published in 1850 and went into five subsequent editions. These men repre-sent three popular views of the heroic but Kingsley argues that they are sham heroics.

the singer can do, unless he chooses to degrade his powers, by setting to rhyme the spiritual dyspepsia of an unhealthy and nerveless time, is to betake himself to the greater dead; to reproduce, as well as he can, their thoughts, their forms; perhaps to awaken men to admire—to make them imitate is now hopeless—the noble deeds of their fore-fathers.'

So they say; and with what apparent truth and weight we know but too well. We cannot controvert their arguments. And yet instinct, truer than all arguments, answers for ever, No! There are the elements of poetry around us now, if we could but see them; there will be for ever. There is poetry in Australian emigrations, Britannia-tubular bridges, Solent steam-reviews; and few who look upon such things but say, in their hearts, 'Oh that I could utter, even to myself, the thoughts which this thing raises in me! Oh that a man would arise, and utter them for me![3] Should I not welcome him as a benefactor and a friend?' There is poetry in nature still; ay, more than our forefathers ever dreamed. If ghosts and fairies have vanished, the microscopist and the geognost are daily revealing wonders to which those of Ariosto and Spenser are bald and tawdry; and if, as yet, they are incapable of being sung, because they seem to connect themselves with no human interest, that is only because the mind of man, as yet stunned and giddy from the vastness of that which has been shown to it, is unable to interweave the new facts with that faith in a living God, which is, paradoxical as it may seem, the root of all truly human poetry, and to recover, again, its part in the great chorus of the Jewish sages, 'Oh all ye works of the Lord, praise Him and magnify him for ever'; which, whensoever truly uttered, has its sure culmination in the higher call, 'Oh ye spirits and souls of the righteous, praise Him and magnify him for ever'.

It is possible, it is to be longed and hoped for, that a poet may arise, even in our days, who will recover for us that our lost part in the harmony of the spheres: but he must be a poet who can see the present; who understands the age in which he lives. It was by virtue of that—of utterly and thoroughly seeing the present, or rather, of being taught it by Him who made it, that the old Hebrew poets, alone of all, saw the

---

[3] 'There is poetry in Australian emigrations . . .': poetry of a kind—eighty thousand persons left for Australia in 1852. '. . . Britannia-tubular bridges, Solent steam-reviews': Stephenson's bridge and displays of power represent the achievements of Victorian technology which are worthy of celebration by modern poets.

future, and were seers, inspired, predicting things to come. For the future is contained in the present; and he who comprehends the one, comprehends the other, and becomes, *ipso facto*, a prophet, telling what will be from what is, and from the eternal laws of it, as a morphologist predicts the plant from the cotyledon; or as Cuvier predicted, from the fragment of a jaw-bone, the yet undiscovered Palaeothere.[4]

But we do not believe that the old classic poets, not even Homer, with all his intense perception of the outward phenomena around him, did see their own time; and in so far we must consider them as defective models. We do not think that either Æschylus or Sophocles saw clearly the age in which they were living. We are sure that Aristophanes did not; sure that Virgil and Horace did not. Socrates saw his age: and wrote no poetry, finding the times too sad for song. Plato saw it, and became a disciple of Socrates, and a prophet for all time: but not till he had burnt all his youthful dramas.

Still, there is the heroic past whereof to sing. It may be that some man may arise, even in our day, who will sing what heroism exists—and heroism does exist—in the present. But if not, a man will arise to do it, after we are dead and gone, and the age of Napoleon and Wellington, of Old England and Young America, will not want its *vates sacer*. And in the meanwhile, how can a poet better employ himself (provided he does not confine his subject-matter to the Greeks, who have already besung themselves far better than we can sing them, and to the Romans, who were besung by our Elizabethan poets better than they ever will be sung again), than in singing whatsoever noble deeds were done of old by men of like passions with ourselves, and above all, by men of our own race, who were our spiritual forefathers, containing in themselves, though undeveloped and unconscious, the seeds of all which England has become since, and may become hereafter. Surely, in the old Norse and Teutonic legends lies a mine of manful teaching for this or any other age; and if, as we do not think, the Middle-ages and the heroisms of the three Edwards' time, be already exhausted, what an untouched field for all noble lessons still lies fallow in the Elizabethan age, its statesmen, generals, sea-rovers, martyrs! If any man does not see the heroism and the poetry of that time, we can only say of him, courteously

---

[4] The revolution in geology to which Kingsley refers was being created and popularised by such works as Charles Lyell's *Principles of Geology* (1830) and Robert Chambers's *Vestiges of Creation* (1844). Baron Georges Cuvier (1769–1832) was one of the pioneers of palaeontology.

but firmly, that he is one who will see the heroism of no time whatsoever, unless he be taught it, as he has been taught the deeds of Leonidas
or Cocles, at second hand, and by accredited authorities; which is,
simply, not to be able to see the heroic element at all, in any true and
real sense, or to any poetic and creative purpose.[5]

These thoughts, or rather hints, desultory and fragmentary—for we
confess to having worked none of them out—have been stirred in us
by Mr Arnold's poems, and the sensible preface which precedes them.

Some four years ago a volume of *Poems by A*, were reviewed in this
magazine, much praised, and much blamed—perhaps somewhat too
severely; the excuse for which fault must be, our honest and kindly
vexation at the strange inequality in the poems which we perceived.[6]
Last year a second volume appeared by the same author entitled
Empedocles on Etna, and other Poems; and this year we have a third
volume, composed of certain new poems, and of some, but in our
opinion, not all of the best, from the two preceding volumes. The *Sick
King in Bokhara*, for instance, one of the wisest, most simple, and
most genial of the poems, has been omitted. *Empedocles* has been
omitted altogether: therefore we shall say nothing of it (being bound
in honour to ignore all words which are retracted by the Author),
except to express our pleasure that one exquisite passage has been preserved, which we here quote at length, as a specimen of Mr Arnold's
quiet grace and scholarly power in handling classic materials:

> Far, far from hence
> The Adriatic breaks in a warm bay
> . . .
> For ever through the glens, placid and dumb.

We think that to this last volume, as a whole, justice has been done
by no reviewer, saving by the *Times* and the *Westminster Review*.[7]

---

[5] Kingsley's historical novel, *Hypatia*, set in fifth-century Alexandria, was
published in 1851, and it is clear that he had no objection to the use of historical
material as long as it was made meaningful to the present and engaged the
imagination. The story of the struggle between Cocles and Porsena is told in
Macaulay's *Lays of Ancient Rome* and Kingsley implies that this is a spontaneous
and imaginative treatment of the story, not an academic, second-hand experience,
but it should not be the *reader's* only experience of heroism.

[6] *Fraser's Magazine*, xxxix (May 1849), 570–86.

[7] *Times*, 4 Nov. 1853, 5: *Westminster Review*, v N.S. (Jan. 1854), 146–59.
J. A. Froude.

Doubtless old faults still linger in it. We confess frankly that there are certain poems in this volume which neither excite nor please us—*Switzerland*, for instance, and the *Scholar-Gipsy*: but after having (with regard to the last) found men whom we know to be sensible, and tasteful, and earnest, praising it as the best poem in the book, and as having taught them lessons worth learning, we feel it far more rational for us as critics to preserve a stoic ἐποχη, and to believe that now and then there may be matters which we do not understand, and honest and wholesome chords of feeling which in ourselves are still dull or dead. Whatsoever word has taught any man—especially a thoughtful and cultivated man—anything whatsoever, is not spoken in vain, and is not without the *divinae particulam aurae.*

But it is pleasant to find all agreeing that the later poems are the best, with the exception of that *Forsaken Merman*, the beauty of which we noticed three years ago, and which neither Mr Arnold himself, nor any other modern ballad-writer, is likely to surpass.

A long poem, *Sohrab and Rustum*—appears for the first time in this new volume, of which we may as well say at once, that it is to our tastes perfectly good. It is doubtless an attempt to reproduce a bygone form of life and old heroic ages; but it is an altogether successful attempt, with one exception, whereof we shall speak hereafter. When a poet brings forward not the mere stage-properties of a past age, the *hartshornen und bürgen, und harnischen* of the German epigram,[8] but the real humanity of it, and instead of going back to the past, brings the past forward to us, by showing the actors in it as men of like passions with ourselves, then, however far back he may go for his subject, it will never fail of interest; for then he gives us that which is both past and present, being eternal in the constitution of man. This it is, surely, which makes, and will make for ever, the oldest book in the world—the Hebrew History—the most modern, the most widely-interesting book in the world, because every peasant and child—ay, and if they would but open their eyes, and see what they are, every statesman and genius —are, while they read, themselves Job, Abraham, Joseph, David, Hezekiah; their own natures, struggles, sorrows, victories, are there in *esse* as well as in *posse*, in that world-wide story of the doings of men in

---

[8] ἐποχή: suspension of judgement. 'divinae particulam aurae': a particle of the divine spirit. Horace, *Satires* 2.2.79. 'hartshornen und bürgen, und harnischen': a puzzling phrase which seems to be an attempt to play with English (hartshorn) and German words rather in the manner of Carlyle.

the little Judaean country, ages ago. So, in a less degree, with Homer. As long as a remnant of the old Norse sea-roving shift and thrift lingers in British hearts, Odysseus will be the ideal sailor; as long as the Anglo-Saxon glories in victorious battle with the wild beasts of the forest and the brute powers of nature, Hercules, Theseus, Perseus, will have ever new and everlasting significance for him. And thus Mr Arnold, out of that old Shah-Nameh, and the mythic struggles of Persians and Tartars, of Iran and Turan, has brought a poem which has to do with any age, and which may raise noble feelings in the heart, and noble tears in the eyes of a modern Englishman, as well as of a Homeric Greek or a Paladin of Charlemagne.

By putting this aim, we suppose, honestly before himself, Mr Arnold has not been afraid of that simple style and those homely words and objects, which we believe to be truly epic, because the epos, by the greatness of its subject-matter and its character—or rather by faith in their greatness—dare and can raise to its own loftiness the whole surrounding scenery, 'the totality of its cosmos', as a German might say.[9] Hence the noble homeliness of the *Iliad* and the *Odyssey*, and hence, also, the everlasting human freshness of them. Ariosto, too—great and forgotten poet—as well as Dante, has this excellence. It is wonderful, if we analyze the *Orlando*, how little 'poetic diction' there is in it; how quietly and faithfully he tells his story just as if he saw it, trusting to the noble metre which he wields almost unconsciously—so completely has he mastered it—to lift the whole into the region of a triumphal music. Even more remarkable is Spenser's stately homeliness, as we should expect from a man of purer mind and loftier purpose. But, no more to compare great things with small, we will say that when we opened *Sohrab and Rustum*, and read thus in the first two pages:

> But when the grey dawn stole into his tent
> . . .
> And he rose quickly on one arm, and said:

When we read thus—though the word 'tent' seemed to us to be repeated somewhat too often—we sprang up with great joy, and cried, 'Thank heaven, here is the man for whom we have been longing for

[9] Such a phrase as the 'totality of its cosmos', used to describe a work of art, could have been found in any of the German Idealist or Romantic writers, for instance in the work of Schelling, Fichte, Hegel, the Schlegels, even Novalis. German philosophy was associated with rather pretentious language of this sort.

years; a man who has written two whole pages without the slightest taint of 'poetry' in it! Farewell Baileys and Smiths, ay, even greater names, till you change to something more like this[10] Here is a man who is doing exactly what you do not do, and not doing exactly what you do; and we will read him every line, and trust him utterly to the very end of his poem, for he evidently has something worth hearing to say, from the quiet way in which he takes his time about saying it, and from his certainty that it is quite beautiful enough in itself, without his decking it up in castoff frippery. And lastly', said we to ourselves, 'here is a man who could translate Homer, as it has never been translated yet.' As we read on, we found that our auguries had not been false. The poem rises gradually, the story evolving itself simply and vividly, and giving the reader, as it proceeds, backward glimpses into the past which make all intelligible; being as an artistic whole, a more complete one, saving the *Merman*, than we know of in any poetry which the young men of the present day have produced.

Through page after page is continued, without apparent effort, a strain of masculine and truly heroical poetry, of which the following is a fair specimen:

> But Sohrab look'd upon the horse and said:
> 'Is this then Ruksh?
> . . .
> Till then, if Fate so wills, let me endure.'

This we call poetry worthy to be written by brave men and read by brave men. Nine-tenths of what we see printed we do not consider worthy to be read by men, or by women either. If we have given a long extract, it is because the general even and stately roll of the poem can hardly be felt in a short one. A poem which depends on its spangles for success may easily be exhibited by producing a sample or two of the spangles. One whose intrinsic value is in the subject, the rhythm, and the key not in the adventitious ornament; which is, in a word, an organic body; cannot be done justice to by a few scraps; and a reviewer must in such cases (rare enough, alas! they are) beware of following the example of the old Greek pedant, and bringing a brick to market as a sample of his house.

---

[10] Alexander Smith and Philip James Bailey were linked together as 'Spasmodic' poets. Bailey's *Festus* was published in 1839 and he went on expanding it in a randomly metaphysical way until 1889.

One point seems questionable about this poem, and that is the end of it. Why, after all the human interest of the poem, are we to turn suddenly off to mere nature and nature-description, beautiful as that may be?

> But the majestic river floated on
> Out of the mist and hum of that low land
> Into the frosty starlight, and there moved
> Rejoicing, through the lone Chorasmian waste
> Under the solitary moon.

And so on, for some twelve or fourteen lines more, every one and all of them life-like, perfect, both as parts and as a whole: but why here?—why end with this? True, the poem began with the Oxus, and ends with it also; but is that right, even in an episode? If the poet cannot always show how his subject arises out of eternity, he should surely show how it returns to it again; there must be some solace; the mind must have something on which to rest, after the chances and changes of this mortal life; something to calm his excitement, without deadening his interest, and to make him feel that after all The Powers are just, that it is better with the righteous in his misery, than with the evil in his prosperity. Sophocles surely always does this; Shakespeare always. And if Mr Arnold was not minded to do it here, he had far better have ended with

> And Rustum and his son were left alone,

so compelling the reader to work out the problem in his own mind, than have tried to turn our human interest and affection from them, by telling us about the Oxus. Who cares whither the Oxus goes, or what becomes of it, while Rustum is lying in the sand by his dead son, like one of 'Giamschid's fallen pillars in Persepolis'? The Oxus, and all the rivers on earth, yea all nature, and the sun and moon, if they intrude themselves at such a moment, are simply impertinences. Rustum and his son are greater than they; nearer to us than they. Our spirits are hovering lovingly round their spirits; and as for the Oxus and its going into the Aral Sea, or the Red Sea—Let it go! Surely Mr Arnold has not fallen into this mistake of malice prepense? Surely this is not a remnant of that old fault of his, the affecting—for no young man really does more than affect—to believe that man is less than phenomenal nature, and a part of it, and that while the Oxus, and the stars, and the Ural Sea, go on right and fulfil their destinies, it is somewhat beneath a wise man to make himself unhappy about the puny little human beings who fight, and love, and do right and do wrong upon its banks? He would not surely wish us to believe that all the noble human pathos, and spiritual experience which he has been displaying throughout the poem, is at heart cold and unreal, a thing which has been put on for forty pages, and then pulled off again at the sight of any river in the world?

Tristram and Iseult is exceedingly beautiful, though there are faults in it which contravene, we think, the very canon which Mr Arnold has learnt so well from the Greeks. The parts are not subordinated enough to the whole; mere scene-painting—admirable painting, nevertheless—occupies too much space, especially in the last part, till one loses the human interest, and, as the old proverb has it, 'cannot see the wood for the trees'; there is at once too much and too little of the dramatic element, the form of the poem being changed again and again from dialogue to description, and *vice versa*, a method which for such subjects is certainly not classic, and can always be escaped by strict labour, working the whole either into drama or into narrative. This fault in form, sadly common in our days, is beneath Mr Arnold's scholarship as it is beneath his powers. And we must complain a little, too, of his having given two children to Iseult of Brittany (Ysonde les blaunches mains), Tristram's lawful wife, and so deserting the old myth of the Mort d'Arthur, and losing the delicate problem of humanity which that wonderful book gives us—how Tristram, on his marriage night, remembered his true love, Ysonde of Ireland, and never consummated his marriage with the innocent Ysonde les Blaunches Mains, 'so that', says the old romancer, in his simple Homeric way, 'she weened that there had been no pleasance save kissing and clipping.' We wish that Mr Arnold had followed even this expedient—deeply natural and human, however fanciful—for helping Tristram out of the blame of open adultery, which deadens our interest in him in the poem, and brings it down painfully near the level of Balzac's *Jane la Pale*. And yet those children and that blighted motherhood, once conceived in his mind, must have been too tempting to be thrown away again; and as they stand, they form an idyllic picture, of which let readers judge:

> This cirque of open ground
> Is light and green;
> . . .
> Told them an old world Breton history.

If the poem has lost as a whole, we cannot deny that we have gained by such a creation as this. Only we complain of that 'Vivian and Merlin' story at the end, much on the same ground that we complained of the impertinent river at the end of *Rustum*. Who cares about Vivian and Merlin, with Iseult and those two children in sight? If it be answered, that the episode completes the poem, by showing that these old sports of the imagination were all the widow had to care for now, and that that is the sort of tale she would have told her children; we must answer that we do not think that the sort of tale at all; that it is not a child's tale, or told in a mother's way; that it is a highly-finished picture —too highly-finished, indeed—and that it is little but a picture, the outward details being over-laboured, to the loss of the dramatic interest, more than in any other part of the poem. It is beautiful, exceedingly beautiful—there is no demur on that score—but it has, we think, absolutely no business where it is.

We find fault: but that is not to be supposed for a moment to countervail our great delight in this volume, or rather, in the principal poems in it, and our high hopes of Mr Arnold's future career. He wants something still—something which he himself can give himself; and what that is, we can hardly define: but we are not fully satisfied with him yet; we fancy him *seipso minor*. If our fancy be true, so much the better for him. Let him develop himself, as his father's son is bound to develop, and do better still.

We had a word to say about Mr Arnold's Greek metres: but we shall postpone it till we know a little more about metre ourselves. The whole science of English metre is still in its infancy; we happen to fancy that wide misconceptions about it are popular just now. But till we have reduced our own thoughts on the point into something more of form, we shall refrain from judging Mr Arnold, having no certain canons whereby to judge him.

One last word. Would that Mr Arnold would employ his great powers in giving us that translation of Homer, at which we hinted before. It is a work which must be done soon, if we wish to have Homer live, as he ought, in the hearts of Englishmen. And in these days of popular education, few greater boons could be conferred on the masses than such a translation as should give them their share of that great world-inheritance of the human race, which we hold to be contained in both the poems, and especially in the *Odyssey*, and instil into the working men who are educating themselves, without injuring their eagerness for progress, their aspirations for the future, something of that self-restraint and stately calm of which they are often now sadly in want, and which Mr Arnold has set forth in the following excellent passage:

> I know not how it is, but commerce with the ancients appears to me to produce, in those who constantly practise it, a steadying and composing effect upon their judgement, not of literary works only, but of men and events in general. They are like persons who have had a very weighty and impressive experience; they are more truly than others under the empire of facts, and more independent of the language current among those with whom they live.[11]

True, there is a darker side to this picture. Many a man, by resting in the study of Greek and Roman literature, has made of himself a moral, as well as an aesthetic dilettante; and has quenched, by a lazy and often a somewhat sensuous optimism, those higher aspirations which would have fitted him to bear a part in the active life of his time. It might be rejoined to Mr Arnold, 'I, again, know not how it is, but commerce with the ancients seems to me to produce, in those who constantly practise it, a paralyzing and effeminating effect upon their judgement of men and events. They are like persons who have had too mighty, and yet too narrow, an experience; they are under the influence of past facts, rather than of present ones, or indeed of any facts which have occurred during the last eighteen hundred years; and so independent of the language current among those with whom they live, that they know nothing of what is going on in the modern mind; cannot address a congregation, if they be parsons, in intelligible English; and when they enter public life, are more liable than any class of men to become helplessly entangled in the pettiest red-tape routine, because they are ignorant of the great canons of action or judgement by which Europe has progressed since the destruction of the Roman empire, and have bound their own hands and weakened their own sympathies by admitting to the title of ancients, and considering worthy of their study, only a few writers in two countries of the whole world, and those men who flourished only during a very few centuries of the world's long existence.'

Here is the darker side of the picture, which has been often enough realized already, and is realized, we much fear, often enough now, in the

[11] 1853 Preface, Allott, p. 604.

common rooms of Oxford. But it is only by being partial and exclusive, by being, in fact, too narrow to allow materials for a fair induction, that the study of the ancients can be hurtful. By this, and also by forgetting what, in spite of the smiles of some of our readers, the world will have to recollect again ere long, that since certain events took place in Judea 1854 years ago, the self-content and calm of the ancients has become impossible for the human race; that from that era aspiration and progress, and a mighty hunger, have become the heritage of every nation which is not dead and rotten; and that, in all its various forms, however fantastical and hideous some of them may be, this hunger after 'the ideal', 'progress', 'salvation', 'a church', 'a republic', 'a kingdom of God', 'a heaven', 'an eternity'—call it what you will— must be looked at, and analysed, and taught to help and to understand itself; and that unless the study of the ancients is presented (as it can well be) in such a form as will not merely lull that hunger, but help it to reach that unseen thing for which it craves, and show it more clearly what that thing is, mankind will toss old Greece and Rome to the winds as unmeaning dilettantisms, and go on in its fierce and confused search after That, which it has not seen, and cannot name, and knows not where to find; but is full sure that it exists, and that it must be found, and will be found at last.

7

Arnold ∾ *The Strayed Reveller and Other Poems* ∾ 1849
Empedocles on Etna and Other Poems ∾ 1852
Poems ∾ 1853
Alexander Smith ∾ *Poems* ∾ 1853

William Caldwell Roscoe, *Prospective Review*, x
(February 1854), 99–118

It would be unfair to Mr Arnold to measure him only by the edition of his poems he has last given to the world; but on the other hand his mode of publishing is a little unfair to the public. In a new edition bearing the author's name, previously concealed, one naturally expects to find embodied, if not all, at least all the best poems contained in the previous impressions. So far is this from being the case in the present instance, that the 'New Edition', while it repeats a great mass of inferior matter, omits from its pages much that gave value to the older ones, and replaces this omission by new poems almost invariably of inferior merit. We are not willing to believe that Mr Arnold has arranged this last volume as a deliberate selection of his best efforts. Its form must have been influenced by some other motive; but whatever may have been the exigencies of the author, they result very unfavourably to the purchaser, who is obliged to buy either a part of the poems only, or many of them twice over. Those whose resources are not unlimited, will perhaps do best to possess themselves of the second set of poems by 'A'. in preference to either of the other two volumes.[1]

William Caldwell Roscoe, 1823–59. Roscoe, with R. H. Hutton and Walter Bagehot, contributed also to the *National Review* (1855–64), which produced some of the freshest criticism of the period.

[1] The *Empedocles* volume was cancelled and the copies withdrawn by Arnold.

It was necessary to dispatch this little preliminary quarrel with Mr Arnold in order to come to his poems with a heart freed from any rankling sense of injury. Once taken in hand, his book must bring genuine pleasure to every one whose judgement it is worth a man's while to interest. Mr Arnold measures himself too justly to claim a place among the kings of song, but below the topmost heights of Parnassus lie many pleasant ranges and happy pastures, among whose denizens he may enjoy a not ignoble rank. He starts from a vantage ground rare in these days. He possesses the uncommon and valuable conviction that poetic art has its nature and its rules which admit of being studied with advantage. Nor does he want the more intrinsic attributes of a poet. A keen and refined sense of beauty, sometimes finding its expression in phrases of exquisite felicity, a mind and artistic faculty, trained, and disciplined to reticence, and an imagination of considerable scope and power, are no mean qualifications.

One of the few observations worth noting (if it be worth noting) in that strangely barren work, the *Life and Letters of Byron*, is one in which his Lordship maintains that there are qualities in poetry closely corresponding with those which distinguish the gentleman in life, and that the same sort of vulgarity may be found in the false assumptions of art as in those of the world.[2] Now Mr Arnold's are eminently the poems of a gentleman, and what is, perhaps, part of this characteristic, they are thoroughly genuine and sincere, the author is always himself and not a pretence at any one else; there is no affectation, no strained effort, no borrowed plumage; he presents himself without disguise, and without false shame; is dignified, simple, and self-restrained. If not always profound, at least he does not affect profundity; his strokes bring his thought or sentiment out clear and decisive; he is never guilty of false

The immediate object of the 1853 Preface was to justify the absence of *Empedocles*.

[2] Thomas Moore's *Letters and Journals of Lord Byron: with Notices of his Life* (2 vols. 1830) was the standard *Life* throughout the nineteenth century, and though other biographies and collections of letters were published, this is probably the 'barren' work to which Roscoe refers. The discussion on vulgarity in literature, particularly the vulgarity of Hunt and Keats, is in Byron's defence of Pope, part of which is reprinted in Moore, *Letters and Journals*, ii, 477–9. For the full text of this see 'Further Addenda' to *Observations on 'Observations'*. *A Second Letter to John Murray on the Rev W. L. Bowles's Strictures on the Life and Writings of Pope* in Byron's *Letters and Journals* (ed. R. E. Prothero, 1901), v, 586–92.

show and glitter, and those who have read some of our modern poets, will recognise the inestimable comfort of not having to press through an umbrageous forest of verbiage and heterogeneous metaphors in order to get at a thin thought concealed in its centre. There is artistic finish too in his verse (though, as we wish hereafter to remark, not in his conceptions); not the finish of high polish, but the refined ease and grace of a taste pure by nature and yet conscientiously cultivated. Hence instead of congratulating ourselves that we have read him, we find a pleasure in actually reading him, and take him up again and again with undiminished freshness and enjoyment. Partly it is that he does not make too great a demand upon us; his light free air refreshes us. Instead of being hemmed in by that majesty and terror which make the vicinity of the Alps oppressive, we stroll with lighter hearts on breezy heaths and uplands. Like Wordsworth, Mr Arnold owes part of his charm to the very absence of deep and engrossing feelings in his nature.

A considerable portion of these poems are self-descriptive, or more properly, self-betraying. These owe their interest chiefly to any fresh indication they may afford us of the tone of feeling and mode of thought prevalent among some of our recent Oxford scholars.[3] Mr Arnold will perhaps be startled to hear that he belongs to an unchristian school, but we hasten to assure him that by saying this we do not mean to charge him with a limited faith in the eternity of punishment, or with nourishing views of his own on baptismal regeneration, or even declining to rest implicit confidence on the verbal inspiration of the Bible. We don't feel it to be our duty, in the phrase of angry brother clergymen, to give him an opportunity of explaining his views on these or any other similar important links in the orthodox manacles. We are indifferent as to whether he overbalances himself towards faith or towards works, and not anxious to inquire into his exact place among the three subdivisions of the three main classes of the *Edinburgh*. We are looking at the matter from the reverse point of view from that gentleman who said, 'Newman on the Soul' was a horribly atheistic book, but that Thomas Carlyle's works contained nothing contrary to sound Christian doctrine.

Probably, however, an error in dogmatic convictions can alone

---

[3] J. A. Froude, whose novel, *The Nemesis of Faith*, was published in 1849, probably represents best the tone of the Oxford doubt to which Roscoe is referring.

entitle us to call a man unchristian in his views; and that it would be more correct to say that Mr Arnold is of a *non*-Christian school. 'Oh, how shocking!' exclaimed a lady, on hearing a certain sonnet of Wordsworth's read aloud: 'he'd rather be a Pagan!' And so Mr Arnold (or his Muse, for it is with the poet not the man we deal) prefers to be a Pagan. In art the Greek is his model, and happily has he sometimes caught the clear Attic note. He is not a modern Greek like Shelley, nor an imitative scholar, but he has familiarised himself with Athenian poetry until the echo rings in his ears, and though when he is most himself he is least Greek, he often, both in force and expression, moulds himself, half consciously and half unconsciously, upon the impressions with which his mind is saturated. One might choose something more exactly in point than the following, but nothing more beautiful.

> Through the black, rushing smoke-bursts,
> Thick breaks the red flame.
> . . .
> The Night in its silence,
> The Stars in their calm.

But though in his art Mr Arnold is Greek, the thought and general feeling of his pieces are tinged with a more modern heathenism.

The greatest intellect of modern times cannot but have had an influence on modern thought even in the English Universities. There is nothing about Goethe in the Articles of the Church of England, and undergraduates at Oxford may read him with impunity. His philosophy and his practice have found echoes—confused and uncertain enough—but still easily recognisable in many English, even many Oxford, minds. We don't allude to his pantheistic tenets, for no sworn member of our English Church can be infected with these; but to his Philosophy of Life—the philosophy which says life is the art of self-development, and claims that we should devote ourselves to conscious self-formation without ulterior object, which would have the nature of a man revolve on its own axis, and treats religion as a step in education, and not the highest step.[4] This is the philosophy which lies hidden in the centre of many an English mind, and it has received an impulse from a very different and less generally suspected quarter. Where Goethe stepped

---

[4] This is very much how a well-read Victorian might summarise Goethe's philosophy of life, whether from reading him in the original or through English versions. The most likely source is *Wilhelm Meister*, possibly from Carlyle's translation.

with conscious searching eyes, the mild egotism of Wordsworth led him without thought or clear perception of his whereabouts. His self-occupation was too simple and complete for him to be conscious of it. It was quiet, inoffensive and unlimited. The most important thing in the world was the cultivation of William Wordsworth for himself, the next important thing his cultivation for the sake of mankind. Goethe puts quietly on one side that central spirit of the Christian revelation which makes the dependent affections the highest element in our nature, and places our noblest attainable life in that service which is perfect freedom. He would have us all patent digesters, or rather assimilaters, of knowledge and experience; and, indeed, his vast ranging genius and cold temperament made him, if any man, capable of the independent position he assumes. But feebler minds that strive to hold this place are constantly and painfully reminded of their own in-sufficiency. They 'stretch weak hands', not 'of faith and prayer', but of the self-distrust begotten by frequent failure, and of the dismay and heart-sinking that arise from finding their steps are not right onward to the proposed goal, but wavering, sliding, too often retrogressive. Their affections, whether strong or weak, outbalance their will: they suffer from all the short-comings of their philosophy, and have not the heart to avail themselves of its consolations, such as they are. Goethe, as Mr Arnold himself says in one of his finest poems,

> Was happy, if to know
> Causes of things, and far below
> His feet to see the lurid flow
> Of terror and insane distress,
> And headlong fate, be happiness.

But to few is it given to taste such happiness. Few have the will and fewer yet the power to sever those threads which knit them up in the common bond of humanity. Some cold tempers there are which can stand aloof and quietly survey the field of circumstance. They quarrel neither with their own short-comings nor those of others; all that is, is if not well, at least not to be helped; they are indifferentists, calm and apathetic ruminators. They lie down in life and chew the cud of destiny. They have opinions; but whether they are true they don't know, nor does it much signify; things must take their course. They are phenomena and content to be phenomena, and they rarely harass them-selves with any stronger feeling than that of a gentle contempt for others. Mr Arnold is far from being of this class, his nature is too genial to permit it, but he is touched with the barren doctrine that it is a man's business to be investigating and following the 'Law of his being', and that therein lies his road to rest and happiness; he yearns to walk by sight, and kneels idolatrously to wisdom, and sings of Fate and 'Unknown Powers' that control the destiny of man; but in such wavering strains, and mixed sometimes with thoughts so much higher, that it is not easy to estimate what real hold the Oxford sublimate of Goethe has upon his mind. Like others of his school, weary of the internecine war of self, his troubled eyes turn to Nature, and he sees in the calm routine of physical nature something that contrasts so peacefully with the jar of his own endeavours, that he not only seeks the soothing balm of loveliness and freshness that she pours into our wounds, but he gives a moral significance to her invariable round of operations, and personifies her as the ideal of voluntary obedience to the law. So vivid is his personification, and so warm his reverence, that it far outpasses the limits of our sympathy and admiration.

> Weary of myself, and sick of asking
> What I am, and what I ought to be
> · · ·
> Resolve to be thyself: and know, that he
> Who finds himself, loses his misery.

Perhaps it is hardly fair to quarrel so much with Mr Arnold's personal philosophy, when his poetry is so much better. He brings this sort of observation on himself however, by inflicting so much of the subject-matter of it upon his readers. His pages are crowded with personal poems when he has it in his power to write others infinitely superior to them. He must pardon us for saying that his own sensations and emotions are scarcely varied and profound enough, his philosophy and meditations on life scarcely valuable enough, to make a poetry employed in developing them capable of deeply moving and widely profiting the public mind. The intricacies of his intercourse with Marguerite are certainly not good love poems, and rarely anything better; and his mourning notes over the perplexities and distracting influences thrust upon the heart and mind in this

> Strange disease of modern life,
> With its sick hurry, its divided aims,
> Its head o'er-tasked, its palsied heart—

are apt to degenerate into mere bewailments. It is the part of a true and
manly poet to raise us above these troubles. We seek him, not to be
reminded of our shortcomings and imbecilities, but to be lifted into a
clearer air which may revive our spirit and purge our eyesight for a
new and more vigorous contest in the dusty plain. And Mr Arnold can
do this for us if he will. His fine, often exquisite sense of beauty, his
power of felicitous narration, his command over varied sentiment and
feeling (he has not attempted the delineation of violent passion), open
a field to him where he might occupy not only a high place, but one
peculiarly his own. Wordsworth and Tennyson have both left a tinge
of their peculiar characteristics in the fountain of Mr Arnold's poetry,
and there is something very charming in having poems analogous to the
short narrative or descriptive pieces in which Tennyson so often revels,
less gorgeous and rich in their beauty, but at the same time less turbid
and sensuous, and purified by something of the quieter insight and
higher refinement of Wordsworth. They are like Greek wine mingled
with water for a draught. In saying this we might convey a false
impression if we did not add that Mr Arnold is no mere compound;
everything he writes is perfectly his own; he has no trace of a copyist,
his genius is truly original and individual, and the resemblances we
advert to are, partly, only the legitimate and perfectly assimilated
influences of minds with which he has come in contact, and yet more
perhaps the traces of other influences so widely and subtly dispersed
that they may be called epidemic.

Tristram and Iseult is by far the most pleasing of these *quasi* narrative
poems, and, on the whole, the best thing in these volumes; and the
mould in which the story is cast, though at the first glance a little
perplexing, is ingenious, and has a charm of its own. No extract can, or
ought to be able to give any idea of a connected story, but we cannot
help indulging ourselves with this delightful picture of 'Iseult with the
white hands', as she watches by the bed of the sick Tristram.

> What Knight is this, so weak and pale
> . . .
> The sweetest Christian soul alive,
> Iseult of Brittany.

Sohrab and Rustum is a fine poem, but less to our taste. Mr Arnold's
forte is description, but here there is a little too much of it. The poem
is too long for the action: but throughout the diction is stately and

sustained, and the ornament and imagery rich, and in keeping with it. Yet it interests us more by the mode of its narration and its decorations, than by the inner kernel of sentiment and action. It is more like a fine carving than a good picture. One merit it has which is very rarely to be found in its author. It is conceived as a whole and executed as a whole, a poem—not a piece of joinery. We wish Mr Arnold could be prevailed on to bestow more pains on some of the main requisites of his art. If he would read his own preface with attention, he might profit by some excellent observations contained in it. No man ever insisted more strongly on the excellence of wholeness and of a due subordination of details to the main composition, on the importance of the choice of a subject and the careful construction of the poem; few men have ever more systematically disregarded their own preaching. It is the one great and prominent defect of these poems that they give the reader no satisfaction as poems, but only scattered rays of enjoyment. Mr Arnold's conceptions want force and unity: what is worse, they some-times want substance. His minor poems especially, even when delight-ing us most, are apt to leave us with a sense of shortcoming, arising from the want of unity in their thought, or some hidden weakness in their conclusion. They are full of flaws. Take the following poem for an example.

> Yes; in the sea of life enisl'd
>   . . .
> The unplumb'd, salt, estranging sea.

The main sentiment and the expression, none will deny to possess beauty, but how abortive the conclusion! To have our expectations raised by the queries in the last verse, and then to be put off with an indefinite deity repeated twice over, as if that solved the whole matter —this is a little too trying; not all the significance and rich cadence of the one last line can restore our equanimity. Again, in *Tristram and Iseult*, it is wonderful how Mr Arnold's sense of completeness could fail him so utterly as to allow him to conclude with a totally new and dis-connected story lying at a tangent to the circle of his original one.

Hazlitt, speaking of painting, says that the 'English school is dis-tinguished by what are called *ébauches*, rude, violent attempts at effect, and a total inattention to the details or delicacy of finish'.[5] This is

[5] From Hazlitt's essay 'On Means and Ends', which Roscoe might have read either in *Literary Remains* (1836), or in *Winterslow* (1850).

applicable to modern English poetry, and Mr Arnold has done good service by the practical protest that his own poems afford against this hasty glaring style. He has both delicacy and purity of finish, and this is one thing which makes his book such agreeable reading. In this respect his classical education and tastes have stood him in good stead; and it is disappointing to find them exercising so disproportionately small an influence over the form of his conceptions and the choice of his subjects.

So fully is Mr Arnold himself aware of the importance of this latter point, that he has excluded one of his larger poems from the last edition on the grounds that the situation embodied in it is one from which no poetical enjoyment can be derived. Apropos of this, and of some difference with his critics, as to the field afforded by ancient subjects for the exercise of modern art, he has written a preface in which he develops a theory of poetry, defends the ancients as models for the artist, and rebukes the false pretensions of the age and of his own critics—but distantly and politely. He is a little sore; but he keeps a steady countenance. 'Non me tua turbida terrent dicta', he says, 'Dii me terrent et Jupiter hostis.' He is not afraid of them. We have as little respect for the critics as Mr Arnold, perhaps less, and are quite at one with him as to the false pretensions of the present age, so we will confine ourselves to a few words upon the earlier part of his preface.

Here again it is the leading idea which appears to be defective, while the subordinate observations are many of them extremely just and valuable. His love for the Athenian Drama has misled Mr Arnold. He has rightly pointed out its most prominent feature when he says that it delineates great *actions*. But he goes on to tell us that great actions can alone afford the subject-matter for excellent poetry. This is not so. It is the main defect of the Greek tragic art, the measure of its shortcoming, that it advanced thus far and no farther; that in its development it rigidly subordinated everything to the delineation of some great action. This Mr Arnold thinks its highest glory. He quotes Aristotle (as conclusively as a lawyer does Coke on Littleton), to prove that our love of poetry is based on the pleasure we take in any imitation or representation whatever; a poetical representation, however, he says, must be one from which men can derive enjoyment, for Hesiod says that the Muses were born that they might be 'a forgetfulness of evils, and a truce from cares'; and Schiller says that 'All art is dedicated to joy, and there is no higher and no more serious problem than how to

make men happy'. Thus it is required of the poet, that he should add
not only to the knowledge but also to the happiness of men. The
eternal objects of poetry, among all nations and at all times, Mr Arnold
goes on to say, are human actions. Hence the highest poetry concerns
itself with the selection of such actions as in their delineation shall give
the highest pleasure. Now all this appears to us narrow and false. It is a
limitation necessarily required indeed, if we are to give the highest place
in the history of poetic art to the Greek drama, but not otherwise.
Without venturing to contradict Aristotle, we may certainly say that
the poetic art is not limited to the representation of human actions, in
however wide a sense we may employ the term. We have poems to the
Lesser Celandine, to a Mouse, to the Skylark—nay, we have abundance
of pieces which involve no picture of any thought or sentiment of the
poet himself, but are purely descriptive of natural objects. Will it be
said that the action here delineated is that of the poet in delineating?
This is as if we should say the picture of a flower was the picture of the
artist painting it; and, at any rate, we should then have in a poem whose
subject is an action in the ordinary sense—two actions delineated, one
the operation of the artist, the other the action he has chosen for his
subject, and it is the latter alone with which we are now dealing. And
an action is not only not the sole, it is not the highest, subject of the
poetic art. Man is higher than his actions, and it is in the representation
of the whole man that the romantic drama soars far beyond its classical
rival. In Sophocles the action is predominant, and the characters are
interesting as they elucidate it. In Shakespeare the characters are predominant, and the events gain their main interest from the insight
which, by their aid, the poet contrives to give us into some human
heart. Types of passion and sentiment suffice for the Greek, he clothes
abstractions in broad if not life-like outlines; but the Englishman must
represent the varied forms which these same passions and sentiments
assume in given individual men. There is no doubt that the easiest and
most effective mode by which the poetic art can interest men, is through
the sympathy of the passions, and that these can only be displayed in
some action; but this is not the highest interest that art can afford. On
the stage, and for some time even in the closet, it is some special scene
that interests us in a great play, some crisis in the action—Lear howling
to the winds, or Macbeth towards his design creeping like a ghost; but
the more cultivated our taste, and the more intimate our knowledge of
the work, the more does our interest centre upon the whole character,

and it is the vivid images of the represented men and women—the noble credulous Moor—the keen, crafty Richard—it is Imogen, Juliet, Hamlet, who live in our hearts and memories, and afford the highest pleasure that art is capable of yielding. We thoroughly coincide with Mr Arnold in his criticism on Shakespeare, and in the necessity of that due subordination of expression to the perfecting of the main conception. But we should scarcely acquiesce in the grounds on which he bases his dicta. Let poetry be what it will, it is valuable to draw a distinction between it and art. Poetry creates, art moulds these creations into the highest forms of which they are capable. The poet moves from an instinctive impulse *qua* poet, *qua* artist he employs this impulse for a remoter purpose. It is art, to quote Mr Arnold's quotation from Goethe, that is '*Architectonicè* in the highest sense'. A man may be a greater poet than artist—Shakespeare was such a one; he may be a far greater artist than poet, such was Goethe. In all this Mr Arnold agrees; indeed, he says almost the same thing; but he makes the attainment of pleasure the highest test of art, and, what makes the matter of interest here, uses it for the education of practical consequences. This is to introduce the doctrines of utilitarianism, exploded from the field of morals, into that of aesthetics. True art never fails to bring enjoyment, as good morals never fail to bring happiness; but the artist is going as far wrong as the moralist if he makes the enjoyment his work is calculated to afford to others, the test and object of his labours. Art seeks the highest, and the rules that lead to the highest admit of no such simple and narrow a gauge.

As to the choice of ancient subjects, we will only just say that, quite acquiescing in the poverty and groundless assumption of the doctrine which would limit the poet to modern interests, it is yet true that the points on which we can touch the ancient world with sufficient closeness to embody in art the materials it affords, are few, and require much tact and skill in the avoidance of the Scylla and Charybdis which beset them—the danger, on the one hand, of making them hybrid and untruthful, by the admixture of modern ideas, and that, on the other, of finding them too remote not only from the interests of the reader, but, what is more important, from the sympathies of the poet himself. More than this, the higher you go in art, the fewer are these points of contact. Restrict yourself to great actions and single exhibitions of the 'permanent passions', and the task is less difficult, but to delineate a complex individual character as it existed in ancient Egypt, would be hard, to say the least of it. *Mycerinus*, we confess, falls dead on our ears.

We will do Mr Arnold the justice to let the last words be his own, and on a field more congenial both to himself and us.

MEMORIAL VERSES

Of Mr Alexander Smith we have not a great deal to say. He belongs to the firework school. He falls upon us in glittering showers, red, blue, and white stars, which vanish into airy nothing, and are succeeded by others; now he delights our eyes with the rapid whizz of a Catharine wheel, and then explodes with a burst of crackers. He fires blank cartridge, and has a fine glow like Bengal lights. His business is neither with thought nor feeling, but with imagery, *pur et simple*. His object is to be amazing, not consecutive. He is exactly like a kaleidoscope, every two or three lines he turns himself round, and, *presto!* all the bits of glass run into new shapes and contrasts of colour, beautiful and glittering, but without much connection with what has gone before. Yet this, perhaps, is too mean a simile, for Mr Smith is *grandiose* and magniloquent. Nothing can be too large or too extravagant. His forte is a power of unbounded exaggeration. One of his habits, and it is not quite peculiar to him, is to dilate the proportions of old fancies. He takes a simile and multiplies it by ten, and seems to think that its intensity is increased in the same proportion. Thus many poets have used the image of a sceptre or a crown to denote how high a price they were willing to pay for some given object. Mr Smith is more lavish, he measures by 'a hundred sheaves of sceptres', or by 'a planet's gathered crowns'. This reminds us of a lady who improved on the expression of armies or legions to denote quantity, and used to speak of a 'hundred thousand barracks' of things. Wordsworth has the fine line, 'Come weak as is a breaking wave'. But Mr Smith says, 'My heart is weak as a great globe all sea'. Weak he may be; but this is to be very weak indeed. A pause in conversation is a 'ghastly chasm in the talk', and we hear of poets 'blanching the braggart cheek of the world'. Most men, our author tells us, are 'shut by sense from grandeur'. His readers are in the reverse case.

What, then, does this author possess? Something he must have to recommend him to his many readers. He has a vivid sense of external beauty; still more, he has a wonderful wealth of diction; and, above all, an unexampled genius for the detection and reproduction of those sort

of analogies on which depend the beauty of similes. Of the art of
making similes, varied, striking, and sometimes even significant, Mr
Smith is a master. Still his fancy, though naturally rich and varied, is
confined by the poverty of the rest of the mind, and runs within narrow
limits ever and ever the same sparkling round. Of him that terrible
French sentence, quoted by Mr Arnold, is terribly true—*Il dit tout ce
qu'il veut, mais malheureusement il n'a rien à dire.* He not only has
nothing to say, he does not seem to wish to say anything. He appears
seriously to believe that poetry is the art of collecting and arranging
descriptions and similes. 'Our chief talk', says the poet, who is the hero
of Mr Smith's *Life Drama*,

> Was to draw images from everything,
> And images lay thick upon our talk
> As shells on ocean sands.

We can well believe it. His personages lead the conversation up to
similes, and, if that fails, ask for them still more definitely. Mr Wilton
is an elderly country gentleman, with a capital cellar. This is what he
says:

> Rain similes upon his corse like tears—
> The youth you spoke of was a glowing moth,
> Born in the eve and crushed before the dawn.

And then all the company take their turn at it. The youth in question
is a hydrophobic young man who, being disappointed in his poetical
ambition, 'foams at God, and dies'. There is one good simile made on
him.

> Mine is pathetic,
> A ginger-beer bottle burst.

This little bit of wit, and very good wit, is the only enlivening thing in
the poem, and as this extends over two hundred pages, they are happy
who have not got to review it, and can put it down when they are tired.
Yet, that there are persons who enjoy this sort of reading, the sale of
these poems has proved beyond dispute. Perhaps they are read because
they demand no effort whatever from the reader. The mere sense of
beauty is gratified; rich and often beautiful imagery (however deformed
by an extravagance and bombast that give one actual pain) comes
crowding, line after line, like the pageantry of a stage procession. For
the first few phrases, and, indeed, as long as one can nourish the hope

that this gorgeous dress contains anything, one thinks it delightful. Soon the endless and empty repetition becomes wearisome, and, before long, intolerable. The Drama of Life is in the school of Festus; but Festus, with all its turgidity, has vigour and ideas, if not profound thought or insight. A man may, perhaps, do without thought. Byron had none, but he had passion and a wide experience. But Mr Smith has neither thoughts, sentiments, nor experience. He has been compared to Keats, but Keats is solid and coherent in comparison, and had, too, a far subtler and wider-ranging sense of beauty. This is mere confectionery. A man rises from it like one who has supped, 'not wisely, but too well', on trifle.

The only genuine sentiment that appears in the whole of this book is a passionate longing to be a poet. Mr Smith does, indeed, attempt to portray the passion of love, but from hearsay evidently. His are but shallow and gorgeous descriptions of that sort of thing, which some modern novelist has well hit off as consisting in the lovers 'looking in one another's eyes, and combing one another's hair with their fingers'.[6] There is nothing either refined or natural in Mr Smith's description of love. It is merely a selection of hyperbolical phrases of passion. But he appears to have a true and genuine desire, however frantically expressed, to be a poet. His writing shows, at least, an ardent love of beauty, and a keen ambition for fame. In spite of the weakest sentimentality about the mission of the Poet, and fabulous notions about setting the Age to music, there may be greater depth than these brilliant bubbles indicate. Supposing this work to be the efflorescence of very early youth, it is yet possible that a sedulous education and patient thought, and, above all, long silence, may enable the author to command materials in some degree worthy of the power of expression he has here displayed. The flattering reception he has had may have the happy effect of stimulating him to higher and more patient effort; it may have the unfortunate consequence of confirming him in the impression that he is already capable of writing a great poem.

[6] I have not been able to discover the source of this quotation.

8

Tennyson ᴖ *The Princess* ᴖ 1847

Charles Peter Chretien, *Christian Remembrancer*, xvii
(April 1849), 381–401

A poet's mind (the world owes the idea to the Poet Laureate) should
be like a cathedral.[1] It should stand in a free space of its own, and
consecrate the soil it stands on. No mean tenements should hem it in,
and hinder it from expanding in its fair proportions. There should be
room for the pilgrim to walk round it, approach and recede at pleasure,
and choose his own points from which to admire its beauty. Seen from
without, it should impress us with the multiplicity of its parts. Porch
and parvise, chantry and oratory, chapterhouse and cloister, should
project themselves in turn boldly forward, in pleasing contrast with the
grey mass behind. But however complex without, it should be eminently *one* within. Here we should trace, in its full solemnity, that Form
which all variety of detail must vary without concealing. Here, the
diversity of individual taste is to be lost in the majesty of the master
mind. In that capacious area, all are instinctively to look one way, to
think one thought, and wonder.

No metaphor, of course, embodies the whole truth. We doubt if
Mr Tennyson would admit, without qualification, even the portion of

Charles Peter Chretien, 1820–75, theologian and fellow of Oriel College,
Oxford, 1843–64. Arnoldian before the Preface, this review adopts Arnoldian
criteria for the form, imagery and action of a poem and criticises Tennyson's self-
conscious modernism.

[1] Wordsworth was poet laureate from 1843 to his death in 1850. Chretien's
image is a free adaptation of Wordsworth's claim in the Preface to *The Excursion*
(first published 1814) that all his work was essentially a whole and that the unpublished *Prelude* was related to that poem: 'the two works have the same kind
of relation to each other . . . as the ante-chapel has to the body of a gothic church
. . . his minor Pieces will be found by the attentive Reader to have such connections with the main Work as do the little cells, oratories, and sepulchral recesses,
ordinarily included in these edifices.'

truth contained in the above image. If his theory coincides with his practice, he would rather insist on the right of the poet to expend his energy in a series of detached efforts, leaving it to circumstance, to the sympathy of the reader, or the ingenuity of the critic, to bring out the unity of result. Be this as it may; many of his admirers have certainly been found not unwilling to accept the comparison. Who has not known Tennysonians, who were living in full and confident expectation of a coming *opus magnum*? Some indeed were more cautious, rejoicing rather in drawing distinctions between quantity and quality, and reminding all who cared to listen to a truism, that the number of consecutive lines under a single title had very little to do with the question, whether their favourite was a minor poet. But more of Mr Tennyson's admirers spoke of the 'crescent promise' of his song, and appealed boldly from the present to the future. They were prepared to allow that his poems, however beautiful, were more fragments than was quite desirable. Much more: in spite of their high finish, they struck more impartial and unfamiliar observers, as wanting in position and arrangement. Here was an antique statue glittering in the whiteness of its marble, and there a picture, somewhat Rubenesque, in a gold frame; on the one hand, Haroun Alraschid sat, in 'merriment of kingly pride', under a canopy; on the other, a weather-beaten S. Simeon prayed, harangued, and soliloquized from the top of his pillar. Sometimes the poet's scroll displayed combinations of grave words—good, and beauty, and duty, and love, and so forth—which puzzled the metaphysician, who endeavoured to make their meaning definite; a turn of the leaf brought the reader to some lucubrations of a half profane, half maudlin tone, and a very vinous and questionable morality. What does it all mean? we asked; or rather, what does the author mean? Is he content that his mind, as reflected in his volumes, should rival an auction room, or an embryo museum, both in the multifariousness and confusion of its beauties? Are the pictures never to be hung up, the statues never to be placed in their niches? Shall the caliph, and the pillar saint, and the Will Waterproof, be crowded together in a capacious tent, or picnic in common on the sward? Shall we never be shown how abstract philosophical speculation is made to bear on the beauties of nature, or cast a reflected light over dim pictures of imaginary ladies, some as sensuous, and all as sleepy, as any that Lely drew? Wait, was the answer to repeated questions—wait, till the longer poem comes.

Well, the world waited; not in the idleness of anxious suspense, for, in these busy times, fifteen years cannot be wasted with impunity. However, long as the pause was, Mr Tennyson was not forgotten in the crush and crowd of things. Poets, poetasters, poetry readers, a little while before the revolutions began, pricked their ears at the title of *The Princess*, like a horse (one of Mr Tennyson's stud, we own) which hears the corn-bin open. And no one who read the poem in simple-hearted-ness, content to seek for nothing more than new images, elaborate diction, a pleasing flow of not too exciting narrative, a day-dream of beauty with which pleasing forms from without could mingle without breaking it, can have been disappointed. But woe to those who had been hoping to see its author rise higher, and mingle with the world's benefactors as his peers. They found his faults and his beauties still the same; an alteration in degree, but not in kind; an improvement, if any, which was not a development. They could at most repeat their praises, but not increase them. Alexander the Great rewarded a skilful pea-shooter with peas. Mr Tennyson also must be paid in kind. His statue must be placed in a larger and more ornate niche, but it must remain on its old level.

One plea, indeed, could it be sustained, would serve to reverse this judgement. Some of the less discreet of Mr Tennyson's admirers have adopted a course in his defence, which we, who admire him with a more guarded prudence, cannot follow. They discover a great artistic construction in *The Princess*. They altogether refuse to consider it as a wonderful specimen of elegant trifling, akin to the 'laborious orient ivory sphere in sphere', which he celebrates at its opening. In spite of the poet's own declaration, they hold that it is at heart, from beginning to end, grave earnest. We ask for the clue which, according to this hypothesis, should serve as our guide through the complexities of the varied scene—

> A Gothic ruin and a Grecian house,
> A talk of college and of ladies' rights,
> A feudal knight in silken masquerade,

and the science of the nineteenth century, in a costume almost equally foreign to its nature, condescending to the prettiness of a toy, and mingling with music, dancing, cricket, and sunshine, as an ingredient in a day's amusement. We inquire where, except in the fantastic playfulness of the *Medley*, we are to find its unity. And we are told, in answer, that *The Princess* is an *allegory*.[2]

We imagine Mr Tennyson would not thank his admirers for this theory. No man less likes to be tied down to a definite meaning. He would no more have a purpose, than Falstaff would give a reason, on compulsion. Of course he would not be displeased, if any one should discover in his poem, as in some great work of nature, a fertile mine of suggestiveness, a noble redundancy of signification. But he would not be willingly committed to the version of the most skilful interpreter. He has spoken prettily on this subject himself.

> So, Lady Flora, take my lay
> . . .
> Should hook it to some useful end.

Nor can we deny his right to wander through the enchanted ground, to sleep in every cool grot and pleasant arbour, to rejoice in dreams which shall be the purest medleys, and only seem to touch upon our every-day world by mistake. We must, indeed, make two provisos. In the first place, his visions shall be either better than our common sights and sounds, or wholly apart from them, that so he may not mar that life which others must live, though poets are exempt from its burden. And secondly, we shall not be blamed for not regarding enthusiastically what he has written sportively, or be accused of shallowness for not seeing depths where there are none. *The Princess* may be an allegory, on Mr Tennyson's own principles. But by the same free method which has been employed in devising for it a profound meaning, we would detect the philosophy of history in the life of King Arthur, or a system of ontology in an ordinary fairy tale.

Let us not then be suspected of any wish to close the open question. Some speculations are so amusing, that nothing but a sense of duty would lead us to stop them. Though giving little promise of satis-factory solution, they might run on for their own sakes. It is so in the present case. Let the Princess Ida represent, to those whom it pleases, 'the passive or feminine principle of the intellect', whatever that may be. Let the struggle which took place in her halls typify a mightier contest even now going on in the civilized world, to be followed, if Mr Tennyson is a prophet (or if he is not), by a reaction. Let even the

[2] Coventry Patmore interpreted *The Princess* as an allegory in the *North British Review*, ix (May 1848), 43–72.

smaller traits have their meaning. Allow that little Aglaia, who sleeps by Lady Psyche's side

> In shining draperies, headed like a star,
> Her maiden babe, a double April old,

is in reality, poor child, most precocious, and indicates, by her name, the splendour of the triumphs which may yet be accomplished by this Daughter of the Soul. Conceive whoever will, that the great principle of the mysterious connection of contraries lies hid in the circumstance that cross Lady Blanche has a pretty and good-natured daughter; and that the mighty Arac has sprung from the loins of the dwarfish Gama; we sit unmoved, and are pleased, both with theories like these, and our own independence of them. *The Princess* is to us as one poem out of many, inferior to none in the novelty of its images and the finish of its language; longer than the rest by far, and therefore of a more complicated structure, but still by no means 'orbed in its isolation'; the chief of several connected powers, but not a sovereign. And as such we proceed to employ it, with the other poems, in illustration of our views of Mr Tennyson. These are simple enough; for we are not prepared to do what the poet himself has not done, and unite the whole of his works under some comprehensive system or theory. Rather, we will follow his own plan, and say what is natural, without much regard to order; bestow praise and blame fairly and frankly; deal more in allusion than quotation; yet not refuse ourselves and our readers the pleasure, on due occasion, of listening to the chiming echo of our author's silvery cadences.

We shall scarcely vary far from Mr Tennyson's own estimate of his works, in assigning the foremost place among their beauties to their *diction*. He has studied long and well the capabilities of language. No man better knows the marvellous art, by which a succession of black and broken lines on a white surface is made to suggest to the mind, through the eye alone, a distinct and articulate melody. No man better knows the exact direction of the boundary, which separates a pleasing originality of style from a forced and affected quaintness. We do not say that his rhythms are never languid even to faintness, and more fit to be sighed forth by 'mild eyed melancholy lotus-eaters', than to swell in 'deep-chested music' from the lips of true-hearted men. We cannot express approval of the extent to which he sometimes trusts to the charms of cadence, or the boldness with which, especially in his last poem, he introduces constructions and turns of expression, which, though neither inelegant nor unintelligible, are foreign to the genius of his native tongue. But who can say, that the potent melody of words is either unemployed or undervalued by an author, who has sung of *The Poet's Song* in music like this?

> The rain had fallen, the poet arose,
> . . .
> When the years have died away.'

Verily, Mr Tennyson is a sweet singer as a poet need wish to be. But a poet should wish to be something more. And we should be glad to be quite sure that language, from being Mr Tennyson's forte, has not shown a tendency to become his foible. It is an unpleasant opinion to entertain of him, but one which has too much foundation, that, as he has become a more practised writer, he has used his skill in spinning out a smaller amount of thought into a tissue of golden words. That which seems to be the earliest of his published poems, *The Ode to Memory*, would well bear expansion. The reader sympathises with the writer in the burden of his song,

> Oh strengthen me, enlighten me,
> I faint in this obscurity,
> Thou dewy dawn of memory.

He would gladly use the poet's assistance in bringing before his mind, with greater distinctness and fuller detail, the decaying image of the past. But who does not feel that *The Talking Oak*, in its sweetly chiming ballad metre, or *The Daydream*, in all the prettiness of its dissolving views, has quite as many words as it can bear? This is not as it should be. Though a poet's thoughts be of the purest gold, this is no reason why he should beat them out into thin leaf, or spin them into wire, though he can twist it into the finest filigree. Genuine fluency is one of the greatest accidental gifts which true genius can enjoy. It is not unfrequently, in the history of a mind, the very last power which is granted. Full-grown souls have rejoiced as in a transmigration to a higher state, on feeling the whole apparatus of language, for years and years a burden and restraint to thought, turning at last into available harness, strong both for attack and defence. But with great minds this readiness has always been something far higher than a mere facility in using well-assorted words. It proceeds from no skill in mechanical contrivance, but from an intellectual harmony. The crowd of thoughts, which formerly jarred and jostled with each other in the attempt to gain expression, are now compacted in orderly array, and march forth to the sound of trumpet-tongued eloquence. But Mr Tennyson is no warrior. He is rather the minstrel, lingering, and trifling, and harping, at the castle gate. He is not content, as higher poets are, to bring out his idea fully, and then to wait till human hearts send back its echo. Like some other skilful musicians, he thinks too little of the air, too much of his control over the instrument. In this he ill consults his true reputation. In spite of the most elaborate variations, we must very soon tire of execution, if its abundance leads us to suspect a poverty of invention.

At the risk of seeming ill-natured, we must add one more stricture on Mr Tennyson's style. *The Princess* has fully developed a disposition, which is traceable to a less extent in his earlier poems, to introduce, in prodigal abundance, forms of expression which are moulded on the type of other languages than our own. The source from which he principally derives these novelties of construction is the Greek. We will not attempt an enumeration of instances; any one who takes up the 'Medley' now before us, will find in it examples of metonymy, synecdoche, and every figure of his schoolboy days, more readily than in his Sophocles. They are often expressive; they have an original sound to the unlearned; they please the scholar from the force of association; they are intertwined with much that is really beautiful. But, meanwhile, they are liable to the one fatal objection, that they are not English.

It is not wise to confuse the genius of any language, living or dead, with that of our own. The result may have the charm of fashion for a time, but it must share the fate of all fashions, and become distasteful at last. Our libraries are the sepulchres of many authors, once considered models of style, but now forgotten. A slight examination generally shows the reason of their past fame, and present insignificance. One glittered a few brief years in the false antithesis of France, and then faded for ever. Another was emulous of Virgilian versification, or endeavoured to train our sturdy Anglo-Saxon into the niceties of Ciceronian prose. Virgil and Cicero still live, but not their imitators. France and Rome have been consulted more than enough, and writers have now learned to try the less-wrought veins of Germany and Greece. They had better trust to their own resources. Time tries severely all refinements of language, but those which are native to the soil will bear most exposure, and suffer least.

It is not often that writers of such perfect smoothness and exquisite finish as the author of *The Princess*, have a keen sense of details in the outward world, a love of minute observation, or a power of bringing its results vividly before their readers. With those who enjoy these gifts, polish generally contributes, not to the even reflection of light, but to point and sparkle. The stone which is cut into many facets, sends back the rays which fall upon it, brilliantly indeed, but unevenly. But Mr Tennyson finds no difficulty here. He has wonderful skill in introducing a multitude of details into his picture without breaking its repose. Whole poems are but a succession of minute touches, and yet are wanting neither in harmony, breadth, nor unity. It is hard to admire enough, for instance, the perfect distinctness with which the image of listless, aimless, half-hoping, half-despairing, and yet withal apathetic melancholy is brought out from the accidents of a lonely locality, the common rural sights and sounds, the every-day associations of a solitary chamber, which surround the dejected Mariana. And throughout Mr Tennyson's volumes, the fidelity of the marsh scenery is most wonderful. He treads in the very steps of Nature. The tangled weeds in the water-courses, the desolate creeks and pools with their silvery flowers, the moss clustering on the sluices, the frequent bridges, the heavy barges trailed by slow horses, sliding along the willow-veiled margin—every feature strengthens, while it half relieves, the impression of level continuity of space. We remember that great men could be born in Boeotia, and congratulate the fens of Lincolnshire on their poet.

But here, too, we must qualify our praise. This microscopic delineation is, to a great extent, artificial; and all artificial beauty easily slides into a defect. These drawings with a fine point are necessarily wanting in power. They betray at every turn the labour of composition. No one could suspect Mr Tennyson of being a rapid writer, and throwing off his noblest passages without a sense of effort. This is one reason why he fails in his attempts to express strong emotion. He betrays none of the characteristic quickness of passion. However great his subject, he knows but one method of treating it. He sits down calmly before hero, saint, or villain, and draws his portrait, stroke by stroke, as a lady would paint a flower.

To this cause, though not to this cause only, we must attribute Mr

Tennyson's failure in the attempt to delineate strong excitement and rapid movement in all their phases. It matters not if he wishes to depict the active powers of nature expanding in their full energy, or the clash and combat of war, and the struggle of contending heroes, or the still more awful conflict of passion in the human heart. In every case there is something wanting. The Daguerreotype process gives the whole of a landscape faithfully, except figures in quick motion, or the leaves of a tree which are trembling visibly in the wind. Like it, Mr Tennyson requires all but a dead calm to display his powers to advantage. Nature must be hushed to sleep, like a baby, to have its likeness taken. This point may bear a little illustration.

Poetry has an obvious advantage over painting, in not being bound to represent any one moment of time. Its interest may be real and vivid, when it is impossible that all its characters should be grouped together on a plane surface, and brought before the eye at once. It can comprehend a whole series of events in a concise and intelligible unity. It can gather up into a verse the beauty of continued motion. We can see the hero on his good steed ride past us, and derive one consistent impression from all that passes between our first glance at the star on the horse's forehead, and the last ring of his hooves which we hear when he is again hidden in the woods. The poet should know his advantage in this respect, and use it.[3]

But this advantage Mr Tennyson singularly neglects. To take the most prominent instance from his last poem, the battle scene; well-drawn as it is, and full of incident, it wants life; we do not start at it as at the sound of a trumpet. The picture changes not so much by alteration of its parts, as by rapid substitution. The climax gives us two figures just as a painter would have chosen them:

> A moment hand to hand,
> And sword to sword, and horse to horse we hung,
> Till I struck out and shouted.

Scarce a battle scene was ever painted in which these two figures do not occur. We have seen the nicely balanced combatants over and over again in all variations of garb, armour, and weapon; in the lighter trappings of the Roman horseman, or the heavier of jousting knights; or in buff coat and jack boots, half hidden in the mingled dust and smoke of a skirmish in our civil wars.

[3] This passage owes a good deal to Lessing's distinction between poetry and painting.

On one occasion Mr Tennyson favours us with an Homeric Echo; and he who does not admire the *Morte d'Arthur*, is a traitor both to English and Greek. But where in Homer have we such a scene of death-like stillness? We see no blow struck; we hear no clang of weapons. No sound of thunder, no tremblings of the soil for which he had fought so long, attend on the departure of the hero. Three or four *tableaux* would bring the whole tale before the eye—the king, lying with broken helm, and dark blood upon his bloodless face, under the light of the full moon, in the ruin which stands upon the neck of barren land between the lake and the ocean: the wondering knight gazing into darkness, while the mystic hand is still holding Excalibur above the waters: an armed figure slowly and painfully bearing down the slippery crag one who will use arms no more: and the funereal barge, with the three dark-robed queens upon its deck, just melting into the distance.

In like manner we are dissatisfied, even while we are pleased, with Mr Tennyson's descriptions of the more violent workings of the heart. He is far from failing when he tells of a fair girl dying slowly of consumption, and untying, through a long year, the knots which bind her affections to things earthly, while, to the last, she is unwilling to let the silken cords quite slip. He takes us wholly with him when he shows us the wife of the lord of Burleigh slowly drooping and fading under the burden of an honour to which she was not born. But, with full knowledge how a whole school will differ from the opinion, we must profess our belief that the passion of *Locksley Hall* is, as such, a failure. This is not to depreciate the excellence of the poem; to deny that it is full charged with thought, at once weighty and rapid in rhythm, and affording very few points where the spear of criticism could be inserted between the junctures of its long and rolling trochaic tetrameters. But we complain of the transitions. Sometimes the mere juxtaposition of thoughts is made to serve instead of their connection. Sometimes we are let fall into a half-line of weakness and obscurity, to rise again, we scarcely know how, to our old level of elevation. Have our readers ever pondered, with us, the appropriateness of such a concise sentiment as— 'here, at least, where nature sickens, nothing'—or been surprised that Mr Tennyson could tolerate the prose, and doubtful prose too, of 'howsoever these things be', in the very climax of his poem? There can be but one reason for these exceptions. Mr Tennyson knows not how passion, like lightning, fuses and blends things most unlike with each other; or rather, knowing it, does not possess that full and energetic flow of soul, which would enable the artist to imitate the process.

The same features characterise our author in dealing with nature, as with man. One instance will suffice: let us observe how he treats the sea. To most minds, it is full of the very spirit of activity. We draw a deeper breath, and walk with a firmer step, by its side. Its colour has a charm, and the freshness of life is recalled by its sparkle. We rejoice much in its ripple, in its dashing wave much more. When we are miles away, and a good strong salt-laden breeze

> Gives to the taste the feeling of the storm,

we are pleased by association. Far from losing its vitality by our familiarity with it, it gains day by day. Those who live much hard by it or upon it, contract from it a pantheistic tinge, and learn to speak and think of it as a great animal. We have no such sea in Mr Tennyson: he confines himself to its gentler aspects, when we can

> watch the crisping ripples on the beach,
> And tender curving lines of creamy spray.

This, it may be said, is just the character it ought to take on the shores of the Lotophagi. But the Prince who succeeded, beyond his will and intent, in subverting the women's Academe, was a child of the north; he must have known the Atlantic; and what seems to have been his dominant impression of Ocean?

> At eve and dawn,
> With Ida, Ida, Ida, rang the woods;
> The leader wild-swan in among the stars
> Would clang it and *lapt in wreaths of glowworm light*
> *The mellow breaker* murmured Ida.

We are right glad to quote the line, itself quite phosphoric with prettiness, even while observing that thus to describe the sea is to describe it by a very separable accident indeed. Nor do we think the force of our remark blunted, because Locksley Hall overlooks 'the hollow ocean billows roaring into cataracts'; or our friend the Prince dreams that he is watching

> A full sea, glazed with muffled moonlight, swell
> On some dark shore, just seen that it was rich;

or even because a soul, which seeks the beautiful without the good, or both the good and beautiful without thought of Him who is source both of goodness and beauty, is likened to

> A salt, still pool, lock'd in with bars of sand;
> Left on the shore; that hears all night
> The plunging seas draw backward from the land
> Their moonlit waters white.

These are pictures, undeniably; and true to nature; but still they are subdued. The waves roar like any nightingale; we see and hear as from a distance; there is a mistiness, a creaminess, a mellowness, a gleam of muffled moonlight (who is richer in words than Mr Tennyson?) cast over all.

If this is really a feature of Mr Tennyson's mind—if beauty is most beautiful in his eyes when it is still and motionless—we can see a peculiar fitness in that taste for the antique which is so prominent in his poems. Classic art, indeed, was no lifeless thing to its contemporaries. The artist wrought from what he saw; his creatures were but a glorified image of the ordinary life of his day. The quick, energetic Greeks knew no higher praise for a picture than that it seemed on the point to speak; for a statue, than that it promised motion. But this is past now; what was a representation to them, is final to us. To our thoughts, an ancient statue is rather a distinct creation than the image of a man. Old associations have died off it; it is a subject for taste, not for feeling. The ties which linked it to our human nature, its personal interest, and its bearing on religion, are departed as completely as the polychrome from the columns of the Parthenon: there is no speculation in its eye, no warmth in the whiteness of its marble.

Among these beautiful forms of the Past Mr Tennyson delights to linger. He does not attempt to animate them; he is not anxious that they should speak or move; he would not have them flush into common life. Far less would he deck them with the gauds of the day, or debase them with ordinary colouring. But it is his pleasure to place them in the garden of the poet's mind, where the shadows of the leaves may fall upon them, or the oblique sunshine give a dark distinctness to their clear-cut features; or bright hues, which are not their own, be reflected upon them from beds of flowers.

His groups are various. A weather-beaten statue of Ulysses, an oar in his hand and his son Telemachus by his side, stands out from a background of grey rock and thundercloud, overspanned by an arch of rainbow. Or, beneath a brighter sky, his sailors are sleeping with the branches of the lotus by their side, while white clouds are sailing over them, as soft as any on which they dream the gods lie reclined in carelessness beside their nectar. Or the forlorn Œnone, leaning on a fragment twined with vine, is singing to the stillness in the loveliest vale of Ida. *The Princess* especially abounds with classical images. A Grecian house was one of the elements which the tale-teller undertook to incorporate in his story; and he amply redeems his promise. The Academe, judging from many of its ornaments, might have stood on the bank of Cephissus. Even the inn hard by its entrance has a bust of Pallas for its sign. When the art manufactures are disposed to extend to such ponderous subjects as college gates, Mr Tennyson has a model at their disposal:

> Two great statues, Art
> And Science, Caryatids,
> . . .
> Spread out at top, and grimly spiked the gates.

The interior is worthy of the entrance. Art is there so fully developed, as to be prominent even over confusion. When the maiden-students throng the court, with a very considerable noise and very doubtful regard of discipline—

> High above them stood
> The placid marble Muses, looking peace.

And in that more general collapse of order which follows when Ida relents after the battle, we are still at leisure to observe how, amid the clash and jingle of intruding armour,

> The day
> Descending, struck athwart the hall,
> . . .
> Now set a wrathful Dian's moon on flame.

What less, indeed, could we expect, in this abode of learning? It is worth attending to the list of the statues in the hall. The catalogue is of sonorous music:

> She
> That taught the Sabine how to rule,
> . . .
> Of Agrippina.

No wonder that, among all this artistic apparatus, the inhabitants themselves become rather statuesque. The Princess strikes us as somewhat affected in this way, with her two tame leopards for constant attendants. Even poor Melissa half owes a lover to the involuntary classicality of her sorrow:

> She, half on her mother propt,
> . . .
> Appealing to the bolts of heaven.

In all this there is some playfulness, and some feeling too. Of thus much, at least, the consideration of Mr Tennyson's classical pictures may serve to assure us: he is not content to be simply a spectator of the antique; he must arrange its models for his own purposes, and place them in his own lights; he must cast over them the hues of his imagination. They shall not speak, but at his touch they shall emit an indefinite harmony, like Memnon at the touch of morning. They shall not cease to be marble; yet they shall glow with a warm, and it may be a fitful, but neither a deep nor a lasting lustre.

The tinge of a ray of light is most easily discovered when it falls on a white surface. May we, in like manner, judge of Mr Tennyson's mind by the tone which it gives to the antique? If so, there can be little doubt what its tinge is. It is soft, almost to enervation. We wonder that objects are seen with such minute distinctness through its golden haze. It is delicate, but the delicacy lies not in the colour itself, but in its degree. A shade deeper, it would become coarse. Like some Claude Lorraine glasses, it gives a better general effect in proportion as the tints of the landscape are less pronounced.[4] Where these are strong, it jars with some unpleasantly, and intensifies others more unpleasantly still. It may light up a harvest field into brighter lustre, or cast a gleam, as of sunshine, over glaucous marshes, ochreous roads, and a cold grey sky; but it would dim the whiteness of an up-piled cloud, make the blue heavens unpleasantly verdant, and only add an additional stare to the flaunting marsh-marigold, an unprofitable accession of gaudiness to the poppy.

We would not have Mr Tennyson paint that which we love. His

---

[4] A Claude Lorraine glass was used to reduce the proportions of a landscape and darkened or coloured, sometimes green or yellow. Chretien, like Ruskin, appears to rate the paintings of Claude rather low: the delicacy and lustre of Claude's paintings he sees as over-intense and garish.

style is unfaithful to that deeper individuality which lies beneath the surface. He applies his peculiar bloom as an unfailing specific for increasing beauty. He peers and pries into details with an intruding minuteness which seems irreverent in the case of high forms of goodness. He is true to himself first, to his subject afterward. If loveliness will not conform to his model, it must suffer. He throws a purple lustre over the violet; and over the lily too. Some of his readers may have observed, for instance, that he is as far from catching the spirit of mountain scenery, as he is close to the very heart of nature in the marsh and the plain. In drawing a hill, he cannot dispense with a luxuriant foreground. The barrenness of its sides needs a compensation which he is most glad to give. It runs up its dark-blue forks beyond the full-leaved platans of the vale; or the gorges in front open wide apart, to reveal some columned citadel. The snow may not rest in cold whiteness on the mountain-top, but is ruddy in the Lotus land with the flash of sunset, or lies on Ida in virgin streaks, to be smitten by the solitary morning. Even the picture which he hangs on the walls of the Palace of Art, to embody the image of desolation, must have one warm touch put in.

> And one, a foreground black with stones and slags,
>   Beyond a line of heights, and higher
> All barr'd with long white clouds and scornful crags,
>   And highest, snow *and fire*.

Some of Mr Tennyson's most highly-finished poems are portraits of ladies, real or imaginary. They are like water-colour drawings, in which we admire, while we are disposed to condemn, the excess both of elaboration and mannerism. We almost expect to see 'jour à gauche' at one corner of the page. These ladies are, we are assured, all of them beautiful, and most of them good. Yet we are not pleased with their likenesses. Be it the fault of artist or sitter, they are not *natural*.

If a style, which is faithful to differences of detail, but monotonous in general effects, is apt to become distasteful when inanimate nature is in question, it is positively disagreeable when applied to men and women. Nature really derives much of its colour from ourselves. We cannot tell accurately, in the complicated scene and its still more complicated impressions, what we create, and what we receive. We animate the thing, with which we afterward hold converse, as with a distinct personality. We wonder at the wisdom of its teaching, when, in fact, it is only sending back an echo to the voice of our soul. But the communication between two minds should be regulated by a different principle from that which prevails in the intercourse of mind and matter. To view other persons mainly as recipients of our character, is to deny that they have a character of their own. This is to degrade those whom we should regard as our fellows, and to extend to both sexes the libel which we blame Pope for wishing to affix to one. To this libel, however, Mr Tennyson practically subscribes. All his ladies are of one school. Nature just creeps humbly in, to vindicate art from the charge of sameness. Margaret is confessedly twin-sister to Adeline, and the rest are first cousins. We never met any of them by daylight, leaping adown the rocks, like Mr Wordsworth's Louisa, or, like his Lucy, listening to the wayward round of the rivulets. A misty moonlight might bring them shawled out of doors; or a red sunset tempt them on to the lawn; but though thus occasionally seen abroad,

> While the amorous, odorous wind
> Breathes low between the sunset and the moon;

yet (as the next two lines run)

> In a shadowy saloon
>   On silken cushions half reclined,

they are much more in place. There they are content to repose; and there we are content to leave them.

We have touched incidentally on several differences between Mr Tennyson and Mr Wordsworth. It will be pleasing to mention one point in which they very decidedly agree, with regard to the duty and vocation of a poet. Neither of them would have him overlook the present in his devotion to the past. Neither speaks or feels despairingly of the age in which he lives; or fears, that while the heart continues to beat, poetry will die for want of depth of earth in which to strike her roots, or of sun and rain to call forth her leaves and flowers. For our own pleasure, as well as that of our readers, we will have the elder bard speak for himself. If prefaces have no other use, they have at least served the purpose of showing us that good poets can generally write good prose.

Poetry is the first and last of all knowledge—it is as immortal as the heart of man. If the labours of men of science should ever create any material revolution, direct or indirect, in our condition, or in the impressions which we habitually receive, the Poet will sleep then no more than at present; he will be ready to follow the steps of the man of science, not only in those general indirect effects, but he will be at his side, carrying sensation into the midst of the objects of the science itself. The remotest discoveries of the chemist, the botanist, or mineralogist, will be as proper objects of the Poet's art as any upon which it can be employed, if the time should ever come when these things shall be familiar to us, and the relations under which they are contemplated by the followers of these respective sciences shall be manifestly and palpably realised to us as enjoying and suffering beings. If the time should ever come when what is now called science, thus familiarised to men, shall be ready to put on, as it were, a form of flesh and blood, the Poet will lend his divine spirit to aid the transfiguration, and will welcome the Being thus produced as a dear and genuine inmate of the household of man.

Thus wrote the father of our living bards long before Mr Tennyson was a poet. But his *Lyrical Ballads* contain very few, if any, exemplifications of the theory thus propounded in their preface. Nor can we recollect a single prominent image in Mr Wordsworth's writings which is taken from that borderland between science and common life, which is every day becoming wider. He is too thoroughly convinced of the poetical character of all natural human feeling, and too deeply engaged in apprehending its essential features, to be very curious as to the exact limits within which, at any particular moment, it is pent by the sand-bank of matter of fact, or the strict and regular masonry of scientific knowledge. Afloat upon that broad ocean, he feels not the change of tide; and, though he knows that its periodic ebb and flow is still going on, does not inquire whether its waves are beating up close under the rocks of the distant shore, or leaving heaps of pebble and sea-weed parching in the sun, and only whitened into greater harshness by the salt of its spray. Mr Tennyson sails in a smaller boat, and has occasion to explore the reefs and shallows more closely. He practises what Mr. Wordsworth has taught; knows well the water-line on the beach, and looks out sharply for any picturesque pebble, or shining piece of crystal, which the sea has cast up, and which he, like a skilful lapidary, may cut and polish. He thus escapes one snare into which Mr Wordsworth is apt to fall. He does not appear as the distinct advocate of the principle which he adopts in practice. He is not committed to an universal, which he is bound to some extent to verify. The author of the *Lyrical Ballads* must endeavour to justify, at least in part, his theoretic positions in his poems. The author of *The Princess* sees only a suggestion where others find a law. Nothing passes as poetical with him, simply because, according to some system, it ought to be so. All is brought before his sense of the beautiful, and adopted or rejected accordingly. He never becomes ludicrous where he means to be simple; or, in adhering to his own crotchet, thinks that he is true to nature.

We will not pretend to quote those smaller touches in which Mr Tennyson gracefully introduces each little conventional grace, which he has culled as pleasing, or as capable of being made so, from our daily life and manners. These, though pretty in their place, would seem jejune out of it. Most of his readers, besides, have probably made the remark for themselves ere now, and verified it for themselves also. But we will mention one or two instances of his skill in weaving the popular aspect of science into poetry. The minds of many will at once revert to the 'circle rounded under female hands with flawless demonstration' on the lecture slate in Ida's College; or the prettily put allusions to the nebular hypothesis in which the Princess and her tutors rejoice. But these, perhaps, are exceptionable examples, as deriving their force either from the attendant circumstances, or from the beauty of expression; not from their own significance or novelty. It is easy to be more definite. What study is more unpoetical than anatomy? Its details are worse than technical and dry; to most constitutions they are, from their nature, necessarily disgusting. And the broad view of the science of the human frame is not more inviting. There seems a profaneness in the rough handling of that wonderful temple of the soul, consecrated as it is to the Christian thought, by a still more wonderful Presence. Mr Tennyson speaks, through the Princess, more feelingly on the subject than is his wont:

> We shudder but to dream our maids should ape
> Those monstrous males who carve the living hound,
> . . .
>
> *Encarnalize their spirits.*

Yet he has contrived to introduce, twice at least, facts of animal chemistry with effect. That strange old king, Gama, who belongs, in virtue of divers touches, to divers centuries, displays knowledge beyond that of the days of tournaments, in his reproach of his daughter's hardness.

> I've heard that there is iron in the blood,
> And I believe it: not one word? not one?
> Whence drew you this steel temper?

And those two metaphysical voices, who, in one of Mr Tennyson's most elaborate poems, contest a difficult question with a skill which seems very nearly matched, till a happy incident, though with rather too fortuitous an air, turns the scale on the side of truth, assume a wide sufficiency of scientific knowledge, and debate of that mysterious time, which was

> *Before the little ducts began*
> *To feed thy bones with lime,* and ran
> Their course, till thou wert also man.

Geology, again, does not readily appear in a poetical aspect. Its hold on the mind is gained mainly by its tempting our curiosity, and often flattering our pride. Except as a matter of knowledge, we can care little for that primitive state of the earth, when molten granite was supreme. Nor do the dynasties of the Saurian races, and their cognate tribes, present any very attractive features. The phraseology, too, is hard and harsh enough:

> Stony names
> Of shale and hornblende, rag and trap and tuff,
> Amygdaloid and trachyte.

Yet a very cursory reader, both of Geology and Poetry, catches the appropriateness of the parallel with which Everard Holmes excuses the work of destruction wrought upon his epic:

> Why take the style of those heroic times?
> For nature brings not back the mastodon,
> Nor we those times.

The Present, indeed, is Mr Tennyson's peculiar sphere. When he views it, however, in its relations to the other parts of time, he casts his looks forward on the future. The Past has no charms for him—that long Past, we mean, which belongs to history, and in which men of another mould in mind, though not in body, trod the world which is now ours. The classical thoughts and associations, with which he is so familiar, please him, not as recalling the system to which they once belonged, but as specimens of fossil beauty which serve to adorn our own. He has no wish to re-animate an intellectual mastodon. On medieval subjects he never fixes his attention. He carries away, it may be, a few touches from them, wherewith to adorn his favourite King Arthur. Or he leaves them far behind in his backward course to the Lotophagi and Ulysses. Here he is once more in the region of the beautiful. But that grotesqueness, which in the middle ages veiled so much that was noble and excellent, has no charm for him. We are thankful that he has not attempted themes so foreign to his nature. A little more elaboration, and even Sir Galahad would become disagreeable. What could be more to be deprecated than a portrait of some medieval saint or hero in the style of S. Simeon Stylites?

Mr Tennyson's province is, we have said, rather the future than the past. Not that here he can claim a high preeminence. He is not ignorant indeed of his privilege to aspire to the rank of a prophet. The poet is to sing of what the world will be when the years have died away. Like all who own the wondrous gift of genius, he is to work mighty works with small means. The viewless arrows of his thoughts are to speed far and wide, and, when at last they light on earth, to take root, and blossom in their season, and produce at last—

> A flower all gold,
> And bravely furnish'd all abroad to fling
> The winged shafts of truth,
> To throng with stately blooms the breathing spring
> Of hope and youth.

His word is to be the lever with which wisdom shall move the world. In this kind of vague anticipation Mr Tennyson delights. He looks forward to a higher state of society, in which some general good shall result from the conflicts of base and noble, of true and false, of knowledge and opinion. The poet is to have no small share in the work. But how he is to forward it, appears not. Only, as he sings, this palace of Art and Morals is to rise like an exhalation. A nobler Amphion, he shall not only bring down from the mountain-top young ashes pirouetting with young beeches, but shall exercise his taming, ordering, humanising influences over the hearts of men. The result, indeed, is altogether above his direct purpose. He is to be great beyond his sense of his vocation; and while he is only thinking to enchant men with his melody, is to instruct them unaware by his words.

It would be hard indeed to expect more than this from Mr Tennyson. We must be content to see him implicitly acknowledge, that the noble task of standing in the van of the world, and leading on to good; of marshalling all that it has of beauty and excellence for the battle; of suggesting new lines of operation, new channels of thought, and thus developing its powers by combining them, belongs to other poets, but not to him. He is not far enough above the common mind to see into futurity. His full and gorgeous foregrounds dim the horizon into indefinite blueness. He paints things as he sees them. He does not lift his half-closed eye from the rounded forms of beauty close at hand, to look into the cold clear distance. He is told that it is beautiful, and that contents him. Or he would imagine it beautiful, if it were not so. His eyes would see pictures, though they were shut. Let the world run its course. Why should its tumult break his dream, if only it is pleasant?

And here we take our farewell of Mr Tennyson, lamenting that, with all his great beauties, he must be, comparatively, a poet of the day. The present is so exclusively his sphere, that he cannot transcend it. On that which is permanent in human nature he has very little hold. Those feelings which beat in the breast of Adam, and will throb in the hearts of his latest posterity, he dwells on only indirectly, in their lesser traits and consequences. The life of struggle and action, of cut and thrust, plot and counterplot, has none of his sympathies. The solemn, the sublime, the terrible both of art and nature; the ideas which are common to man, woman, and child; which all recognise, as if by some Platonic instinct, and love in their shadows, even when they dread them in their substance, he looks at and passes by.

It is not then as a poet of our common humanity that Mr Tennyson can hope for lasting fame. We must look to some other quarter for his patent of intellectual nobility. And where shall we hope to find it? He has raised no structure of mighty verse on the platform of philosophy. He knows that age succeeds to age, blowing before it a noise of tongues and deeds, of creeds and systems. But he is never bold enough to hope that he has discovered the key which can open the mystery of the world, and detect order in its confusion. His poems are not pregnant with sweet wisdom, or studded with the sententiousness of a refined morality. We seldom like him less than when he buries himself in a cloud of allegory and parable, which is meant to be luminous, but is obscure. He is far from the depths of human sympathy: he is almost as far from the calm height of philosophical enthusiasm.

In the halls of Divine song, Mr Tennyson never ventures to tread. No one could call him a Christian poet. We do not say that his poems are never touched even by a reflected beam of the sun of religion. A purer, calmer light than that of his common day, falls by the bed-side of the dying May-queen, gleams on the helmet of the maiden-knight Sir Galahad, and whitens into silver the first snow-drop of the year, as it lies in the bosom of S. Agnes. But this does not amount to much. Most poets have written on sacred subjects, as most painters have drawn Madonnas. And Mr Tennyson's good taste has given him the advantage over many of either tribe, by leading him to modify, if not to alter, his style to suit his subject.

But we are in danger of digressing; the more so, because we are unwilling to say what must be said after all. We have searched for a place for Mr Tennyson among the ideal artists, and cannot find one. We are obliged to confess, that his world is the world of sense; his beauty, is the beauty of colour and form and touch, not of mind. He is neither intellectual nor spiritual. Though it spoil the regularity of our terminations, we will rather say that he is sensuous than sensual.

Mr Tennyson, in a word, swims in the shallow waters of taste. We admire and appreciate his beauties at present; but we feel that they would not be half understood, if any wide-sweeping change passed over society. And if time do the work gradually, the effect will at last be the same.

A hundred years may pass, and the genius of the English language may have slightly altered. Shakespeare and Pope will still in that case be admired; but Mr Tennyson will not. He will seem to the reader of those days, frigid and affected in style, in proportion as he now seems original and novel.

His similes will be as difficult for others to appreciate, as they were for him to discover. Where their material is genuine, they will have to be melted down and remodelled before they can be employed. *The Princess* will be a mine of conceits, to be opened occasionally for the benefit of the curious.

His men and women—we hope our descendants will not like them. A figure here and there may be picked out for approval; but half their graces will be gone, and the other half faded; society will have changed its tone; new conventionalities will have rendered the old unpleasing; and the very ordinary clay of which the figures are made, will show through as their wrappings fall off them.

It is in the present age that Mr Tennyson must look for honour.

Happily, it is not slow to grant it. He has laboured for us most success-fully, and should receive all due acknowledgement of his labours. We must grant him thanks and praise and, in some sense, admiration. But, in justice to ourselves, we must deny him the title of great. That poet is not great who can amuse us, but cannot awe us; who, when he opens to us the treasury of his thoughts, shows us only the counterpart of our own; at whose feet we feel less disposed to sit, than to call him before us to receive our judgement; whose beauty is without elevation, whose effort is without strength, whose repose is without dignity, and whose philosophy is without wisdom.

Mr Tennyson is not a great poet. We can scarcely any longer hope that he will achieve greatness. Into that highest circle of the sons of song, who are wise beyond their generation, and belong only acci-dentally to the age in which they live, and compete for no honours which are not wider than their own time and country, he cannot ask to enter. But he is the poet of the day; nor has any rival yet appeared who seems likely to dethrone him. The loss is more the world's than his own. He is far enough above mediocrity for the full vindication of his dignity. He may sit in his place many years. We will pay him due homage, with one reservation. If he is king, it is not in a generation of giants.

9

Tennyson ❧ *In Memoriam* ❧ 1850

Franklin Lushington, *Tait's Edinburgh Magazine*, N.S. xvii
(August 1850), 499–505

Without assuming for the present age either an unprecedented sharpness of curiosity or an unparalleled acuteness of criticism, we may safely assert that the most unostentatious publication, the most exemplary secrecy, and the blankest title-page, could not long have kept the public in doubt as to the authorship of these poems. No one moderately conversant with the style, diction, and deep thought of the other works of the gifted writer could have read many pages without becoming aware of their parentage. No one endowed with a perception of what poetry is, could have closed the volume without a full conviction that it was the creation of the first poet of the day.

Such a trial of its merits was, however, not reserved for *In Memoriam*. The thin veil was lifted by too curious hands. Before the lapse of twenty-four hours, the circulating libraries had advertised the new birth in large type. The attractive announcement of 'Fifty copies of Tennyson's new poem this day in circulation!' undoubtedly paid its own expenses. The close of the first week brought with it the notices of the various Sunday papers; not, indeed, destitute of misconceptions and misconstructions, but all (except in one instance, where the literal tendencies of the critic discovered a female hand, and hailed the rising of a new poetical star in a widow's cap[1]) assuming the notoriety of the authorship, and of all, or more than all, the facts connected with the production of these poems. On the whole, we do not complain of the

Franklin Lushington, 1823–1901. The Lushington family had close connections with Tennyson. Edmund, Franklin's brother, married Tennyson's sister, Cecilia, in 1842. This review is extraordinarily sensitive in its claim that *In Memoriam* appeals to what Arnold was later to call the great primary feelings.

[1] *Literary Gazette*, 15 June 1850, 407.

premature solution of the mystery, as, in fact, it may be considered rather convenient than otherwise. That considerable portion of the public which is content to defer entirely to the influence of authority in matters of poetical opinion is, by the announcement of a well-known name, spared the thankless labour of exercising an unbiassed judgement, the expression of which might possibly hereafter have been found inconsistent with its received formulas of criticism. Those who are ready and willing to use the Protestant right of private opinion, and therefore are less liable to be prejudicially affected by this disclosure, have had their attention earlier drawn to the pleasure and profit which this volume had in store for them, than if the secret had oozed out more gradually.

Nevertheless, we are glad to record our full sympathy with the feelings which prompted the author to omit his own name on the title-page; and we feel it to be, if not our bounden duty, at any rate our better course, to treat this work as it appears, *per se*; to consider it without any unnecessary reference to his earlier poems; and, as far as is possible, without the *prestige* attaching to his established reputation. And we have no hesitation in saying, not only that *In Memoriam* contains finer passages of poetical thought than have been published for many years, but that it is perfect and unique as a whole, to a degree and in a style very rarely reached. It is one of the most touching and exquisite monuments ever raised to a departed friend—the pure and unaffected expression of the truest and most perfect love; and as such, it ought to be, and (unless some great and sudden psychological convulsion overlays and buries, throughout the whole human world, the present fabric of poetical sympathies and conceptions), will be, a memorial more lasting than bronze.

Taking into our account nothing beyond the facts which come out on the internal evidence of the poems themselves, and relying on these implicitly, the history of *In Memoriam* may be given briefly as follows: A. H. H. was the dearest friend of the poet, and betrothed to one of his sisters. He was endowed with singularly clear and comprehensive intellectual powers: loved and revered among his college contemporaries for the truth and earnestness of his views, and by old and young alike for the irresistible grace and gentleness which clothed their expression. He had quitted college, and commenced the study of the law; his friends were anticipating a brilliant political future for the exercise of his noble talents; when, in the autumn of 1833, he died suddenly at Vienna. His remains were conveyed to England, and interred on the banks of the Severn.

> So runs the round of life from hour to hour.

It is the fate of many men of promise to die early—of many more to be prevented by bad fortune from attaining the eminence of which their powers were worthy, and for which the aspirations of their contemporaries had already destined them; but to few of them is allowed the compensating glory of being associated in life and after death with the deepest and dearest thoughts of so great a writer. Indeed, the interest of such a memorial arises, not merely from the exercise of the highest genius, but from the irresistible truth and strength of feeling, arguing so forcibly the enduring impression made by the character and the continual influence exerted by the memory of A. H. H. on his friend. The Sicilian muses may begin and end the bucolic strain—the sisters of the sacred well may sweep the string loudly or lowly for their loved Lycidas; we must always linger gladly in the charm of their divine melody; but neither the Daphnis of Theocritus, nor 'Mr King, son of Sir John King, Secretary for Ireland', have for us any durable personal interest beyond the mere beauty of the elegies which are sacred to their *manes*. To this very day, the personality of 'Mr W. H., the only begetter of Shakespeare's sonnets', is an unresolved problem. Even the wonderful lyrical passion and prophetic melancholy of the *Adonais* of Shelley cannot enlarge our love and regret for Keats. The interest of Laura is entirely derived from her permanent influence on the character of Petrarch; and our vivid persuasion of the charms of Beatrice (for we will not believe her to be Theology 'whate'er the faithless people say'), from the sense that Dante's passion for her was the origin and life of the *Vita Nuova*, while it gave form and colour to the *Divine Comedy*. It is not only the momentary absorption of self in the contemplation of that which has been loved and lost, but the entire and enduring devotion to the self-imposed task of recording its excellences, which still has, after the lapse of five hundred years,

> Virtù di far piangere altrui.[2]

We have said that, in reviewing *In Memoriam*, we would not make any unnecessary reference to the earlier works of the same author; but

---

[2] 'The power to make other men weep'. Dante, 'Deh peregrini che pensosi andate', sonnet from ch. xl of the *Vita Nuova*.

we must begin by recalling to the attention of our readers one of the sonnets in his first collection, published in 1830. We mean that entitled *Love and Death*. Love is turned out of the 'thymy plots of Paradise' by Death, who, with the insolence of a mortal 'man in possession', is talking to himself beneath a yew. Love submits to the temporary ejectment with a sorrowful but confident protest:

> —This hour is thine.
> . . .
> But I shall reign for ever over all.

Sun and shadow, love and death, yew-trees and thymy plots, are the contrasts of which the world is made. The sonnet of 1830, filled with the imaginative hopefulness of a young artist, passes lightly over the sting of Death, and the victory of the Grave, to dwell on the glorious end of the contest. The aim of *In Memoriam* is identical with the moral deduced in the youthful Paradise-picture; but the interval has turned the imagination of grief into the stern consciousness of experience. Years of toil and danger are required to change the recruit into the veteran; and the simple assertion of our 'sure and certain hope' is very different from the actual struggle which must be gone through before overcoming the shock of pain and despair consequent on a sudden bereavement. It is one thing to deny a fear of ghosts, and another to face and lay the spectres of the mind.

In a late article, we had occasion to refer to Goethe as being in the habit of writing calm reviews of his past feelings, and even, in certain cases, writing himself deliberately out of a waning phase, in contrast to Wordsworth, whose practice it was to set down a pure and simple transcript of his then present mood.[3] In the composition of *In Memoriam* we have to remark an intermediate principle, the result of which is the reconciliation and harmonious fusion of the two methods. Each separate poem of the series is a true expression of the particular shade of feeling under which it was written; but each poem is also a necessary link in the great chain of thought by which the progressive enlargement of faith is worked out. The various moods of hope and sorrow often contradict each other; but they all lead towards the same end. The despair of the moment is fixed and deep; but in its very depth there is a vague but irresistible longing to look forward.

---

[3] *Tait's Edinburgh Magazine*, xvii (July 1850), 393–8; 394. The article is actually on Wordsworth, not Goethe.

As the final state of perfect resignation cannot be immediately reached by a simple submission to reason, it must be gradually won by the actual workings of the feelings themselves; and it is only from the full and simple frankness with which these workings are confessed, and their inevitable contradictions grappled with, that we can unreservedly sympathise in the reconciliation of love and destiny. The process is slow, but sure; and to the very last the rights of the original feelings are asserted, so as to maintain satisfactorily what we may term the personal identity of the soul.

With such a text we might write many a sermon; but we prefer to illustrate our meaning by quoting the first poem of the series, in which the ground-plan of the whole is indicated. The author referred to in the first stanza is, as our readers will see, Goethe himself.

> I held it truth, with him who sings
> . . .
> But all he was is overworn!

The general law enunciated by the German poet—that we may rise on stepping-stones 'of our dead selves'—had been theoretically accepted; but the application of it to the practice of life must be modified by the opposition of our deepest and most divine feelings, or its proud logic will fail. The 'large discourse' of sight with which we are made must not, in 'looking before and after', stoically overlook the present; or we may run the risk of falling where we thought to rise. The higher the tower of intellect rises the broader moral base does it require. There can be no true security for the future where all the past 'is overworn'. But there are times when the blind despair of sorrow almost overpowers faith, alternating with the strong reaction of reason, which prompts the sufferer to 'crush her like a vice of blood'. The purely physical revulsions of feeling, from the weary passiveness of midnight to the stronger pulse of waking manhood in the morning, are drawn by the rigid hand of iron experience in the poem numbered IV. Under such pressure, it is an unmingled good for the overburdened heart to betake itself to the relief of song. It is the most natural substitute for the Gaelic moaning or the Greek wail over the dead. The best answer (if any is needed) to the objections of all who hold that if a man is merry he should sing only psalms, and that his singing anything whatever is a proof of the unreality of his sadness, is to be found in the following lines:

> I sometimes hold it half a sin
>   To put in words the grief I feel
> . . .
> Is given in outline and no more.

Where so mutual an interchange of love had bound together the writer and the object of *In Memoriam*, it is not wonderful that every familiar place, every returning anniversary, every strain of thought or feeling, should 'breathe some gracious memory' of his friend. Each poem is a record of some single affectionate fancy, some tender detail of past years, some well-known picture in which the two friends had been prominent figures, some high or deep thought or yearning evoked by the terrible contrast of present circumstances. The subject runs through the whole diapason of human sympathy; the founts of sorrow and love are always flowing, for every one that thirsteth to come to the waters.

Here and there the poems naturally arrange themselves into smaller self-contained systems. The succession of feelings and fancies, while waiting for the arrival of the ship which conveyed the remains to England, forms the matter of a most beautiful and touching series. The mind, strained by indefinite expectation, falls into the most contradictory moods, of which, nevertheless, the music is as true and deep as that produced by the fusion of the clashing discords of Beethoven. The 'wild unrest that lives in woe' alternates with calm despair; the longing which annihilates space spends itself in forming the most distinct pictures of the vessel sailing under southern skies, and dwells with magnetic attraction upon the sacred relics nearing their native land; till the reaction of fancy almost brings back the bitter-sweet hope that the present sorrow is a dream, and refuses to realise the mourner's loss, until the desperate certainty of vision has dispelled his affectionate scepticism. The sad aim and end of the voyage, the final resting-place of the remains, is indicated with a grand simplicity which will find its way to the bosoms of all whose losses have taught them to endow some particular spot with the attributes of a sacred city, the most frequent and revered goal of the heart's silent pilgrimage.

> The Danube to the Severn gave
>   . . .
> And I can speak a little then.

It is through the assertion of these broad relations with nature—

colouring with our individual passions the largest features of the universe—that we exercise our most direct (if our most unconscious) action upon the sympathies of our fellow-beings, who are creatures of time and space like ourselves. The simplest and most familiar images are those which flatter most our home-bred fancies, and, consequently, those through which the artist can work on us most easily. The illustration of the deepest feelings through the commonest uses of daily life, through the most necessary and primeval (and therefore the widest) laws of society, will awake the most distant echoes between 'the slumber of the poles'. The shepherd in the plains of Chaldaea, the ferryman over the waters of the Euphrates, the most untaught agricultural intellect that ever stepped behind an English plough, would all be able to see dimly and in part the beauties of the terrestrial imagery contained in the following verses:

> Sad Hesper o'er the buried sun,
>   And ready, thou, to die with him,
>   Thou watchest all things ever dim
> And dimmer, and a glory done:
>
> *The team is loosened from the wain,*
>   *The boat is drawn upon the shore:*
>   *Thou listenest to the closing door,*
> *And life is darkened in the brain.*
>
> Bright Phosphor, fresher for the night,
>   By thee the world's great work is heard
>   Beginning, and the wakeful bird;
> Behind thee comes the greater light:
>
> *The market-boat is on the stream,*
>   *And voices hail it from the brink;*
>   *Thou hears't the village hammer clink,*
> *And see'st the moving of the team.*
>
> Sweet Hesper-Phosphor, double name
>   For what is one, the first, the last,
>   Thou, like my present and my past,
> Thy place is changed: thou art the same.

We should take especial delight in pointing out to the Chaldaean shepherd, whose astronomical tendencies are matter of the world's earliest history, how the simplicity of the local images prevents them from unduly interfering with the fixed contemplation of the star. The whole earth is reduced to a single point, on which the spirit may stand while gazing through the heavens. To our present readers we need hardly remark the beauty of the love which enshrines its object in so glorious a likeness, or the imitation of the celebrated epigram of Plato—

> Thou, that did'st shine a morning star among the living,
> Now shinest dead among the dead, the star of even.

The English poet carries the analogy one step farther; after the dusk of death, and the night of doubt, the serene hope of re-union brings back to its place in heaven the fallen star of the morning.

We have quoted these lines earlier than their place in the volume, or, indeed, their relations in time and feeling, may apparently justify us in doing, to illustrate the witchcraft that lies in the indication of landscape by a few broad touches. For a specimen of a very opposite manner of painting, where the infinities of perspective are drawn with a careful truth of graduation not surpassed by Claude, we must return to one of the earlier series, written during the homeward voyage of the sacred ship. We look beyond the forcible and characteristic foreground over the mellowing colours and blending details of the middle distance, back to the extreme horizon of the sea, where it is lost under the harmonious airy canopy which embraces all.

> Calm is the morn without a sound
> . . .
> Which heaves but with the heaving deep.

The same power of accurate delineation of the charms of an English landscape is visible everywhere through the volume; but the peculiar handling of this description of autumn strikes us as displaying a wonderful mastery over the materials of art. It is an almost unique instance of transferring into a word-picture the magic of the pencil. There is, however, a pendant to it, in the aerial perspective of the following 'Frühlingslied':[4]

> Now fades the last long streak of snow,
> . . .
> And buds and blossoms like the rest.

We now return to an analysis of the story, for such, although the

---

[4] 'Frühlingslied': spring song.

incidents are few, it may well be called; or rather a most intricate history of the growth of love and faith. The ship has reached the port; the mortal relics are interred in English ground; the vague dreams of an unwilling fancy have yielded to the stern certainty which accompanies the sound of the dropped handful of emblematic dust; but the mourner lingers still. He has no present aim in life, except to prolong the sad farewell—to sing to him that rests below. He takes no heed of the sneers or wonder of the unsympathising crowd, or answers them with the shortness of sorrow, strong in the rights of necessity:

> Behold, ye speak an idle thing—
> . . .
> Because her brood is stolen away.

He reviews the years of their sweet companionship, bright with the joy of youth and love; he recalls in vain the happy trust in the goodness of all created things, the emulation of mutual fancy, the unwearied freshness of spirit, the gaiety of endless sunshine, which lightened the necessary burdens of life; but all the avenues of recollection converge to the Valley of the Shadow of Death. It is only by a firm but agonised clinging to the faith that man is made in the Divine image that he can reconcile his grief to the confession:

> I hold it true, whate'er befall;
> I feel it, when I sorrow most;
> 'Tis better to have loved and lost
> Than never to have loved at all.

The first return of Christmas, with its sacred household festivities, now so sad, or, at any rate, so changed, by the loss of the beloved partaker, as to raise the doubt whether they would be more honoured in the breach or the observance, excites mingled feelings in the mourning circle. The well-known games, songs, and dances are gone through at first with the ghastly hollowness of pretended merriment, till finally the overwrought nerves are roused into the temporary exaltation of lyrical enthusiasm. The holly boughs and the yule-log are at once melancholy reminders of the past, and vague whispers of a more cheerful future; but most of all, the village bells. That simple music, of which the associations stretch over the world—'the merry, merry bells of Yule'—brings to the troubled spirit 'sorrow touched with joy'. How should it be otherwise? In spite of all the songs, good, bad, and indifferent, that have been written and sung on the subject of village bells, there is an invincible freshness in their merry peal. In spite of the *Lied der Glocke*, one of the few among Schiller's poems for which we can prophesy immortality, there is yet infinite and most excellent fancy to be drawn out of the inexhaustible theme. Ignorant as we are of the scientific mysteries of ringing, we yet feel a pathos associated with the very name of a triple bob-major. The unimaginative sailor in the calms of the tropics, and the *blasé* wanderer in the Syrian desert, hear the distant notes of the church-bells of England booming through the thin air, and are changed by the magnetic influence of the illusion into unalloyed masses of poetical feeling. Even those of our readers whose unhappy tympana have ever vibrated to the *scherzi, fantasie involontarie*, and general *charivari* of a Maltese festa, will pardon us for being slightly sentimental on the topic of village bells.

Between this Christmas and the next point in time which is distinctly marked, the first anniversary of the death, a calmer and more speculative element enters into the spirit of 'these brief lays, of sorrow born'. They touch on all the mysteries of life and death; they unfold 'grave doubts and answers', proposed, not with the dogmatic confidence or irrefragable arguments of professed science, but by the blind inspiration and instinctive reasoning of the heart, which will not submit to the *reductio ad absurdum* of its holiest feelings. Their continuity of thought is often assisted by what is the greatest proof of their unfailing truth, the unsparing revision, in one poem, of the assertions or results contained in the one immediately preceding; as, for instance, in Nos. XLIX and L. The natural yearning for the presence and aid of the loved spirit is the *motive* of the first; the severest self-questioning as to the sincerity and reality of this wish is expressed as follows in the second:

> Do we *indeed* desire the dead
>   Should still be near us at our side?
>   Is there no baseness we would hide?
> No inner vileness that we dread?

when the heart justifies itself by the noble answer:

> I wrong the grave with fears untrue;
>   Shall love be blamed for want of faith?
>   *There must be wisdom with great Death:*
> The dead shall look me through and through.

The same intense honesty and persevering spirit of inquiry is pre-eminent in the 'Natural Theology' of the three poems LIII, LIV, and LV.

The touching and graceful modesty of all the comparisons drawn between the writer's self and the 'nobler tone' of the soul which has passed away, reminds us again of the sonnets of Shakespeare. Whether he sighs in solitude, like the

> Poor girl, whose heart is set
> On one whose rank exceeds her own,

or, like the old playmate of 'some divinely-gifted man', who had risen from the 'simple village green' to be 'the pillar of a people's hope, the centre of a world's desire', stands musing in the furrow of the field of his childhood, within which the fate of his own manhood is as firmly bound,

> Does my old friend remember me?

or whether he looks upward in happy trust, like the simple wife of some great philosopher, who, while her husband's weight of learning and abstraction of thought rarely condescend to the expression of playful tenderness, still preserves a fixed faith in the depth of his attachment, and 'darkly feels him great and wise'; we cannot but feel that, however dwarfed the living may appear to the dead, however small a point our own planet occupies in the realms of space, the earnestness of such love is a warrant for its being reciprocated on equal terms.

> I loved thee Spirit, and love, nor can
> The soul of Shakespeare love thee more.

It is the soothing certainty of this return of affection which creates the calm cheerfulness amid general society, so exquisitely compared to the gaiety of the blind man, whose 'inner day can never die'. The still-ness of night hushes the noise of everyday life, and lets us hear the whispered communion with the unseen world.

> When on my bed the moonlight falls
> . . .
> Thy tablet glimmers to the dawn.

The *dies carbone notandus*, a chilly, stormy, colourless day of autumn, is quickly followed by the second Christmas. The regret for the fair guerdon of fame, which, but for the premature death, must sooner or later have 'burst out into sudden blaze', is consoled by the trust that it 'lives and spreads aloft' by the pure eyes and perfect witness of a higher judge. The old games no longer jar upon the sense: the tears of sorrow are dry, although 'her deep relations are the same'. The mind can afford to look forward to the springing beauty of the new year; to enjoy in anticipation the colour and scent of the woods, the fresh 'ambrosial air', and the overflowing passion of the nightingale. But the re-awakening to a fuller sympathy with the outer world only strengthens and expands the inner life of love. The hunger for a nearer intercourse, for some picture more strong than that of memory, some inner sight more true than that conveyed by the fallible nerves of vision, grows with the growth of the summer, to an intensity which, at last, we are told,

> By its own energy fulfilled itself,
> Merged in completion.

Towards the end of the second autumn, the family of the poet quit the home of their childhood. The memories of infancy are mingled with the traces of this departed friend into 'one pure image of regret'. It does not require any abnormal development of the organ of inhabitativeness to enter thoroughly into the feeling of the following picture:

> Unwatched the garden bough shall sway,
> . . .
> From all the circles of the hills.

On the last night before leaving his first home the poet dreams a dream, into which the presence of his friend is interwoven, here described with the force and grandeur of Dante. The next Christmas is passed in 'the stranger's land', and kept sacred by solemn thoughts alone, instead of song, or dance, or feast, for 'change of place, like growth of time, has broke the bond of dying use'. But in spite of the snapping of local ties, always most strongly felt at such a season, the merry bells of New Year's Eve ring out with a new vigour, and cause a more world-wide echo to thrill over the harp of faith. The prophetic enthusiasm which chants a noble accompaniment to the wild peal culminates in the last stanza:

> Ring in the valiant man and free,
>   The larger heart, the kindlier hand;
>   Ring out the darkness of the land,
> Ring in the Christ that is to be.

And so the story draws to a conclusion. The spirit has risen 'to something greater than before'; but what he was is not overworn. The meeting with Death has not paralysed Love, but made him rise on stronger wings. Before the saying of the words which must at last be said, AVE, AVE, DILECTISSIME, he can express, as follows, the sum of his own infinity:

> Strange friend, past, present, and to be,
>   Loved deeplier, darklier understood;
>   Behold, I dream a dream of good,
> And mingle all the world with thee.

Only once more, after the lapse of some years, are the same chords touched; the appropriate occasion being the marriage of another of the writer's sisters. The poem which is placed as the preface to the whole series, written after another long interval, is, from its tone and subject, beyond criticism.

We are loth to mingle one or two slight hints of imperfection with the praise of such a book. For those who are content to read poetry only once, a great deal of its beauty must remain unintelligible; even those who are willing to study it as fully as it deserves must, after many readings, find some parts exceedingly hard. The thoughts themselves are not always adequately expressed in clear language, nor is their connection always so fully within the logical view of the reader as to make him feel sure that all, as in some piece of art, 'is toil co-operant to an end'. There are one or two of the poems from which we should like to cut off the final stanza. The 'grand old name of gentleman', referred to in CIX, has not only been 'defamed by every charlatan', and 'soiled with all ignoble use' of theatrical and other parodies of the original 'good old song', but has even crossed the seas, and naturalised itself in Paris as *un vrai gentleman*, till, we fear, nothing can be done to retrieve its character. The agonies, and energies, and undulations of CXI remind us too forcibly of the wounded snake that drags its slow length along. We should be glad to ask the Chaldaean shepherd, who should know (potentially) all about mythology as well as astronomy, (for the Chaldaeans taught the Assyrians, who taught the Egyptians, who taught the Greeks, who taught the world), for the elucidation of a conceit, which, we fear, will otherwise take up its residence in that undiscovered country of Cloudland to which many of the pictures of Turner, with their unearthly limpets and black dogs, emphatically belong. What, O Chaldaean—*in te spes ultima*, is the mystery of 'the crimson-circled star' that falls 'into her father's grave'?

These, however, are but small and almost invisible specks on the beauty of *In Memoriam*; and we can only conclude by repeating what we have said before, and what we trust the feling of our readers, and of all who already know or may hereafter become acquainted with the work itself will justify, that it is the finest poem the world has seen for very many years. Its title has already become a household word among us. Its deep feeling, its wide sympathies, its exquisite pictures, its true religion, will soon be not less so. The sooner the better.

Further Reading in Periodical Reviews

A selection of reviews which discuss the same issues as those raised in Arnold's 1853 Preface.

TENNYSON

Discussions of Tennyson (by this date established as the major poet of the time) reflect the concerns of the Preface with extraordinary fidelity and for this reason I have included in this bibliography more discussions of his poetry than that of any other poet. Reviews of *The Princess* listed here are those which discuss the notion of form implied by the 'medley', Tennyson's language and his place and importance as a poet of the age. Discussions of *In Memoriam* are concerned with the appeal of the poem to the universal affections and with its subjectivity. The morbidity of the poem and the difficulties of the contemporary subject dominate discussions of *Maud* (although critics often takes sides on the special issue of the war philosophy without seeing the importance of the larger issue of contemporaneity). Discussions of *Idylls of the King* concentrate on the appropriateness of the legendary subject and on the importance of simplicity of style. Walter Bagehot (see *National Review* below) bases his discussion of the poem on a sympathetic acceptance of the principles of the 1853 Preface.

Athenaeum, 1 Jan. 1848, 6–8, *The Princess*, 1847. J. W. Marston. (Shannon, p. 171.)

Examiner, 8 Jan. 1848, 20–1, *The Princess*, 1847. John Forster. (Shannon, p. 171.)

Howitt's Journal, 3, 8 Jan. 1848, 28–9, *The Princess*, 1847. William Howitt? (Shannon, p. 171.)

Christian Reformer, 4 N.S. (Feb. 1848), 111–13, *The Princess*, 1847.

Quarterly Review, 82 (March 1848), 427–53, *The Princess*, 1847. Sara Coleridge. (*W.I.*, p. 731.)

Rambler, 1 (11 March 1848), 210–13, *The Princess*, 1847.

North British Review, 9 (May 1848), 43–72, *The Princess*, 1847. Coventry Patmore. (*W.I.*, p. 671.)

The Times, 12 Oct. 1848, 3, *The Princess*, 1847. Manley Hopkins? (Shannon, p. 172.)

Westminster Review, 51 (July 1849), 265–90, *Poems*, 1842 (fifth ed.).

Edinburgh Review, 90 (Oct. 1849), 388–433, *The Princess*, 1847. Aubrey De Vere. (*W.I.*, p. 499.)

Examiner, 8 June 1850, 356–7, *In Memoriam*, 1850. John Forster. (Shannon p. 173.)

Inquirer, 22 June 1850, 389–90, *In Memoriam*, 1850.

Britannia, 29 June 1850, 410, *In Memoriam*, 1850.

British Quarterly Review, 12 (August 1850), 291–2, *In Memoriam*, 1850.

North British Review, 13 (August 1850), 532–55, *In Memoriam*, 1850. Coventry Patmore. (*W.I.*, p. 673.)

Eclectic Review, 28 N.S. (Sept. 1850), 330–41, *In Memoriam*, 1850.

English Review 14 (Sept. 1850), 65–92, *In Memoriam*, 1850 (also Browning and Taylor).

Fraser's Magazine, 42 (Sept. 1850), 245–55, *In Memoriam*, 1850. Charles Kingsley. (*W.I.*)

Christian Socialist, 2 (Aug.-Sept. 1851), 140–2; 155–7; 187–90, 'Tennyson and his Poetry'. Gerald Massey (signed).

The Times, 28 Nov. 1851, 8, *In Memoriam*, 1850. Manley Hopkins? (Shannon, p. 174.)

Critic, 14 N.S. (15 Aug. 1855), 386–7, *Maud*, 1855.

The Times, 25 Aug. 1855, 8. E. S. Dallas. (Shannon, *P.M.L.A.*, p. 417.)

Blackwood's Magazine, 78 (Sept. 1855), 311–21, *Maud*, 1855. W. E. Aytoun. (*W.I.*, p. 100.)

Irish Quarterly Review, 5 (Sept. 1855), 453–72, *Maud*, 1855.

Tait's Edinburgh Magazine, 22 N.S. (Sept. 1855), 531–9, *Maud*, 1855.

British Quarterly Review, 22 (Oct. 1855), 467–98, *Maud*, 1855. David Masson. (*W.I.*)

Edinburgh Review, 102 (Oct. 1855), 498–519, *Maud*, 1855. Coventry Patmore. (*W.I.*, p. 505.)

National Review, 1 (Oct. 1855), 377–410, *Maud*, 1855, W. C. Roscoe. (*W.I.*)

Scottish Review, 111 (Oct. 1855), 347–57; 353–7, *Maud*, 1855.

Westminster Review, 8 N.S. (Oct. 1855), 596–601, *Maud*, 1855. George Eliot. (Shannon, *P.M.L.A.*, p. 417.)

Oxford and Cambridge Magazine, 1, 2, 3 (Jan., Feb., March 1856), 7–18; 73–81; 136–45, Tennyson's work up to *Maud*, 1855. William Fulford. (Shannon, *P.M.L.A.*, p. 417.)

Christian Remembrancer, 31 (April 1856) 267–70, *Maud*, 1855.

London University Magazine, 1 (May 1856), 1–11, *Maud*, 1855.

Eclectic Review, 2 N.S. (Sept. 1859), 287–94, *Idylls of the King*, 1859.

Bentley's Quarterly Review, 2 (Oct. 1859), 159–94, *Idylls of the King*, 1859. Anne Mozley. (*W.I.*)

British Quarterly Review, 30 (Oct. 1859), 481–510, *Idylls of the King*, 1859.

London Review, 13 (Oct. 1859), 62–80, *Idylls of the King*, 1859.
National Review, 9 (Oct. 1859), 368–94, *Idylls of the King*, 1859. Walter
 Bagehot. (N. St John Stevas, *T.L.S.*, 26 April 1963.)
Quarterly Review, 106 (Oct. 1859), 454–85, *Idylls of the King*, 1859. W. E.
 Gladstone. (*W.I.*, p. 742.)
Westminster Review, 16 N.S. (Oct. 1859), 503–26, *Idylls of the King*, 1859.
 John Nichol. (*W.I.*)

BROWNING

Browning criticism during this period is dismal in its failures of understanding. He was attacked for his beliefs (see *Christian Remembrancer* below), for
his style and coarseness of subject matter. The most perceptive attack is by
a reviewer who complained that his poetry consisted merely of lumps of
thought and lacked the 'blended' effect of true poetical associative language
(see *Prospective Review* below). The *Christian Remembrancer* finally made
amends by saying (see third reference to *C.R.*) that irony was not necessarily
irrelevant but the effort it costs the writer to reach this position suggests how
difficult it was for the Victorian critic to assimilate Browning's poetry. Some
critics manage to catch the difficulties of Browning's language in vivid
phraseology but otherwise critical insight is lacking. W. M. Rossetti's
discussion of Browning's poetry and that of William Morris (see *Art and
Poetry* and *Oxford and Cambridge Magazine* below) are exceptionally free
from common presuppositions, though Morris's escape route from hostility
is not very inspiring. His is one of the first of the discussions of Browning
which make claims for the poet's philosophical teaching.

Art and Poetry, 4 (May 1850), 187–92, Browning's poetry up to *Christmas
 Eve and Easter Day*, 1850. W. M. Rossetti.
Prospective Review, 6 (July 1850), 267–79, *Christmas Eve and Easter Day*,
 1850 (also Bailey). R. H. Hutton. (*W.I.*)
Fraser's Magazine, 43 (Feb. 1851), 170–82, *Poems*, 1849 (also Elizabeth
 Barrett Browning). Charles Kingsley. (*W.I.*)
Christian Remembrancer, 21 N.S. (April 1851), 346–99, *Poems*, 1849 (also
 Elizabeth Barrett Browning, Bailey and others).
Bentley's Miscellany, 39 (Jan. 1856), 64–70, *Men and Women*, 1855.
Fraser's Magazine, 53 (Jan. 1856), 105–16, *Men and Women*, 1855. George
 Brimley. (Broughton, p. 97.)
Westminster Review, 9 N.S. (Jan. 1856), 290–6, *Men and Women*, 1855.
 George Eliot. (*W.I.*)
Oxford and Cambridge Magazine, 1 (March 1856), 162–72, *Men and Women*,
 1855. William Morris.
Christian Remembrancer, 31 N.S. (April 1856), 267–308, *Men and Women*,
 1855 (and others).

Christian Remembrancer, 34 N.S. (Oct. 1857), 361–90, *Men and Women*, 1855. J. G. Cazenove or John Gibson. (*W.I.*)

CLOUGH

Clough's poems were sometimes reviewed with Arnold's first volume, *The Strayed Reveller*. I have chosen reviews which suggest how writers are divided between appreciating Clough's response to everyday realities and suspecting his 'morbid conscientiousness', as the *Guardian* put it (see below). It is noticeable that Clough and Arnold were often seen in relation to the influence of the established poets, Tennyson and Browning. Arnold is often included in hostile discussions of Clough's Wertherism. The *English Review* (see below) summed them up: ' "A's" singing is like the musical wind wailing through the forest tops on the high mountains far away. "Clough" resembles rather the monotonous heaving of the sea against a rock-bound shore.'

Fraser's Magazine, 39 (Jan. 1849), 103–10, *The Bothie*, 1848. Charles Kingsley. *Correspondence of A. H. Clough*, ed. F. Mulhauser (Oxford, 1957), i, 229.

Spectator, 20 Jan. 1849, 65, *Ambarvalia*, 1849.

Fraser's Magazine, 39 (March 1849), 342–7, *Ambarvalia*, 1849. William Whewell (R. M. Gollin, W. E. Houghton, M. Timko, *Clough: A Descriptive Catalogue*, New York, 1967, p. 67.)

Guardian, 28 March 1849, 208–209, *Ambarvalia*, 1849, and Arnold's *The Strayed Reveller*, 1849.

Germ, 1 (Jan. 1850), 36–48, *The Bothie*, 1848. W. M. Rossetti.

Prospective Review, 6 (Jan. 1850), 112–37, *Ambarvalia*, 1849.

English Review, 13 (March 1850), 207–13, *Ambarvalia*, 1849; *The Bothie*, 1848, and Arnold's *The Strayed Reveller*, 1849.

ARNOLD

I have chosen reviews prior to 1853 to suggest how common it was for writers to criticise the melancholy, the standoffish aloofness of Arnold's poems and their lack of involvement with contemporary life—'Resignation! To what? To doing nothing? To discovering that a poet's business is "swinging on a gate" . . .' (see *Fraser's Magazine*, 1849, below). In choosing reviews of the 1853 volume I have tried to illustrate the intelligence with which the issues of the Preface were discussed. The debate is still very much alive in discussions of *Merope*.

Spectator, 10 March 1849, 231, *The Strayed Reveller*, 1849.

Fraser's Magazine, 39 (May 1849), 570–86, *The Strayed Reveller*, 1849. Charles Kingsley. (Coulling, p. 239, n. 18.)

Blackwood's Magazine, 66 (Sept. 1849), 340–6, *The Strayed Reveller*, 1849. W. E. Aytoun. (*W.I.*, p. 87.)

Germ, 2 (Feb. 1850), 84–96, *The Strayed Reveller*, 1849. W. M. Rossetti.

North British Review, 19 (May 1853), 209–18, *Empedocles on Etna*, 1852. Coventry Patmore or George David Boyle. (*W.I.*, p. 676.)

Times, 4 Nov. 1853, 5, *Empedocles on Etna*, 1852. Goldwin Smith. (Coulling, p. 239, n. 17.)

Spectator, 26, 1853, Supplement, 5–6, *Poems*, 1853.

Leader, 4, 1853, 1147; 1170, *Poems*, 1853. G. H. Lewes. (Coulling, p. 251.)

Westminster Review, 5 N.S. (Jan. 1854), 146–59, *Poems*, 1853. J. A. Froude. (*W.I.*)

Fraser's Magazine, 49 (Feb. 1854), 140–9, *Poems*, 1853. Charles Kingsley. (*W.I.*)

Blackwood's Magazine, 75 (March 1854), 303–14, *Poems*, 1853. W. E. Aytoun. (*W.I.*, p. 97.)

Christian Remembrancer, 27 N.S. (April 1854), 310–33, *Poems*, 1853. John Duke Coleridge. (Coulling, p. 250, n. 31.)

Putnam's Monthly Magazine, 3 (April 1854), 452; 6 (Sept. 1855), 235–8, Arnold's work up to *Poems*, 1855.

Dublin University Magazine, 43 (June 1854), 736–52, *Poems*, 1853. John Francis or more prob. J. F. Walker. (*W.I.*)

North British Review, 21 (August 1854), 493–504, *Poems*, 1853. J. C. Shairp. (*W.I.*, p. 678.)

Eclectic Review, 9 N.S. (March 1855), 276–84, *Poems, Second Series*, 1855.

Dublin University Magazine, 51 (March 1858), 331–44, *Merope*, 1858. William Alexander. (*W.I.*)

National Review, 6 (April 1858), 259–79, *Merope*, 1858. W. C. Roscoe. (*W.I.*)

Fraser's Magazine, 57 (June 1858), 691–701, *Merope*, 1858. John Conington? (*W.I.*)

North British Review, 29 (August 1858), 124–48. *Merope*, 1858. Coventry Patmore. (*W.I.*, p. 682.)

Browning, Clough and Tennyson in the 1860s

10

Browning ∾ *The Ring and the Book* ∾ 1868–9

John Morley, *Fortnightly Review*, v N.S. (March 1869), 331–43

When the first volume of Mr Browning's new poem came before the critical tribunals, public and private, recognised or irresponsible, there was much lamentation even in quarters where a manlier humour might have been expected, over the poet's choice of a subject. With facile largeness of censure, it was pronounced a murky subject, sordid, unlovely, morally sterile, an ugly leaf out of some seventeenth-century Italian Newgate Calendar. One hinted in vain that wisdom is justified of her children, that the poet must be trusted to judge of the capacity of his own theme, and that it is his conception and treatment of it which ultimately justify or discredit his choice. Now that the entire work is before the world, this is plain, and it is admitted. When the second volume, containing *Giuseppe Caponsacchi*, appeared, men no longer found it sordid or ugly; the third, with *Pompilia*, convinced them that the subject was not, after all, so incurably unlovely; and the fourth, with *The Pope*, and the passage from the Friar's sermon, may well persuade those who needed persuasion, that moral fruitfulness depends on the master, his eye and hand, his vision and grasp, more than on the this and that of the transaction which has taken possession of his imagination.

The truth is, we have this long while been so debilitated by pastorals, by graceful presentation of the Arthurian legend for drawing-rooms, by idylls, not robust and Theocritean, but such little pictures as might adorn a ladies' school, by verse directly didactic, that a rude inburst of

John Morley, 1838–1923, scholar and man of letters, social critic and statesman, edited the *Fortnightly Review* from 1867–82. One might point to Morley's agnosticism and his writings on Voltaire (1872) and Rousseau (1873) as examples of the change in the intellectual atmosphere of the late sixties which is noted by Sidgwick in his review of Clough (see below, p. 289).

air from the outside welter of human realities is apt to spread a shock, which might show in what simpleton's paradise we have been living. The little ethics of the rectory parlour set to sweet music, the respectable aspirations of the sentimental curate married to exquisite verse, the everlasting glorification of domestic sentiment in blameless princes and others, as if that were the poet's single province and the divinely-appointed end of all art, as if domestic sentiment included and summed up the whole throng of passions, emotions, strife, and desire; all this would seem to be turning us into flat valetudinarians. Our public is beginning to measure the right and possible in art, by the superficial probabilities of life and manners within a ten-mile radius of Charing Cross. Is it likely, asks the critic, that Duke Silva would have done this, that Fedalma would have done that?[1] Who shall suppose it possible that Caponsacchi acted thus, that Count Guido was possessed by devils so? The poser is triumphant, because the critic is tacitly appealing to the normal standard of probabilities at Bayswater or Clapham; as a man who, having never thought of anything mightier or more turbulent than the village brook or horse-pond, would most effectively disparage all stories of wreck and storm on the great main. In the tragedy of Pompilia we are taken far from the serene and homely region in which some of our teachers would fain have it that the whole moral universe can be snugly pent up. We see the black passions of man at their blackest; hate, so fierce, undiluted, implacable, passionate, as to be hard of conception by our simpler northern natures; cruelty, so vindictive, subtle, persistent, deadly, as to fill us with a pain almost too great for true art to produce; greediness, lust, craft, penetrating a whole stock and breed, even down to the ancient mother of 'that fell house of hate',

> The gaunt grey nightmare in the furthest smoke,
> . . .
> The while she lets youth take its pleasure.

But, then, if the poet has lighted up for us these grim and appalling depths, he has not failed to raise us too into the presence of proportionate loftiness and purity.

> Tantum vertice in auras
> Aetherias quantum radice in Tartara tendit.[2]

[1] Duke Silva and Fedalma: characters in George Eliot's *The Spanish Gypsy*.
[2] '[the oak above all, whose] head reaches as far into the heavens as its roots stretch into the world below'. Virgil, *Georgics* 2. 292.

Like the gloomy and umbrageous grove of which the Sibyl spake to the pious Æneas, the poem conceals a golden branch and golden leaves. In the second volume, Guido, servile and false, is followed by Caponsacchi, as noble alike in conception and execution as anything that Mr Browning has achieved. In the third volume, the austere pathos of Pompilia's tale relieves the too oppressive jollity of Don Giacinto, and the flowery rhetoric of Bottini; while in the fourth, the deep wisdom, justice, and righteous mind of the Pope, reconcile us to endure the sulphurous whiff from the pit in the confession of Guido, now desperate, satanic, and naked. From what at first was sheer murk, there comes out a long procession of human figures, infinitely various in form and thought, in character and act; a group of men and women, eager, passionate, indifferent: tender and ravenous, mean and noble, humorous and profound, jovial with prosperity or half-dumb with misery, skirting the central tragedy, or plunged deep into the thick of it, passers-by who put themselves off with a glance at the surface of a thing, and another or two who dive to the heart of it. And they all come out with a certain Shakespearian fullness, vividness, directness. Above all, they are every one of them frankly men and women, with free play of human life in limb and feature, as in an antique sculpture. So much of modern art, in poetry as in painting, runs to mere drapery. 'I grant', said Lessing, 'that there is also a beauty in drapery, but can it be compared with that of the human form? And shall he who can attain to the greater, rest content with the less? I much fear that the most perfect master in drapery shows by that very talent where his in weakness lies.'[3] This was spoken of plastic art, but it has a yet deeper meaning in poetic criticism. There too, the master is he who presents the natural shape, the curves, the thews of men, and does not labour and seek praise for faithful reproduction of the mere moral drapery of the hour, this or another; who gives you Hercules at strife with Antaeus, Laocoon writhing in the coils of the divine serpents, the wrestle with circumstance or passion, with outward destiny or inner character, in the free outlines of nature and reality, and not in the outlines of a dress-coat, either of Victorian or Arthurian time. The capacity which it has for this presentation, at once so varied and so direct, is one reason why the dramatic form ranks as the highest expression and measure of the creative power of the poet; and the extraordinary grasp with which Mr Browning has availed himself of this double capacity,

[3] Lessing, *Laokoon,* ch. v.

is one reason why we should reckon *The Ring and the Book* as his masterpiece.

One may say this, and still not be blind to the faults of the poem. Many persons agree that they find it too long, and if they find it so, then for them it is too long. There were probably some among the Greeks who could find nothing to remark about Phidias's famous statue of Zeus at Olympia, except that it was monstrous that a statue should be sixty feet high. Others, who cannot resist the critic's temptation of believing that a remark must be true if it only look acute and specific, vow that the disclosure in the first volume of the whole plan and plot vitiates subsequent artistic merit. If one cannot enjoy what comes, for knowing beforehand what is coming, this objection may be allowed to have a root in human nature; but then two things might perhaps be urged on the other side, first, that the interest of the poem lies in the development and presentation of character, on the one hand, and in the many sides which a single transaction offered to as many minds, on the other; and therefore that this true interest could not be marred by the bare statement what the transaction was or, baldly looked at, seemed to be; and, second, that the poem was meant to find its reader in a mood of mental repose, ready to receive the poet's impressions, undisturbed by any agitating curiosity as to plot or final outcome. A more valid accusation touches the many verbal perversities, in which a poet has less right than another to indulge. The compound Latin and English of Don Giacinto, notwithstanding the fun of the piece, still grows a burden to the flesh. Then there are harsh and formless lines, bursts of metrical chaos, from which a writer's dignity and self-respect ought surely to be enough to preserve him. Again, there are passages marked by a coarse violence of expression that is nothing short of barbarous (for instance, ii. 190, or 245). The only thing to be said is, that the countrymen of Shakespeare have had to learn to forgive terrible uncouthnesses, blunt outrages on form and beauty, to fine creative genius. If only one could be sure that readers, unschooled as too many are to love the simple and elevated beauty of such form as Sophocles or Corneille gives, would not think the worst fault the chief virtue, and confound the poet's uncouthnesses with his admirable originality. It is certain that in Shakespeare's case, his defects are constantly fastened upon, by critics who have never seriously studied the forms of dramatic art except in the literature of England, and extolled as instances of his characteristic mightiness. It may well be, therefore, that the grotesque caprices which Mr Browning unfortunately permits to himself may find misguided admirers, or, what is worse, even imitators. It would be most unjust, however, while making due mention of these things, to pass over the dignity and splendour of the verse in a great number of places, where the intensity of the writer's mood finds worthy embodiment in a sustained gravity and vigour and finish of diction not to be surpassed. The concluding lines of the *Caponsacchi* (comprising the last page of the second volume), the appeal of the Greek poet in *The Pope*, one or two passages in the first *Guido* (e.g. vol. ii, p. 156, from line 1957), and the close of the *Pompilia*, ought to be referred to when one wishes to know what power over the instrument of his art Mr Browning might have achieved, if he had chosen to discipline himself in instrumentation.

When all is said that can be said about the violences which from time to time invade the poem, it remains true that the complete work affects the reader most powerfully with that wide unity of impression which it is the highest aim of dramatic art, and perhaps of all art, to produce. After we have listened to all the whimsical dogmatising about beauty, to all the odious cant about morbid anatomy, to all the well-deserved reproach for unforgivable perversities of phrase and outrages on rhythm, there is left to us the consciousness that a striking human transaction has been seized by a vigorous and profound imagination, that its many diverse threads have been wrought into a single rich and many-coloured web of art, in which we may see traced for us the labyrinths of passion and indifference, stupidity and craft, prejudice and chance, along which truth and justice have to find a devious and doubtful way. The transaction itself, lurid and fuliginous, is secondary to the manner of its handling and presentment. We do not derive our sense of unity from the singleness and completeness of the horrid tragedy, so much as from the power with which its own circumstances as they happened, the rumours which clustered about it from the minds of men without, the many moods, fancies, dispositions, which it for the moment brought out into light, playing round the fact, the half-sportive flights with which lawyers, judges, quidnuncs of the street, darted at conviction and snatched hap-hazard at truth, are all wrought together into one self-sufficient and compacted shape.

But this shape is not beautiful, and the end of art is beauty? Verbal fanaticism is always perplexing, and, rubbing my eyes, I ask whether then beauty means anything more than such an arrangement and disposition of the parts of the work as, first kindling a great variety of dispersed emotions and thoughts in the mind of the spectator, finally concentrates them in a single mood of joyous, sad, meditative, or interested delight. The sculptor, the painter, and the musician, have each their special means of producing this final and superlative impression; each is bound by the strictly limited capability in this direction and in that of the medium in which he works. In poetry it is because they do not perceive how much more manifold and varied are the means of reaching the end than in the other expressions of art, that people insist each upon some particular quiddity which, entering into composition, alone constitutes it genuinely poetic, beautiful, or artistic. Pressing for definition, you never get much further than that each given quiddity means a certain Whatness. This is why poetical criticism is usually so little catholic. A man remembers that a poem in one style has filled him with consciousness of beauty and delight. Why conclude that this style constitutes the one access to the same impression? Why not rather perceive that, to take contemporaries, the beauty of *Thyrsis* is mainly produced by a fine suffusion of delicately-toned emotion; that of *Atalanta* by splendid and barely rivalled music of verse; of *In Memoriam* by its ordered and harmonious presentation of a sacred mood; of the *Spanish Gypsy*, in the parts where it reaches beauty, by a sublime ethical passion; of the *Earthly Paradise*, by sweet and simple reproduction of the spirit of the younger-hearted times? There are poems by Mr Browning in which it is difficult, or, let us frankly say, impossible, for most of us at all events and as yet, to discover the beauty, or shape. But if beauty may not be denied to a work which, abounding in many-coloured scenes and diverse characters, in vivid image and frank portraiture, wide reflection and multiform emotion, does further, by a broad thread of thought running under all, bind these impressions into one supreme and elevated conviction, then assuredly, whatever we may think of this passage or that, that episode or the other, the first volume or the third, we may not deny that *The Ring and the Book*, in its perfection and integrity, fully satisfies the conditions of artistic triumph. Are we to ignore the grandeur of a colossal statue, and the nobility of the human conceptions which it embodies, because here and there we notice a flaw in the marble, a blemish in its colour, a jagged slip of the chisel? 'It is not force of intellect', a fine writer has said, 'which causes ready repulsion from the aberration and eccentricities of greatness, any more than it is force of vision that causes the eye to explore the warts in a face bright with human expression; it is simply the negation of high sensibilities.'[4]

Then, it is asked by persons of another and differently rigorous temper, whether, as the world goes, the subject, or its treatment either, justifies us in reading some twenty-one thousand and seventy-five lines, which do not seem to have any direct tendency to make us better or to improve mankind. This objection is an old enemy with a new face, and need not detain us, though perhaps the crude and incessant application of a narrowly moral standard, thoroughly misunderstood, is one of the intellectual dangers of our time. You may now and again hear a man of really masculine character confess that though he loves Shakespeare and takes habitual delight in his works, he cannot see that he was a particularly moral writer. That is to say, Shakespeare is never directly didactic; you can no more get a system of morals out of his writings, than you can get such a system out of the writings of the ever-searching Plato. But, if we must be quantitative, one great creative poet probably exerts a nobler, deeper, more permanent ethical influence than a dozen generations of professed moral teachers, including under the latter head such poets, too, as forgetful of their earlier skill, now strum us dolefully forth the tracts in polished verse of blameless Arthurs and prodigious Enochs. It is a commonplace to the wise, and an everlasting puzzle to the foolish, that direct inculcation of morals should invariably prove so powerless an instrument, so futile a method. As though one should wonder why flower-stems stuck into the casual earth must droop and perish. The truth is that nothing can be more powerfully efficacious from the moral point of view than the exercise of an exalted creative art, stirring within the intelligence of the spectator active thought and curiosity about many types of character and many changeful issues of conduct and fortune, at once enlarging and elevating the range of his reflections on mankind, ever kindling his sympathies into the warm and continuous glow which purifies and strengthens nature, and fills men with that love of humanity which is the best inspirer of virtue. Is not this why music, too, is to be counted supreme among moral agents, soothing disorderly passion by diving down into the hidden deeps of character where there is no disorder, and touching the diviner mind? Given a certain rectitude as well as vigour of intelligence, then whatever stimulates the fancy, expands the imagination, enlivens meditation upon the great human drama, is essentially moral. Shakespeare does all this,

---

[4] I have been unable to find the source of this quotation.

as if sent Iris-like from the immortal gods, and *The Ring and the Book* has a measure of the same incomparable quality.

There is a profound and moving irony in the structure of the poem. Any other human transaction that ever was, tragic or comic or plain prosaic, may be looked at in a like spirit. As the world's talk bubbled around the dumb anguish of Pompilia, the cruelty and hate of Guido, so it does around the hourly tragedies of all times and places.

> The instinctive theorizing whence a fact
> . . .
> Talked over, bruited abroad, whispered away:

if we reflect that these are the conditions which have marked the formation of all the judgements that we hold by, and which are vivid in operation and effect at this hour, the deep irony and the impressive meaning of the poem are both obvious:

> So learn one lesson hence
> . . .
> And human estimation words and wind.

It is characteristic of Mr Browning that he thus casts the moral of his piece in an essentially intellectual rather than an emotional form, appealing to hard judgement rather than to imaginative sensibility. Another living poet of original genius, of whom we have much right to complain that he gives us so little, ends a poem in two or three lines which are worth quoting here for the illustration they afford of what has just been said about Mr Browning:

> Ah, what a dusty answer gets the soul,
> When hot for certainties in this our life!—
> In tragic hints here see what evermore
> Moves dark as yonder midnight ocean's force,
> Thundering like ramping hosts of warrior horse,
> To throw that faint thin line upon the shore?[5]

This is imaginative and sympathetic in thought as well as expression, and the truth and the image enter the writer's mind together, the one by the other. The lines convey poetic sentiment rather than reasoned truth; while Mr Browning's close would be no unfit epilogue to a scientific essay on history, or a treatise on the errors of the human

[5] George Meredith, *Modern Love*, L.

understanding and the inaccuracy of human opinion and judgement. This is the common note of his highest work; hard thought and reason illustrating themselves in dramatic circumstance, and the thought and reason are not wholly fused, but exist apart and irradiate with far-shooting beams the moral confusion of the tragedy. This is, at any rate, emphatically true of *The Ring and the Book*. The fullness and variety of creation, the amplitude of the play and shifting of characters and motive and mood, are absolutely unforced, absolutely uninterfered with by the artificial exigencies of ethical or philosophic purpose. There is the purpose, full-grown, clear in outline, unmistakeable in significance. But the just proprieties of place and season are rigorously observed, because Mr Browning, like every other poet of his quality, has exuberant and adequate delight in mere creation, simple presentment, and returns to bethink him of the meaning of it all only by-and-by. The pictures of Guido, of Pompilia, of Caponsacchi, of Dominus Hyacinthus de Archangelis, of Pope Innocent, are each of them full and adequate, as conceptions of character in active manifestation, apart from the truth which the whole composition is meant to illustrate, and which clothes itself in this most excellent drama.

The scientific attitude of the intelligence is almost as markedly visible in Mr Browning as the strength of his creative power. The lesson of *The Ring and the Book* is perhaps as nearly positive as anything poetic can be. It is true that ultimately the drama ends in a vindication of what are called the ways of God to man, if indeed people are willing to put themselves off with a form of omnipotent justice which is simply a partial retribution inflicted on the monster, while torture and butchery fall upon victims more or less absolutely blameless. As if the fact of punishment at length overtaking the guilty Franceschini were any vindication of the justice of that assumed providence which had for so long a time awarded punishment far more harsh to the innocent Pompilia. So far as you can be content with the vindication of a justice of this less than equivocal quality, the sight of the monster brought to the

> Close fetid cell,
> Where the hot vapour of an agony,
> Struck into drops on the cold wall, runs down
> Horrible worms made out of sweat and tears,

may in a sense prove satisfactory enough. But a man must be very dull who in reading the poem does not perceive that the very spirit of it points to the thousand hazards which even this thrum and fragment of justice had to run in saving itself and bringing about such partially righteous consummation as destiny permits. True opinion fares yet more perilously. *Half-Rome*, the *Other Half-Rome*, the *Tertium Quid*, which is perhaps most masterly and finished of the three, show us how ill truth sifts itself, to how many it never comes at all, how blurred, confused, next door to false, it is figured even to those who seize it by the hem of the garment. We may, perhaps, yawn over the intermingled Latin and law of Arcangeli, in spite of the humour of parts of it, and over the vapid floweriness of his rival; but for all that, we are touched keenly by the irony of the methods by which the two professional truth-sifters are made to darken counsel with words, and make skilful sport of life and fact. The whole poem is a parable of the feeble and half-hopeless struggle which truth has to make against the ways of the world. That in this particular case truth and justice did win some pale sort of victory does not weaken the force of the lesson. The victory was such and so won as to stir in us awful thoughts of fatal risks and certain defeats, of falsehood a thousand times clasped for truth, of fact a thousand times banished for fancy:

> Because Pompilia's purity prevails,
> . . .
> Beauty made blank and harmlessness destroyed!

Or, to take another simile from the same magnificent passage, in which the fine dignity of the verse fitly matches the deep truth of the preacher's monitions:

> Romans! An elder race possessed your land
> . . .
> Each vulgar god that awes the market-place?

With less impetuosity and a more weightily reasoned argument the Pope confronts the long perplexity and entanglement of circumstances with the fatuous optimism which insists that somehow justice and virtue do rule in the world. Consider all the doings at Arezzo, before and after the consummation of the tragedy. What of the Aretine archbishop, to whom Pompilia cried 'Protect me from the fiend!'—

> 'No, for thy Guido is one heady, strong,
> . . .
> —Come to me, daughter,—thus I throw him back!'

Then the monk to whom she went, imploring him to write to Rome:

> He meets the first cold sprinkle of the world
> And shudders to the marrow, 'Save this child?
> Oh, my superiors, oh, the Archbishop here!
> Who was it dared lay hand upon the ark
> His betters saw fall nor put finger forth?'

Worst of all, the Convent of the Convertites, women to whom she was consigned for help,

> They do help; they are prompt to testify
> To her pure life and saintly dying days.
> . . .
>   They unsay
> All the fine speeches,—who was saint is whore.

It is not wonderful if his review of all the mean and dolorous circumstance of this cycle of wrong brings the Pope face to face with the unconquerable problem for the Christian believer, the keystone of the grim arch of religious doubt and despair, through which the courageous soul must needs pass to creeds of reason and life. Where is 'the gloriously decisive change, the immeasurable metamorphosis' in human worth that should in some sort justify the consummate price that had been paid for man these seventeen hundred years before?

> Had a mere adept of the Rosy Cross
> . . .
> Well, is the thing we see, salvation?

It is certain that by whatever other deficiencies it may be marked *The Ring and the Book* is blameless for the most characteristic of all the shortcomings of contemporary verse, a grievous sterility of thought. And why? Because sterility of thought is the blight struck into the minds of men by timorous and halt-footed scepticism, by a half-hearted dread of what chill thing the truth might prove itself, by unmanly reluctance or moral incapacity to carry the faculty of poetic vision over the whole field; and because Mr Browning's intelligence, on the other hand, is masculine and courageous, moving cheerfully on the solid earth of an articulate and defined conviction, and careful not to omit realities from the conception of the great drama, merely for being unsightly to the too fastidious eye, or jarring in the ear, or too bitterly perplexing to faith or understanding. It is this resolute feeling after and grip of fact which is at the root of his distinguishing fruitfulness of thought, and it is exuberance of thought, spontaneous, wellmarked, and sapid, that keeps him out of poetical preaching, on the one hand, and mere making of music, on the other. Regret as we may the fantastic rudeness and unscrupulous barbarisms into which Mr Browning's art too often falls, and find what fault we may with his method, let us ever remember how much he has to say, and how effectively he communicates the shock of new thought which was first imparted to him by the vivid conception of a large and far-reaching story. The value of the thought, indeed, is not to be measured by poetic tests; but still the thought has poetic value, too, for it is this which has stirred in the writer that keen yet impersonal interest in the actors of his story and in its situations which is one of the most certain notes of true dramatic feeling, and which therefore gives the most unfailing stimulus to the interest of the appreciative reader.

At first sight *The Ring and the Book* appears to be absolutely wanting in that grandeur which, in a composition of such enormous length, criticism must pronounce to be a fundamental and indispensable element. In an ordinary way this effect of grandeur is produced either by some heroic action surrounded by circumstances of worthy stateliness, as in the finest of the Greek plays; or as in *Paradise Lost* by the presence of personages of majestic sublimity of bearing and association; or as in *Faust* or *Hamlet* by the stupendous moral abysses which the poet discloses fitfully on this side and that. None of these things are to be found in *The Ring and the Book*. The action of Caponsacchi, though noble and disinterested, is hardly heroic in the highest dramatic sense, for it is not much more than the lofty defiance of a conventionality, the contemplated penalty being only small; not, for example, as if life or ascertained happiness had been the fixed or even probable price of his magnanimous enterprise. There was no marching to the stake, no deliberate encountering of the mightier risks, no voluntary submission to a lifelong endurance. True, this came in the end, but it was an end unforeseen, and one, therefore, not to be associated with the first conception of the original act. Besides, Guido is so saturated with hateful and ignoble motive as to fill the surrounding air with influences that preclude heroic association. It has been said of the great men to whom the Byzantine empire once or twice gave birth, that even their fame has a curiously tarnished air, as if that too had been touched by the evil breath of the times. And in like manner we may say of Guido Franceschini that he was such that even to have touched him in the way of resistance detracts from pure heroism. Perhaps the same consideration explains the comparative disappointment which most people seem to have felt with *Pompilia* in the third volume. Again, there is nothing which can be rightly called majesty of character visible in one personage or another. There is high devotion in Caponsacchi, a large-minded and free sagacity in Pope Innocent, and around Pompilia the tragic pathos of an incurable woe, which by its intensity might raise her to grandeur if it sprang from some more solemn source than the mere malignity and baseness of an unworthy oppressor. Lastly, there is nothing in *The Ring and the Book* of that 'certain incommensurableness' which Goethe found in his own *Faust*. The poem is kept closely concrete and strictly commensurable by the very framework of its story:

> pure crude fact,
> Secreted from man's life when hearts beat hard,
> And brains, high-blooded, ticked two centuries since.

It moves from none of the supernatural agencies which give the impulse to our interest in *Faust*, nor from the sublimer passions and yearnings after things unspeakable in *Faust*, and in *Hamlet* as well.

Yet, notwithstanding its lack of the accustomed elements of grandeur, there is a profound impressiveness about *The Ring and the Book* which must arise from the presence of some other fine compensating or equivalent quality. Perhaps one may say that this equivalent for grandeur is a certain simple touching of our sense of human kinship, of the large identity of the conditions of the human lot, of the piteous fatalities which bring the lives of the great multitude of men to be little more than 'grains of sand to be blown by the wind'. This old woe, the poet says, now in the fulness of the days again lives,

> If precious be the soul of man to man.

This is the deeply implanted sentiment to which his poem makes successful appeal. Nor is it mocked by mere outpouring of scorn on the blind and fortuitous groping of men and societies of men after truth and justice and traces of the watchfulness of 'the unlidded eye of God'. Rather it is this inability to see beyond the facts of our condition to some diviner, ever-present law, which helps to knit us to our kind, our brethren 'whom we have seen'.

Clouds obscure—
But for which obscuration all were bright?
Too hastily concluded! Sun-suffused,
A cloud may soothe the eye made blind by blaze,—
Better the very clarity of heaven:
The soft streaks are the beautiful and dear.
What but the weakness in a faith supplies
The incentive to humanity, no strength
Absolute, irresistible, comports?
How can man love but what he yearns to help?
And that which men think weakness within strength
But angels know for strength and stronger get—
What were it else but the first things made new,
But repetition of the miracle,
The divine instance of self-sacrifice
That never ends and aye begins for man?

I I

Browning ❧ *The Ring and the Book* ❧ 1868–9

Richard Simpson, *North British Review*, li
(October 1869), 97–126

'The Title', says Remigius on Donatus, 'is the key or porch of the
work to which it is prefixed.' 'And note', adds pseudo-Aquinas upon
Boethius, after quoting it, 'that Title is so called from Titan, that is the
Sun. For as the Sun enlighteneth the world, so doth the Title the book.'
The title of Mr Browning's new poem is so far from doing this, that he
is obliged to set apart a book of the poem to shed light on the title. At
first sight it might appear that it referred to the ring or circle of cantos
of which the book consists; or that it hinted at the poet's solicitude for
proportion, and his care that the architecture of his poem should be as
good as its masonry, and that the whole should be symmetrical as a
circle. These ideas may be implied; but the author's primary meaning
is something far more material and realistic. He presents himself to us
with a ring in one hand and a book in the other. The first, he tells us,
is Roman work by Castellani;[1] and he explains by what art so delicate

Richard Simpson, 1820–76, Roman Catholic writer and Shakespearian scholar,
was editor of the *Home and Foreign Review* from 1862–4. He contributed some
outstanding criticism to the *North British Review*. This essay is one of the most
perceptive of nineteenth-century discussions of Browning.

[1] Browning's 'Castellani' is not a person, as Simpson suggests, but a firm of
Roman jewellers. The opening sentences of the review refer to scholastic
writers and philosophers, all with legendary reputations as men of learning
in the middle ages. This rather ponderous opening is probably an attempt
to poke fun at Browning's display of learning. Aelius Donatus, who taught
at Rome in the middle of the fourth century A.D., was the author of the *Ars
Grammatica*, widely used in the middle ages, and his name, a *donet*, was given
to any treatise setting out the elements of a subject. Remigius, who died in
A.D. 533, was influential as the bishop of Rheims. Boethius was, of course,
widely known for his *De Consolatione Philosophiae*. I have not been able to

a filigree is produced—how, in order to render the thin gold capable of bearing the tools which are to emboss it, it is mixed with alloy, and the composite mass hammered out into its proper shape, when, with a spurt of acid, the alloy is burnt away, leaving the gold pure and all its embellishments perfect. The book, he tells us, is a volume, half print, half manuscript, which he found at a stall in Florence, and which contains all the documents and pleadings in the case of a murder committed in Rome in 1698 by Count Guido Franceschini upon his wife, Pompilia Comparini, and her supposed father and mother. This book he compares to the pure gold of fact, which he alloys with a sufficient amount of poetical fiction to be able to round it off into a perfect and living work of art. As it will be necessary afterwards to inquire how far he has complied with the conditions which he has set himself, we may pass on for the present, because, as one of the characters says,

> we must not stick
> *Quod non sit attendendus Titulus*
> To the Title.

There can be little doubt that this poem is the masterpiece of the writer. With a timely consciousness that he has hitherto failed to be generally understood, he has set himself in the early afternoon of his power to repeat what he had to say in a tongue more comprehensible. Once, it seems, he thought that if he could understand himself, any one else could understand him; that if his eyes were focused, and his ears attuned for the cave,

> Where brooding darkness spreads his jealous wings,
> And the night raven sings,

all other eyes and ears would be equally piercing and equally pleased. But he acknowledges that the British public has decreed otherwise; therefore, with a self-denying modesty, he has determined to write for the many, and not for the few. He has entered into himself, felt the pulse of his Muse, found where its beats were out of sympathy with the national pulse, and has at last attempted to produce a national poem,

> Perchance more careful whoso runs may read
> . . .
> Was apt to find himself the self-same me.

ascertain which late medieval writer was known as pseudo-Aquinas in the nineteenth century.

The simple confession that he never knew he was too hard for the most cursory reader sheds a flood of light on the author of *Sordello* and *Paracelsus*. If he was unintelligible, it was not on theory, . . . but with a consciousness of a secret gift which genius spontaneously reveals. . . Criticism, indeed, is hardly to be trusted in appraising novelties; nor is it quite its business to announce to the world the advent of the poet of the future. It can see the revolution, can perceive the negation, but cannot determine the positive worth of the new phenomenon. It is not criticism, but sympathy, which catches at once the whispers of genius, and readily recognises a new poet in the bud. Such an apparition appeals to the critic, not on the critical side of his nature, which proceeds by rules and precedents, but on the side of his feelings, which it is his business to control and prune. The plodding critic sees too little; the enthusiastic critic sees too much; the genuine critic is suspected of enthusiasm. Amongst them the new poet remains unacknowledged, and has to make his way painfully by his own weight. Mr Browning has experienced this long struggle, and, though forcing himself to be cheerful under the trial, has, at least vicariously, grumbled at his audience,

> The public blames originalities.
> You must not pump spring-water unawares
> Upon a gracious public, full of nerves.

With 'patience perforce', he has resigned himself to be his own audience and his own critic; but fortunately for himself, he has also kept his ears open to the sounds of the outer world, and at last the happy thought has struck him that he would try to say what he meant in a language common to himself and his fellow-men. This has worked well for his poetry. There is a new sense of freedom in his present book. The man who writes for himself only, his own sole reader and sole judge, can never satisfy himself; for, knowing both terms, the ideal and its embodiment, he knows also the gulf between them. In writing for others, he writes for those who can only guess at his ideal, and cannot tell whether his expression of it falls short or runs over; he must therefore be more careless of their judgement than of his own. Writing for other men thus delivers the scrupulous author from his own most importunate carper, himself, without making him the thrall of his new masters. It delivers him from his domestic slavery without selling him to a new servitude.

In availing himself of his new freedom, Mr Browning has wrought no notable change in himself. He is the same man, the same thinker, the same speaker, as formerly, but delivered at last from the bonds of the anxious and minute self-inspection and examination which, he confesses, qualified his former utterances. The present poem of 21,000 lines, the product of four years' thought, has evidently not been distilled by driblets with a bar's rest between each drop, in the alternate fire of invention and frost of criticism. Mr Browning has never been one

> To strain from hard-bound brains eight lines a year.

On the contrary, his gush is, if anything, too easy; he sometimes squanders himself in a debauch of words, and, rather than fall short of his tale of bread, when wheat-flour fails will make use of sawdust and chopped hay. Such stuffing is omitted in this, the first poem which the author has written avowedly and of set purpose, not for himself but for his audience, and with the express intention of converting the 'British public', who hitherto have 'liked me not', into admirers who 'may like me yet, marry and amen'. It is not that the coarse love of reputation has replaced the refined craving for sympathy, but that the sense of power urges him to assay his force upon a larger mass.

In the explanation which he gives of the title of his poem, Mr Browning invites attention to the matter of which he makes it, to the form in which he ultimately leaves it, and to the alloy which he lends it, by projecting into it his own 'surplusage of soul'. The poet, his method, and his materials, make up his poem.

Mr Browning has been long before the world. As a poet he seeks to be not a mere rhymer, not a mere expresser of ordinary thoughts in uncommon language, but a vates, a prophet, and expounder of the mysteries of things. He is a theological poet, a Christian, orthodox in the main, but tempering his creed with universalist notions about the ultimate salvation of all men. He is, moreover, a moralist, especially in relation to causes of love and marriage. Both as theologian and moralist he is a confirmed casuist. With a secondary sympathy for creeds which he does not profess, and for habits which he disallows, he takes a special pleasure, and shows an extraordinary facility, in throwing himself into the states of mind of the professors of such creeds, or the thralls of such habits, groping tenderly his assumed conscience, explaining and defending to himself his hypothetical position, and making out the best case he can in the assertion, or defence, or palliation, or simple exposition, of the mental and moral situation. He possesses this power to so remarkable a degree, that he can enter into phases of intellect which are even beneath humanity, and belong, if to anything, to inferior beings. One of his strongest points is the faculty of seizing the lower and more bestial currents of thought and feeling, and translating them into human language. Nothing is more known to a man's obscure self-consciousness than the importunate proofs of his animality and his degradation. But nothing is more uncommon than the translation of these sullen and darkness-haunting feelings into coherent and articulate thought. In all men, civilized or savage, there is a possibility of the generation of superstition out of sottish ignorance or panic terror. But it would be miraculous to see such ignorance and terror contemplating themselves, arguing upon themselves, and formulating their conclusions, as in Mr Browning's *Caliban upon Setebos*. He sees that the intellect can express all things, even what is most contrary to itself. There may be a science of ignorance; there may be a fine bust of an unrefined face, an amusing personation of bore, and a philosophical reflection of the workings of the dull and embryo intellect, of a lump neither alive nor dead. Mr Browning even goes so far as to strive to enter the animal brain, to open a new intercourse with fishes and insects, to feel in his own fibres the irrational consciousness, and to express in words what birds and beasts express in cries and pipings. He, if any one, is the man for whom

> Pigs might squeak love odes, dogs bark satire.

He has a power of seeing things in their chaotic rudiments, of ranging them in lines one behind the other, so as to see one thing through another, of tracing the perfect form in the germ, and finding kindred not only in likeness but in contradiction. Such a power might result in Hudibras's confusion of vision, whose

> notions fitted things so well,
> That which was which he could not tell.

In Mr Browning it only leads to a metaphorical habit, full of comparisons, which looks at things not centrally, in their own characteristic qualities and acts, but collaterally in their relations, and

> With windlaces, and with assays of bias
> By indirections finds directions out.

Mr Browning thinks in blocks, by images and pictures, not by abstract notions, and forms his ideas not by clearing away the superfluous, but by conglomerating all possible details. He adopts not Goethe's ideal of simplicity and repose, but the Shakespearian ideal, and therefore cuts off no excrescence, though it be ugly, prefers substance to form, truth to ornament, the raw thing, with all its natural complications and irregularities, to the manufactured thing, with all its prunings, transformations, artificialities, and arrangements. To embody this ideal a poet must have, besides subtlety and tenderness, a coarse, round-about common sense, and a freedom and familiarity of mind which jumbles together the great and the little, and jests about its creed as naturally as it rails with its friend or toys with its mistress.

The same habit of mind which prefers the free forest scenery of Shakespeare's school to the clipped and prim parterres of Racine, usually magnifies nature and disparages art, and distributes art into two classes, that which follows nature, and that which expels it. The first kind of art Mr Browning allows, because in all its workings the art itself is nature.

> For nature is made better by no mean,
> But nature makes that mean.

The unnatural kind of art he rejects, and under its category he includes such things as the speech which hides instead of revealing our thoughts, and the political contrivances which keep up artificial social relations and the conventionalities of civilisation. The moral which he draws at the end of the present poem is

> This lesson—that our human speech is naught,
> Our human testimony false—our fame
> And human estimation words and wind.

Truth, he tells us, comes out, not in the long-drawn collections of reason, but in the sudden interjections of feeling. Testimony is for him a perversion of facts to prove a foregone conclusion; this conclusion, mere words and wind, and life itself—at least artificial, correct, externally-ordered life—only a tale told by an idiot, full of sound and fury, signifying nothing. Sir Humphry Davy has remarked, that the first effect of incipient civilisation, in the way of clothing, is to make man rebel against nature by tattoing his skin, boring his ears, or slitting his nose; and Mr Browning takes up the parable and delights in framing cases, which shall expose the unexpected but universal contradictions that crop up between nature and artificial life. He finds everywhere baseness, emptiness, and hollowness, but always, where Rousseau finds it, in the conventional and made-up part of life. The men and women whom he offers to our scorn, ridicule, or disapproval, are very often mere painted bladders distended with the wires and buckram of social machinery. He delights in placing a cold colourless soul within some special social forcing-house, in order that he may study the influence which some political situation, or some wheel of the mechanism of society, would exercise upon it. This is the prescription according to which he has made up *Luria* and *The Soul's Tragedy*. In *The Flight of the Duchess* and *My Last Duchess*, he carries out the principle so logically that the two Dukes become not men but apparitions of abstract dukeness. They hardly exist as persons; they impose themselves as institutions; and their wives, who ought to be nourished on their warm humanity, are starved, and either die or elope. Lord Tresham in *The Blot on the Scutcheon*, is rather abstract rank than a man of rank. Mr Browning is a master in exhibiting how a system or creed, or conviction, or craze, imposes itself on a man, enters into him, possesses him, and takes the place of his soul. In his hands the abstract essence of an age, or society, or school, becomes a kind of goblin, a *simulacrum* of a soul, which may on occasion serve instead of a soul for his men and women. The quintessence of the Renaissance is impersonated in *The Bishop's Tomb in St Praxed*.

But even the better part of human energy, its spontaneous action, is affected with an imperfection analogous to that of its premeditated action—incompleteness. Wherever the element of contrivance or thought comes in it leaves its mark. Art is marred by 'the particular devil that makes all things incomplete'. Even when reason is apprenticed to feeling, and is made blind to give passion eyes, it still retains its infectious virus. Human passion and human action become, not hollow like reason, but incomplete.

> All success
> Proves partial failure; all advance implies
> What's left behind; all triumph, something crushed
> At the chariot wheels.

Love is linked to what it hates, or is divided from what it loves, or is ejected by jealousy, or fades away into indifference. Hate destroys itself by its very success. And passion, not intellect, is

> Indisputably mistress of the man.

Life then, made up as it is of the empty contrivances of reason, and the imperfect utterances of passion, becomes itself vanity, and would be merely a failure and a jest if it were not for its teleological consequences. But Mr Browning, theologian as he is, can rarely help looking chiefly at its grotesque side, and speaking of it somewhat in Thersites's vein, without reference to its more serious aspects; or rather, he jumbles up its comic and tragic sides, and illustrates them by the first metaphors which come to hand, with the indifference of nature planting a hedge-row with nettles and honeysuckles, roses and toadstools.

The recklessness with which he squanders his similes is rather a characteristic of his mind than of his style. Next to Shakespeare, he is the most comparative of poets, because, like Shakespeare, he thinks by images, not by abstractions. And he treats each image as a word, not to be followed by a consequent image, as pictorial effect might demand, but by another image-word, which may carry on the sense, without reference to the congruity of the metaphor. He will describe a murder thus: 'Vengeance, like a mountain wave that holds a monster in it, burst o'er the house, and wiped clean its filthy walls with a wash of hell-fire, and bathed the avenger's name clean in blood.' A courtly canon, beginning life at Arezzo to end it at Rome, is

> A star, shall climb apace and culminate,
>   . . .
> Ere it sweep chastened, gain the silver sphere.

What would Boileau or Pope say to such confusion of metaphor? It is only defensible on the ground that the writer is dissatisfied with the coldness of our bleached abstract terms, and is making a new pictorial or hieroglyphic vocabulary to represent his thoughts.

Sometimes the similes are prolonged into episodes; and in such cases the reader is almost certain to find that in the long-run the picture and the thought are only partially consistent. Incompleteness, first the devil of art, soon comes to receive a Pagan worship, and is then enthroned as a god. It is a grief which the poet learns to wear

> like a hat, aside,
> With a flower stuck in it.

One of the cantos of this poem is a speech of Bottini, an advocate, who, in about a hundred lines of exordium, discourses touching the way in which an artist composes a picture; then, for about forty lines, the principle thus illustrated is applied to his own business, when the orator suddenly finds the application unmanageable, and so takes to a new metaphor. Half-a-dozen lines further on he finds that he must let his new simile go, and invent still another. Perhaps Bottini is no more astray in his application of painting to oratory than the poet himself is in his comparison between ring-making and poetry, from which *The Ring and the Book* has its title. The gold is the dead matter of the poem; the alloy is the 'surplusage of soul', which the poet projects into the dead matter to make it malleable; the embossing and shaping is the poetic form; the spurt of acid by which the alloy is washed away is some final act of the poet, by which he removes all traces of himself, and leaves the poem quite impersonal. This Mr Browning claims to have done:

> So I wrought
> This arc, by furtherance of such alloy
> And so, by one spurt, take away its trace
> Till, justifiably golden, rounds my ring.

But the reader, who will see that each speaker in these idylls talks unmistakeable Browningese, that, however varied the character, the turns of thought and expression always remain similar, and that with the rough hands of Esau we still have the voice of Jacob, will justifiably wonder what spurt it is which has caused that which was only just now alloy suddenly to have become pure unalloyed gold. He may think the process as imaginary as that of the scrupulous Abbot, who, finding himself seated before roast chicken on a Friday, commanded the capon to be carp, and then canonically fell to with clear conscience. For in truth we cannot find that Mr Browning makes any special spurt to clear away his own additions to the story, except an argument to prove that the alloy is no alloy, but spirit and life. According to him, historical fact is gold, but gold in the ingot. The gold is unformed; the fact unvivified, lifeless, unremembered. An old and dead fact can only be re-created by being infused, transfused, inspired, by the living force of a creative, or rather re-creative, fancy, which is related to fact as alloy is related to gold in making the ring—necessary to prepare it for the hammer and file which are to give it artistic shape and imagery. All facts, as they are performed, live their day, and then fade into oblivion. Some leave their shrunk skin and dry bones in annals, and are entombed in archives. These too are dead, but, like dry sponges, are able to suck up the living water, and so to be raised to a second life, which the artist, from whose breast that water flows, confers on them. God gives the first life; the artist gives the second. The creative force proceeds forth from the poet, mixes itself with the deceased fact, makes the shrunk skin plump, the dead bones to live, and the corpse to stand on its feet, and run on its own legs. However true all this may be, it does not seem to account for any double action of the poet. The alloy is added by one act. An apprentice in the art will make this alloy so personal that the dramatic element will be nil; each speaker will only be a mask to conceal the poet's face, not his voice. A great artist will make the alloy entirely impersonal, and will allow it to contain none of the elements of his own biography. But whatever alloy the poet first contributes remains in the perfect poem, unless he writes it all over again. There are not two distinct acts—first of infusing surplusage of soul, and next of washing it away. Here, as elsewhere, Mr Browning seems, of set purpose, to let an element of incompleteness, or even error, remain in his similes. An amusing instance occurs in Bottini's speech, where he tells a very good story of the apostles Peter, John, and Judas. It is somewhat of an anticlimax when, in the application, the faithful apostles stand for two knaves, and the traitor for the hero whose conduct Bottini is defending.

Allied with the incompleteness of his more elaborate similes is the indirectness of his passing metaphors. As he gives life to his story, so he wishes also his diction to be alive and liquid; and to effect this he does not kill and anatomize his images, and make a cabinet of the bits, but gives each in its natural and living totality, even though it may be too great or too little for the matter in hand. As the Chinese represents a foreign word, not by any alphabetical spelling, but by a combination of the nearest syllables which his monosyllabic dictionary contains, so Mr Browning communicates his ideas, not by images which have been worn down to mere symbols and abstract words, but by whole pictures. It is as if he tried to represent a circle with a number of rough sticks. He could only make a polygon, each side of which would be represented by a most unmathematical piece of rusticity. And this inadequacy of representation he seems to accept, not as a painful necessity, but as a condition of poetical beauty. He compels his eye to view things askance. His metaphors, which are his new words, are generally one-sides and incomplete; so are his poems. The concluding canto of the present poem is like the conclusion of a firework—an empty tube and a stick. It will not do to say of this poem that the end crowns the work; a better motto would be—

Acribus initiis, incurioso fine.[2]

He leaves his work to end in a flourish, like a torso in arabesque. And this gives his poetry an appearance of coarseness of design and execution. There is nothing like vulgarity in it, if vulgarity is a conventional coarseness; nor is his coarseness one of exaggeration, like that of the flabby imitators of Rubens: it is rather akin to the coarseness of the earlier Flemings, in pictures of martyrdoms or of the last judgement. They ransack Noah's ark for monstrous reptiles, obscene birds, poisonous insects, hogs and hyænas, each of which suggests some special ugliness and wickedness, and which altogether make a very grotesque, but a very effective suggestion of hell. Or, to come down to later days, his coarseness is something like that of Gustave Doré, who made a mistake in choosing the sculptured and classical imagery of Mr Tennyson to illustrate, rather than the Rembrandt-like obscurities of Mr Browning.[3] The poet of *Childe Roland* has surely more than the poet of the *Idylls of the King* in common with the artist of the *Wandering Jew*. But though Mr Browning has no conventional coarseness, yet he is hardly enough on his guard against mannerism. Mannerism of thought is more or less inseparable from individuality of character; but mannerism of representation is a routine unworthy of a great artist. No good painter would paint all his reds with vermilion; Mr Browning can never see the colour without talking of blood. With him a crimson sunset is blood-red, tulips are bubbles of blood. If he introduces us to anything painted red, he must hasten to assure us that it is not painted with blood, as if that thought was an inevitable temptation and the first suggestion of Satan.

The satirical element in Mr Browning's mind is strong; but he is too serious a theologian and moralist to be a genuine satirist. His humour lacks not only the keen edge and fine incisiveness, but the playful and careless dallying, of satire. Satire should appeal to the inner consciousness of the person satirized; he should be made to feel, not only that

---

[2] 'Rigour at the outset, negligence at the end'. Tacitus, *Annals* 6. 17.
[3] Gustave Doré illustrated *Idylls of the King* in 1868.

the cap was made to his measure, but that it fits him. It would be too great a stretch of imagination to suppose that any prelate could ever in his inmost heart have recognised Blougram's apology as correctly representing his own moral situation. This, and several similar poems, wherein the speaker is introduced dragging to public light hidden tendencies and byways of thought which he could scarcely see clearly enough to confess to himself, are beyond the range of satire, and come within the category of casuistry. And they assume quite a prophetic character, when we remember the assumptions and pretensions of the poet. For Mr Browning, in analysing as he does the processes and the characters of men's minds, attributes to himself a kind of infallibility, which ought to be enough to make his judgements haunt his victims like an evil conscience. After giving us his theory of dead fact restored to life by the alloy of poetical fiction, he asks whether this fiction is truth:

> Are means to the end themselves in part the end?
> Is fiction which makes fact alive fact too?

He gives no very coherent answer to the question; but he makes it very evident that he considers that the artist is the real and only truth-teller. For him the fictions of art, combined with the facts of nature, are of a higher grade of truth than the facts by themselves. Moreover, all human attempts, by means of logic or theories of probabilities, or criticism, to sift and tell the truth, are failures; 'our human speech is naught, our human testimony false'; but

> art remains the one way possible
> Of speaking truth,—

at least, he adds modestly, to mouths like his. It is fair to say that this truthfulness of art does not in his view apply to personal satire, but only to such art as speaks not to man, but to mankind. The artist, however infallible in his analysis of special character, may be mistaken in attributing it to any special person. . . But in the present poem he has introduced a person as well known as Pope Innocent XII, and has assigned him a long and searching soliloquy. The main outlines of the character show a careful regard of Ranke;[4] the fillings-up smack rather

[4] Leopold Von Ranke, *The Popes of Rome* (1834–7). Ranke helped to revolutionise the methodology of historians by the scrupulous and systematic examination of documents and sources in such a way as to take into account the bias of writers and documents.

of the poet's surplusage of soul than of any probable opinions of any Pope. Innocent XII would hardly have propounded as part of his creed the opinions of modern Universalism, nor have gone far towards identifying God with Nature; nor, because he was the first of his line who exhibited either justice or mercy to the Jansenists, would he necessarily have proceeded to compare an 'irregular noble scapegrace', whom he meant to praise, with Augustine, or a 'fox-faced horrible priest', whom he abhorred, with Loyola; nor, without the gift of prophecy, would he have alluded to and joined in the condemnation of modern civilisation in the Syllabus of Pius IX; nor, without a kind of presentiment of Hegel's doctrine of the genesis of being out of not-being, would he have formulated his fine theory of the restoration of faith in the latter days through the antagonism of doubt. The poet knows how far he is here wandering from probability; and before the end of the poem he harks back to this supposed Papal doctrine, and says,

> If he thought doubt would do the next age good,
> 'Tis pity he died unapprised what birth
> His reign may boast of, be remembered by—
> Terrible Pope, too, of a kind,—Voltaire.

The alloy which attributes an elaborate theory to a historical person, followed by the spurt of acid which washes out the fiction with an 'if', is perhaps the most noteworthy exhibition of this typical process of ring-making to be found in the whole poem.

The artistic truth, then, which is brought out in such an exhibition of a historical character, is not historical truth or verity of fact, but that verity of congruity which allows one to say that if it was not so it ought to have been so. By this rule, the artist shows us not what a man was, but what he ought to have been, in order to place him in conformity, not with the moral law, but with the artist's ideal. For, after all, the truth which the artist contends for is his own ideal—himself. Much must be forgiven to genius; the superior man may well be supposed to have also a superior Ego, besides higher motives to thrust his own personality upon others. But the man of genius should be the first to find out that of all human qualities personality is at once the most familiar and the least communicable, that a man's intercourse with himself, if it is the first object of his own intelligence, is the last object for the intelligence of other people. He that speaketh in this unknown tongue edifieth himself, for in the spirit he speaketh mysteries; but he is a barbarian to others. He speaks, but says nothing; his puzzling no-meaning is as hopeless an enigma as a bankrupt's books. There are thoughts which are not transferable, autochthons that can only live where they are born, and cannot be naturalized in another soil. The youth of genius often makes volcanic efforts to colonize with such thoughts. . . Knowing well what he did, but not knowing what he could do best, he [Browning] always tried to be a dramatist; but he is, and ever will be, a critical poet. The author is never off the scene. Like Thackeray, he is always commenting on the sayings and doings and meanings of his dramatic personages. And when he is not formally doing so his readers feel that the process is still going on underground. He is his own chorus, the ideal spectator of his own dramas; and the chorus is often, perhaps generally, more important than the dialogue.

Such appear to be a few of the main characteristics of the poet who infuses his surplusage of soul into the tale told in *The Ring and the Book*. And they show how it is that, in spite of his theological bias and undeniable Christianity, he is acceptable to the materialistic and positivist thought of the day. The man whose imagination can interpret the soul of brute matter seems to show to other imaginations how thought and soul may be only secretions of matter specially organized, while his decided contempt for reason in comparison with the senti-ments must endear him to all friends of Comte's law, 'que l'esprit doit être subordonné au coeur'.[5] If we turn to the form into which he has moulded his story, we must be struck with a novelty which has at the same time the merit of simplicity and obvious naturalness. In some respects the design follows the plan of Chaucer's *Canterbury Tales*; there is a similar prologue, which introduces to the reader the narrators of the poem, followed by a series of cantos or idylls, in which each of them tells his tale. But Mr Browning's design has a more compressed unity than Chaucer's; for in the twelve books of this poem there is only one complete action, one tune, the subject of twelve variations. He has a theory that the life of a fact consists in the variety of ways in which it is regarded. A truth in which all are agreed gradually fades and dies. A living fact looks differently to each beholder. The 'variance and event-

---

[5] This does not appear to be an exact quotation from Comte. Simpson's view of Comte is more applicable to the later Comte than valid as a general account of Comte's position. He over-simplifies both Comte and Browning when he stresses a contempt for reason in comparison with the sentiments.

ful unity' of opinion regarding it make up its thread of life; and therefore the poet, who has to quicken a dead fact, must, as it were, throw its
carcass into the arena to be fought over and dragged hither and thither
by the lions of thought.

> See it for yourselves,
> This man's act, changeable because alive.

The poet has forgotten to tell us how it is that human speech and
human judgement, which he thinks are naught, and which prove their
naughtiness by their inconstancy, are able by this very inconstancy to
rise to the most sublime function of humanity—poetical creation. But
perhaps this is only one instance out of many where our weakness is our
strength. Perhaps generalization rests on confusion of memory and
forgetfulness of special details; and the absence of logical accuracy and
metaphysical abstraction may be a condition for the picturesqueness of
metaphor and abundance of imagery which distinguish the poet. It is
however a truth, that facts, as mirrored in men's minds, are infinitely
variable; and it is this changeableness which makes judicial investiga-
tions so interesting, and makes it possible to write a great poem on the
present plan. To tell the same story in the same way a dozen times over
would be to overdo the loquacious imbecility of Mrs Quickly or
Juliet's nurse. But, in its place, repetition is one of the fundamental laws
of art. As nature begins with uniform repetition, and ends with differentiated repetition, so does art. Indeed, a scale of arts might be con-
structed on this principle. The less articulate and intellectual the art is,
the more readily it admits simple repetition, even in its highest works.
In music, the repetition of the tune, the subject, or the figure, is one of
the most imperative rules of the art. In Beethoven's pastoral symphony
a single bar is repeated ten times successively; fugues, imitations,
variations, figures of accompaniment, are all instances of the same law.
In architecture, the ranges of repeated members—arcades, columns,
pinnacles, the arrangement of the elevation, where mass answers to
mass, and tower is flanked with tower—are examples of repetition as
simple as that of music. When we advance to the higher efforts of
sculpture, painting, and poetry, we find the repetitions veiled, as they
are in the differentiated segments of a highly organized vertebrate,
though in their lower examples—the frieze, the arabesque, the ballad
with its burden—we find the same simplicity as in the less articulate
arts. But the same rule of repetition holds good throughout; all the

subtleties of rhythm, proportion, and measured flow, depend on the law of repetition and variation. One of the most honoured traditions of the Elizabethan dramatists was the composite plot, in which the subsidiary action answered to the main one as its supplement, its contradictory, or its parody. Much of the stereoscopic solidity of their work may be due to this binocular vision which they afford us of it. The law of repetition applies not only to the creation but to the enjoyment of art. A thing of beauty is a joy for ever, not for a moment merely, like a peach, which is eaten and done with; the picture, the play, the poem, is visited and revisited, heard and reheard, read and re-read, by the same people, and by their children, generation after generation. If Raphael never wearied of repeating his Madonnas, the public have never grown tired of gazing on them. Poet after poet, tragedian after tragedian, has taken up the same tale; and the masterpieces of literature have been written on stock stories, familiar as nursery tales. If Mr Browning's design is new, it is founded on old analogies, and obeys a well-known law.

Another trait of this poem is its hybrid character. Mr Browning, in his essays to be a dramatist, has gradually been sliding back till he has landed in the archaic simplicity of Thespis. His drama is long monologue, only made dramatic by faithfully portraying the actual and present workings of the speaker's passions and intellect. But this vitality at once gives the monologue or the narrative a lyric character. The monologues are dramatic, because the speakers are placed in dramatic situations, where the event depends upon their suasive power. They are narrative; for they set before us the history, not the actual development, of an event. But they are eminently lyric, because their chief interest is reflective, lying not in the deed or narrative itself, but in the psychological states of the speakers, and in the various hues which the history assumes when refracted through their various minds. It is with reason then that the poet makes an invocation to lyric love the posy of his ring. This invocation has been everywhere quoted, and everywhere read, rather, probably, for its music than for its intelligence; for it can hardly speak plainly except to those who know the poem. The poet gazes on lyric love, half angel and half bird; and as he gazes its form becomes transfigured, and it seems to be a lost companion, whose presence was once his best gift of song. He still gazes, and the well-known features are glorified into those of the Redeemer, dropping down 'to toil for man, to suffer or to die'. For to him, poetry, love, and religion, are but three aspects of one great creative force, not logic or reason, though he identifies it with the Logos, but 'all a wonder and a wild desire', a pure passion, which he enthrones as Queen of man and the world. Lyric love accepts not the world as it is; that is the dramatist's realm. The dramatist knows that

> there is no art
> To find the mind's construction in the face,

and so employs himself in exposing the contradiction between the mask and the brain beneath it. But lyric love spurns this world, feathered with deceitful promises and false truths, and makes to itself another world, where the inside corresponds to the outside, where the face is the mind, and the grace of the body is the shadow of the grace of the soul. Such a world is the ideal of art; for art itself is but the expression of truth in its most natural symbols. Its problem is to make the invisible visible, and give articulate voice to the mute feelings of the heart. Shapes and colours, and sounds and words, are its only materials. With these it has to express the shapeless, colourless, inaudible, inarticulate motions of the mind; and therefore, in the interests of its own life, it has to assume a constant relationship, even an identity, between the convex and concave of its world. Words become things, colours become moral qualities; the face is no longer merely the index of the heart, but becomes the heart itself. In the lyric world of art

> What the breast forges, that the tongue must vent;

there is no opposition between being and seeming. Hence the very first doctrine of the lyric philosopher is love at first sight. No other love is love, as Marlowe declares in the saw which Shakespeare quotes. A face, as Mrs Browning says, strikes like a symbol on a face, and fills with its silent clangour brain and heart, transfiguring the man to music. So it is with the love in this poem. Caponsacchi sees Pompilia once for a moment, and she sees him. He describes the result:

> That night and next day did the gaze endure
> Burnt to my brain, as sunbeam through shut eyes,
> And not once changed the beautiful sad smile.

In that instant he learns her whole character. Evil reports come to him; vile papers which purport to be her own letters are brought to him. He knows them to be false and forged. The lips of one of Raphael's

Madonnas might as soon drop scorpions as she be foul. He might say of her, as Pericles of Perdita,

> Falseness cannot come from thee; for thou look'st
> Modest as Justice, and thou seem'st a palace
> For the crowned Truth to dwell in.

In the same way Pompilia knows Caponsacchi at a glance; his face is sufficient refutation of all scandal against him:

> Thus I know
> All your report of Caponsacchi false
> . . .
> I ever see his own face.

This love at first sight is but one stone of the temple of Lyric Love. The whole constitutes a complete philosophy, distilled from Plato, and coming down to us in a succession of poets, of whom Dante, Petrarch, and Shakespeare in his sonnets, are the chief. It is a philosophy which does not fit things as they are, but perhaps would fit them if they were as they ought to be. If applied to life, it sets it to a higher pitch, translates it to a more refined language, representing it not as it is, but 'as you like it', as it may be supposed to go on in the mythical forest of Arden. It lends itself to the drama, and produces a Romeo and Juliet. It is the poet's means for raising man above himself. It is the idealism which, joined to the realism of natural representation, gives an elevation more than human to human life and human energy. . .

Lyric art, in embodying this ideal, has to deal with many other things besides lyric love. Like the chorus in a Greek tragedy, it has to be the supposed spectator of all that happens, and to convey to the spectator of the play a lyrical and poetical expression of the emotions which he ought to feel. It contrasts not only the doings of men with the lyric ideal, but much more their feelings. It has to trace the various ways in which Job's comforters judge him, and to judge their judgements. The Greek chorus represented a whole population; and Mr Browning introduces populations—half Rome, and the other half Rome—delivering their sentiments upon the actors and action of his story. In this again his ideal approaches that of the earliest Greek drama. There is no such popular running commentary on the action in Shakespeare, except sometimes in the observations of the fool or clown. We know of nothing quite like it in modern literature, except perhaps the social opinion which comes in as Chorus in George Eliot's novels, and gives the judgement of the Raveloe alehouse or the Florentine barber's shop upon the action and persons of the history. The parliamentary and representative fancy that makes an idyll of popular opinion, though a novelty, is yet an advance in the grooves of the great movement of thought. When philosophical criticism regards the hero of literature simply as the spokesman of his age, it proposes to writers the problem of making the characters they invent not individual and idiosyncratic, but samples of common opinion. We have indeed crowds and mobs and citizens in Shakespeare; but they are rather yielding material in the hands of the individual demagogue or orator than masters of the situation. Public opinion has now become a constraining force, as often directing as following those whose hands turn the wheels of society and the State. Literature can represent all that is, and after a time will be able to embody public opinion as poetically as it has exhibited the action of the heroic will or the individual prudence. There is no reason why some of the persons of a drama should not be collective corporations, organized aggregates of men; and there is no reason why these composite persons should not be truly poetical. The people is in its way a poet. To it we owe proverbs and ballads. It seizes on the skeletons of facts, and, like a poet, projects its 'surplusage of soul' into them, giving them its own colouring, and making them 'alive' with its own fictions. On the narrow basis of a telegram it can set up a tower of Babel huge enough to cast a shadow over a whole empire. It can be as wayward and wilful as a baby; it can also be patient and persevering as a spider. As the poet strives to enter into the minds of his heroes, to possess himself of their springs of action, to think and feel in their grooves, so, when he makes public opinion his hero, he can possess himself of its national spirit, of its corporate logic, and represent collective humanity as easily as he can represent individuals. Collective humanity individualizes itself in the average man, and in him manifests its way of lookings at things. And in an age of democratic advance the average man's toe comes so near the heel of the hero that he galls his kibe. Some people think that the day of novelists has passed its meridian, and that the sun of journalists is about to rise. For society, they suppose, is growing tired of the exceptional, and is beginning to feel its interest centre in the common action of mankind. The age of chivalry is gone, when one man engrossed all interest, and the rest were only chaff and bran, porridge after meat. The hero has already been served up in every variety of cookery—plain for simple palates, devilled for the uncertain feverish appetite, minced for children to swallow. There is no more gold to be found in these diggings. Those who still work at them are apt to give us the strained products of an imagination groping in the sewers for new spawn of Belial, new networks of improvised fatalities, new atrocities of noble-minded crime. Men turn from this to the dull matter-of-fact of reporters and correspondents and journalists, and find it more interesting. There is on the whole a movement of thought among those who feed on light literature, similar to that which has changed the aspect of historical books. The novel of exceptional character and intrigue is analogous to the history which makes the world depend on politicians and diplomatists, and governs the chariot of progress by the will of the strong checked by the plots of the wise. The history, on the other hand, which no longer looks exclusively to the erratic course of the eccentric hero, but finds force in the multitude, and law in the uniform flow of average society, obtains in journalism its popular literary expression. When it is commonly recognised that the hero and statesman is no original creator, no imposer of his own private dreams upon mankind, but one who represents their average opinions, and enforces them with extraordinary ability, the hero of literature must become not the eccentric but the sample man. The vagaries of sensationalism seem to herald its dissolution. A moribund school, whether of theology or philosophy or art, is always most rabid in its anathemas, most uncompromising in its logic, most extravagant in its one-sided consistency. There is an autumnal and painted gorgeousness, which is the precursor not of life but of death. Sensationalism may be the last fitful glare of the novel of exceptional character and situation, and journalism the first twilight and the model of a school about to arise. Mr Browning's poem is cousin-german to a series of newspaper articles. His 'horrid murder' is not led up to, hidden, and discovered as in a novel, but bursts upon us like an announcement in a journal. Its interest lies not in its sensational atrocity or pathos, but in its ambiguous character, the various interpretations which may be given to the acts and motives of the murderer, his wife, her parents, and her friend. And these are just the qualities which would make it fit material for the journalist. A cruel murder, stupidly conceived and clumsily executed, where justice has no trouble in tracing the evidence, and where the motives are apparent and the provocation imaginary, does not become a celebrated cause. It is only when it involves terrible uncertainties of inferential evidence, or when the motives urged in justification are capable of various explanations, that the case becomes meat and drink for journalists. Then society is moved. Then all classes contribute their comments, and improve the occasion to enforce their various social theories, their belief in the corruption of the aristocracy, their distrust of trial by jury, their contempt for the English law of evidence, their conviction of the connection between the increase of crime and the advance of democracy. It is just such a series of comments which three out of twelve of Mr Browning's cantos furnish. 'Half Rome' might be a summary of the articles and correspondence of the daily Liberal journal on the subject, 'the other half Rome' a similar digest of the opinions of the Tory paper, while the 'Tertium quid' would be the acrid and impartial distribution of universal condemnation administered by a weekly journal reviewing the perturbations of the world from a region of sweetness and light. These cantos resemble leading articles done into verse, in that they are the lyrical expressions of a chorus of public opinion, exercising itself on the deeds which move its interest, delivering its judgement on their evidence and motives, and recording its sentiments about them. They do not dramatize public opinion; to do so, it would be necessary to exhibit a common wish and will using its own instruments, performing its own functions, and controlling events, with multitudes instead of persons as actors. Here the aggregates of men simply record their sentiments through the mouth of an average member.

Although Mr Browning makes use of these expositors of opinion, he does not cease to accompany their utterances with a running commentary of his own, sometimes expressed, sometimes understood, forming a perpetual gloss on the text, and ever making us alive to the relationship in which the sentiments dramatically expressed stand to those of the poet himself. He writes with a didactic purpose. He claims to have a mission; and the most direct way of accomplishing it would be to look his brethren in the face, and tell them that they have eyes and see not, ears and hear not, and that what they count faith is foolishness. But besides the peril of making one's-self a common enemy by calling all things by their right names, such a way of delivering his message would be obnoxious to the common charge against all human testimony and human speech. He must therefore deliver his message in the way of art, which 'nowise speaks to men, only to mankind', which tells truth obliquely by painting the picture that shall breed the thought, and thus both satisfy the imagination and save the soul. It is not to be forgotten, in considering the complex form of Mr Browning's poem, that it is in some sense a sermon.

With regard to the materials of the poem, the first thing that strikes one is that it is, both in the plot and in the characters, a renewal of old productions. A comparison of it with the poet's earlier writings will show that it stands to them in that relation of finished picture to previous studies on which Bottini enlarges in the beginning of his monologue. Up to the publication of the poem, it was generally thought that *The Flight of the Duchess* was Mr Browning's most considerable work. But as the individual characters of that piece are mostly only developments of previous isolated studies—studies of neglected wives and of heartless husbands—so the whole complex play of characters, their mutual action and reaction, in *The Ring and the Book*, is very much a reproduction and improved version of the play of moral forces exhibited in *The Flight of the Duchess*. In both there is the child-wife, great in moral nature and in possibilities of development, but ignorant, innocent, and unformed; in both the icy, formal, heartless husband; in both the 'gaunt grey nightmare' of the mother-in-law; in both a deliverer whose presence is like a flash of light to the pining wife, transfiguring her to a daring heroine. In one poem this character is borne by the gipsy, in the other by the canon Caponsacchi. In both there is a censor who relates the story, and delivers his judgement upon the motives and acts of the persons. In one, this office is borne by the old huntsman; in the other it is divided between the three representative speakers who utter the opinions of Roman society, and the Pope who sums up the case, and makes the final award. . . In his more extensive studies, where the reaction of the characters on each other had to be exhibited, he has always shown a deficiency in the power of inventing plots. . . If the writer in the exercise of his self-criticism ever felt this weakness, the discovery of his Florentine book, with an interesting story ready made, supplying not merely a likely but a true plot, furnished with the best possible machinery and incidents for a new display of his favourite types of character, must have appeared even whimsically providential. He seized on his treasure, gloated over it, talked of it, investigated the records connected with it, brooded over it for four years, and told its story over again, with the additions of his own fancy, using it as a mould for recasting all his favourite characters, in the composition of whose metal almost his whole life had been spent.

While he designed moulds for himself, he had generally remained perilously near the edge of the impossible or the grotesque.

> Amphora coepit
> Institui; currente rota cur urceus exit?[6]

Now he has found a mould, or rather a collection of moulds, which admits of a variegated display of his potter's craft, and requires a large collection of vessels, some to honour, some to dishonour. All that he could not do he found ready to hand; all that he could do best, he saw room for. His characters were ready; he had only to adapt them, and make them act over again in poetry a drama which had once been really acted by persons more or less resembling his masks.

The story had perhaps another attraction for Mr Browning in its being Italian. Dutch as he is in his realism, in his distance from the abstract ideal, and in a complexity which buries a fire under the abundance of fuel, he yet shares the Dutch artist's love for the

> Woman country, never wed,
> Loved all the more by earth's male lands.

But if he goes to Italy and studies there, he paints Italian subjects in the Dutch manner, and is most attracted by the deposits of the Teuton admixture in the strata of the Italian mind. He may decorously display on his table the masterpieces of Latin art, but under them we find the open volumes of Rabelais, Montaigne, Annibale Caro, Pietro Aretino, or the burlesques of Ariosto and Tassoni. To adduce but one example, the grotesque onomatopoeia of the Italians exercises quite a magnetic attraction over him. A nation which delights in giving its most re-nowned families such names as Head-in-a-bag, Beggar-my-neighbour, Wish-you-well, and Rags, has a certain underground fibre of sym-pathy with a poet who delights in inventing such noises as Blougram, Gigadibs, or Bluphocks. 'Uncouth, unkissed', says Chaucer; but an uncouth name has so great an attraction for Mr Browning that he not only kisses it, but absolutely chews it, and licks it into shape with the affection of a she-bear for her cubs. The fatted calf, Dominus Hyacin-thus de Archangelis, who in one of the cantos is exhibited alternating between the pains of composing a defence of the murderer, and the pathos of intercalary benedictions of his little boy Hyacinth, whose

---

[6] 'That object began life as a wine-jar; why then does it come out of the potter's wheel as a ewer?' Horace, *Epistula ad Pisones, de Arte Poetica*, 21–2.

birthday it is, ransacks the whole armoury of Italian increments for variations on the child's name—Giacinto, Giacintino, Cinino, Ciniccino, Cincicello, Cinone, Cinoncino, Cinoncello, Cinotto, Cinozzo, Cinuzzo, Cinarello, Cinuccio, Cinucciatolo, Cineruggiolo, where affection prompts a homeliness of sound analogous to the homeliness of meaning in the mother who calls a child by the endearing terms of pig or duck. . . It must have delighted him [Browning] to find that the story would fill his lines with Pompilia and Caponsacchi, and would give him occasion to lug into his verse such agglomerations of syllables as Panciatichi and Acciaiuoli.

Italians would probably condemn Mr Browning's latinizing as a corrupt following of his apostles, and repeat their old proverb, *Inglese italianizzato diavolo incarnato*. If the intricate and rapid rhymes, of which he has heretofore shown such management, have an Italian example in Leporeo, Leporeo is but a corrupt follower of the rhyming Latin of the medieval monks. Mr Browning is Saxon, and not Latin, when he hunts the letter with clash and clatter like Holophernes, and ambles along with the artificial aid of alliteration. If he affects crabbed and club-fisted words like Marston, it was just for this that the more classical taste of Ben Jonson made him so indignant with that poet. But all these things are probably connected with the retrospective attitude of the poet. As he draws his story and characters from old books, so he draws up whatever he can find in the well of old English, and transfers to his own pages whatever he finds most characteristic. This proceeding has been common to our poets, of all ages and of all calibres. They have all been news-gleaners from old archives, wise scribes bringing out of their treasures things new and old.

The chief value of the story of Mr Browning's poem is to form the framework for the display of the characters. These are, first, Count Guido Franceschini, the murderer, a poor nobleman who, having fished all his life in the antechambers of a cardinal at Rome, and caught nothing, in the wane of his years baits his hook with his nobility, and catches the wife, and through her the supposed daughter, of a wealthy Roman burgess. Guido is Mr Browning's Iago; in him we have his ideal of wickedness. Guido is not a man of strong passions urged by his nature to vice. He is, on the contrary, an artificial man, one whose hinges turn not on the pivot of passion but on that of reason. He is a walking example of Rousseau's aphorism, 'L'homme qui raisonne est un animal dépravé'. His master passion is a made-up one, the love of money, which, in common with medieval moralists, Mr Browning considers the least human and most diabolical of all, because it is simply artificial. Whoever stands in the way of this passion is simply vermin to Guido—first to be provoked to suicide, and in default of that to be led into some crime which may excuse deadly vengeance, and in default of that to be poisoned or stabbed. Add to him pride, not the natural pride of his far-reaching intelligence, or any other natural gift, but the pride of station, another artificial passion, and we have a reason for the cruel vengeance, the 'lust and letch of hate' which he exhibits. . . Like Iago, he is a man of logical and powerful mind, knowing the world, wary in observation, prophetic in political forecast, looking quite through the deeds of men. This cold, satanic intellect, with the artificial heart organized out of gold and rank, Mr Browning incarnates in a body almost like a tragic Hudibras—short, thick-shouldered, hook-nosed, dark, with a bushy red beard, capable of enduring pain like a brute, but deficient in physical courage. The man is one whose language has a relation to his own interests, but not the slightest relation to truth, except at the last moment, when the terror of death compels him to invoke his murdered wife as a saint, and who, again like Iago, permits himself on all occasions the utmost licence in talk. Indeed, Mr Browning may be charged with not sufficiently trapping the gullies of Guido's uncircumcised imagination.

In contrast with the cold reason and active conventionality of Guido, we have the nature and passion of Pompilia, his wife, and Caponsacchi, her deliverer. Each, either devoid of education or ill-educated, puts to shame the artificial power of education by the natural flow of right feeling and instinct. The woman exhibits this in her innocence and ignorance; the man, in the midst of the frivolities and wild-oats sowing of courtly Italian life. They are both essentially lyrical characters; and in obedience to the lyrical law, they both lack active originating power, but sit down in a boat, without oars or sails, to be luckily wafted over the wild waters of life by the breezes of good feeling and the gales of passionate instinct. Hence they lack striking individuality. Mr Browning tells us miles more about them than we are told about Hotspur or Cordelia; yet they come miles behind Hotspur and Cordelia in definiteness, dramatic energy, and elevation of individual character. They neither of them flash upon the reader; he has to gather their characters from a multitude of sayings or doings or sufferings. He has to credit them with what they tell him of their own feelings and intentions, and to believe them chiefly because their features are so handsome, and their countenances so open. Nevertheless they are real characters; and the cumulative, painfully heaped up conceptions of them which we gradually agglomerate in our minds become, if not grand outlines, at least grand patches of massive and yet subtle colour. They constitute the masculine and feminine ideals of the poet; and there is great pathos and lyrical power in the monologue and sallies of Caponsacchi, explaining how, like Prince Hal, he lived amidst pleasures which he loved not, and how he was saved from them by a sudden passion. But there is more pathos when Pompilia, like a dying swan, intones the plain song of her life, and gives the history of her weary walk with Guido, and her exciting run with Caponsacchi. The story is a convenient one for a man who can put together last speeches, and knows that

> the tongues of dying men
> Enforce attention, like deep harmony.

Guido's speech to his confessors before execution is one of the most powerful in the poem. But perhaps the most satisfactory on the whole is the monologue of the aged Pope, who investigates the case as if it were his last earthly work, and speaks of his decision as the crowning effort of his life. The ripe observation and mature wisdom with which he characterizes the persons of the drama, and at the same time delivers himself of a multitude of religious, moral, political, and even artistic theories, makes his speech a model of Mr Browning's lyrico-didactic style. The poet himself speaks behind the mask. It is not however that the poet becomes romanized, but the Pope becomes tinctured with his presenter, as we have already sufficiently seen. In this canto of the poem, consequently, Mr Browning's whole circle of teaching, feeling, and criticism may be most conveniently studied. He will be found to possess great unity of principle. It is not only in human characters that he contrasts the gush of nature with the creeping contrivances of art. He exhibits a general scepticism, not about the observed laws, but about deduced precepts and conventional rules of morals, politics, and economy. He includes in the same condemnation premeditated proofs, prepared speeches, made-up marriages, codified rules, regulated education, and routine in general. He enforces his argument by examples of the failure of special contrivances. The clergy are in the world to humanize mankind; yet it was not the clergy who objected to the torture chamber. The seminary and the monastery should wean priests

from the world, and harden them for their sharp duties; yet in Mr
Browning's poem it is the regularly educated priests who timidly
follow the world, while the 'irregular noble scapegrace', the man who
should be a priest but is a desultory lover and poet, alone rushes from
the ball-room to the battle-field at the call of duty. The physician falls
sick, the lawyer cheats, the divine is damned, and the aimless saunterer
finds health, success, and salvation. . . In the astutest villains he puts
such a mixture of the fool as brings to nought the knave. In the extremely moderate Roman jurisprudence he exhibits the mild flame of
justice, hidden under the bushel of that plausible desire to avoid dis-
putes which is the palladium of all establishments, and which drives
them to let souls perish rather than themselves lose credit; and he shows
how the intemperate sallies of those who are right are always matters of
righteous blame for those who are temperately and methodically
wrong. Nature against art is a central thought with him; but in his view
the fine arts are nature.

After those described, the two most prominent speakers in the poem
are two Roman advocates, of whom one argues for Guido and one for
Pompilia. For each his brief is his rule of faith. This is an offence as
great in the poet's eyes as a marriage of convenience. One is the unpardonable sin against passion, the other against truth. Guido sins in
one way, and is foiled; the advocates in another, and become ludicrous.
Each, with his piebald language, his forensic quotations, his oratorical
conceit, his jealousy of his opponent, his childish arguments, fitter for
Euphues than for an advocate, becomes, however tedious, a comic and
burlesque personage. One of them, the lean bachelor Bottini, blue-
eyed, bright-haired, treble-voiced, screaming

> in heights of head
> As, in his modest studio, all alone,
> The tall wight stands a tiptoe, strives and strains
> Both eyes shut, like the cockerel that would crow,

seems painted after Chaucer's pardoner. These are the persons who are
dramatically brought out. The rest have only an existence in the
narrative. These more undefined characters have a great range, from
the neutral tints of the Comparini to the black, scarlet, and yellow of
Guido's family. A number of them are twin brothers or sisters with
men or women in Mr Browning's former poems, many of whom seem
to have missed their vocation in appearing where they did. They would

certainly have been more at home in *The Ring and the Book* than where their premature birth has placed them.

Among the materials of the poem would be the place to discuss the minute realism of the poet, his theory of rhythm, his grammar, his style, as distinct and special in verse as Mr Carlyle's in prose, his felicitous power of working at once upon contradictory models, consciously copying Euripides but producing something even more like Æschylus, and, in attempts to advance beyond the most advanced of the Greek dramatists, falling back upon the mythical beginnings of the Greek drama. His great virtue is that he has an impetus, a rush, which, to a great extent, hides his contradictory faults. It carries the reader over pages of 'prose swell'd to verse, verse loitering into prose', over sheets where thoughts lie jumbled together, close packed and without room to move. It carries him over pitfalls of grammar, over empty holes and hard stones, where a slow coach would be upset or stopped. It carries him on in such wise that he is content only half to understand, to forgive more than he takes in, and to retain but a little of that which passes through his ears. If there were not positive evidence to the contrary, Mr Browning might be considered a careless poet, bestowing ample pains on amassing his materials, but little on their organization. But whatever trouble he may take he evidently lacks the power to give any great unity to the multifariousness of his farrago. Loaded as his pictures are with details, they can only please at a considerable distance. He writes a symphony carefully, and scores it for an orchestra of 'saltbox, tongs, and bones'. A minute critic might ask in vain for a plausible defence of line after line of his verse. He must be read running, and read with the eye more than with the ear. To read him aloud, or to let the ear pore over his verse is mortal. But to the intelligence he repays minute study. He presents a boundless chaos of accidental knowledge. The wide horizon of dim distance teeming with suggestions of facts outside the action of the poem gives it an air of reality, life, domesticity, and truthfulness, such as we are conscious of in Homer and Shakespeare. It is as plausible as a letter from home or a police report in the newspaper. Yet the laboured accumulation of appropriate allusions is sometimes rather overdone. In reading his lines also we perpetually arouse fleeting and impalpable memories of the great poets of the reign of James I. But there is at least one of them who knew how in a few paragraphs to anticipate many of Mr Browning's chief characteristics. The Old City Captain in Beaumont and Fletcher's

Philaster does not say much. But what he does say is so richly streaked with peculiar metaphor, that he reminds one very strongly of Mr Browning. When, at the head of the insurgent apprentices, he catches and threatens the Spanish prince, he speaks the purest Browningese—

> Nay,
> My beyond-sea-sir, we will proclaim you:
>> You would-be king!
> Thou tender heir-apparent to a church-ale,
> Thou slight prince of single sarcenet,
> Thou royal ring-tail, fit to fly at nothing
> But poor men's poultry.

The difference is that the burlesque of Beaumont becomes serious in Mr Browning. He knows how infinite should be the changeful flash of the facets of a poem which is destined to live; and he seeks this variety rather in the costume of his characters than in their differences of expression. Each of them is saturated with his profession. His lawyers speak in terms of the pleas and bench; his divines in those of the pulpit and the schools; and his nobles are all heralds. All are vexed with an itch of making metaphors corresponding to the circumstances of their lives. Hence the style is rather a pudding-stone of dialects, all formed on the same principle, but out of different materials, than a smooth amalgam in which all the materials are made fluid, and worked up into the one comprehensive and dignified language of the cultivated man. There is enough of observation, learning, humour, wit, wisdom, but little charm; 'nihil hic nisi carmina desunt'. Yet there is more to admire than to forgive in Mr Browning. Like Plato he is a poet because he is a poetical philosopher, though it may be a question whether his philosophy does not tend to strangle his poetry. His power may be guessed by the opposition he has encountered. Smashers clip gold, not copper.[7] But to some his very power is repulsive. There are still many wise men, and men of taste, who would have their teeth drawn or toes amputated rather than read him. And those who can appreciate him are often so struck with the multifariousness of his merits in detail that, without appraising him higher than he deserves, they are apt in criticising him to raise expectations which the reading of his poems will fail to satisfy.

[7] A smasher, one who passes or utters counterfeit or debased coin: to clip, to mutilate current coin by paring the edges. *N.E.D.* gives these words as slang current in the nineteenth century. Browning deals with important things, just as smashers deal in the most precious metal, and the opposition they provoke is proportionate to the value of their materials.

12

Clough ∽ *Poems and Prose Remains* ∽ 1869

Henry Sidgwick, *Westminster Review*, xcii
(October 1869), 363–87

These two volumes contain all that will now be given to the world of a very rare and remarkable mind. The editor has, we think, exercised a wise confidence in transgressing what is usually a safe rule in post-humous publications, and including in the volume some prose that the author had probably not composed for permanence, and some verse that is either palpably unfinished, or at any rate not stamped with the author's final approval. Clough's productive impulse was not ener-getic, and only operated under favourable conditions, which the circumstances of his life but scantly afforded. Therefore the sum total of his remains, when all is included, does not form an unwieldy book; and on the other hand his work is so sincere and independent that even when the result is least interesting it does not disappoint, while his production is always so rigidly in accordance with the inner laws of his nature, and expresses so faithfully the working of his mind, that nothing we have here could have been spared, without a loss of at least biographical completeness. There is much that will hardly be interest-ing, except to those who have been powerfully influenced by the individuality of the author. But the number of such persons (as every evidence shows), has not diminished, but largely increased during the ten years that have elapsed since his death: the circle of interest has gone

Henry Sidgwick, 1838–1900, moral philosopher, economist and reformer of women's education. This essay is reprinted in *Miscellaneous Essays and Addresses* (1904), pp. 59–90. His particularly sensitive criticism of Clough's work may perhaps stem from his realisation of the similarity between Clough's position and his own: educated at Rugby, he resigned his fellowship at Trinity College, Cam-bridge, in October 1869, the month this essay was published, because he could no longer assent to the religious tests. For the same reasons Clough had resigned his fellowship at Oriel in October 1848.

on widening without becoming fainter, and now includes no small portion of a younger generation, to whom especially the publication of these volumes will afford timely and welcome gratification.

The tentative and gradual process by which Clough's remains have been published is evidence and natural result of the slow growth of his popularity. For this there seem to have been several reasons. It is partly due to the subject matter of his writings. He was in a very literal sense before his age. His point of view and habit of mind are less singular in England in the year 1869 than they were in 1859, and much less than they were in 1849. We are growing year by year more introspective and selfconscious: the current philosophy leads us to a close, patient, and impartial observation and analysis of our mental processes: and the current philosophy is partly the effect and partly the cause of a more widespread tendency. We are growing at the same time more unreserved and unveiled in our expression: in conversations, in journals and books, we more and more say and write what we actually do think and feel, and not what we intend to think or should desire to feel. We are growing also more sceptical in the proper sense of the word: we suspend our judgement much more than our predecessors, and much more contentedly: we see that there are many sides to many questions: the opinions that we do hold we hold if not more loosely, at least more at arm's length: we can imagine how they appear to others, and can conceive ourselves not holding them. We are losing in faith and confidence: if we are not failing in hope, our hopes at least are becoming more indefinite; and we are gaining in impartiality and comprehensiveness of sympathy.[1] In each of these respects, Clough, if he were still alive, would find himself gradually more and more at home in the changing world. In the second place his style, at least in his longer poems, is, though without any affectation, very peculiar: at the same time he has not sufficient loudness of utterance to compel public attention. Such a style is naturally slow in making way. Even a sympathizing reader has to get accustomed to its oddities before he can

---

[1] By 'the current philosophy' Sidgwick means Comtean positivism with its sociological bias and historicism. Frederick Harrison was becoming known, and J. S. Mill published his *Auguste Comte and Positivism* in 1865. The change in the intellectual atmosphere which he describes and the erosion of confidence and certainty in established ideas and institutions is more difficult to pin down and obviously a matter of the 'feel' of his culture to Sidgwick, but one might point to the appearance of *Essays and Reviews* at one end of the decade (1860) and T. H. Huxley's *The Physical Basis of Life* (1868) at the other as signs of this change.

properly feel its beauties. Afterwards, if it has real excellence, its peculiarity becomes an additional charm. Again, the chief excellence of Clough's style lies in a very delicate and precise adaptation of form to matter, attained with felicitous freshness and singular simplicity of manner; it has little superficial brilliancy wherewith to captivate a reader who through carelessness or want of sympathy fails to apprehend the *nuance* of feeling.

To this we may perhaps add, that the tone which many of Clough's personal friends have adopted in speaking of the author and his writings has, though partly the result, been also partly the cause of the slow growth of their popularity. It was, for example, certainly a misfortune that in issuing the first posthumous edition of these poems, Mrs Clough prefaced them with a notice by Mr Palgrave, a critic of much merit, but quite inappreciative of his friend's peculiar genius, and whose voluble dogmatism renders his well-meant patronage particularly depressing.[2] There is a natural disposition among personal friends to dwell upon unrealized possibilities, and exalt what a man would, could, or should have done at the expense of what he actually did; and to this in Clough's case circumstances were very favourable. In the first place he produced very little, and the habit of demanding from candidates for literary fame a certain quantum of production seems inveterate, though past experience has shown the fallacy of the demand, and we may expect it to become still more patent in the future. Indeed, if we continue as we are now doing, to extend our own literary production and our sympathy and familiarity with past and alien literature *pari passu*, the reader of the future will have so much difficulty in distributing his time among the crowd of immortal works, that he certainly will contract a dislike to the more voluminous. And in the case of poems like these, that are attractive chiefly because they are characteristical and representative, because they express in an original and appropriate manner a side of human life, a department of thought and feeling, that waited for poetical expression, voluminous production seems not only unnecessary but even dangerous. On a subjective poet continence should especially be enjoined; if he writes much he is in danger of repeating words or tune; if he tries to write much he is in danger of mistaking his faculties and forcing his inspiration.

But besides this scantiness of production, there is much in the external aspect of Clough's career which justifies the disposition to

[2] *Poems* (1862), with a memoir by F. T. Palgrave.

regard his life as 'wasted'—at best an interesting failure. We have before us a man always trying to solve insoluble problems, and reconcile secular antagonisms, pondering the 'uralte ewige Rathsel'[3] of existence, at once inert and restless, finding no fixed basis for life nor elevated sphere of action, tossed from one occupation to another, and exhausting his energies in work that brought little money and no fame; a man who cannot suit himself to the world nor the world to him, who will neither heartily accept mundane conditions and pursue the objects of ordinary mankind, nor effectively reject them as a devotee of something definite; a dreamer who will not even dream pleasant dreams, a man who 'makes the worst of both worlds'.

This is no doubt a natural complaint from a practical point of view, but it ignores the fact that the source of Clough's literary originality and importance lies precisely in what unfitted him for practical success. He was overweighted with certain impulses, felt certain feelings with a too absorbing and prolonged intensity, but the impulses were noble, at least an 'infirmity of noble minds', they are incident to most fine natures at a certain stage of their development, and generally are not repressed without a certain sense of loss and sacrifice. This phase of feeling is worthy of being worthily expressed, and it is natural that it should be so expressed by one who feels it more strongly than other men, too strongly for his own individual happiness. It is the same with other phases of feeling. Out of many poets there are few Goethes; the most are sacrificed in some sort to their poetical function, and it is but a commonplace sympathy that loudly regrets it. Those at any rate who had no personal knowledge of Clough, may recognise that this life, apparently so inharmonious, was really in the truest harmony with the work that nature gave him to do. In one sense, no doubt, that work was incomplete and fragmentary; the effort of the man who ponders insoluble problems, and spends his passion on the vain endeavour to reconcile aspirations and actualities, must necessarily be so; the incompleteness is essential, not accidental. But his expression of what he had to express is scarcely incomplete, and though we have no doubt lost something by his premature death, we can hardly think that we have lost the best he had to give. His poetical utterance was connected by an inner necessity with his personal experience, and he had already passed into a phase of thought and feeling which could hardly lead to artistic expression so penetrating and stirring as his earlier poems.

[3] 'age-old eternal riddles'.

But we shall better discuss this question after a closer examination of his work, of what he had to express and how he expressed it.

In this examination we shall treat Clough as a poet. It is necessary to premise this, because he was a philosophic poet; a being about whose nature and *raison d'être* the critical world is not thoroughly agreed. Philosophic poetry is often treated as if it was versified philosophy, as if its primary function was to 'convey ideas', the only question being whether these should be conveyed with or without metre. Proceeding on this assumption, an influential sect maintains that there ought to be no philosophic poetry at all; that the 'ideas' it 'conveys' had much better seek the channel of prose. To us it seems that what poetry has to communicate is not ideas but moods and feelings; and that if a feeling reaches sufficient intensity, whatever be its specific quality, it is adapted for a poetical form, though highly intellectual moods are harder to mould to the conditions of metrical expression than others. The question is often raised, especially at the present day, when our leading poets are philosophic, whether such and such a poem—say Browning's *Christmas Eve*, or parts of *In Memoriam*—would not have been better in prose. And the question is often a fair one for discussion, but a wrong criterion is used for determining it. If such a poem is really unpoetical, it is not because it contains too much thought, but too little feeling to steep and penetrate the thought. Tried by this test, a good deal of Browning's thought-laden verse, and some of Tennyson's, will appear not truly poetical; the feeling is not adequate. Although Clough sometimes fails in this way, it may generally be said that with him the greater the contention of thought, the more intense is the feeling transfused through it. He becomes unpoetical chiefly when he becomes less eagerly intellectual, when he lapses for a moment into mild optimism, or any form of languid contentment; or when like Wordsworth he caresses a rather too trivial mood; very rarely when the depths of his mind are stirred. He is, then, pre-eminently a philosophic poet, communicator of moods that depend on profound and complex trains of reflection, abstract and highly refined speculations, subtle intellectual perceptions, and that cannot be felt unless these are properly apprehended. He is to a great extent a poet for thinkers; but he moves them not as a thinker, but as a poet.

We do not mean to say that Clough was not a thinker; but the term is somewhat indefinite, and in one sense he was not. His mind brooded over a few great questions, and was rather finely receptive than eagerly discursive; he did not enjoy the mere exercise of thought for its own sake. This is evidenced by the first of the volumes before us, especially the letters, which, except in the rare instances where he drops to his habitual depth of meditation, are perhaps somewhat disappointing. There is humour in them, but the vein is thin; and subtlety, perpetual subtlety, and from time to time a pleasant flow of characteristically whimsical fancy; there is also a permanent accuracy, propriety, *justesse* of observation, remarkable in compositions so carelessly thrown off; but fertility and rapid movement of ideas are wanting. They do not seem the work of a mind that ranges with pleasure and vigour over all subjects that come in its way. The critical essays, again, that have been republished, though exceedingly just, careful, and independent, and therefore always worth reading, are not very striking; with the exception of occasional passages where passionate utterance is given to some great general truth. But though he was too much of a poet to care greatly for the mere exercise of the cognitive faculties, though no one could less have adopted the 'philosopher's paradox' of Lessing, we may still Call him philosophic from his passionate devotion not to Search after Truth, but to Truth itself, absolute, exact truth.[4] He was philosophic in his horror of illusions and deceptions of all kinds; in his perpetual watchfulness against prejudices and prepossessions; against the Idols, as Bacon calls them, of the Cave and the Theatre, as well as of the Tribe and the Market-place. He was made for a free-thinker rather than a scientific inquirer. His skill lay in balancing assertions, comparing points of view, sifting gold from dross in the intellectual products presented to him, rejecting the rhetorical, defining the vague, paring away the exaggerative, reducing theory and argument to their simplest form, their 'lowest terms'. *Lumen siccum,* as he calls it in one of his poems, is the object of his painful search, his eager hope, his anxious loyalty.

The intellectual function, then, which Clough naturally assumed was scepticism of the Socratic sort, scepticism occupied about problems on which grave practical issues depended. The fundamental assumptions involved in men's habitual lines of endeavour, which determined their ends and guided the formation of their rules, he was continually endeavouring to clear from error, and fix upon a sound basis. He would not accept either false solutions or no solutions, nor, unless very

---

[4] It is not clear what sort of paradox Sidgwick has in mind here.

reluctantly, provisional solutions. At the same time, he saw just as clearly as other men that the continued contemplation of insoluble problems is not merely unpractical, but anti-practical; and that a healthy and natural instinct forces most men, after a few years of feverish youthful agitation, resolutely to turn away from it. But with this instinct Clough's fine passion for absolute truth conflicted; if he saw two sides of a question, he must keep seeking a point of view from which they might be harmonized. In one of the most impressive of the poems classed in this edition as 'Songs of Absence', he describes his disposition

> To finger idly some old Gordian knot,
> Unskilled to loosen and too weak to cleave:

but the reluctance to cleave knots, in the speculative sphere, does not proceed from weakness.

It is this supreme loyalty to reason, combining and conflicting with the most comprehensive and profound sympathy with other elements of human nature, that constitutes the peculiar charm of Clough's scepticism, and its peculiar adaptation to poetical expression. Towards the beliefs to which other men were led by their desires, he was as strongly, or more strongly, impelled than others; the assertions in which they formulated their hopes he would gladly have made with the same cheerful dogmatism. His yearning for the ideal he never tried to quench or satisfy with aught but its proper satisfaction; but meanwhile the claims of the real, to be accepted as real, are paramount. He clings to the 'beauty of his dreams'; but—two and two make four. It is the painfulness, and yet inevitableness of this conflict, the childlike simplicity and submissiveness with which he yields himself up to it; the patient tenacity with which he refuses to quit his hold of any of the conflicting elements; the consistency with which it is carried into every department of life; the strange mixture of sympathy and want of sympathy with his fellow-creatures that necessarily accompanies it, that makes the moods which he has expressed in verse so rare, complex, subtle, and intense.

We may classify these moods, according to a division suggested by this edition, into first, those of religious scepticism, where the philo-sophic impulse is in conflict with the mystical; secondly, those of ethical scepticism, where it contends with habitual active principles; thirdly, those where it is perplexed with the most clamorous and absorbing of human enthusiasms, the passion which forms the peculiar topic of poetry. It is this latter division that at once completes the consistency of Clough's scepticism, and forms its most novel, original, and least understood application. As he himself says, not only 'saint and sage', but also 'poet's dreams',

> Divide the light in coloured streams;

the votary of truth must seek *lumen siccum*.

The personal history of Clough's religious scepticism has rather to be guessed than known from the records of his life that lie before us. The memoir prefixed to the volume, written with great delicacy and dignity, but with an unreserve and anxious exactness in describing his phases of thought and feeling worthy of the subject and most grateful to the reader, can tell us little on this head. Nor do the letters that lead us up to the time when he must in effect have abandoned the beliefs of his childhood at all prepare us for so deep a change. At Rugby he seems to have yielded himself entirely to the influence of Arnold, and to have embraced with zealous docility the view of life which that remarkable man impressed so strongly, for good or for evil, on his more susceptible pupils. But though somewhat over-solemn and prematurely earnest, like many Rugby boys of the time, he was saved from priggishness by his perfect simplicity. At Balliol he shows nothing of the impulsiveness, vehemence, and restlessness, the spirit of dispute and revolt, which are supposed to precede and introduce deliberate infidelity. Thrown upon Oxford at the time when the 'Newmanitish phantasm', as he calls it, was startling and exciting Young England, he writes of the movement to his friends with a mild and sober eclecticism—a tranquil *juste-milieu* temper which would become a dean. He is candidly observant, gives measured admiration for good points, notes extravagances, suggests the proper antidotes, seems disposed, on the whole, to keep out of the atmosphere of controversy and devote himself to his studies. Nothing could give smoother promise of untroubled orthodoxy. It is true that he speaks of being 'exhausted by the vortex of philosophism'; and he must have been much more powerfully influenced by Newmanism than these letters indicate. He said afterwards, that for two years of this time he had been 'like a straw drawn up the vortex of a chimney'. His mind seems habitually to have been swayed by large, slow, deep sea currents, the surface remaining placid, even tame; such a steady hidden movement it seems to have been that floated him away from his old moorings of belief. Gradually or suddenly the theologico-juridical, ecclesiastico-mystical dialectics that went on around him became shadowy and unreal; all his religious needs, hopes, aspirations remaining the same, a new view of the universe, with slowly accumulating force, impressed itself irresistibly on his mind, with which not only the intellectual beliefs entwined with these needs and aspirations seemed incompatible, but even these latter fundamentally incongruous. And thus began a conflict between old and new that was to last his life, the various moods of which the series of his religious poems, solemn, passionate, and ironical, accurately expresses.*

Perhaps the first characteristic that we notice in these is their rare reality and spontaneity. We feel that they are uttered, just as they appear, from an inner necessity; there was no choice to say them or not to say them. With some poets religious unbelief or doubt seems an abiding attitude of intellect, but only occasionally to engross the heart; their utterances have the gusty force of transitory passion, not the vitality of permanent feeling. But with Clough it is different: the whole man is in the poems, they spring from the very core of his being. The levity of some of them is as touching as the solemnity of others; it is a surface-mood, showing explored depths beneath it, in which an unrestful spirit finds momentary relief. Another characteristic is, that over the saddest cries of regret and struggles of checked aspiration is spread a certain tranquillity—not of hope, still less of despair, but a tranquillity that has something Aristotelian in it, the tranquillity of intellectual contemplation. It is curious, for example, to contrast the imperishable complaint of Alfred de Musset:

* A similar account is to be given of another event in his life, his abandonment of outward conformity to Anglicanism and its material appurtenances of an Oriel fellowship and tutorship. No reader of his life and writings can doubt that with him this step was necessarily involved in the change of opinions: yet many years elapsed between the two, and his biographer thinks that it was 'some half-accidental confirmation of his doubts as to the honesty and usefulness of his course' that finally led him to resignation. Such accident can surely have been but the immediate occasion, expressing the slow hidden growth of resolve. Lax subscription to articles was the way of Clough's world: and it belonged to his balanced temper to follow the way of his world for a time, not approving, but provisionally submitting and experimentalizing. To do what others do till its unsatisfactoriness has been thoroughly proved, and then suddenly to refuse to do it any longer, is not exactly heroic, nor is it the way to make life pleasant; but as a *via media* between fanaticism and worldliness, it would naturally commend itself to a mind like Clough's.

> Quand j'ai connu la verité,
> J'ai cru que c'etait une amie;
> Quand je l'ai comprise et sentie,
> J'en etais dejà degouté;[5]

with Clough's,

> It fortifies my soul to know
> That though I perish, Truth is so.

The known order of the world, even without the certainty of a personal God, source or correlate of that order, afforded somewhat of philosophic satisfaction, however little it could content the yearnings of his soul. It was a sort of *terra firma*, on which he could set his feet, while his eyes gazed with patient scrutiny into the unanswering void. Further, we remark in these moods their balanced, complex character; there is either a solemn reconciliation of conflicting impulses, or a subtle and shifting suggestion of different points of view. Specimens of the former are two hymns (as we may call them), headed *Qui laborat, Orat*, and ὕμνος ἄυμνος; they attempt to reconcile the intellectual resolve to retain clear vision with religious self-abandonment. The latter of these has a little too much intellectual subtlety and academic antithesis; but the former is one of Clough's most perfect productions; there is a deep pathos in the restrained passion of worship, and the clear-cut exactness of phrase, as it belongs to the very essence of the sentiment, enhances the dignity of the style. Somewhat similar in feeling, but more passionate and less harmonious, is the following fragment:

> O let me love my love unto myself alone,
> . . .
> And say, what is not will be by-and-bye.

Sometimes the intellectual, or as we have called it, philosophical element, shows itself in a violence of sincerity that seems reckless, but is rather, to use a German word, 'rücksichtslos',[6] it disregards other considerations, not from blind impulse but deep conviction. The tone of the poem is then that of one walking firmly over red-hot plough-shares, and attests at once the passion and the painfulness of looking facts in the face. In the fine poem called *Easter Day* (where a full sense of the fascination of the Christian story and the belief in immortality

---

[5] 'Tristesse' in *Poésies Nouvelles*.   [6] 'rücksichtslos': ruthless, inconsiderate.

depending on it, and of the immensity of its loss to mankind, conflicts with scientific loyalty to the modern explanation of it), the intensity of the blended feeling fuses a prosaic material into poetry very remarkably.

> What if the women, ere the dawn was grey,
> . . .
> This is the one sad Gospel that is true,
>   Christ is not risen!

The complex and balanced state of Clough's moods shows itself in an irony unlike the irony of any other writer; it is so subtle, frequently fading to a mere shade, and so all-pervading. In the midst of apparently most earnest expression of any view, it surprises us with a suggestion of the impossibility that that view should be adequate; sometimes it shifts from one side of a question to the other, so that it is impossible to tell either from direct expression or ironical suggestion what the writer's decision on the whole is. In some of the later stanzas of the poem we have quoted the irony becomes very marked, as where the 'Men of Galilee' are addressed:

> Ye poor deluded youths, go home,
> Mend the old nets ye left to roam,
> Tie the split oar, patch the torn sail:
> It was indeed an 'idle tale',
>   He was not risen.

The truth is, that though Clough from time to time attempts to reconcile and settle, his deepest conviction is that all settlement is premature. We meet continually phrases like the

> Believe it not, yet leave it not,
> And wait it out, O man,

of one of his earlier poems. To use a favourite image of his, the universe, by our present arithmetic, comes to much less than we had fondly imagined. Our arithmetic is sound, and must be trusted; in fact, it is the only arithmetic we have got. Still the disappointing nature of the result (and let us never pretend to ourselves that it is not disappointing) may be taken as some evidence of its incompleteness.

This irony assumes a peculiar tone when it is directed to vulgar, shallow, unworthy states of mind. It is not that Clough passionately repudiates these, and takes up a censorial position outside and over against them; these, too, are facts, common and important facts of humanity; *humani nihil*—not even Philistinism—*a se alienum putat.* His contempt for them is deep, but not bitter; indeed, so far from bitter that a dull pious ear may misperceive in it an unpleasing levity. His mode of treating them is to present them in extreme and bald simplicity, so that the mind recoils from them. A penetrating observer describes something like this as a part of Clough's conversational manner. 'He had a way', says Mr Bagehot, 'of presenting your own view to you, so that you saw what it came to, and that you did not like it.'[7] A good instance of this occurs in an unfinished poem, called *The Shadow* (published in this edition for the first time). We quote the greater part of it, as it also exemplifies Clough's powerful, though sparingly exercised, imagination; which here, from the combination of sublimity and quaintness, reminds one of Richter, only that we have antique severity instead of romantic profuseness:

> I dreamed a dream: I dreamt that I espied,
>   . . .
> And on the grave the Shadow sat all day.

The effect of the latter part is like that of stripping an uncomely body, familiar to us as respectably draped and costumed, and showing it without disguise or ornament. That 'the world' has never seen himself in this nakedness we feel: but we also feel that here is the world which we know. The two lines before the three last show the felicitous audacity with which Clough sometimes manages metre: nothing could more sharply give the shallowness of the mood in contrast with the solemnity of the subject than the careless glibness of the lines

> It was a comfortable thing to think upon
> The atonement and the resurrection of the dead.

The longest of the religious poems is an unfinished one called *The Mystery of the Fall.* The fundamental idea seems to be this. The legend of the Fall represents a permanent and universal element of human feeling, the religious conviction of sin, but only one element: the beliefs corresponding to it, even if intuitive consciousness is relied upon as their evidence, are not affirmed by the sum total of valid consciousness—taking 'Sunday and work-days' together. Not only do our practical necessities and active impulses require and generate

[7] Walter Bagehot, *National Review*, xiii (Oct. 1862), 310–26; 326.

other conceptions of the universe which seem incompatible with the religious, but the latter is unsatisfying in itself: the notions of perfect creation, lapse, wrath, propitiation, though they correspond to a part of our religious experience, yet do not content our religious feeling as an adequate account of the relation of God to man. This Clough has tried to express, keeping the framework of the old legend, in dialogues between Adam, Eve, Cain, and Abel after expulsion from the garden. The transitions and blendings of the different moods are given with a close and subtle fidelity to psychological truth: and this putting of new wine into old bottles is perhaps justified by the prominence in human history of the Hebrew legend. There is no reason why Adam and his family should not be permanent machinery for serious fable, as Jove and his subordinates are for burlesque. Still the incongruity between the modern moods (and especially the perfect self-consciousness accompanying them) and the antique personages and incidents is here too whimsical: and, for poetry, the thought is too predominant, and the feeling not sufficiently intense; to some parts of the subject, as the murder of Abel, Clough's imagination is inadequate: and on the whole the result is interesting rather than successful, and we doubt whether the poem could ever have been completed so as to satisfy the author's severe self-criticism.

We take a very different view of the other unfinished long poem, *Dipsychus*. If it had received the author's final touches, a few trivialities and whimsicalities would no doubt have been pruned away: but we doubt whether the whole could have been much improved. It has certain grave defects which seem to us irremovable, and we should rank it as a work of art below either of his hexameter poems. There is not sufficient movement or evolution in it; the feeling is too purely egoistic to keep up our sympathies so long; and it is not sufficiently framed. The Venetian scenes in which the dialogue goes on, though appropriate to some of the moods, have no particular connection with the most important: whereas in *Amours de voyage*, and still more in the *Bothie*, the harmonizing of external and internal presentments is admirably managed. At the same time the composition is one of great interest. The stress of feeling is so sustained, the changes and fluctuations of mood are given with such perfect propriety, the thought and expression are so bold and novel yet free from paradox, so subtle without a particle of mere ingenuity. The blank verse too in parts, though only in parts, seems to have been carefully studied, and, though a little too suggestive of Elizabethan models, to attain a really high pitch of excellence. Perhaps no other poem of Clough's has so decidedly this one 'note' of genius, that its utterances are at once individual and universal, revealing the author to the reader, and at the same time the reader to himself.

The constructive idea of the poem, which is a dialogue between a man and an attendant spirit, is taken of course from *Faust*. But Goethe (as his half-apologetic prologue hints) sacrificed something in adapting his idea to the conditions of drama: and the issues in Clough's debate are so much finer, that we feel nothing imitative in his development of the conception. The suggestions of the spirit are never clearly fiendish in themselves; with much skill their fiendishness is made to lie in their relation to the man's thoughts. The spirit, in fact, is the 'spirit of the world'; and the close of the debate is not between clear right and wrong (however plausible wrong), but between two sides of a really difficult question, how far in acting on society rules and courses repugnant to the soul's ideal are to be adopted. True to himself, Clough does not decide the question; and though his sympathies are on the side of the ideal, we never know quite how far he would pronounce against the fiend.

The second part of the poem is almost too fragmentary to discuss. In it the man appears at the close of a successful career, having been attuned and attempered to the world by an immoral liaison. How far this means is justified by that end seems to us a disagreeable specialization of the general problem of the first part, much more easy to decide. It is worked out however with much force. Several songs included in this poem were in the first edition published separately; by a great mistake, we cannot but think, as they have more force and beauty in their original setting; and it was a little unfair to Clough (though less than might be expected) to publish his fiend's utterances as his own.

We turn now to what we may call the amatory scepticism. This is a more proper subject of poetry, as thought here is in no danger of being too predominant over feeling; at the same time it is more novel and original, as on no subject do poets in general less allow thought to interfere with feeling. Poets, in fact, are the recognised preachers of the divinity, eternity, omnipotence of Love. It is true that with some of them fits of despair alternate with enthusiasm, and they proclaim that Love is an empty dream: but the notion of scrutinizing the enthusiasm sympathetically, yet scientifically, and estimating the precise value of its claims and assertions, probably never entered into any poetic soul before Clough. Nor is it less alien to the habits of ordinary humanity. That the lover's state is a frenzy, innocuous indeed, delightful, perhaps even laudable as a part of nature's arrangements for carrying on the affairs of the world, but still a frenzy; that we all go into it and come out of it, take one view of things in general when in it and another when out of it: is what practical people accept with more or less playful or cynical acquiescence. Poets have a licence to take an opposite view, in fact we should be disappointed if they did not; but we listen to them not for truth but for pleasant illusion. It will be seen how impossible it was for Clough's nature to acquiesce in this. Goethe sings of

> Den Drang nach Wahrheit und die Lust am Trug[8]

as part of the poet's endowment. It was Clough's peculiarity, perhaps his defect, as a poet, that he had not the 'Lust am Trug'. He feels the rapture that illusion gives, he quotes more than once with sympathy.

> Wen Gott betrügt ist wohl betrogen,[9]

but such 'wohl' he could not himself appropriate. Nor could he serenely separate idea from fact, as his friend Emerson does in the following passage.

> And the first condition [of painting Love] is, that we must leave a too close and lingering adherence to the actual, to facts. . . Everything is beautiful seen from the point of the intellect. But all is sour, if seen as experience. Details are always melancholy: the plan is seemly and noble. It is strange how painful is the actual world, the painful kingdom of time and place. There dwells care and canker and fear. With thought, with the ideal, is immortal hilarity, the rose of joy.[10]

This well illustrates by contrast the fundamental mood of Clough. For his imagination at any time thus to abandon *terra firma* and console itself with cloudland would have been impossible. The fascination of the ideal was as strong for him as for other poets, but not stronger than the necessity of making it real. Hence in that period of youthful

---

[8] 'The striving for truth and the delight in deception'. Goethe, *Faust*, Vorspiel auf dem Theater, I, 193.

[9] 'He whom God deceives is well deceived'.

[10] R. W. Emerson's essay on 'Love', *Essays* (1841).

forecast and partial experience of passion, in which the finest love-fancies of most poets are woven, he perpetually feels the need of combining clear vision with exaltation. He keeps questioning Love as to what it really is, whence it comes, whither it goes: he demands a transcendental evaluation of it.

> Whence are ye, vague desires?
> . . .
> Whence are ye?

'Is love spiritual or earthly?' is the passionate perplexity that tinges many of his songs. Or if this pearl of great price is to be found on earth, how shall we know it from its counterfeits, by what criterion discern the impulses that lead us to the true and the false? In one of the finer passages of the *Mari Magno* tales, this longing for direction is uttered.

> Beside the wishing gate which so they name,
> . . .
> To awake to life the mind within the mind.

But if love be after all only 'a wonderous animal delight' in which nature's periodic blossoming culminates, the philosophic spirit, however deep its yearning, cannot submit to it, but has to contemplate it from the outside with tender and curious sympathy. This mood tinged with playfulness inspired the charming song in which he describes how he

> Watched in pleasant Kensington
> . . .
> To feed the youthful heart?

The rapture of this sympathetic contemplation is expressed in *Amours de Voyage*.

> All as I go on my way, I behold them consorting and coupling
> . . .
> Life were beatitude, living a perfect divine satisfaction.

This leads us to the deepest issue of all—a thoroughly Platonic problem. Be this love as noble as it may, is its exaltation compatible with clear vision? Does not this individualized enthusiasm of necessity draw away from the centrality of view and feeling after which the philosophic spirit aspires? Is it not unworthy of us, for any pleasure's sake, to be tricked by its magic and take its coloured light for white?

But we are tired of reducing to prose the various phases of this subtle blending and conflict of enthusiasms. As expressed by Clough they have the perfect vitality and reality of all his moods. None of these perplexities are arbitrarily sought; the questions raised must each have been raised and decided by many human beings since self-consciousness began. If no poet has uttered them before, it is because in most men the state of mind in which they were felt is incompatible with the flow of feeling that poetry requires. Clough's nature was, perhaps, deficient in passion, but it had a superabundant tenderness and susceptibility to personal influence, which made him retain the full feeling of personal relations while giving free scope to his sceptical intellect.

In one of the two long hexameter poems published in his lifetime, *Amours de Voyage*, Clough has given a dramatic embodiment to the motives that we have been analysing. The poem is skilfully composed. Thoroughly apprehending the aversion which practical humanity feels for these perplexities, he somewhat exaggerates the egotism of the hero of the piece to whom he attributes them, handles him with much irony throughout, and inflicts a severe but appropriate Nemesis at the close. The caricature in 'Claude' is so marked that we are not surprised that Clough, the least egoistical of men, was indignant when a friend appeared to take the poem as an account of the author's own experiences. 'I assure you', he writes, 'that it is extremely not so.' Still this attitude of the author could not reconcile the public to a hero who (as the motto has it) *doutait de tout, même de l'amour*. That the poem never attained the success of the *Bothie* we are not surprised. It has not the unique presentations of external nature which give such a charm to the earlier poem: it wants also the buoyant and vivacious humour which is so exuberant in the *Bothie*, and of which the fountain in Clough's latter years seems almost to have dried up. But it shows greater skill in blending and harmonizing different threads of a narrative, and a subtler management of the evolution of moods; it has deeper psychological interest, and in its best passages a rarer, more original imagination. The *Amours* is very closely interwoven with the incidents of the French siege of Rome (of which, by the way, Clough's letters give us interesting details) so that the two series of events together elicit a complete and consistent self-revelation of the hero. The amative dubitations turn principally on two points—the immense issues that depend on amative selection compared with the arbitrary casual manner in which circumstances determine it, and the imperious claim of passion for a concentration of interest which to the innermost, most self-conscious, self is profoundly impossible. These play into one another in the following very characteristic passage.

Juxtaposition, in fine; and what is juxtaposition?

. . .

But for assurance within of a limitless ocean divine, o'er
Whose great tranquil depths unconscious the wind-tost surface
Breaks into ripples of trouble that come and change and endure not,—

. . .

Yes, and contented sit down to the victual that He has provided.

The three lines that we have italicized seem to us almost perfect specimens of the English hexameter, showing the extreme flexibility which the metre has in Clough's hands, and his only, and none of the over-accentuation which neither he nor any one else can generally avoid. Very opposite opinions have been delivered as to the merits of this hexameter. Some most appreciative readers of the poems declare that they read them continually under protest; that no interest in the subject and no habit can make the metre tolerable. Mr Arnold, how-ever, on this subject an especially Rhadamanthine critic, considers the success of Clough's experiment to be so decided as to form an import-ant contribution to the question (which has occupied a most dis-proportionate amount of human intellect in our time), How Homer is to be translated?[11] We do not take either view. We think Clough's metre, as he uses it, felicitous; but we do not think that this proves anything as to the appropriateness of the hexameter for translating Homer, or for any other application of 'the grand style'. Clough has not *naturalized* the metre. He has given it ease, but not simplicity; he has not tried to give it simplicity, and therefore he has succeeded with it. All English hexameters written quite *au sérieux* seem to us to fail; the line ought to be unconscious of being a hexameter, and yet never is. But Clough's line is, and is meant to be, conscious of being a hexa-meter: it is always suggestive of and allusive to the ancient serious hexameters, with a faint but a deliberate air of burlesque, a wink imply-ing that the bard is singing academically to an academical audience, and catering for their artificial tastes in versification. This academic flavour suits each poem in a different way. It harmonizes with the Oxonian studies of the *Bothie*; and here, indeed, the faint burlesque inseparable from the metre becomes from time to time distinct mock-heroic. In

[11] Matthew Arnold, *On Translating Homer* (1861), pp. 78–80.

Amours de Voyage, it suits the over-culture, artificial refinement of the hero's mind: he is, we may say, in his abnormal difficulties of action and emotion, a scholastic or academic personage. In short the metre seems to belong to a style full of characteristic selfconscious humour such as Clough has sustained through each of the poems; and we cannot analyse its effect separately. Clough we know thought differently; but we are forced to regard this as one instance out of many where a poet takes a wrong view of his own work. His experiment of translating Homer into similar hexameters is nearly as much a failure as Mr Arnold's, or any other; and his still bolder experiment of writing hexameters by quantity and not accent results, in spite of the singular care and even power with which it is executed, in a mere monstrosity.

We consider then that it was a happy instinct that led him to the metre of the *Bothie*. In more ordinary metres he often shows a want of mastery over the technicalities of verse-writing. He has no fertility of rhymes, he is monotonous, he does not avoid sing-song, he wearies us with excessive, almost puerile, iterations and antitheses. It is very remarkable, therefore, how in this new metre, self-chosen, he rises to the occasion, how inventive he is of varied movements, felicitous phrases, and pleasant artifices of language, how emphatically yet easily the sound is adapted to the sense, in a way which no metre but blank verse in the hands of a master could rival. Another evidence of the peculiar fitness of this instrument for his thought is the amount that he can pack without effort into his lines; as e.g. in the following description of one of the members of the Oxford reading-party—

> Author forgotten and silent of currentest phrase and fancy
> . . .
> Hope an Antinous man, Hyperion of calves the Piper.

It is hard to imagine so much said so shortly in any other style.

The flexibility of the metre aids in bringing out another great excellence of these poems; the ease and completeness with which character is exhibited. There is not one of the personages of the *Bothie*, or even of *Amours de Voyage*, where the sketching is much slighter, whose individuality is not as thoroughly impressed upon us as if they had been delineated in a three-volume novel by Mr Trollope. We are made to understand by most happily selected touches, and delicately illustrative phrases, not only what they are in themselves, but precisely how they affect one another. It becomes as impossible for us to attribute a remembered remark to the wrong person as it would be in a play of Shakespeare. To say that Clough's dramatic faculty was strong might convey a wrong impression, as we imagine that he was quite devoid of the power of representing a scene of vivid action; but the power of forming distinct conceptions of character, and expressing them with the few touches that poetry allows, is one of the gifts for displaying which we may regret that he had not ampler scope.

The descriptions of natural scenery in the *Bothie* form probably the best-known and most popular part of Clough's poetry. In this, as in some of his most important poetical characteristics, he may be called, in spite of great differences, a true disciple of Wordsworth. His admiration for the latter appears to have been always strongly marked; and one of the more interesting of the prose remains now published is an essay on Wordsworth, perhaps somewhat meagre, but showing profound appreciation, together with the critical propriety and exactness of statement characteristic of Clough. His simplicity, sincerity, gravity, are all Wordsworthian; but especially his attitude towards nature. Through a manner of description quite different we trace the rapt receptive mood, the unaffected self-abandonment, the anxious fidelity of reproduction, which Wordsworth has taught to many disciples, but to no other poet so fully.

In the essay referred to we find a view of Wordsworth's poetical merits, which to many persons will appear paradoxical, but which seems to us perfectly true, and applicable to some extent to Clough himself. He says that Wordsworth, the famous prefaces notwithstanding,

really derives from style and diction his chief and special charm . . . he bestowed infinite toil and labour upon his poetic style; in the nice and exquisite felicities of poetic diction he specially surpassed his contemporaries: and his scrupulous and painstaking spirit, in this particular, constitutes one of his special virtues as a poet. He has not the vigour and heartiness of Scott or the force and sweep and fervour of Byron: but that permanent beauty of expression, that harmony between thought and word, which is the condition of 'immortal verse', they did not, I think—and Wordsworth did—take pains to attain. There is hardly anything in Byron and Scott which in another generation people will not think they can say over again quite as well, and more agreeably and familiarly for themselves: there is nothing which, it will be plain, has in Scott or Byron's way of putting it, attained the one form which of all others truly belongs to it: which any new attempt will, at the very utmost, merely successfully repeat. For poetry, like science, has its final precision; and there are expressions of poetic knowledge which can no more be re-written than could the elements of geometry. There are pieces of poetic language which, try as men will, they will simply have to recur to, and confess that it has been done before them.

And he goes on to say that 'people talk about style as if it were a mere accessory, the unneeded but pleasing ornament, the mere put on dress of the substantial being, who without it is much the same as with it: whereas really some of the highest truths are only expressible to us by style, only appreciable as indicated by manner.'

With all this we agree: but it seems to us that two conditions are necessary for the success in style spoken of, and that Clough has only given one. In order to attain it, a man must be conscious of very definite characteristic moods, and must have confidence in them, take an interest in and value their definite characteristics; then in expressing them he must work with a patient, single-minded effort to adapt the expression to the mood, caring always for the latter more than for the former. This was certainly the manner of Clough's composition, and hence many of his poetic utterances have, as he phrases it, 'final precision'. We do not mean to compare their effect to Wordsworth's. Clough has none of the prophetic dignity of his master, of the latter's organ-music he has not even an echo: and he far surpasses him in subtlety. There is a peculiar combination of simplicity and subtlety in his best things, the simplicity being as it were the final result and outcome of the subtlety, so that the presence of the latter is felt and not distinctly recognised, which we find in no other poet except Goethe. It is this combination that fits him for his peculiar function of rendering conscious the feelings that pass half unconsciously through ordinary minds, without seriously modifying them. There is a pretty instance of this in an idyllic song which we will quote. Most of the song is rather commonplace; a peasant girl driving she-goats homeward thinks alternately of the scene, and of her absent lover. Suddenly we are surprised with this very Cloughian sentiment.

> Or may it be that I shall find my mate,
> And he returning see himself too late?

> *For work we must, and what we see, we see,*
> *And God he knows, and what must be, must be,*
> When sweethearts wander far away from me.

The excellence of the lines that we have italicized we should describe paradoxically by saying that their naïveté is at once perfect, and, as naïveté, impossible.

On the other hand, if Clough has many of Wordsworth's excellences, he certainly has his full share of the cognate defects. It is natural, perhaps, to the man who values the individuality of his thought and feeling so much as to spend great care on its expression, to want the power of discriminating between those parts of it that are, and those which are not worth expressing. Certainly Clough has not, any more than his master, the selective faculty that leads to the sustained elevation and distinction which we expect from a great poet, and which the adoption of a simple manner renders peculiarly indispensable. Commonplace thought and feeling in strikingly simple language does not make, perhaps, more really worthless poetry than commonplace thought and feeling in ornate language; but its worthlessness is more patent. There is this one advantage, that the critic is not forced to dwell upon it: no one's taste is perverted, except perhaps in the first charm of the poet's novelty. No one now pretends to admire the dullness and twaddle in Wordsworth; and in Clough even more than in Wordsworth the expression rises and falls with the matter: the dullest and most trivial things are the worst put. We will only say that the genius of twaddle, which often hovers near his muse, makes its presence especially felt in his last poems, the *Mari Magno* tales. These must, of course, be judged as unfinished productions; but no retouching could have enabled them to rank very high as poetry. They are easy, pleasant, even edifying reading, and they essentially want effectiveness. They are written in obvious emulation of Crabbe; and in a natural and faithful homeliness of style, which occasionally becomes a transparent medium for a most impressive tenderness, they certainly rival Crabbe; but their general level is much lower. The charm of Crabbe, when he is not tender, lies in the combination of unobtrusive dignity, and a certain rustic raciness and pregnancy, with a fair share of the artificial point and wit that properly belong to the Popian measure. Clough has nothing of this; and though in the best passages his characteristic fineness of apprehension makes amends, on the dead levels of narration the style is much inferior to Crabbe's: its blankness is glaring. In the first tale especially the genius of twaddle reigns supreme; it reminds us of—we will not say the worst, for it has no bad taste, but—the second-rate portions of Coventry Patmore.

The inferiority of these poems is due, as we before hinted, to a deeper cause than a temporary defect of vigour or a mistaken experiment of style. It is evident that we have here Clough without his peculiar inspiration—his talent, we may say, but not his genius. As an artist he is noteworthy—his production has many high qualities, viewed as technically as possible; it is not, however, as a mere artist, but as an utterer of peculiar yet representative moods, that he has the power to excite our deepest interest. But these moods are the moods, in the main, of youth; and when Clough, after a period of more than usually prolonged adolescence, finally adopted the adult attitude towards life, they ceased to dominate his habitual thought and feeling. Not that any abrupt change shows itself in him. There were two tempers singularly entwined in him throughout: his letters for the most part present a striking contrast to the contemporary poems. In the latter we find chiefly absorbing effort after an ideally clear vision, a perfect solution of problems: in the former mild practical wisdom, serene submission to the imperfections of life, cheerful acquiescence in 'the best under the circumstances'. And this quieter tone naturally grew upon him. Not that he could ever separate speculation from practice, or in either sphere settle down into smooth commonplace: but he grew tired of turning over the web of commonplace notions and rules, and showing their seamy side: he set himself rather to solve and settle instead of raising and exposing difficulties. At the same time the sincerity which had led him to emphasize his passionate perplexities, still kept him from exaggerating his triumph over them: he attains no fervour of confident hope, nor expansion of complacent optimism: he walks in the twilight, having adapted his eyes to it somewhat, but he does not mistake it for dawn. Whether in such twilight he would ever have seemed to see with sufficient clearness to impel him to utter his vision to the world, is doubtful: at any rate the utterance would, we imagine, have taken a prosaic and not a poetical form. He was looking at life steadily till he could see it whole: aspiring, as he says in an early poem,

> To bring some worthy thing
> For waiting souls to see.

But the very loftiness of this aspiration, and the severity with which he

would have judged his own claims to be a teacher, incline us to think
that he would never have uttered the final outcome of his life's thought.
What he wished to do for the world no one has yet done: we have
scarcely reason to believe that he could have done it: and he would
have been content to do nothing less. His provision views, the temporary substitutes for 'demonstrated faith' by which he was content
to walk, he would hardly have cared to publish. That they would,
however, have been interesting, we can see from the only fragment of
them that the editor has been able to give us, a paper on 'The Religious
Tradition'. From this, as it illustrates a different side of Clough's mind
to that on which we have been led chiefly to dwell, we will conclude
by quoting some extracts:

> The more a man feels the value, the true import, of the moral and
> religious teaching which passes among us by the name of Christ-
> ianity, the more will he hesitate to base it upon those foundations
> which, as a scholar, he feels to be unstable. Manuscripts are doubtful,
> records may be unauthentic, criticism is feeble, historical facts must
> be left uncertain. Even in like manner my own personal experience
> is most limited, perhaps even most delusive; what have I seen, what
> do I know? Nor is my personal judgement a thing which I feel any
> great satisfaction in trusting. My reasoning powers are weak; my
> memory doubtful and confused; my conscience, it may be, callous
> or vitiated. . .
>
> I see not what other alternative any sane and humble-minded man
> can have but to throw himself upon the great religious tradition. But
> I see not either how any upright and strict dealer with himself—how
> any man not merely a slave to spiritual appetites, affections, and
> wants—any man of intellectual as well as moral honesty—and
> without the former the latter is but a vain thing—I see not how any
> one who will not tell lies to himself can dare to affirm that the
> narrative of the four gospels is an essential integral part of that
> tradition. I do not see that it is a great and noble thing to go about
> proclaiming that Mark is inconsistent with Luke . . . it is no new
> gospel to tell us that the old one is of dubious authenticity. I do not
> see either that it can be lawful, for the sake of the moral guidance
> and the spiritual comfort, to ignore all scientific and historic doubts,
> or if pressed with them to the utmost, to take refuge in Romish
> infallibility. . .

Where then, since neither in Rationalism nor in Rome is our refuge, shall we seek for the Religious Tradition?

Everywhere; but above all in our own work: in life, in action, in submission; so far as action goes in service, in experience, in patience, in confidence. I would scarcely have any man dare to say that he has found it, till that moment when death removes his power of telling it. Let no young man presume to talk to us vainly and confidently about it. Ignorant, as said Aristotle, of the real actions of life, and ready to follow all impressions and passions, he is hardly fitted as yet even to listen to practical directions couched in the language of religion. But this apart—everywhere: among all who have really tried to order their lives by the highest action of the reasonable and spiritual will.

13

Tennyson ⌒ *The Holy Grail and Other Poems* ⌒ 1869

British Quarterly Review, li (January 1870), 200–14.
Authorship unknown

The chief part of Mr Tennyson's new volume is occupied with
Arthurian restorations, aiming at the completion, after a certain
arbitrary and ideal manner, of the cycle of the Round Table romances.
These now given are meant to be read in relation to those which went
before; and we are led to understand that, so read, the sense of a complete scheme of truth will arise upon us. This we take to be the intent
of the short advertisement prefixed to the work; but as no clue whatever is here given to the underlying idea or *motif* presumed to link
together into a studied whole a series of somewhat disparate legends
arbitrarily chosen

> As right thro' ring and ring runs the djeered,
> And binds the loose, one bar without a break,

criticism is compelled to suspend its terms till it can find a standpoint
of interpretation. Mr Stuart Glennie, who has made a study of the
Arthurian myths, and has endeavoured to find in their substance the
proper body for a great dramatic allegory, has carefully enunciated his
idea in plain terms; but not so the Laureate.[1]

Now, there are two lines which criticism might legitimately take in
the attempt to fix the point of view. It might inquire into the condition
of the people among whom these traditions took their rise, and to
whom they stood for a whole literature; and, dealing with Mr Tennyson's poems as mere restorations or reproductions, test them by the
results of this search; or it might detach Mr Tennyson wholly from the
historical or antiquarian circle, and view him as a modern interpreter,
using these old-world myths merely as the form or body for a new

---

[1] J. S. S. Glennie, *King Arthur: or, the Drama of the Revolution* (2 vols., 1867–
1870).

truth—the bottles into which he pours the liberal wine of a new
revelation. The first process is one which would involve vast labour,
in fact it would be needful to go over the whole ground traversed by
Mr Skene in the preparation of his laborious work, *The Four Ancient
Books of Wales*, and much more than even that.[2] For this we profess
ourselves incompetent. It is evident that Mr Tennyson is minutely
learned in all that concerns the period during which these legends were
gradually crystallizing into literature. But his laborious learning is
nowhere obtruded: he contents himself with isolating whatever seems
willingly to lend itself to reflect the complex lights and colours—the
shy reserves and involved experiences of modern life. Here we can see
how possible it is for two opposite lines of criticism to take their rise.
Viewing the matter from a certain positivist ground, it were easy to
demonstrate that Mr Tennyson often wanders far away from the quaint
directness, the naïve simplicity and near naturalness of the old legends;
and while passing by what are evidently later adhesions that glance with
a kind of phosphorescent, unhealthy glimmer of self-conscious light,
he seems, nevertheless, to have been so deeply influenced by them as to
be unable to escape from some persecuting sense of their falseness and
impropriety. A critic of one school, determined to make points against
Mr Tennyson on this ground, might probably urge in evidence his
peculiar refinements of meaning; his vague hold of real character; his
inability to face the whole facts, and to master and mould them into
true dramatic agents; that, in one word, he has never mastered the
Arthurian period, but has been mastered by it, and has been led to
carry some of the moonshiny magic and glamour that touched and
took hold of him as he wandered in that fairy-land into the very wrestle
and rush of modern life, with its settled scepticism and unsentimental
reserve, if not even into the thick of scientific discussion and contest.
Nay, the very restlessness and openness to varied impressions, out of
which comes his proclivity to assume scientific attitudes, only to be, as
it were, shyly scared and startled out of them, might be made the
ground of a more serious charge, involving a question as to his right
to be elevated into the supremest rank of poets. But assuredly all this
must, at the same time, be held to make him peculiarly representative
of the aspiration and despondent fickleness, as well as of the reaction
from the mere sensuous delights and expectations, which are so
characteristic of the present time. And doubtless the Arthurian period,

[2] W. F. Skene, *The Four Ancient Books of Wales* (Edinburgh, 1868).

as apprehended by Mr Tennyson, has taken a deep hold upon his imagination, and formed a kind of amalgam, at all events, underneath the upper surface of his mind.

But there is another point of view, and one in which the critic of another school, regarding Mr Tennyson primarily in his relations to the peculiar needs and demands of science and criticism in the present day, finds a deeper dramatic significance in the very defects on which our other friend dwelt so fondly, and of which he made such proud parade. This critic would hold that the essence of Mr Tennyson's genius, and the secret of his power and popularity in the present time, is the subtle manner in which, like Dante in the under world, he skirts the margin of the darkest places of modern doubt and difficulty, and faithfully overseeing them, yet returns with the image of a fairer reality ever present to the eye of his imagination. It is the continued yearning after this, indeed, rather than any inability to face the separated demands of thought in their last result, which makes him advance and then wistfully turn back, to break into sad, yet not despondent song. Mr Tennyson, for instance, sees very clearly all that Heine or Clough saw of the dividedness and the dissatisfaction which seem to lie in the way of any positive form of belief or of enjoyment, a difficulty enhanced by the very multiplicity of artificial means; and he certainly has in him a touch of the cynical nonchalance of the one, and of the helpless suspense and wistful, eager, far-outlooking anxiety of the other. Yet he shrinks not from the arena either to sport, and laugh, and grin, in sheer despite of anything better, or to give himself up by fits to mere passive dalliance in the delight of nature and natural enjoyments. The curiosity which so characterises the present age, and which with a certain school of French critics has become a seemingly innocent formula for unbounded scepticism, is included in the sum of Mr Tennyson's intellectual energies, and is transported by him into a more sublime medium, in such a way, indeed, that no man can say how much we owe to him for saving us from the last results of this very curiosity.[3]

Mr Tennyson is not intensely individual or powerfully dramatic; that, in view of both estimates of him, may be admitted. But, in a period when

The individual withers, and the world is more and more,

[3] The writer probably means by the 'school of French critics' Renan as a French exponent of the higher criticism, or, if he is thinking in more literary terms, Saint-Beuve.

may there not be a significance in the fact, that its accredited poet deals more with individual characters as forms setting forth or measuring the strength and volume of the various currents that are pulsing through our present existence, than as mere *dramatis personae*, with no significance beyond themselves? We think there may be something in this; a something which, well understood, will throw light on Mr Tennyson's relation to the Round Table.

Our age, by virtue of its very artificiality and scientific culture, is so far unfitted to catch the significance of life in its broadest and most individual aspects. Its self-consciousness makes it as unable to receive and accept this highest and most unconscious art as it is to produce it. It glances beyond the actor to the scene, and struggles to seize or to find a hidden significance in details. It is not content with simple traits; it must have accessories, charged with vague suggestion, if not with grandeur of effect. Nor is it a valid objection to this statement to refer us to the peculiar realism for which, alike on the stage and in literature, such a hunger is now exhibited. It is a realism which carries a false, extravagant, and perverted idealism in its bosom, before which all health and truth is prostrated, as to a ruthless Juggernaut. The excitement of many ideas is unfavourable to such a steady and patient view of a limited range of character, as would enable the spectator to relish a thoroughly natural representation, and to sympathize with it. Mr Tennyson has evidently felt this keenly; and in looking about for a form into which to throw what to him was the true epical idea of the century, he fixed on the legend of Arthur, as that which most readily lent itself to imposing accessories and details charged with enough of the ideal element to relieve the baldness of modern ideas. Following up this line of thought, we find a starting-point in the fact of Mr Tennyson's having embodied, without alteration or modification, what was printed in the first volume of poems as the *Morte d'Arthur*, in the last idyll here given—*The Passing of Arthur*. This poem, as is the case with the preface or introduction to the *In Memoriam*, is the *summa* or result of the whole, and in it the essence of the Arthurian idea, as conceived by Mr Tennyson, finally concentrates itself. 'The Round Table' is the world of today, and King Arthur is 'a gentleman of stateliest port', the ideal of true knighthood and all noble activity, falling helpless, in midst of the fatal complexity alike of natures and of circumstances among which it was cast; yet yielding itself up in serene and absolute dependence on Providence, as fitly typified by the deliberate surrender of 'Excalibur' in the appointed way, and passing, firm in the faith that the true follower would get his own call:

> The old order changeth, yielding place to new,
> And God fulfils himself in many ways.

It is true that Mr Tennyson has not, in the completed idyll, maintained the recitative in which the idea was plainly announced; but the reproduction of the poem in this form shows that the poet's relation to the Arthurian period has been one and unchanged; and that this relation has involved the idea of translating the central elements of modern life and thought through these old-fashioned symbols, in order to their better illustration.

The six idylls proper may therefore be taken to exhibit as many phases of individual experience, deemed to be in their ultimate issue specially characteristic of the present time. Some attention may not unfitly, therefore, be directed to the new idylls in their relation to the whole scheme. There can be no doubt that the legend of the 'Search for the Holy Grail', though it came late in the series, is one of the most important centres of the Arthurian romance; so important, indeed, that one may well express some little surprise that Mr Tennyson did not deal with it in the first series. It undoubtedly presented a great theme for treatment by such a poet; and, considered in reference to his acknowledged purpose, seemed to offer the choicest material and situations. But a moment's reflection gives us pause. *The Holy Grail* is, perhaps, that which is least distinctly marked, and besides, it is the one which, in the whole current of its development, seems most to be dimmed by the breath of allegory resting upon it. Now, the whole tendency of Mr Tennyson, in dealing with the Arthurian legends, is to lift up on the wave of a freer and more advancing faith these half-empty forms of fancy so as to impart to them a rarer reality. But to do this effectively, it seemed that the very capability of their being thus lifted up lay in their being in themselves so far empty. Now, notwithstanding that there were certain essential elements of the Arthurian story which Mr Tennyson had to draw into the background—the double adultery, and the mystery of Arthur's birth—yet he naturally had recourse to those points which stood forth before the imagination as mere story. And wherever Mr Tennyson has found that his modern conception would flow into the prepared medium without unnaturally expanding it on any side, he certainly has been most successful.

Professor Cheetham, in the *Contemporary Review* for April, 1868, has put this point well, claiming the pre-eminence for the *Morte d'Arthur*, although it is the first of the series. 'Nowhere', he writes, 'is the old romance so simply solemn, and nowhere has the modern poet followed it so closely, as in the story of the "death of Arthur".'[4] A true, and, in our idea, an effective criticism might be advanced upon all the later idylls, to the effect that the old story is too much puffed out and too perfectly rounded off under stress of the breath of inner meaning blown into it. The conscious intention speaks too plainly through the elaborate sensuous finish of the verse. The old story seems now and again to be too directly divorced from its real ground—from its deepest, because undefined human interest and meaning; and the thread of allegory round which it is sought to gather it is too thin and fragile to support the real earthly pressure of the materials; and here and there it sharply breaks through and nakedly exposes itself. We feel that the whirl of the poet's fancy by which the Elaines and Viviens are translated into abstractions is too sudden; and we have really a vague impression of two characters, as revealed to eyes looking through unpaired prisms. This is emphatically the case with *The Holy Grail*, as treated by Mr Tennyson. The cross play of allegorical meanings has really, to some extent, put under water the genuine human interest of the story. Added to this grave fault, Mr Tennyson has adopted an involved, inverted mode of narration, to which he is apt to have recourse. In separated pictures we have had nothing finer from him, and, regarded as the story of the search for the Supreme Good—where each finds what he brings—it is full of significance; but it fails in true unity and simplicity of conception. It is intricate and involved beyond any allowance of symbolic reference or justification.

Perhaps the most skilful point in *The Holy Grail* is the manner in which Mr Tennyson, while doing full justice to Galahad as the greatest in the quest, yet gains relief and a kind of gracious, neutral tone from the position of Sir Percivale and his sister, the nun, as the direct tellers of the tale. Nothing could well be more delicate and graceful than the way in which the transitions are managed. To have made Galahad appear directly in sustained blank verse monologue would undoubtedly have tended to suggest too readily to the minds of those familiar with the earlier poems incessant parallels with that dewy-fresh, serenely-

[4] *Contemporary Review*, vii (April 1868), 497–514, 'The Arthurian Legends in Tennyson'. S. Cheetham (signed).

pure, and saintly *Sir Galahad*, which, indeed, appears still to exhaust Mr Tennyson's conception of the character. How perfect, how composed, and sustained the strain—

> When down the stormy crescent goes,
> . . .
> Until I find the Holy Grail.

The great difficulty of Mr Tennyson, therefore, was to devise a new form which should not confuse and cross the associations of this lyrical monologue, and yet present Galahad with new accompaniments, but in all his old serenity of saintliness and conquering odour of devotion. Very probably some of the involvedness or intricacy of which we have spoken may be traced to this as its proximate cause; and consequently, some deductions from the force of the criticism may, in simple justice, have to be made. The first portion of the following extract is the only direct utterance of Galahad's, and it contrasts in many ways with the early poem, and, in our opinion, not in every point to the clear advantage of the blank verse:

> I, Galahad, saw the Grail,
> The Holy Grail, descend upon the shrine:
> . . .
> To whence I came, the gate of Arthur's wars.

The allegorical idea of making each knight's mind or will—or what Mr Tennyson would perhaps call the sum of his life-long conscious energies—find clear correspondent reflection in what the incidents of the Quest reveal to him, furnishes a sort of ground for bringing the inner life and destiny of Galahad and Percivale, of Lancelot and Gawain and Sir Bors into close contact; but it is only one of those instances where the modern refinement, that so pursues Mr Tennyson, throws tantalising and irregular gleams over the simple current of the story. It is felt to be too forced and artificial; and, on oft-repeated and careful readings, it becomes rather oppressive, somewhat as a close and over-heated, though perfumed atmosphere is oppressive to one whose wont has been to abide much out in the open air. Percivale's want is defect of true humility, without which, in the spiritual world, all effort, divorced from the sweet claims of human affection, is but self-seeking —a grasping at shadows, which shrink into dust at a touch:

> All men, to one so bound by such a vow,
> And women, were as phantoms.

King Arthur from the first tells his knights that in the Quest they would only 'follow wandering fires', and this gives a note of peculiar tragic fatefulness, which sounds through the story, imparting to it depth and sombre grandeur; and this simplicity of conception contrasts strangely with the wealth and almost fantastic variety of the rhythms, and brilliancy of richly-wrought imagery.

The Coming of Arthur, as respects its form, is marked to some extent by these faults. This arises from the mystery of Arthur's birth, and the necessity for the poet's shrouding it and refining it away. The following song, however, is in Mr Tennyson's best manner—an arabesque, beautiful in varied colour and tessellated mosaic of light and shade, too aptly significant of the shifting uncertainty that pertains to all forms of thought and opinion in our time:

> Rain, rain, and sun! a rainbow in the sky!
> . . .
> From the great deep to the great deep he goes.

Pelleas and Ettarre, we think, is the gem of the book. Graciously move the quivering lights of later meaning over the dimpling current of the story, and, dwelling for a little on its darker pools, showing depths with only uncertain glimpses of a pebbly bed, they glance on towards the final depths. Ettare is the false lady, but false only because others are false—a fit symbol of the involved duties and claims of the present, which seem to make us all false, and false even when and where we seem true.

Take the opening and the closing passages, and observe what a transition there is from the dewy, morning-like clearness and freshness of the first, to the awful gloom and doom of the second, the active cause of which terrible change is failing belief in true affection, which, sapping the roots of the virtues of constancy and faith, and even of honesty in all the ordinary relations of life, bring social chaos:

> Sir Pelleas of the isles—
> But lately come to his inheritance,
> . . .
> And all her damsels too were gracious to him
> For she was a great lady.

And then this, the ending:

> Lancelot slowly rode his war-horse back
> . . .
> And Modred thought, 'The time is hard at hand'.

Thus we have now an idealized and modernized King Arthur—a cycle of fable charged with real and subtle meanings, and addressed to the self-questioning and restless spirit of the present. If the men of the present will but thoughtfully regard the reflection, and take warning from the tragic destiny of many of the knights—no less than from the confusion and misery that finally fall on Arthur—it will be all the better for us and for them.

Notwithstanding our perception of the modern element residing in these idylls, and brooding over them, we must confess to feeling very much, in passing on from them to the *Northern Farmer—New Style*, as though we had been suddenly thrown out of a warm temperature into a cold bath. This is in Mr Tennyson's most powerful, realistic, dramatic manner, of which he has already given specimens in the first *Northern Farmer* and *The Grandmother*. Each sentence seems to fix, with a sense of determinate finality, a characteristic trait, so that, at the last, a real character stands before the imagination, as completely known as though we had lived beside him for half a lifetime. The new *Northern Farmer* will not, of course, come with a sense of surprise to readers, as the former did, but he is certainly not so far from being novel as the dialect might lead one to suppose. This 'Farmer', unlike the other, is not lifted up and made half-poetical by sheer devotion to the land which he is grieved to leave, as much because it will now inevitably be given up to new methods of working, as for anything else; but, with a touch more of garrulousness, he is equally dogged and wrapt up in his 'Proputty, proputty', and the conviction that, after all, property is the one thing needful—'the poor in a loomp being bad'. The 'Farmer' is trying to argue his son Sammy out of a foolish passion for a poor curate's daughter, and this is his style:

> Do'ant be stunt: taäke time: I knaws what maäkes tha sa mad.
> . . .
> Proputty, proputty, proputty—canter an' canter awaäy.

But the interest of the poem plays within narrower and more conventional limits than in the former one; it is, moreover, lacking in the peculiar undercurrent of pathos which gave such a wondrous charm and relief to the humour of the first, so that we fear the *Northern Farmer—New Style* may not prove quite so popular as the other, though as a work of art it is in several respects superior. Here greater difficulties have been overcome in the more *un*poetical nature of the material.

The Golden Supper has unmistakeable value, as enabling us to trace certain developments of Mr Tennyson's mind, and to see the effect upon him of some influences which were very marked at one time, but of which there is now hardly any direct trace. Undoubtedly his study of the great Italians has been great, and we fancy he has made a decisive effort to shake off once for all the great Florentine's influence. Are we right in presuming that this was only achieved by a kind of reactionary devotion to writers like Boccaccio and Petrarch, with side glances thrown wistfully towards Boiardo, Berni, and even Cecco? Certainly we have in this *Golden Supper* some hint of the hidden *finesse*, the playing with the outer fringes of passion where, like the sea-marge, it touches and turns up the settled sand of social convention, and where only the most dainty and watchful handling prevents a suggestion of something morbid. We have a little of this feeling, completely relieved and justified, however, by rare English honesty and healthy moral conviction, alike in *The Princess*, in *Maud*, and in *Enoch Arden*; and certainly we trace in the form of even the latest of Mr Tennyson's works an inwrought richness and love of brooding over separate conceits and images, for which we find no match elsewhere than in some of the more elaborate Italians, such as Bembo. Evidently Mr Tennyson has successfully drawn strength from the sweetness of the elaborate medievalism of that circle of writers, and has so far enriched English literature with the sense of new movements and new rhythms.

The Golden Supper is a poem of great power and passion, and since we presume that it is not quite a recent poem, it may have some value in showing Mr Tennyson's gradual progress towards a complete command of that peculiarly rich, fluent, cunningly rhythmical blank verse for which he is now so distinguished.

The only other poems in the volume are *Lucretius* and *The Higher Pantheism*; the latter a semi-mystical answer to the ravings of more recent philosophy, but conveyed in a form so scientific and unpoetical, that we are somewhat astonished to find it here.

Further Reading in Periodical Reviews

As there is a mass of material in the 1860s, this section is limited to reviews which contrast sharply with the opinions expressed in previous decades. A survey by J. R. Mozley (*W.I.*, p. 751) of all four poets, Tennyson, Browning, Clough and Arnold, suggests the kind of re-evaluation of contemporary poetry, particularly of Tennyson and Browning, that was going on in the sixties. Mozley (*Quarterly Review*, 126 (April 1869), 328–59) says that Tennyson has been both over-rated and misinterpreted: he is neither a philosophical nor a dramatic poet but a simple, sometimes simple-minded, lyric poet; he praises the violence and introspection of *Maud* at the expense of the *Idylls*, and is sceptical about the importance of the notion of the poet of the age. Browning is praised for intellectual adventurousness, Clough for the honesty of his analytical reflections. The mood of his poetry is likened, with admiration, to *Hamlet*, an analogy which has none of the pejorative associations of the earlier decades. Another touchstone is Alfred Austin's series on *The Poetry of the Period* in *Temple Bar* in 1869. His 'Summary' (28, Dec. 1869), with its attack on the deficiencies of the Victorian age, is in strong contrast to, for instance, John Sterling in 1842.

TENNYSON

It became customary for reviewers to refer to Tennyson's enormous popularity and there are many reviews which express an uncritical admiration. The reviews listed here, however, are mainly those in which disappointment, doubt and hostility are predominant. Tennyson's limited range and lack of complexity is frequently discussed. The *London Quarterly* in 1870 asserts, borrowing from Taine, that Tennyson's art is in its decadence.

Dublin Review, 2 N.S. (April 1864), 363–85. Prob. Charles William Russell. (*W.I.*)

North British Review, 41 (August 1864), 231–52, *Enoch Arden*, 1864. H. H. Lancaster. (*W.I.*, p. 689.)

The Times, 17 August 1864, 9, *Enoch Arden*, 1864.

British Quarterly Review, 40 (October 1864), 463–90, *Enoch Arden*, 1864.

London Quarterly Review, 23 (Oct. 1864), 153–69, *Enoch Arden*, 1864.

Westminster Review, 26 N.S. (Oct. 1864), 396–414, *Enoch Arden*, 1864.

Blackwood's Magazine, 96 (Nov. 1864), 555–72, *Enoch Arden*, 1864. Elizabeth J. Hasell. (*W.I.*, p. 121.)

Temple Bar, 26 (May 1869), 179–94. Alfred Austin (signed).
Contemporary Review, 13 (Jan. 1870), 104–25, *The Holy Grail*, 1869. Henry Alford (signed).
Quarterly Review, 128 (Jan. 1870), 1–17, *The Holy Grail*, 1869. J. R. Mozley. (*W.I.*, p. 752.)
Dublin Review, 14 N.S. (April 1870), 418–29, *The Holy Grail*, 1869.
London Quarterly Review, 34 (April 1870), 154–65, *The Holy Grail*, 1869.

BROWNING

The familiar attitudes of the earlier decades persisted and are represented here by reviews in *Fraser's Magazine* for 1863 and the *Contemporary Review* for 1867 (see below). Even in these discussions, however, there is a greater respect for Browning's intellectual powers and an attempt to grapple with the notion of the impersonality of the dramatic poet. Tennyson and Browning were regarded as equals (the publication of *Enoch Arden* and *Dramatis Personae* in 1864 occasioned frequent comparisons) and although Browning could always be redeemed for some critics by his optimism (see the *Edinburgh* below) there is an increasing willingness to abandon criteria and categories which are irrelevant to Browning and to evolve ones more appropriate to his poetry. Hutton, and H. B. Forman are particularly intelligent and understanding critics of Browning.

Saturday Review, 7 Feb. 1863, 179–80. William Bodham Donne. (Broughton, p. 101.)
Fraser's Magazine, 67 (Feb. 1863), 240–56. John Skelton, signed 'Shirley'. (*W.I.*)
National Review, 17 (Oct. 1863), 417–46. R. H. Hutton. (Broughton, p. 101.)
National Review, 19 (Nov. 1864), 27–67. Walter Bagehot. Reprinted in *Literary Studies*, 1879.
Contemporary Review, 4 (Jan., Feb. 1867), 1–15; 133–48.
North British Review, 49 (Dec. 1868), 353–408. J. H. Stirling. (*W.I.*, p. 692.)
Macmillan's Magazine, 19 (Jan. 1869), 258–62, *The Ring and the Book*, 1868. J. A. Symonds.
British Quarterly Review, 49 (March 1869), 435–59, *The Ring and the Book*, 1868. Montina Collins. (*W.I.*)
Temple Bar, 26 (June 1869), 316–33. Alfred Austin (signed).
Edinburgh Review, 130 (July 1869), 164–86. J. H. C. Fane. (*W.I.*, p. 518.)
London Quarterly Review, 32 (July 1869), 325–57, *The Ring and the Book*, 1868. H. B. Forman. (Broughton, p. 111.)
Fraser's Magazine, 80 (Nov. 1869), 670–8, *The Ring and the Book*, 1868. John Skelton. (*W.I.*)

ARNOLD

Criticism of Arnold at this time does not show the same striking shift of emphasis to be found in discussions of Tennyson and Browning. Very little is of the quality of Swinburne's outstandingly perceptive essay in the *Fortnightly* (see below). There is a calmer and less critical acceptance of what earlier would have been called the 'subjective' or 'Wertherish' elements in Arnold's work and a more emphatic demand for energy and vigour. There are some lively discussions of *On Translating Homer* and of Arnold's conception of culture.

Fraser's Magazine, 63 (June 1861), 703–14, *On Translating Homer*, 1861. James Spedding. (*W.I.*)

Westminster Review, 24 N.S. (Oct. 1863), 468–82, 'The Critical Character' (on Ruskin and Arnold). Samuel Henry Reynolds. (*W.I.*)

Macmillan's Magazine, 16 (Aug. 1867), 271–80, 'The Prophet of Culture'. Henry Sidgwick (signed).

British Quarterly Review, 46 (Oct. 1867), 565–7, *New Poems*, 1867.

Fortnightly Review, 2 N.S. (Oct. 1867), 414–45. A. C. Swinburne. (*Essays and Studies*, 1875.)

St James's Magazine, 21 (Feb. 1868), 375–82, *New Poems*, 1867.

Temple Bar, 27 (Aug. 1869), 35–51, 'The Poetry of the Period' Arnold and Morris. Alfred Austin (Signed).

CLOUGH

Clough comes into his own in the sixties. Apart from one or two unsympathetic critics (see G. H. Lewes in the *Cornhill* below) there was an increasing respect for the range and analytical and introspective qualities of his poetry.

Guardian, 15 Jan. 1862, 2. A. P. Stanley. (Gollin, p. 72.)

Fraser's Magazine, 65 (April 1862), 527–36. F. T. Palgrave. (Gollin, p. 72.)

Macmillan's Magazine, 6 (Aug. 1862), 318–31, *Poems*, 1862. David Masson. (Gollin, p. 72.)

Cornhill Magazine, 6 (Sept. 1862), 398–400, *Poems*, 1862. G. H. Lewes. (Gollin, p. 71.)

National Review, 13 (Oct. 1862), 310–26, *Poems*, 1862. Walter Bagehot. (Gollin, p. 70.)

North British Review, 37 (Nov. 1862), 323–43, *Poems*, 1862. W. Y. Sellar. (Gollin, p. 72.)

Fortnightly Review, 4 N.S. (Dec. 1868), 589–617. John Addington Symonds (signed).

Athenaeum, 14 Aug. 1869, 205–6, *Poems and Prose Remains*, 1869.

Spectator, 11 Sept. 1869, 1073–5, *Poems and Prose Remains*, 1869. R. H. Hutton. (Gollin, p. 76.)

Saturday Review, 18 Sept. 1869, 383–5. *Poems and Prose Remains*, 1869.

Academy, 9 Oct. 1869, 3–4, *Poems and Prose Remains*, 1869. H. de B. Hollings. (Gollin, p. 76.)

Contemporary Review, 12 (Dec. 1869), 513–24, *Poems and Prose Remains*, 1869.

Spectator, 5 Feb. 1870, 166–7. R. H. Hutton. (Gollin, p. 77.)

Appendix

E. S. Dallas ∾ *Poetics* ∾ 1852
Alexander Smith ∾ *Poems* ∾ 1853

David Masson, extracts from 'Theories of Poetry and a new Poet', *North British Review*, xix (August 1853), 297–344

. . . In short, and to close this discussion with a phrase which seems to us to fall like a block of stone crush through all our puny contemporary reasonings about art imitating nature, being true to nature, and the like—'Art is *called* art', said Goethe, 'simply because it is *not* nature.' This, it will be seen, is identical with Bacon's poesy 'submitting the shows of things to the desires of the mind'. Only in one sense can it be said that art itself comes under the denomination of nature. Thus, Shakespeare—

> E'en that art,
> Which, you say, adds to nature, is an art
> That nature makes.

True, as Goethe would have been the first to admit! In this sense, Spenser's grim-hued Horror beating his iron wings *was* a part of nature, seeing that, in this sense, the poet's own soul, with that very imagination starting out of it, was involved and contained in the universal round. But in any sense in which the words art and nature are available for the purposes of critical exposition, Goethe's saying is irrefragable—'Art is *called* art simply because it is *not* nature.' Dissolve the poet through nature, regard the creative act itself as a part of nature, and then, of course, poetry or art is truth to nature; but keep them distinct, as you must do if you talk of imitation, and then the poet is nature's master, changer, tyrant, lover, watcher, slave, and mimic,

David Masson, 1822–1907, prolific contributor to the periodicals and professor of English literature at University College, London, from 1853–65. Some of his best work is in *Essays, Biographical and Critical* (1856) and *British Novelists and their Styles* (1859).

all in one, his head now low in her lap, and again, a moment after, she
scared and weeping, that, though he is with her, he minds her not.

All this, we believe, is very necessary to be said. Pre-Raphaelitism
in painting, like Wordsworth's reform in poetical literature, we regard,
so far as it is a recall of art to truth and observation, as an unmixed good.
But it is essentially, in this particular respect, a reform only in the
language of art; and art itself is not language, but the creative use of it.
We think the Pre-Raphaelites know this; for though, in theorizing,
they naturally put forward their favourite idea of imitation or truthfulness, as if it were the sum and substance of art, yet in their practice, as
Coleridge remarked of Wordsworth, they are as much imaginative
artists as imitative. Take any of the higher Pre-Raphaelite paintings,
and while the *language* of the painting—that is, the flowers, and
grasses, and foliage, and brick-walls, and costumes—are more real and
true imitations than are to be seen elsewhere, the *thought* which this
language is used to convey is at least as ideal, as much a supposition,
imagination, or recombination, as much a mere wish or *utinam*, as in
the majority of other pictures. Still, in our theory of art at the present
day, or at least in our theory of literary art, the notion of imitation is
beginning to exist in excess. The very power of that most admirable
of our novelists, Thackeray, is beginning to spoil us. We will have
nothing but reality, nothing but true renderings of men and women as
they are; no giants or demigods any more, but persons of ordinary
stature, and the black and the white in character so mixed that people
shall neither seem crows nor white doves, but all more or less magpies.

. . .

In short, poesy is what the Greek language recognised it to be—
ποίησις, or creation. The antithesis, therefore, *is* between Poetry and
Science—ποίησις and νόησις.[1] Let the universe of all accumulated
existence, inner and outer, material and mental, up to the present
moment, lie under one like a sea, and there are two ways in which it
may be intellectually dealt with and brooded over. On the one hand,
the intellect of man may brood over it inquiringly, striving to penetrate
beneath it, to understand the system of laws by which its multitudinous
atoms are held together, to master the mystery of its pulsations and
sequences. This is the mood of the man of science. On the other hand,
the intellect of man may brood over it creatively, careless how it is
held together, or whether it is held together at all, and regarding it only

[1] ποίησις: the poetic faculty. νόησις: thought, intelligence.

as a great accumulation of material to be submitted farther to the operation of a combining energy, and lashed and beaten up into new existences. This is the mood of the poet. The poet is emphatically the man who continues the work of creation; who forms, fashions, combines, imagines; who breathes his own spirit into things; who conditions the universe anew according to his whim and pleasure; who bestows heads of brass on men when he likes, and sees beautiful women with arms of azure; who walks amid Nature's appearances, divorcing them, rematching them, interweaving them, starting at every step, as it were, a flock of white-winged phantasies that fly and flutter into the heaven of the future.

All very well; but, in plain English, what is meant by this imagination, this creative faculty, which is allowed by all to be the characteristic of the poet? Mr Dallas will tell you that psychologists differ in their definitions of imagination. Dugald Stewart, and others, he says, have regarded it solely as the faculty which looks to the possible and unknown, which invents hippogriffs and the like ideal beasts, in short, the creative faculty proper. Mr Dallas properly maintains that this is not sufficient, and that the faculty unphilosophically called Conception, that is, the faculty which mirrors or reproduces the real, must also be included in the poetic imagination. And this is nearly all that he says on the subject.

Now, if we were to venture on a closer definition, such as might stand its ground, and be found applicable over the whole length and breadth of poetry, we should, perhaps, affirm something to the following effect: The poetic or imaginative faculty is *the power of intellectually producing a new or artificial concrete;* and the poetic genius or temperament is *that disposition of mind which leads habitually, or by preference, to this kind of intellectual exercise.*[2] There is much in this statement that might need explanation. In the first place, we would call attention to the words 'intellectually producing', 'intellectual exercise'. These words are not needlessly inserted. It seems to us that the distinct recognition of what is implied in these words would save a great deal of confusion. The phrases 'poetic fire', 'poetic passion', and the like, true and useful as they are on proper occasion, are calculated sometimes to mislead. There is fire, there is passion in the poet; but that which is peculiar in the poet, that which constitutes the poetic tendency as such, is a special *intellectual* habit, distinct from the intellectual habit of

[2] The phrase 'artificial concrete' is taken over from Hegel's aesthetics.

the man of science. The poetic process may be set in operation by, and accompanied by, any amount of passion or feeling; but the poetic process itself, so far as such distinctions are of any value, is an *intellectual* process. Farther, as to its kind, it is the intellectual process of producing a new or artificial concrete. This distinguishes poetry at once in all its varieties, and whether in verse or in prose, from the other forms of literature. In scientific or expository literature the tendency is to the abstract, to the translation of the facts and appearances of nature into general intellectual conceptions and forms of language. In oratorical literature, or the literature of moral stimulation, the aim is to urge the mind in a certain direction or to induce upon it a certain state. There remains, distinct from either of these, the literature of the concrete, the aim of which is to represent the facts and appearances of nature and life, or to form out of them new concrete combinations.

. . .

Connected with this [the poet's ability to conceive of other beings] in practice, but distinguishable from it, is another variety of imaginative exercise, which may be called the imagination of *states of feeling*. Here is an example:

> A fig for those by law protected!
>   Liberty's a glorious feast;
> Courts for cowards were erected;
>   Churches built to please the priest.
>   Burns, *Jolly Beggars.*

This stanza, it will be observed, and we have chosen it for the purpose, is, in itself, as little poetical as may be; it is mere harsh Chartist prose. But in so far as it is an imagined piece of concrete, that is, in so far as it is an imagination by the poet of the state of feeling of another mind, or of his own mind in certain circumstances, it is poetical. This is an important consideration, for it links the poet not only with what is poetical in itself, but with a whole, much bigger, world of what is unpoetical in itself. The poet may imagine opinions, doctrines, heresies, cogitations, debates, expositions—there is no limit to his traffic with the moral any more than with the sensuous appearances of the universe; only, as a poet, he deals with all these as concrete things, existing in the objective air, and from which his own soul stands royally disentangled, as a spade stands loose from the sand it shovels, whether it be sand of gold or sand of silex. The moment any of the doctrines he is dealing with melts subjectively into his own personal state of being (which is necessarily and nobly happening continually), that moment the poet ceases to be a poet pure, and becomes so far a thinker or moralist in union with the poet. As regards the literary range of this kind of imaginative exercise—the imagination of states of feeling—it is only necessary to remember what a large proportion it includes of our lyric poetry, and how far it extends itself into the epic and the drama, where (and especially in the drama) it forms, together with the imagination of costume, the greater part of what is called the invention of *character*.

The foregoing is but a slight enumeration of some of the various modes of imaginative exercise as they are popularly distinguishable; and, in transferring them into Creative Literature at large, they must be conceived as incessantly interblended, and as existing in all varieties and degrees of association with personal thought, personal purpose, and personal calm or storm of feeling. It is matter of common observation, however, that some writers excel more in one and some more in another of the kinds of imagination enumerated. One writer is said to excel in descriptions, but to be deficient in plot and incident, nay, to excel in that kind of description which consists in the imagination of form, but to be deficient in that which consists in the imagination of colour. Another is said to excel in plot, but to be poor in the invention of character, and in other particulars. In short, the imagination, though in one sense it acts loose and apart from the personality, flying freely round and round it, like a sea-bird round a rock, seems, in a deeper sense, restricted by the same law as the personality in its choice and apprehension of the concrete.

. . .

Every thought of the poet, about whatever subject, is transacted not wholly in propositional language, but for the most part in a kind of phantasmagoric, or representative language of imaginary scenes, objects, incidents, and circumstances. To clothe his feelings with *circumstance*; to weave forth whatever arises in his mind into an objective tissue of imagery and incident that shall substantiate it and make it visible; such is the constant aim and art of the poet. Take an example. The idea of life occurs to the poet Keats, and how does he express it?

> Stop and consider! Life is but a day;
> . . .
> Riding the springy branches of an elm.

This is true ποίησις. What with the power of innate analogy, what with the occult suasion of the rhyme, there arose first in the poet's mind, contemporaneous with the idea of life, nay, as incorporate with that idea, the imaginary object or vision of the dew-drop falling through foliage—that imagined circumstance is, therefore, flung forth as representative of the idea. But even this does not exhaust the creative force; the idea bodies itself again in the new imaginary circumstance of the Indian in his boat; and that, too, is flung forth. Then there is a rest; but the idea still buds, still seeks to express itself in new circumstance, and five other translations of it follow. And these seven pictures, these seven morsels of imagined concrete, supposing them all to be intellectually genuine, are as truly the poet's *thoughts* about life as any seven scientific definitions would be the thoughts of the physiologist or the metaphysician. And so in other instances. Tennyson's *Vision of Sin* is a continued phantasmagory of scene and incident representative of a meaning; and if the meaning is not plain throughout, it is because it would be impossible for the poet himself to translate every portion of it out of that language of phantasmagory in which alone it came into existence.

. . .

Now, as the very essence of the poet consists in the incessant imagination of concrete circumstance, a language rich in imagery is in itself a proof of the possession of poetical faculty in a high degree. *Ceteris paribus*, that is, where there is an equal amount of imagination and of the same quality, in the bodying forth of the main circumstance of a poem or a poetical passage—whether that is a circumstance of visible scenery, of incident, of physiognomy, or of mental state—the more of subsidiary circumstance evolved in intellectual connection with the main one the higher the evidence of poetical power. There is an analogy, in this respect, between poetical and scientific writers. Some scientific writers, as, for example, Locke, attend so rigorously to the main thought they are pursuing as to give to their style a kind of nakedness and iron straightness; others, as, for example, Bacon, without being indifferent to the main thought, are so full of intellectual matter of all kinds that they enrich every sentence with a *detritus* of smaller propositions related to the one immediately on hand. So with poets. Some poets, as Keats, Shakespeare, and Milton in much of his poetry, so teem with accumulated concrete circumstance, or generate it so fast, as their imagination works, that every imagined circumstance as it is put forth from them takes with it an accompaniment of parasitic fancies. Others, as the Greek dramatists and Dante, sculpture their thoughts roundly and massively in severe outline. It seems probable that the tendency to excess of imagery is natural to the Gothic or Romantic as distinct from the Hellenic or Classical imagination; but it is not unlikely that the fact that poetry is now read instead of being merely heard, as it once was, has something to do with it. As regards the question *when* imagery is excessive, *when* the richness of a poet's language is to be called extravagance, no general principle can be laid down. The judgement on this point in each case must depend on the particular state of the case. A useful distinction, under this head, might possibly be drawn between the liberty of the poet and the duty of the artist. Keats's *Endymion*, one might safely, in reference to such a distinction, pronounce to be too rich; for in that poem there is no proportion between the imagery, or accessory concrete, and the main stem of the imagined circumstance from which the poem derives its name. In the *Eve of St Agnes*, on the other hand, there is no such fault.

Index

Modern secondary authorities cited in the notes have not been indexed. The figures in italics refer to the footnotes to the Introduction which appear between pp. 59 and 68.